Communications
in Computer and Information Science 1313

More information about this series at http://www.springer.com/series/7899

Weitao Song · Feng Xu (Eds.)

VR/AR and 3D Displays

First International Conference, ICVRD 2020
Hangzhou, China, December 20, 2020
Revised Selected Papers

 Springer

Editors
Weitao Song
Beijing Institute of Technology
Beijing, China

Feng Xu
Tsinghua University
Beijing, China

ISSN 1865-0929   ISSN 1865-0937 (electronic)
Communications in Computer and Information Science
ISBN 978-981-33-6548-3   ISBN 978-981-33-6549-0 (eBook)
https://doi.org/10.1007/978-981-33-6549-0

This Springer imprint is published by the registered company Springer Nature Singapore Pte Ltd.
The registered company address is: 152 Beach Road, #21-01/04 Gateway East, Singapore 189721, Singapore

Preface

We are honored to organize the International Conference on VR/AR and 3D Displays 2020 (ICVRD 2020). The conference was hosted by the Chinese Institute of Electronics. The conference has been influenced by COVID-19 during this year, but it still received a lot of attention and support from scholars at home and abroad. In this special year, we are excited to see the successful continuation of this event.

ICVRD is a professional meeting and an important forum for virtual reality, augmented reality, 3D displays, and related topics, including but not limited to human-computer interaction, near-eye displays, naked-eye 3D displays, modeling, simulation, animation, and applications.

The ICVRD 2020 conference attracted 29 technical reports from different countries and regions. Despite the influence of the pandemic, the paper selection remained highly competitive this year. Each manuscript was reviewed by at least two reviewers, and 12 manuscripts were selected for publication based on careful evaluation.

On behalf of the conference general chairs, I would like to thank all our committee and staff members for all their hard work for this conference, and I really appreciate the contributions from all authors and the support of the reviewers.

Finally, we firmly believe that we will overcome the pandemic soon, and we look forward to seeing you face to face at ICVRD 2021 next year.

November 2020   Chinese Institute of Electronics

Organization

General Chairs

Qionghai Dai   Tsinghua University
David Brady   Duke University

Executive Chair

Yongtian Wang   Beijing Institute of Technology

Steering Committee

Hujun Bao   Zhejiang University
Aimin Hao   Beihang University
Xun Luo   Tianjin University of Technology
Tongsheng Mou   Zhejiang University
Xinzhu Sang   Beijing University of Posts and Telecommunications
Xukun Shen   Beihang University
Qionghua Wang   Beihang University
Zhaoqi Wang   Institute of Software Chinese Academy of Sciences
Xiaokang Yang   Shanghai Jiao Tong University
Jingyi Yu   ShanghaiTech University
Fengjun Zhang   Institute of Software Chinese Academy of Sciences
Ninghua Zhu   Institute of Semiconductors Chinese Academy
     of Sciences

Program Committee Chairs

Weitao Song   Beijing Institute of Technology
Feng Xu   Tsinghua University

Publication Chair

Liming Gong   Chinese Institute of Electronics

Contents

Research on the Application of 3D Visualization of Marine Environmental Data in Underwater Sub-mersibles Route Planning 1
Jun Fu, Yang Chang, Zhiwen Ning, and Hongxiang Han

Integral Imaging Tabletop 3D Display System Based on Compound Lens Array.. 14
Yun-Peng Xia, Yan Xing, Hui Ren, Shuang Li, and Qiong-Hua Wang

High-Quality Facial Expression Animation Synthesis System Based on Virtual Reality... 21
Yang You, Limei Song, and Yangang Yang

Performance Evaluation of 3D Light Field Display Based on Mental Rotation Tasks... 33
Jingwen Li, Peng Wang, Duo Chen, Shuai Qi, Xinzhu Sang, and Binbin Yan

Large Horizontal Viewing-Angle Three-Dimensional Light Field Display Based on Liquid Crystal Barrier and Time-Division-Multiplexing 45
Renxiang Dai, Xinzhu Sang, Shujun Xing, Xunbo Yu, Xin Gao, Li Liu, Boyang Liu, Chao Gao, Yuedi Wang, and Fan Ge

Extended-Depth Light Field Display Based on Controlling-Light Structure in Cross Arrangement 56
Fan Ge and Xinzhu Sang

Stereoscopic 3D Depth Perception Analysis of H.264/AVC Coded Video ... 66
Wenfei Wan, Hong Ren Wu, Jinjian Wu, and Guangming Shi

AR Application Research Based on ORB-SLAM 78
Baihui Tang, Zhengyi Liu, and Sanxing Cao

Virtual Reality App for ASD Child Early Training 89
Lei Fan, Wei Cao, Yasong Du, Jing Chen, Jiantao Zhou, and Guangtao Zhai

Convolutional Neural Networks for Face Illumination Transfer 103
Zhonglan Li, Xin Jin, Xiaodong Li, and Yannan Li

Modeling the Self-navigation Behavior of Patients with Alzheimer's Disease in Virtual Reality.. 121
Jinghui Jiang, Guangtao Zhai, and Zheng Jiang

A Large-Scale VR Panoramic Dataset of QR Code and Improved
Detecting Algorithm 137
    Zehao Zhu, Guangtao Zhai, Jiahe Zhang, Jun Jia, and Fuwang Yi

Author Index 149

Research on the Application of 3D Visualization of Marine Environmental Data in Underwater Sub-mersibles Route Planning

Jun Fu$^{(\boxtimes)}$ (iD), Yang Chang$^{(\boxtimes)}$ (iD), Zhiwen Ning$^{(\boxtimes)}$, and Hongxiang Han

Naval University of Engineering, Wuhan 430033, China
fjsd@21cn.com, 624227230@qq.com, 653433856@qq.com

Abstract. The traditional vast marine environment data acquisition and processing are usually independent and presented in a numerical way, which is not good for the intuitive and quick use of the ordinary end-users. Due to this, based on the point data of the environmental data field of marine 3D space, we carry out 3D visualization to the complex and changeable marine environment, and key feature information, to turn the complex and single marine environment data into easily understandable 3D graphics. Combining with different task-assistant decision algorithms, end-users can abandon the traditional decision-making methods of checking forms and reading data, which realized the assistant decision in terms of underwater navigation safety assessment, navigation path planning and trail control, and effectively improved the global analysis and judgment and scientific decision-making ability of end-users in complex dynamic environment, forming the optimal behavioral decision-making scheme that matches with the specific task.

Keywords: Marine environmental data · Underwater submersibles · 3D visualization · Assistant decision

1 Introduction

The vast ocean contains abundant aquatic and mineral resources, and it will certainly provide more food and energy for human with the development of science and technology. Compared with land, humans know little about the ocean, especially the marine underwater world. In recent years, our country has invested a lot of resources in marine construction, and is now focusing on the construction of marine environment monitoring system,consisted of ships, aircraft, satellites, buoys, submersibles, and shore-based radar, and has obtained a large amount of marine environment observation data [1]. Therefore, it's significant to use scientific and effective means to intelligently organize, manage and extract large amounts of marine environment observation data, realize the visual expression of complex environmental information, improve the transparency of the marine environment, form an intuitive interactive decision space based on simulated visual data, and create a new generation 3D visualization application engine of the marine environment, which plays an important role in mining and utilizing marine

© Springer Nature Singapore Pte Ltd. 2021
W. Song and F. Xu (Eds.): ICVRD 2020, CCIS 1313, pp. 1–13, 2021.
https://doi.org/10.1007/978-981-33-6549-0_1

environment data and improving its application level in the fields of national economy and national defense.

The types of marine environmental data are complex, including weather, sea conditions, temperature, salinity, density, gravity, geomagnetism, and seafloor topography. At the same time, the data is highly correlated in time and space. At present, the description and expression of marine complex environmental information are still at a low level. For the situation of the underwater environment, there are more local descriptions and less global descriptions. Complex marine environment information expressions have more static forms and less dynamic presentations. It is still difficult to make timely and accurate measurements [2] and predictions of some changes in the marine environment. Compared with developed countries, there are still large gaps in the marine environment data processing efficiency, data joint analysis, and convenience of end-user applications.

This paper starts with the needs of underwater route planning and track control of underwater vehicles, uses the 3D visualization technology of marine environment data [3–6], and assists decision-making algorithms to explore the establishment of a 3D visualization system of marine environment data to realize the feature extraction of under complex marine environment conditions and provides a dynamic visualization and statistical analysis platform for ocean observation data and forecast models.

2 Demand Analysis of 3D Visualization of Marine Environment Data

2.1 Basic Function Demand

Marine environmental data can be divided as marine geographic information data, marine management and business application service data, and observation, monitoring and prediction data of marine environmental information from the aspect of data content. If divided from the data source and format of marine environmental data, mainly includes topographic data, image data, toponymic data and marine environmental element data.

The extraction, analysis and visualization of marine environment elements [7] is the basis to achieve the 3D visualization, release and customization services of elements like marine basic geography, marine environment, marine resources [8], including the basic functions of marine environment visualization and feature extraction, marine environment element query, spatial analysis and so on [9, 10].

Marine environment visualization and feature extraction are under the conditions of 3D Virtual Earth [11], present the marine environment data in a multi-dimensional, dynamic visualization way, achieving the dynamically interactive and multidimensional continuous visualizations. For the marine environment elements scale field data, such as elements reflecting the marine hydrological characteristics of temperature, density and salinity, to achieve the marine data multidimensional information display. Supporting visualization ways for marine environment elements scale includes: section drawing, contour drawing, isosurface drawing, and body drawing of the scale field. Provide processing tools of slicing and cutting for visualization data.

Marine environment factors query should be based on its different characteristics, to realize information query in time space (anytime, specified time period, specified time interval), air space (any point, line and area within the forecast range), and display the spatial characteristics and changing trends of multi-dimensional dynamic marine environment data in different ways.

Space analysis offers functions like measurement (distance and area), section analysis and bathymetric contour analysis.

2.2 Assistant Decision Function Demand

When the underwater vehicle sails, it is necessary to do reasonable path planning in terms of navigation depth and speed. For example, when the underwater vehicle goes from point A to point B, if there is a mesoscale vortex between the two points, the different route will directly affect the economics and time of the arrival of the underwater vehicle. If the underwater vehicle is carrying out underwater searching emission, we need to conduct assistant decision optimization for regional search methods based on visual image information formed by the sound velocity profile of the sea area. When searching at area and water where ocean sound velocity is transmitted better, can increase the search interval appropriately; when sailing at area and water where ocean sound velocity is transmitted worse, we need to reduce the search interval.

The traditional navigation path planning method is difficult to timely consider the influence of environmental elements, and by quantifying and graphically representing the marine environment data information in the mission area, and using it as a constraint condition for the model of the safe navigation path of the underwater vehicle. Carry out safe navigation path according to the temperature leap, different density of water mass, and density leap, so that the underwater vehicle can dynamically optimize the route under the condition of taking full account of the marine environment.

3 Marine Environment Data 3D Visualization Processing Technology and Assistant Decision Algorithm

Faced with the diverse marine environment data obtained by ocean survey, this paper designed the hierarchical processing structure consist of resource layer, data layer, application service layer and application display layer (Fig. 1).

The resource layer is mainly composed of computer hardware resources and software platforms which support the operation of meteorological marine environment simulation platform. The data layer is the basis of supporting the operation of the system, mainly refers to various database. The data types include ocean observation data, re-analysis data, marine simulation products and other data, the specific content covers the marine basic geographic data, remote sensing image data, topographical data, seafloor topography data, place data, hydrological data and other marine environmental survey data. Data of the data layer can be called and loaded directly by the business module of application service layer. The application service layer is used to manage and publish various services, achieve the request and response for multi-source data, extract and convert and load raw data, scientifically store, extract, clean up and integrate unprocessed data, visual display and analyze the marine environmental data, and to achieve the feature extraction of complex marine environmental elements and assistant decision analysis based

Fig. 1. Hierarchical processing structure of marine environment data

on visual data of the marine environment. This layer consists of a series of business modules and is the core modules of the system. Application display layer offers function interface and interactive control. Function interface designs the interface to perform the operation of the system and determine the interface parameters based on system function demand. Interactive control responses to user operation and provide friendly interactive interface for users.

3.1 Fast Access to Marine Environment Database

Because of the wide variety of ocean data obtained and the huge amount of data, traditional centralized file storage is difficult to meet the efficient management and analysis needs of big data, which can easily cause over load and reduce query performance. In order to improve the performance of the database, we designed a mixed shard storage method nested vertical partition based on attributes, horizontal partition based on time, and horizontal partition based on space by combining with the characteristics of marine environment data and different business needs to balance the database load and make up for the deficiency of single shard method, and achieve the efficient storage and management of marine environmental data.

Vertical partition is a disjointed subset divided by relation and combined with attributes, projection operation of the global relationship in a vertical direction, and each fragment after sniping contains some properties of the original table and its main code, meant to correctly dividing the attribute groups according to the application requirements. However, there is a problem of low reading and writing efficiency and uneven node load due to the large amount of date resulting from single business table.

Horizontal partition based on time is numerous logical fragments divided by all tuples of data table according to certain constraint, each logical fragment does not intersect. On the basis of vertical partition, through horizontal partitioning of time rules of logical tables to realize the horizontal partition based on time, so that resources can be fully utilized and the operational efficiency is improved. However, when the query task involves a large spatial range, the data at the same time is over-concentrated in one node, time-based partition are difficult to distribute the task evenly, and the waste of resources also leads to the load tilt of the server node.

Horizontal partition based on space is sharded on the basis of spatial location, and the relevant records for all spatial position points are equally distributed to each node. The result set of query target based on spatial partition is evenly distributed among the nodes, and for the large-scale query task, make parallel query of each node and full use of the performance of each node.

In order to further improve the efficiency of data reading, a Spatio-temporal indexing mechanism is adopted, that is, establish a composite index of the time and space attribute fields of the data in the database in order to reduce the scope of the query and locate quickly. The marine environment data is continuous in time and space. After being stored in pieces, it is in a discrete and disordered state in the distribution database. Considering the characteristics of the "Leftmost prefix" of the composite index and the spatiotemporal nature of the data, a composite index was designed for the database in the order of time, latitude, and longitude. During the query process, by the gradual filter of time and spatial indexes, we locate the data table with the physical address value provided by the filtering result and obtain corresponding data. The index table has a simple structure, a small amount of data, and a fast traversal speed, which is of great significance to improve the overall query speed. The designed query process is shown in Fig. 2.

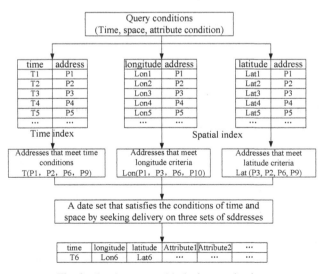

Fig. 2. Spatio-temporal indexing mechanism

3.2 Contour Extraction and Visualization of 2D Scalar Field Based on GPU

For data like the temperature, salinity and in the marine environment data, it can be regarded as a two-dimensional scalar function $F = F(x, y)$ defined on a certain surface. For a two-dimensional scalar field, the data is often distributed on regular grid points. Common contour extraction methods include the grid sequence method and the element division method. We use the GPU-based grid sequence method to achieve real-time 2D scalar field contour extraction and visualization. For the regular grid data shown in Fig. 3(a), we can see that the grid lines are orthogonal to each other, and each grid unit is a rectangle, with four vertices as $(x0, y0), (x0, y1), (x1, y0), (x1, y1)$, the corresponding values are $F_{00}, F_{01}, F_{10}, F_{11}$.

The intersection calculation of grid cells and contours is mainly to figure out the intersection of the edges and contours of each cell. Assuming that the function is showing a linear change within the unit, the intersection point can be calculated by vertex determination, edge interpolation method, and the grid point is divided into two states, "IN" and "OUT", indicating that the point is within the contours, or outside the contours. If $F_{ij} \leq F_t$, the vertex (x_i, y_j) is "IN" and it is recorded as "−"; if $F_{ij} > F_t$, the vertex (xi, yj) is "OUT" and it is recorded as "+". If the four vertices of the cell are all "+" or all "−", the grid element has no intersection with the contour with the value Ft. For two cell edges where the vertices are "+" and "−", you can use linear interpolation to calculate the intersection of contours on this edge.

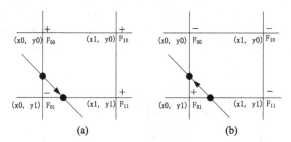

(a)   (b)

Fig. 3. Contour links situation

For the regular grid data of type 3 (b), $(x0, y0)$ is "−" and $(x0, y1)$ is "+", then the intersection point is obtained by Eq. (1).

$$\begin{cases} x_t = x_0 \\ y_t = y_0 + \dfrac{F_t - F_{00}}{F_{01} - F_{00}}(y_1 - y_0) \\ \quad = \dfrac{y_0 \bullet (F_{01} - F_t) + y_1(F_t - F_{00})}{F_{01} - F_{00}} \end{cases} \tag{1}$$

After calculating the intersection of contours with the edge of the grid cell within each cell, these intersections can be used to form contour segments within the cell. In order to correctly connect intersections to generate contour segments, we must determine the direction of the contours.

The direction of the contour is defined as along with the contour, a point that is greater than the contour value to the left of the contour, and a point less than the contour value to the right of the contour. That is, the "−" point is to the right of the contour, and the "+" point is to the left of the contour. After the direction of the contours is specified, the connection of contours for rectangular cells can be divided into vertex all as "+", or all as "−", no contour segments. There is a vertex for "+" or "−", a total of two intersections, an equidistant segment, two "+", two "−" and totally three vertex situation. The above processing can be placed in the GPU's Geometry Shader for real-time contour extraction and visualization.

3.3 Isosurface Extraction and Visualization of 3D Scalar Field Based on GPU

The processing of various equipotential, isosurface, isobaric, and isothermal surfaces in the visualization of marine environment data can be summarized as the extraction and rendering of isosurfaces. In addition to generating geometric representations of isosurfaces, isosurface technology also includes display technologies [12]. If we consider the appropriate lighting models and solve mutual occlusion of isosurfaces, the generation and display of isosurfaces are also important problems needed to be solved in visualization applications.

The commonly used isosurface extraction algorithm is MarchCube algorithm. This paper uses GPU to realize real-time 3D isosurface extraction and visualization. The algorithm flow of extracting and drawing isosurfaces using MC method based on GPU is shown in Fig. 4.

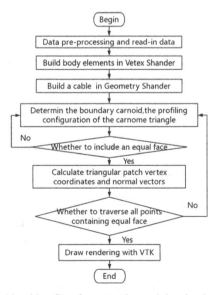

Fig. 4. Algorithm flow for extracting and drawing isosurfaces

3.4 Pre-integration RayCast Visualization of 3D Data Field Based on GPU

Because of the own features of the marine environment elements, volume visualization can mostly describe the spatial and temporal changes of marine environment elements. Volume rendering technology is a direct drawing method, which directly draws the structure that the users are interested in, and even interactively selects part of the data for drawing, which can accurately and clearly reproduce the original 3D data field, so that the users can intuitively feel the distribution and change of data values at any position in the 3D data field. The GPU realization method steps of pre-integral volume visualization are shown in Fig. 5:

Fig. 5. GPU realization steps for pre-integral volume visualization

Based on the above methods, it can realize the rapid visualization and related calculation of various marine physical fields such as the ocean density field, magnetic field, gravity field, and temperature field. It can also realize the real-time 3D dynamic visual expression of various marine mesoscale phenomena based on measured marine environment data, deeply dig into the spatial distribution and dynamic evolution of marine environment data, and conduct comprehensive analysis and knowledge extraction of key features of the marine environment.

3.5 Auxiliary Decision-Making Algorithms

By adding marine environment information as constraints based on the original navigation behavior and state of underwater vehicle, we can effectively carry out assistant decision optimization on underwater vehicle navigation and state control by using visual information after visualization of marine environmental data [13]. This article takes underwater vehicle safe navigation assistant decision as goal, constructs underwater vehicle safety navigation index curve based on marine environment visualization results. In special application fields like national defense, we can take the probability of detection of underwater vehicle as target function of safe navigation planning equations to further construct safe index curve targeting the probability of detection.

Set the current moment as t_c, and predict Δt behind. Current underwater vehicle speed is V_m, the opposite side's underwater vehicle speed is V_d, A is safe navigation index of underwater vehicle, set the current marine environment sound field information as N(x, y, z), bottom elevation is H(x, y, z) set the sonar detection probability field of the opposite side's underwater vehicle at position P(x, y, z) is TCP(x, y, z), the composition of the predictive safety navigation index curve L(t) is shown in Eq. 2.

$$
\begin{cases}
L(t) = (\lambda_1 * D_P(t) + \lambda_2 * D_N(t)\lambda_3 * D_H(t)) \\
D_P(t) = TCP_{t(x_d,y_d,z_d)}\left(P_t(x_m, y_m, z_m), \bar{V}_m\right) \\
D_N(t) = f_N(x_m, y_m, z_m) \\
D_H(t) = \begin{cases} A(H(x_m, z_m) - y_m), H(x_m, z_m) - y_m > 0 \\ 1, H(x_m, z_m) - y_m < 0 \end{cases} \\
P_t(x_m, y_m, z_m) = P_{tm}(x_m, y_m, z_m) + \bar{V}_m * (t - t_c) \\
P_t(x_d, y_d, z_d) = P_{tc}(x_d, y_d, z_d) + \bar{V}_d * (t - t_c) \\
t_c < t < \Delta t
\end{cases}
\tag{2}
$$

Among it, D_P, D_N, D_H is sonar detection threats, marine environmental threats and undersea terrain (reefs, shoals) threats of the current underwater submarine position, Dp not only rely on both positions but also related to the current speed. λ_1, λ_2, λ_3 is weight factor corresponding to each threat. This curve can be used to sense the distribution of the current underwater vehicle safe navigation status over time during the forecast time period in real time, and decision can be made in advance according to the forecast results. The assistant decision model can always construct action strategies based on safe navigation guidelines and change action strategies if necessary, according to the environmental prediction values of the current marine environment and after to assist in the dynamic completion of decision-making behavior (Fig. 6).

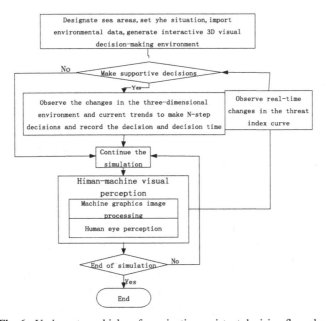

Fig. 6. Underwater vehicle safe navigation assistant decision flow chart

4   Implementation of Marine Environment Data Application Software

The specific implementation of the software system uses the Model-View-Controller framework mode [14]. The adoption of the MVC framework development makes it easier to develop applications on the system architecture.

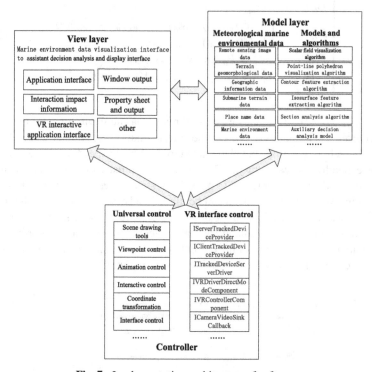

Fig. 7. Implementation architecture of software

In Fig. 7, the controller acts as a bridge to connect the view and model, which is mainly responsible for forwarding and processing the request. The view is used to encapsulate the graphical interface, realize the user-defined interface and interactive information, and the model stores the algorithm for the visualization of marine environment data, feature extraction, and data analysis and assistant decision. For the access requirements of VR scenes, VR interface control module and VR interactive application interface are provided at the control layer and the view layer respectively. VR interface processing and VR interactive application adopt open source OpenVR API implementation.

Figures 8(a) and (b) are the 2D scalar field contour extraction and visualization of the January temperature and January salinity of the ocean based on the GPU. Through the selection of marine environmental elements in a specified space-time area. The accelerated visualization algorithm by the GPU realizes the real-time visual presentation of the marine environment elements, and reflect the real-time characteristics and rules of the

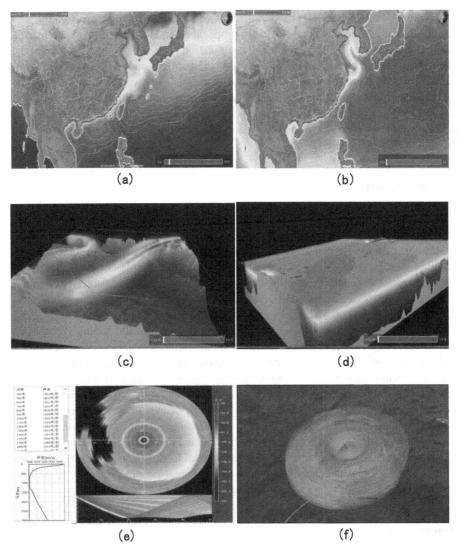

Fig. 8. (a) Ocean temperature contour extraction and visualization in January ocean. (b) Ocean salinity temperature contour extraction and visualization in January ocean. (c) Real-time 3D isosurface extraction and visualization based on GPU. (d) Temperature field visualization of the marine environment. (e) Visualization of 3D sound propagation loss. (f) Route planning.

marine environment elements in space and time through contour extraction. Figure 8(c) shows the isosurface extraction and visualization of the ocean temperature scalar field based on the GPU. Figure 8(d) shows the volume visualization effect of the ocean temperature scalar field based on the GPU, which respectively reflects different digital graphics reproduction methods for displaying the value information of marine hydrological environment elements through the 3D display processing methods of surface rendering and volume rendering. Figure 8(e) is a visualization of the ocean acoustic propagation loss calculated using the ocean sound velocity propagation model according to the marine environment. Figure 8(f) is the effect of the simulation of the safe navigation path of the underwater vehicle based on the visualization results of the underwater acoustic propagation loss and the navigation aid decision algorithm. The green route planned in the figure, its direction and sailing depth are based on the principle of high acoustic propagation loss, avoiding areas with low marine acoustic propagation loss, and effectively use the characteristics and rules of marine underwater sound propagation, so as to achieve the goal of improving navigation safety.

5 Conclusion

With the increasing tension of land resources, the human will increasingly rely on the ocean in the future. At present, in addition to accelerating the construction of the national marine observation system and conducting extensive marine environment surveys, more attention must be paid to how to fully and effectively use marine environment data to serve the national economic development and national defense construction. Aiming at the actual needs of assistant decision-making for underwater vehicles mission planning, this article analyzes and discusses from the aspects of requirements analysis, algorithm design, and specific implementation, and proposed specific technical paths for the storage, management, and visualization applications assistant decision-making of multi-source, multi-dimensional, dynamic, massive marine environment data, construct a marine environment data application system based on 3D visualization technology, which solves the problems of lack of connection between different types and different sources of marine environment data and the difficulty of overall presentation and comprehensive utilization, providing users with a three-dimensional visualization platform for management and analysis of marine environmental data, assistant decision-making and comprehensive applications, and has the potential for further application in a series of fields such as big data analysis and marine fishery, marine transportation, near-shore environmental monitoring, and sea area management.

References

1. Zhang, F., Jin, J.Y., Shi, S.X.: Progress of China's digital marine information infrastructure. Marine Inf. 1, 1–16 (2012)
2. Lin, X.H.: Research on publishing method of marine environment forecast information service. Zhejiang University (2014)
3. Xu, W.J.: Research on 3D seawater visualization based on GIS. China University of Mining and Technology (2017)
4. He, S.F., Sun, J.H., Wei, H.L., Lin, W.R.: Development and implementation of 3D visualization system of marine geology based on sky line. Front. Marine Geol. 34(3), 54–67 (2018). 1009-2722(2018)03-0054-10
5. Xu, J.H., Gu, H., Wang, X.D., Zeng, Y.Y.: Research on 3D visualization of virtual ocean battlefield based on visual entropy. Comput. Simul. 3, 312–316 (2019). 1006-9348(2019) 03-0312-05

6. Chen, Y.: Design and implementation of 3D visualization platform for real-time marine water quality data. Zhejiang University of Technology (2018)
7. Li, X.J., Zhan, H.F., Tang, Z.Q., Chen, S.J.: Design and implementation of 3D visualization system for mining roadway. Surv. Mapp. Geogr. Inf. **1**, 1–14 (2020)
8. Liu, W.: Research on 3D visualization technology for integrated monitoring of shipwreck salvage. Dalian Maritime University (2018)
9. Zu, W.G., Lei, W.G., Pan, Y.F.: Three-dimensional visualization management system of marine survey comprehensive data. Surv. Sci. Technol. **S1**, 38–41 (2016)
10. Xin, W.P., Fang, J., Xia, W.: Design and implementation of a three-dimensional ocean visualization system based on WebGL. Ocean Inf. **3**, 44–48 (2018)
11. Zhang, J.D.: Research on 3D visualization technology of marine environment data field. National University of Defense Technology (2013)
12. Sun, Q., Wang, S.H., Lu, F.: Research on 3D visualization of ocean scalar field data under network environment. Mod. Electron. Technol. **42**(8), 104–107 (2019). https://doi.org/10.16652/j.issn.1004-373x.2019.08.023104
13. Shan, Y.H., Yang, X.D., Wu, B.: Research on safe concealed route planning of underwater submarine based on improved ant colony algorithm. Ship Sci. Technol. **4**(17), 1–5 (2019). https://doi.org/10.3404/j.issn.1672-7649.2019.07.009
14. Li, J.S.: Research and design of marine oil spill dynamic visualization and emergency decision support system based on I4Ocean platform. Ocean University of China (2013)

Integral Imaging Tabletop 3D Display System Based on Compound Lens Array

Yun-Peng Xia[1], Yan Xing[2], Hui Ren[1], Shuang Li[1], and Qiong-Hua Wang[2,3]([⊠])

[1] School of Electronics and Information Engineering, Sichuan University,
Chengdu 610065, China
[2] School of Instrumentation and Optoelectronic Engineering, Beihang University,
Beijing 100191, China
qionghua@buaa.edu.cn
[3] Beijing Advanced Innovation Center for Big Data-Based Precision Medicine,
Beihang University, Beijing 100191, China

Abstract. Tabletop 3D display is a new type of display that gives a collaborative way for multiple viewers standing or sitting in lateral 360° viewing zone. One important technique for tabletop 3D display is integral imaging. Compared with the other tabletop 3D display technologies, integral imaging tabletop 3D display is easier to implement and lightweight, but the viewing angle in the longitudinal direction is limited because of the restriction of the lens array. We present an integral imaging tabletop 3D display system based on a compound lens array. The compound lens array can increase the longitudinal viewing angle by improving the 3D imaging quality in large viewing angle. Experimental results verify that the total longitudinal viewing angle of the proposed system has been widen to 70°.

Keywords: Integral imaging · Tabletop 3D display · Compound lens array

1 Introduction

In recent years, the collaborative working and entertainment become popular because of high-efficiency and convenience. Tabletop 3D display is a promising display technology that enables lateral 360° viewing zone production for shared viewing of multiple viewers, so it can overcome the viewer number limitation of the conventional wall 3D display that only a few viewers can observe 3D Images [1]. Recently, tabletop 3D display is gradually getting more attention and has made great progress.

Depending on difference of the used display technologies, the tabletop 3D display is classified into projection light field tabletop 3D display [2–4], integral imaging tabletop 3D display [5–8], volumetric tabletop 3D display [9, 10] and holographic tabletop 3D display [11, 12]. The projection light field tabletop 3D display can achieve the large-scale and bright 3D images on the table, but the longitudinal parallax is hard to realize. Besides, the hardware architecture of the projection light field tabletop 3D display system is bulky and complex. Volumetric tabletop 3D display and holographic tabletop 3D display are essentially free of convergence-accommodation conflict. However, the size

© Springer Nature Singapore Pte Ltd. 2021
W. Song and F. Xu (Eds.): ICVRD 2020, CCIS 1313, pp. 14–20, 2021.
https://doi.org/10.1007/978-981-33-6549-0_2

and resolution of the 3D images are limited. Integral imaging tabletop 3D display can reconstruct impressive, full-color and full-parallax 3D images, and the system architecture is lightweight and practical. However, the longitudinal viewing angle is narrow, and the imaging quality of 3D image in the large longitudinal viewing angle is deteriorated, which worsen the tabletop 3D display result.

In this paper, we propose an integral imaging tabletop 3D display system with a compound lens array to achieve large viewing angle. The compound lens array is comprised of three pieces of lenses to explore the optimization space of the lenses. Taking the image quality analysis of single lens as the starting point, we optimize the compound lens with the aim of reducing the RMS radius of Spot diagram, enlarging the viewing angle and reducing the distortion in the large field of view. Experimental results demonstrate the total longitudinal viewing angle of 70°, and show improved 3D image quality compared with the conventional system with a single lens array.

2 Principle

2.1 Integral Imaging Tabletop 3D Display System

Integral imaging uses a lens array to capture spatial and directional information of the light rays from 3D objects into the elemental image array (EIA). Then, the recorded light rays can be restored by the modulation of the lens with the same parameters array from the EIA. The conventional integral imaging 3D display uses a micro-lens array with small pitch of 1–3 mm to reconstruct the 3D image, so the viewing angle of the integral imaging 3D display is very narrow, which cannot satisfy the requirement of large viewing angle of the tabletop 3D display. In order to improve the viewing angle, the size of each lens element in the lens array should be increased firstly. However, the aberration of lens increases rapidly with the increase of the aperture and the field of view. The traditional flat convex lens only has a single curvature surface, and its aberration control ability is restricted. Thus, we propose an integral imaging tabletop 3D display system by using a compound lens array.

The principle of the proposed system is demonstrated in Fig. 1. This system includes a flat panel display device, a compound lens array and a light shaping diffuser screen. They are placed horizontally from bottom to top in turn. The flat panel display device is utilized to display the EIA. The compound lens array modulates the light rays from the flat panel display device and project the light rays onto the diffuser screen to create a lateral 360° continuous viewing zone. The diffuser screen diffuses the rays emitted by the reconstructed 3D points with a specific diffusing angle to ensure that the observers can view consecutive 3D images and eliminate the gap between the adjacent lenses. The mathematical model of the light shaping diffuser is a normal distribution model, and its modulation function can be referenced as Ref. [13].

Fig. 1. Configuration of the integral imaging tabletop 3D display system based on the compound lens array.

2.2 Compound Lens Array

In order to improve the control ability of the aberration and provide more freedom for optimization, the number of the lenses is increased from 1 to 3 pieces. For designing and optimizing the compound lens, the relevant optical parameters should be determined, such as the aperture size D of each lens, the curvature radius r of each surface, refractive index n of the glass, Abbe number v and other structural parameters. We need to do aberration analysis for each optical parameter and modify it according to the design requirements. Based on the initial structure and image quality evaluation function of the system, the optical automatic design software ZEMAX is used to find the local optimal solution of the image quality of the system.

The compound lens structure is shown in Fig. 2. We use different glass materials to control the chromatic aberration of the compound lens. The lens barrel and spacer provide mechanical support for the lens assembly and ensure optical spacing between the lenses. The optical parameters of the compound lens are shown in Table 1. When the aperture size of the lens rises from millimeter to centimeter level, the integral imaging 3D display system has large aberration. Therefore, we adopt the image quality evaluation method based on the geometric optical ray tracing rather than the diffraction theory. Ray tracing result of the proposed compound lens is shown in Fig. 3. The compound lens mesh distortion is shown in Fig. 3(a). The Spot diagram of the compound lens is shown in Fig. 3(b), where the maximum RMS value reaches 229.29 μm at the half longitudinal viewing angle of 35°. Other research groups adopted to defocus in the center field of view to compensate the partial aberration in the large field of view, which would sacrifice the imaging quality of the central field of view [7]. While in our proposed scheme, all of field of views are considered in a balanced way to ensure the 3D image quality wherever the viewers are. From Fig. 3(b), we can see that the RMS values of all fields of view are close.

Table 1. Optical parameters of the compound lens array

Lens aperture size	Entrance pupil diameter	ZF1 refractive index	ZF1 Abbe number	H-K9L refractive index	H-K9L Abbe number	Maximum half field of view
12.0 mm	8.0 mm	1.647	33.836	1.516	64.212	35°

Fig. 2. Structure of the compound lens array.

(a) Mesh distortion

(b) Spot diagram

Fig. 3. Evaluation results of the imaging quality of the compound lens array.

3 Experiments

In order to verify the proposed method, a prototype of the proposed integral imaging tabletop 3D display system is developed, as depicted in Fig. 4(a). The presented integral imaging tabletop 3D display prototype is composed of the a 31.5-in. 60 Hz LCD (Dell UP3218K, with resolution 7680 × 4320) used as the flat panel display device, the compound lens array and the custom-built light shaping diffuser [14]. The compound lens array consisting of 50 × 30 lenses is placed in front of the display device. The focal length of the compound lens is 11 mm. The aperture size and the pitch of each lens unit are 12 mm and 13 mm, respectively. The light shaping diffuser screen is placed on the imaging plane of the compound lens array. The imaging distance is 200 mm and the diffuser angle θ is 5°. The parameters of the display prototype are shown in Table 2. Figures 4(b) and 4(c) show the EIAs of *food* and *town* respectively. The partial magnification of the EIA of *food* and *town* is also given.

Fig. 4. (a) Photograph of the proposed integral imaging tabletop 3D display prototype, and EIAs of (b) *food* and (c) *town* models.

Table 2. Parameters of the proposed integral imaging tabletop 3D display system

Focus length of compound lens	Resolution of flat display device	Size of flat display device	Number of compound lens	Pitch of compound lens array	Diffusing angle of light shaping diffuser screen	Lateral viewing angle of 3D image	Longitudinal viewing angle of 3D image
11 mm	7680 × 4320	31.5 in.	50 × 30	13 mm	5°	360°	70°

The 3D images are captured at different viewing positions with a constant longitudinal half viewing angle of 35° (total longitudinal viewing angle of 70°), as shown in Fig. 5. Figures 5(a) and 5(b) are the reconstructed 3D images of *food* model and *town* model, respectively. We can see the different perspectives of 3D images *food* and *town* from 0° to 360°, which verifies the lateral 360° viewing zone and sharing viewing of multiple viewers around the table.

A comparison experiment using cube model between the proposed system with the compound lens array and the conventional system with single lens array is performed, and the 3D images at different longitudinal half viewing angles are shown in Fig. 6. Both the focal length and the aperture size of the single lens in the conventional system are 12.7 mm. The refraction index is 1.517 and Abbe number is 64.167. The Maximum half field of view is only 25°, and the RMS value is more than 20000 μm, which is much larger than that of the compound lens at 35°. Compared with the 3D images produced by the conventional system shown in Fig. 6(a), the quality of the 3D image produced by the proposed system is significantly improved, as shown in Fig. 6(b).

(a)

(b)

Fig. 5. 3D images of (a) *food* and (b) *town* models captured at different positions with a constant longitudinal half viewing angle of 35°.

(a)

(b)

Fig. 6. (a) 3D images of the proposed system and (b) of the conventional system with the single lens array at different longitudinal half viewing angles.

4 Conclusion

We develop an integral imaging 3D tabletop display system based on the compound lens array to improve the viewing angle and ensure the 3D image quality. Three pieces of lenses are designed to suppress aberrations. The experiment results verify that the proposed system enhances the longitudinal viewing angle and improves the 3D image quality. In the future, we will focus on developing a more compact system and natural interaction to promote the commercialization.

Acknowledgement. This work is supported by the National Key R&D Program of China under Grant No. 2017YFB1002900.

References

1. Ren, H., Ni, L.X., Li, H.F., et al.: Review on tabletop true 3D display. J. Soc. Inf. Disp. **28**(1), 75–91 (2020)
2. Li, H., Ni, L., Liu, X., et al.: 360-degree large-scale multi-projection light-field 3D display system. Appl. Opt. **57**(8), 1817 (2018)
3. Yoshida, S.: fVisiOn: 360-degree viewable glasses-free tabletop 3D display composed of conical screen and modular projector arrays. Opt. Express **24**(12), 13194–13203 (2016)
4. Su, C., Zhou, X., Li, H., et al.: 360 deg full-parallax light-field display using panoramic camera. Appl. Opt. **55**(17), 4729–4735 (2016)
5. Luo, L., Wang, Q.H., Xing, Y., et al.: 360-degree viewable tabletop 3D display system based on integral imaging by using perspective-oriented layer. Opt. Commun. **438**, 54–60 (2019)
6. Su, B., Zhao, D., Chen, G., et al.: 360 degree viewable floating autostereoscopic display using integral photography and multiple semitransparent mirrors. Opt. Express **23**(8), 9812–9823 (2015)
7. Gao, X., Sang, X.Z., Yu, X., et al.: 360° light field 3D display system based on a triplet lenses array and holographic functional screen. Chin. Opt. Lett. **15**(12), 121201 (2017)
8. Zhu, Y., Sang, X., Yu, X., et al.: Wide field of view tabletop light field display based on piece-wise tracking and off-axis pickup. Opt. Commun. **402**, 41–46 (2017)
9. Liu, X., Dong, G., Qiao, Y., et al.: Transparent colloid containing upconverting nanocrystals: an alternative medium for three dimensional volumetric display. Appl. Opt. **47**(34), 6416–6421 (2018)
10. Miyazaki, D., Hirano, N., Maeda, Y., et al.: Floating volumetric image formation using a dihedral corner reflector array device. Appl. Opt. **52**(1), A281–A289 (2013)
11. Inoue, T., Takaki, Y.: Table screen 360-degree holographic display using circular viewing-zone scanning. Opt. Express **23**(5), 6533–6542 (2015)
12. Lim, Y., Hong, K., Kim, H., et al.: 360-degree tabletop electronic holographic display. Opt. Express **24**(22), 24999–25009 (2016)
13. Ren, H., Xing, Y., Zhang, H.L., et al.: 2D/3D mixed display based on integral imaging and a switchable diffuser element. Appl. Opt. **58**(34), G276–A281 (2019)
14. https://www.luminitco.com/

High-Quality Facial Expression Animation Synthesis System Based on Virtual Reality

Yang You[1], Limei Song[1(✉)], and Yangang Yang[2]

[1] Key Laboratory of Advanced Electrical Engineering and Energy Technology,
Tiangong University, TianJin 300387, China
lilymay1976@126.com
[2] School of Mechanical Engineering, Tianjin University of Technology and Education,
Tianjin 300222, China

Abstract. In order to realize a virtual teacher online visual teaching system based on virtual reality, a high-quality facial expression animation synthesis technology for virtual reality is proposed. First use the depth camera to track the expression of the performer, extract the facial feature point data and transmit it to the local. Then for the specific organs with low matching degree between the model and the performer's facial feature points and prone to errors, the method of establishing local coordinate system for the feature points of the specific organs of the model is used to optimize the feature point data of the model. Finally, the improved Laplacian deformation algorithm is used to calculate the facial coordinates of the virtual avatar, and the face model is driven to simulate the same expression as the performer, and the accuracy and efficiency of the algorithm are optimized. Experimental results show that the algorithm can achieve high-quality and real-time transfer of captured facial expressions to any virtual facial model, and meet the needs of practical applications.

Keywords: Expression synthesis · Expression capture · Kinect · Virtual human · Online education

1 Introduction

The outbreak of the COVID-19 outbreak in 2020 has made online teaching and virtual teaching the main modes of teaching in many countries. Educational models, forms, content and learning methods are undergoing profound changes. Traditional classroom teaching methods are limited by time, venue, equipment and teachers, they can no longer meet the growing learning needs of the people. With the development of science and technology, virtual reality technology has become a new educational method to promote the development of education. Compared with the traditional boring education, it just blindly instills knowledge into students. The use of virtual reality technology can help students create

© Springer Nature Singapore Pte Ltd. 2021
W. Song and F. Xu (Eds.): ICVRD 2020, CCIS 1313, pp. 21–32, 2021.
https://doi.org/10.1007/978-981-33-6549-0_3

a vivid and realistic learning environment, so that students can enhance their memories through real feelings, and finally achieve immersive learning with deep perception.

Real-time facial expression animation synthesis technology [1] has always been a research hotspot in the field of computer vision, and has important applications in many aspects. An online virtual teacher system that combines virtual reality technology with facial expression animation synthesis and driving technology brings a refreshing feeling to a wide audience of student groups. Customizing the personalized virtual teacher image according to the students' preferences enhances the students' interest in learning, provides a more colorful teaching experience, and has broad application prospects and value in the future.

At present, facial expression animation synthesis technology mainly includes expression animation tracking and model driving. From the establishment of the first facial model by Parke in the 1970s [1] to the present, facial expression animation tracking technology has been relatively mature, but the realization of high real-time and high-reality facial animation reconstruction technology is still currently research Puzzles. For remote interactive teaching, the real-time and realism of virtual teacher expression synthesis are important indicators, so this paper focuses on how to improve the efficiency and accuracy of expression synthesis methods to meet the real-time and realism requirements of virtual teaching.

In the field of facial feature point tracking, Williams proposes to attach reflective points on the user's face to track facial feature point motion information [2]. This method has high accuracy but poor user experience. He et al. used Kinect to capture 3D facial expression parameters, and passed the extracted expression parameters to OGRE to generate real-time facial expression animation [3], but the avatar's expression is delayed compared to the performer. Bulat et al. adopted deep learning methods based on convolutional neural networks to achieve real-time tracking of 3D facial feature points based on RGB video[4], due to the limitation of training data, the detection accuracy is not high. In the field of data-driven expression synthesis technology, common methods include expression animation based on muscle models, expression-based synthesis and deformation algorithms. Although the method based on the muscle model is realistic, it has poor real-time performance, the expression-based synthesis method has the disadvantage that the personalized features are not obvious. Pighin et al. proposed a video-based facial expression simulation technology, after collecting feature point motion data, a three-dimensional curving interpolation algorithm was used to drive the model to generate expression animation [5]. The commonly used algorithms of face model deformation include deformation based on radial basis function (RBF) and radial basis interpolation deformation algorithm. The efficiency of the RBF algorithm is high, and the local subtle expressions are lacking [6,7]. Radial basis interpolation deformation algorithm has good smoothness, but when applied to the face surface of complex topology, local distortion will occur, and the calculation amount is large [8,9]. Suwajanakorn et al. proposed an expression reconstruction method based on voice data [10]. Guo et al. used deep learning methods based on convolutional neural networks to realize the real-time reconstruction of faces using a single picture [11]. However, this method requires a lot of work to establish a database with three-dimensional feature point data, and requires high hardware performance. In summary, as people are very familiar with all kinds of facial expressions, it is easy to detect the small implausibility in the synthesized expression. Therefore, achieving high-real-time and high-fidelity facial animation reconstruction is still a challenging task.

After a comparative analysis of the above methods, combined with the application background, this paper proposes a high-quality synthesis technology of facial expression animation based on depth camera. Compared with traditional expression capture methods that require wearing specific physical devices or using facial markers, the use of depth camera is inexpensive and has low requirements for the environment. It is more convenient and accurate in face data collection and expression parameter extraction, and is more suitable for use in teaching. First we use the depth camera device to track the movement information of face feature points in the natural state, and then establish a local coordinate system for the model specific organs with low feature point matching and prone to errors, the purpose is to optimize the model data. Finally, the improved Laplacian deformation algorithm is used to drive the facial model to output facial expression animation, and the accuracy and efficiency of the algorithm are optimized to achieve high-quality transfer of the captured facial expression to any virtual facial model without geometric restrictions.

2   Our Approach

2.1   System Framework

This system is used to synthesize and drive the virtual teacher's expression in the remote visual teaching. The facial expression animation synthesis system constructed in this paper mainly includes an expression acquisition module, a data processing module, an expression synthesis module, and a model driving module. The technical method framework of the facial expression animation synthesis system is shown in Fig. 1.

The first part is the facial expression acquisition and data processing module. We first track the human face in real time through the depth camera. After acquiring the source data of the human face, we preprocess the data to obtain the main feature points. The second part is the expression synthesis module. Because of the difference between the model and the face, for the special organs that do not directly correspond to the face on the model, we adopt the method of establishing a local coordinate system for the feature points of the special parts. By calculating the conversion relationship between the local coordinate system and the world coordinate system, we transfer the data changes of the built local coordinate system to the world coordinate system. For feature points that do not have a local coordinate system, directly map the coordinates of the corresponding feature points, and finally we integrate all the data to get the model's face. The third part is the real-time drive module. We use the improved Laplacian facial expression synthesis algorithm to calculate the real-time change data of the model feature points according to the data changes of the feature points, and continuously obtain the new positions of the changed feature points. We pass the coordinates of the new position to the array that stores the feature point data of the model, so as to obtain the model after the expression changes, presenting the virtual teacher image that changes in real time with the performer's expression.

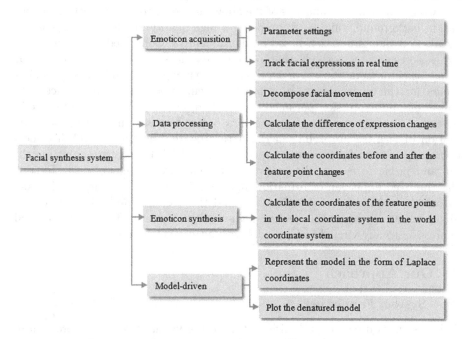

Fig. 1. The framework of our facial animation system.

Finally, a system with comprehensive functions, convenient operation, smooth control and perfect interactivity is realized.

2.2   Facial Data Collection

First, we use the depth camera to collect 1347 original feature points from the performer's face image, and select important feature points from the 1347 feature points. The selection of important feature points will directly affect the final virtual teacher expression synthesis effect. Based on the definition of the MPEG-4 standard and the observation of facial expression deformation, we found that the changes in facial expressions were mainly concentrated on feature points such as eyebrows, eyes and mouth. After a comparative analysis of facial features, we finally selected 68 main facial feature points The distribution of the 68 important feature points selected is: 12 eyes, 10 eyebrows, 20 lips, 9 noses, 17 cheeks, as shown in Fig. 2.

Fig. 2. The left image shows the 1347 original feature points of the face, the middle image shows part of the facial feature points defined in the MPEG-4 standard, the right image shows the 68 main facial feature points finally selected.

2.3   Model Data Optimization

After the depth camera collects the performer's facial data and extracts the required parameters, we also need to build a three-dimensional model of the face. In this paper, Autodesk Maya modeling software is used to build a 3D model. We first model the face with natural expressions, as shown in Fig. 3, and then attach the texture material to get the original model of the virtual teacher.

Fig. 3. Head model created by Maya.

We first manually select the corresponding feature points of the model face based on the positions of the 68 feature points of the performer's face. Through intuitive analysis of the face of the virtual teacher model, we find that the feature points of the model and the performer's eyes and lips are low in matching, and there is no direct correspondence. However, we can find through observation that the eyes and lips of each model can be directly corresponded to the eyes and lips of the performer after rotating a specific angle. In order to ensure that the facial feature points of the model correspond to the facial feature points of the performer, we propose a method of establishing a local coordinate system for the model, and optimize the data of the model's eyes and lips.

Taking the center position of the entire face coordinates as the coordinate origin, the coordinates of 68 feature points corresponding to the performer's face are output to construct the overall world coordinate system with the origin $o_G(0,0,0)$. The position coordinates of each facial image can be represented by a vector of 204 elements,

$$F = (X_1, Y_1, Z_1, X_2, Y_2, Z_2, \ldots X_{68}, Y_{68}, Z_{68}) \tag{1}$$

Among them, $X_i, Y_i, Z_i (i = 1, 2, \ldots, 68)$ are the three-dimensional position coordinates of each feature point.

We select four feature points $x_{La}, x_{Lb}, y_{La}, y_{Lb}$ in the eye and lip regions of the model. Establish the local coordinate system with the origin of $o_L(x_0, y_0, z_0)$ respectively. The unit vectors of the established coordinate system are $u_L(u_1, u_2, u_3)$, $v_L(v_1, v_2, v_3)$, $w_L(w_1, w_2, w_3)$. The unit vector representation of the coordinate system is as follows,

$$\begin{cases} u_L = \dfrac{\left(x_{Lb}^T - x_{La}^T\right)}{\left|x_{Lb}^T - x_{La}^T\right|} \\ w_L = \dfrac{\left(u_L\left(x_{Lb}^T - x_{La}^T\right)\right)}{\left|x_{Lb}^T - x_{La}^T\right|} \\ v_L = u_L * w_L \end{cases} \tag{2}$$

After the area required to establish the local coordinate system of the model face is successfully established, we need to calculate the coordinates of the feature points in the local coordinate system in the world coordinate system. The local coordinate system is transformed into the world coordinate system through transformations such as translation and rotation. Assuming that any point A in the coordinate system has the coordinates of $A(x_L, y_L, z_L)$ and $A(x_G, y_G, z_G)$ in the local coordinate system and the world coordinate system, we use T to represent A from the local coordinate system. The conversion matrix to the world coordinate system, then the conversion relationship can be expressed as:

$$[x_L, y_L, z_L, 1]\, T = [x_G, y_G, z_G, 1] \tag{3}$$

Only need to find the transformation matrix T, we can find the coordinates of any feature point in the world coordinate system. The transformation matrix T can be expressed as:

$$T = \begin{bmatrix} T_L & 0 \\ T_0 & 1 \end{bmatrix} \tag{4}$$

where T_L is the rotation matrix, T_O is the offset matrix, and $T_0 = o_L - o_G$. The rotation matrix T_L we obtained from this can convert the coordinates of all points in the local coordinate system to coordinates in the global coordinate system.

$$T_L = \begin{bmatrix} u_1 & v_1 & w_1 \\ u_2 & v_2 & w_2 \\ u_3 & v_3 & w_3 \end{bmatrix} \tag{5}$$

After the coordinate conversion, we get the coordinate positions of the eye and lip feature points in the local coordinate system in the world coordinate system, and render the facial feature point coordinates into the model, after rendering the facial feature point coordinates to the model, we solved the problem that there is no direct correspondence between the same organ of the model and performer's face, and realized the accurate matching of the model and the performer's face.

2.4   Data-Driven Facial Expression Animation

In order to improve the authenticity of the facial expressions of the model and make the expressions more refined, we propose a data-driven facial expression synthesis algorithm based on improved Laplace deformation.

We decompose the acquired motion data of the performer's facial feature points into facial expression motion data and head rigid body motion data. The motion F_t of the captured facial feature points and the corresponding facial expression change F_t' and head rigid body motion A_t, where A_t includes rotation transformation R_t and translation transformation T_t, satisfy the following formula,

$$F_t = R_t F_t' + T_t \tag{6}$$

Calculate the Laplacian coordinates of all vertices on the model according to the following formula,

$$\delta_i = (\delta_i^x, \delta_i^y, \delta_i^z) = V_i - \frac{1}{d_i} \sum_{j \in N_i} V_j \tag{7}$$

where δ_i is the Laplacian coordinate of the vertex V_i, $d_i = N_i$ is the number of elements in the set N_i, and N_i is the set formed by the subscripts of all adjacent vertices of the vertex V_i.

We fix the vertices of the model unchanged, and migrate the expression movements of the feature points extracted from the motion data of the captured face features of the performer to the corresponding feature points in the model. Keeping the Laplacian coordinates of the vertices of the model unchanged, according to the following error function, a target face consistent with the expression of the performer can be obtained,

$$E(V') = \sum_{i=1}^{n} \|\delta_i(v_i) - \delta_i(v_i')\|^2 + \sum_{i=1}^{m} \|v_i' - u_i\|^2 \tag{8}$$

where V' is the face model to be solved, v_i is the vertex on the initial model, δ_i is the Laplacian coordinate of vertex v_i, v_i' is the vertex on the model to be solved, u_i is on the model Feature points and fixed points.

We migrate the decomposed head rigid body motion to the facial model with the same expression as the performer, so that the final model has the same facial expression and head pose as the performer. The calculation process is as follows,

$$M_t'' = R_t M_t' + T_t \tag{9}$$

Among them, M_t' is a facial model with expressions, and M_t'' is a facial model with corresponding facial expressions and head gestures.

3   Experimental Results and Analysis

The equipment we used for this experiment included a second-generation Microsoft Kinect For Windows and a computer with a CPU model of Intel Core i7-7700HQ. In order to test the practicability of our facial expression synthesis algorithm, we selected three different types of models for the experiment, namely female facial model, male facial model and cartoon kid model. Figure 4 shows several common expressions of performers selected in the experiment and facial expressions synthesized using the algorithm of this paper. Experimental results show that, according to the entire system flow given in this paper, the expression of the performer can be captured and real-time animation simulation, the system can finally output a virtual character expression animation with good display effect.

Fig. 4. Simulation effects of common expressions.

For comparison, we compared two classic expression-driven methods: RBF-based facial transfer method and feature point-based method. In terms of fineness, we showed three similar expressions, namely smile, laugh and surprise. In order to show the details more clearly, we extracted the magnification effect of the expression synthesized by these three methods near the lips. Figure 5 shows the final experimental results. The first line of the picture is the face image of the performer. The second line of the picture is the three expressions synthesized by our method, and the third line and the fourth line of the picture are the results generated by the other two methods. Through the comparison of images, it is easy to find that although the expression based on the RBF method is more natural, the amplitude is relatively small, mainly because the topology and geometric information of the facial model are not considered. The method based on feature points will cause the mouth of the synthesized expression to stretch and deform. The expression synthesis effect of our method in the local area is the most natural and most similar to the performer's expression.

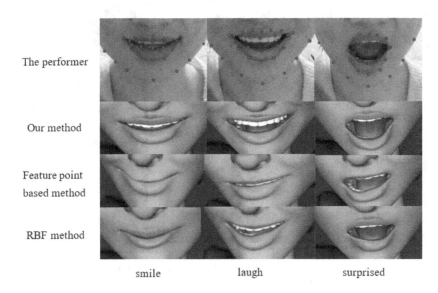

Fig. 5. The results of the region near the mouth using our method, the RBF, and the feature point based method respectively.

In terms of efficiency, in order to check the reconstruction efficiency of the three deformation algorithms, the experiment calculates the time of expression synthesis for the three target models with three deformation algorithms in each frame of expression in real time. Table 1 shows the use of three Comparison of the average time spent by the deformation algorithm in real-time synthesis of the three models.

Table 1. Synthetic efficiency comparison.

Algorithm	Our method (ms)	RBF method (ms)	Feature point based method (ms)
The female model	0.536343	1.326543	10.336753
The male model	0.615430	1.565936	8.4304368
The kid model	0.638634	1.440653	9.6854578

The research purpose of this paper is to realize the virtual teacher's expression synthesis function and apply it to online visual teaching. Based on the real-time facial expression animation synthesis technology proposed in this paper, the virtual teacher interaction interface shown in Fig. 6 is designed. Students can switch between different virtual teacher images and real teacher images by clicking buttons, and choose their favorite teacher images for teaching.

Fig. 6. Virtual teacher online teaching system.

At present, the virtual teacher teaching system has been applied to many basic teaching occasions and video recordings of our school, as shown in Fig. 7.

Our virtual teacher online teaching system also includes virtual teacher voice switching function. It uses a self-developed virtual teacher voice changing system. By changing the timbre and pitch of the virtual teacher's voice, the output sound is changed. And there are many star and cartoon sound simulators. The system can synthesize a variety of voice effects in real time, and students can switch to the voice that matches their favorite image to teach.

We also built a virtual teacher holographic projection exhibition hall, which covers an area of about 20 square meters and consists of a holographic rear projection screen, tempered glass, a control computer, and a high-definition projector. The teaching scenes built by Unity3D and the experimental teaching aids used in teaching, based on 5G holographic projection technology, can present virtual teachers in any built-up supporting teaching scenes, enhancing the interaction between students and virtual teachers in distance teaching. Through this technology, famous teachers and experts who are thousands of miles away can conduct experiments, explain and interact with students at home or in the office. Make students feel the holographic teaching experience with experts and famous teachers in front of them.

Fig. 7. Application of virtual teacher system.

4   Conclusion

In this paper, how to synthesize highly effective and realistic simulated facial animation expressions is studied. Since people are very familiar with various facial expressions, it is easy to perceive distortions in synthetic expressions. In this regard, this paper proposes a high-quality synthesis technology of facial expressions based on depth cameras. For the specific organs with low matching of feature points and easy to produce errors, the model is optimized for feature point data by establishing a local coordinate system. The improved Laplacian deformation algorithm is used to drive the facial model to output facial expression animation, thereby improving the precision and synthesis efficiency of facial expressions. We compared two classic expression-driven methods, the RBF method and the feature point based method. Experiments show that in terms of fineness, the face synthesized by the method proposed in this paper is the most natural and most similar to the performer's expression. In terms of efficiency, the facial synthesis method proposed in this paper is significantly faster than the other two methods. The expression synthesis method proposed in this paper can satisfy the real-time required by the application while guaranteeing realism. We also designed a virtual teacher online teaching system based on real-time expression animation synthesis technology. It can build vivid 3D characters for multimedia applications such as video conferencing, education systems and virtual simulations. There are still defects in the detailed processing of texture mapping, such as the folds of the forehead during head-up and facial folds during laughter. These problems need to be resolved in the next step.

Acknowledgement. We thank Tianjin Research Program of Application Foundation and Advanced Technology for the support. Special thanks to our project partner Huazhong Normal University for providing an innovative platform for experimental design, technology development and engineering practice for this project. This research is supported by the State Key Laboratory of Precision Measuring Technology and

Instruments (Tianjin University) and the Program for Innovative Research Team in University of Tianjin (No. TD13-5036). This research is also supported by the National Key Research and Development Program Project (2017YFB1401302), National Natural Science Foundation of China (NO. 51806150), Natural Science Foundation of Tianjin (NO. 18JCQNJC04400).

References

1. Parke, F.: Computer Generated Animation of Faces. AVM'72 Proceedings of the ACM Annual Conference 1972, pp. 451–457 (1972)
2. Williams, L.: Performance driven facial animation. ACM SIGGRAPH Comput. Graph. **24**(4), 235–242 (1990)
3. He, Q., Wang, Y.: Research on system of facial expression capture and animation simulation based on kinect. J. Graph. **37**(3), 290–295 (2016)
4. Bulat, A., Tzimirpopilos, G.: How Far are We from Solving the 2D & 3D Face Alignment Problem. In: 2017 IEEE International Conference on Computer Vision, pp. 1021–1030 (2017)
5. Pighin, F., Hecker, J., Lischinski, D., Szeliski, R.: Synthesizing realistic facial expressions from photographs. In: Proceedings of SIGGRAPH 1998, pp. 75–84 (1998)
6. Yao, S., Li, W., Su, Z.: Facial expression simulation technology for virtual avatar. J. Graph. **40**(03), 525–531 (2019)
7. Zhang, M., Huo, J., Shan, X.: Facial expression animation based on kinect and mesh geometry deformation. Comput. Eng. Appl. **53**(14), 172–177 (2017)
8. Zhang, M., Yao, J., Ding, B.: Fast individual face modeling and animation. In: Proceedings of the Second Australasian Conference on Interactive Entertainment, pp. 235–239 (2015)
9. Wan, X., Jin, X.: Spacetime facial animation editing. J. Comput.-Aid. Des. Comput. Graph. **25**(8), 1183–1189 (2016)
10. Suwajanakorn, S., Seitz, S., Kemelmache, I.: Synthesizing Obama. ACM Trans. Graph. **36**(4), 1–13 (2017)
11. Guo, Y., Zhang, J.C., Cai, J.: CNN-based real-time dense face reconstruction with inverse-rendered photo-realistic face images. IEEE Trans. Pattern Anal. Mach. Intell. **41**(6), 1294–1307 (2018)
12. Wan, X., Jin, X.: Data-driven facial expression synthesis via Laplacian deformation. Multi-media Tools Appl. **58**(1), 109–123 (2012)
13. Bickel, B., et al.: Multi-scale capture of facial geometry and motion. ACM Trans. Graph. **26**, 33–41 (2007)
14. Bickel, B., Lang, M., Botsch, M., Otaduy, M., Gross, M.: Pose-space animation and transfer of facial details. In: Proceedings of Symposium on Computer Animation Dublin Ireland, pp. 57–66 (2008)
15. Lipman, Y., Sorkine, O., Cohen, D., Levin, D., Rossl, C., Seidel, H.: Differential coordinates for interactive mesh editing. In: Proceedings of the Shape Modeling International IEEE Computer Society, pp. 181–190 (2004)
16. Oka, M., Tsutsui, K., Ohba, A.: Real-time manipulation of texture-mapped surface. In: ACM SIGGRAPH Computer Graphics. SIGGRAPH'87 Proceedings of the 14th Annual Conference on Computer Graphics and Interactive Techniques, pp. 181–188. ACM Press, New York (1987)
17. Seitz, S., Dyer, R: View morphing. In: ACM SIGGRAPH Computer Graphics. SIGGRAPH'96 Proceedings of the 23rd Annual Conference on Computer Graphics and Interactive Techniques, pp. 21–30. ACM Press, New York (1996)

Performance Evaluation of 3D Light Field Display Based on Mental Rotation Tasks

Jingwen Li, Peng Wang$^{(\boxtimes)}$, Duo Chen, Shuai Qi, Xinzhu Sang, and Binbin Yan$^{(\boxtimes)}$

State Key Laboratory of Information Photonics and Optical Communications, Beijing University of Posts and Telecommunications, Beijing 100876, China
{wps1215,yanbinbin}@bupt.edu.cn

Abstract. Three-dimensional light field display, which can provide human with natural 3D images in the way of humans observing the real world without any glasses, has attracted more and more attentions in recent years. However, most of studies focus on the performance improvement of 3D light field display, and there is rarely work on the performance evaluation of 3D light field display. In this paper, a quantitative performance evaluation method of the 3D light field display based on cognitive measurement of the observer with a specifically designed mental rotation task is proposed. The procedure of the performance evaluation experiment design is demonstrated, some pairs of complex images with either same structure or mirror structure are displayed, and the participants are required to distinguish whether the displayed images are the same. Three different control experiments including 2D display with fixed viewpoint, 3D light field display with fixed viewpoint and 3D light field display with a free view are designed. 45 participants which are divided into three groups are assigned to take part in three difference control experiments, and the rate of mission success and the completion time are evaluated. By comparing the results on different experimental conditions and using a statistic analysis method called *T-test*, the superiority of 3D light field display is proved quantitatively.

Keywords: 3D light field display · 2D displays · Mental rotation · Viewing angle · Performance evaluation

1 Introduction

Recently, the 3D light field display (LFD), which is considered as a promising technology to reconstruct the light rays' distribution of the real 3D scene without any additional equipment, has drawn great public attention [1–6]. Unlike the traditional autostereoscopic display which simply directs parallax images for the viewer's eyes to form 3D depth impression, the LFD optically redistributes the 3D spatial information precisely, which provides vivid and natural 3D images similar to how humans observe the real 3D scene [7]. In addition to its high resolution and full color, the 3D LFD also has the characteristics of wide viewing angle and dense viewpoints which provides viewers with smooth and continuous motion parallax. One of the most common technique to realize

© Springer Nature Singapore Pte Ltd. 2021
W. Song and F. Xu (Eds.): ICVRD 2020, CCIS 1313, pp. 33–44, 2021.
https://doi.org/10.1007/978-981-33-6549-0_4

the wide viewing angle (even 360 degrees) [8] is the multi-projection LFD, which can achieve smooth motion parallax and high definition with its high dense projectors. However, researchers pay so much attention to the system performance improvement of 3D LFD, but lacking the understanding of displays' task performance. Maurice H.P.H et al. investigated the performance effects of stereoscopic displays for applications and they suggested that there is a clear need for more empirical evidences to quantify the added value of stereoscopic displays [9]. Thus, this paper focused on the task performance of 3D LFD.

The mental rotation (MR), a concept provided by Shepard and Metzler in 1971, is an excellent way to evaluate the performance of stereoscopic displays [11]. It is well-known that the essential difference between 2D displays and 3D LFDs is that 3D can provide depth information to the viewer. The MR task tests the participants' spatial visualization ability which requires participants to determine the relationship (rotation or mirror image) of the paired three-dimensional models on the display [11]. Therefore, it is significant to evaluate the performance of MR tasks on different stereoscopic displays. So far, there have been some studies using MR tasks to measure the task performance of stereoscopic displays. Sabine Bergner et al. demonstrated training effects on MR performance by using computer games with MR-related content on VR devices and 2D screen [12]. Y. Aitsiselmi et al. compared the performance of 2D and a kind of autostereoscopic displays by asking participants to complete MR task on different displays [10]. Ware et al. chose a path tracing in a graph as the task completed with a head-coupled display to demonstrate that 3D gets better performance than 2D in the field of image understanding [13]. Hubona G S et al. assessed the effects of four variables which included stereo vs. mono viewing etc. on the accuracy and speed of decision performances based on a task similar to MR [14].

In addition to the use of MR as the experimental task, there have been other studies that use different experimental tasks to evaluate the performance of 3D displays. David Drascic conducted an experiment to examine the performance of stereoscopic video system on the task of teleoperation, whose result showed that the stereoscopic video system can aid teleoperation by reducing task execution times, reducing error rates and reducing the time needed for training compared to standard monoscopic video systems [15]. N. Rehfeld et al. carried out an experiment to compare the performance parameters and qualitative subjective evaluations of different display types including monoscopic, anaglyph, polarization, shutter and autostereo on the image analysis task. The results indicated that stereoscopic display technologies were found to be very good and appropriate for image analysis tasks [16]. K. Votanopoulos et al. conducted an experiment on six laparoscopic skills using 2D or 3D imaging systems to assess whether 3D imaging ameliorates laparoscopic performance for surgeons who have already adapted to working within a 2D surgical environment. The results showed the 3D imaging had an advantage on the group of inexperienced participants by requiring less time and/or making less errors than 2D imaging [17]. McKee et al. conducted an experimental task of motion perception to compare the performance of participants between 3D condition and 2D condition and the results showed that stereoscopic 3D was more useful for the detection of static targets within clutter compared to the detection of straight-moving targets [18]. Willemsen et al. [19] designed related experiments to assess the effect of stereoscopic 3D to distance judgment tasks and they found that distance judgments in a virtual environment to be comparable over the non-stereo and stereoscopic 3D conditions. However, from all the above related studies, there have been few researches concerning performance evaluation of the three-dimensional LFDs which is a kind of true stereoscopic display technology. In this case, it is of great significance to assess the task performance of 3D LFD.

In this paper, a quantitative performance evaluation method of the 3D light field display based on cognitive measurement of the observer with a specifically designed mental rotation task is proposed. The procedure of the performance evaluation experiment design is demonstrated, some pairs of complex images with either same structure or mirror structure are displayed, and the participants are required to distinguish whether the displayed images are the same. Three different control experiments including 2D display with fixed viewpoint, 3D light field display with fixed viewpoint and 3D light field display with a free view are designed. 45 participants which are divided into three groups are assigned to take part in three difference control experiments, and the rate of mission success and the completion time are evaluated. By comparing the results on different experimental conditions and using a statistic analysis method called *T-test*, the superiority of 3D light field display is proved quantitatively and the display types and information of motion parallax with large viewing angle are demonstrated to have significant difference on the task performance. In addition, genders are proved to hardly make significant difference on the MR task performance.

2 Method

2.1 Participants

29 male and 16 female volunteers participate in the experiment and they are all graduate students and teachers in the Beijing University of Posts and Telecommunications. The participants range in age from 21 to 31 (23.7 ± 2.32) years old and all report normal or corrected to normal vision. All participants are naïve to the tasks that they are to perform in this experiment.

2.2 Experimental Setup

According to the reference [20], the 3D LFD used in our experiment is shown in Fig. 1. The 3D LFD is fabricated with a 32 inches LCD which has a resolution of 7680×4320. A 3D light field with a spatial resolution of about 1920×1080 and an angular resolution of 100 in a viewing angle of 80 degrees can be reconstructed with this LFD in a depth range of [-150 mm, 150 mm]. Due to the high spatial resolution, a high definition 2D image can also be displayed with this LFD by changing the parallax of different view to be zero. The software generating the experiment images is implemented based on the OpenGL graphics programming library. By using OpenGL graphics programming library, we write the rendering pipeline and generated virtual cameras to shoot multi-angle pictures of the three-dimensional cube model constructed in advance in Blender. After a process of the 3D LFD coding, the generated 3D model will be presented on the

(a)   (b)

Fig. 1. Experimental setup: (a) Frontal view of the 3D Light Field Display used in our experiment. (b) Side view of the 3D Light Field Display used in our experiment.

3D LFD. And by changing the number of virtual cameras into one, we can transfer the same 3D LFD into a traditional 2D display.

In addition to the display device above, the study also need to use keyboard input. Participants are asked to determine the relationship between two models displayed by pressing the appropriate S (same, rotated) or D (different, mirrored) key on the keyboard. Since all participants are graduate students and teachers of Beijing University of Posts and Telecommunications, it was reasonable to assume that the vast majority of participants would be familiar with using a computer keyboard and therefore there is no need for additional training work on the use of keyboard. Figure 2 shows some examples of participants participating in our experiment.

Fig. 2. Examples of experimental procedure

3 Procedure

(1) Preliminary Spatial Ability Test

Before the actual experiment, 46 potential participants are tested for the ability to see stereoscopically. Stereopsis is tested with the TNO-test for stereoscopic vision which demands participants to distinguish figures from a background in random dot figures within 30 s [21]. One participant of insufficient stereoscopic ability is excluded from further participation. And then the remaining 45 participants are tested for spatial ability using Vandenberg and Kuse's MR test in the form of paper questionnaire, who are ranked according to scores of spatial ability and gender factors, and evenly split over the three conditions of the experiment later. This provides an equal distribution of spatial ability and gender factors over the 3 experimental conditions.

(2) Experimental Task

A variant of the MR paradigm, first introduced by Shepard and Metzler, is used in this research. As shown in Fig. 3, participants are presented with a pair of objects, whose task is to distinguish the relationship between the two objects on the display. If relationship of the model pair is rotated, participants are expected to press the S key on the keyboard; while if the relationship turns to mirrored, they need to press D key instead. Right before the formal experiment, a 3D model library has been built in Blender with 35 different kinds of 3D models from which the experimental questions are generated randomly. Each participant needs to complete 50 such S or D model pair questions and they are expected to finish each question within a time threshold of 25 s otherwise the program will record the present answer to be an error.

Participants are informed of the details and precautions in the following formal experiments and have 5-7 questions for practice. After all the preparations are settled down, they need to click the start button and start formal experiment by giving their answers of the relationship between model pair presented on the display, whose results of correct rate and response time will be recorded automatically by platform system. The

Fig. 3. Examples of the model pairs on the display. Participants' task was to determine the relationship between the left and right objects of one model pair. The answer or the relationship of the left example image is rotated (S) and the relationship of the right example image is mirrored (D).

model pair on the display will be updated to the next as soon as participants give their answer and this process will loop until 50 model pairs are all presented to the participant.

(3) Experimental Design
A fully between-subjects measure design is used in this study. There are three independent variables in the experiment, including the display types (2D display, 3D LFD), the information of motion parallax with large viewing angle (with fixed viewpoint, with free view) and the genders (male, female), and two dependent variables including scores (i.e. the number of correct responses per participant per trial) and response time (i.e. the time from model pair presented to an answer given by participants). Repeated measures of the dependent variables are automatically recorded by the test software. According to the independent variables above, we divide all participants into 3 different groups, one group carried out the task on a 2D display with fixed viewpoint (since it has no difference on the 2D display with fixed viewpoint or with the free view, cause motion parallax in 2D cannot offer any depth information like 3D), one group on a 3D LFD with fixed viewpoint and one group on 3D LFD with free view. The test software system will record the scores/50 and the response time per model pair per participant.

4   Results

In this section, experimental results are presented and analyzed. The means and standard deviations of scores and response times on 3 different conditions are shown in the form of table (see Table 1) and scatter graphs (see Fig. 4, 5), from which performance difference can be seen intuitively. In order to deduce the population trend from the sample statistic results in this research, a statistical analysis method called *T-test* is used, from which we can evaluate if the population also has the significant difference like sample's tendency on performance results. The *T-test* uses the T-distribution theory to deduce the probability of the difference so as to compare whether the difference between two sets of data is significant [22]. By using *T-test* to compare and analyze the sample results of 2D group with fixed viewpoint vs 3D LFD group with fixed viewpoint, the 3D LFD group with fixed viewpoint vs 3D LFD group with free view, male vs female under each experimental group respectively, the significant difference of display types, the information of motion parallax and genders on task performance can be assessed and we can draw related conclusions on the population.

4.1   Measurement Results

The means and standard deviations of scores and response times are shown in Table 1. The results are classified by display types (2D display or 3D LFD), motion parallax in a large viewing angle (with fixed viewpoint, with free view) and genders (female, male).

In terms of the scores, the mean scores of the 3D LFD group with fixed viewpoint (43.07 ± 2.76) is higher than the 2D group (40.20 ± 3.55), but is much lower than the 3D LFD group with free view (45.27 ± 2.46). Specifically, comparing with the score of 2D display with fixed viewpoint, the results of 3D LFD with fixed viewpoint get 2.87 higher scores on average which shows an improvement of 7.14%, and the results of the 3D LFD with free viewpoint get 5.07 higher scores on average which show an improvement of 12.61%.

This trend can also be seen intuitively from Fig. 4, which is a scatter graph that shows the results of all participants when ordered form lowest to highest scores. Figure 4 confirms the fact that participants on 3D LFD conditions do better than participants on 2D conditions. And in the comparison between the condition of 3D LFD with fixed viewpoint and 3D LFD with free view, it can be intuitively seen that participants on the 3D LFD with free view do better than participants on the 3D LFD with fixed viewpoint. Meanwhile, we notice that no matter under which experimental conditions, the scores of the participants are mainly concentrated in the range of 35 to 45 from Fig. 4.

Figure 5 is a scatter graph that shows the results of all participants when ordered from shortest to longest response time over the 3 different experimental conditions. From the average results we can see a trend that participants take the longest response time under the 3D LFD with free view (6061.90 ± 2192.29 ms), followed by the 2D with fixed viewpoint (4745.09 ± 2272.54 ms), while the group under the 3D LFD with fixed

Table 1. Means and standard deviations of scores and response times

Experimental conditions		2D Display with Fixed viewpoint		3D LFD with fixed viewpoint		3D LFD with free view	
Scores/50	female: male	1:1.5		1:2		1:2	
	Mean	39.33	40.78	42	43.6	43.6	46.1
		40.2		43.07		45.27	
	Std. dev.	3.55		2.76		2.46	
Average response time (ms)	Mean	4319.09	5029.08	5631.23	4062.38	7099.15	5543.27
		4745.09		4585.33		6061.9	
	Std. dev.	2272.54		1576.7		2192.29	

Fig. 4. Scatter graph of the scores of all participants when ordered from lowest to highest

Fig. 5. Scatter graph of average response time per model pair of all participants when ordered from lowest to highest.

viewpoint condition takes the shortest time (4585.33 ± 1576.70 ms). Specifically, the 3D group with free view takes more time than the other two, about 27.75% longer than the 2D group and about 32.20% longer than the 3D group with fixed viewpoint. This is not a surprise, because it takes time for participants to observe the different perspective views to gather more information about the scene. But at the same time, participants in 3D group with free view achieve higher scores than the other two groups due to the additional information, which improves the accuracy of spatial relationship cognition in the cost of extra response time. In addition, we also notice that no matter under which experimental conditions, the response time of participants are mostly concentrated in the range of 3000 ms to 7000 ms and it is rare that participants' response time exceeds 11000 ms.

4.2 T-test Analysis

The *T-test*, also known as student's *T-test*, is a typical statistical analysis method which uses the T-distribution theory to deduce the probability of the difference, so as to compare whether the difference between the two sets of data is significant [22]. Specifically, the *T-test* calculates a p-value, which is the probability that two sets of results are not significantly different. In statistics, the p-value of 0.05, which means that we can be 95% confident that there was a difference between the two sets of results, is generally used as the boundary of significant and not. That is, if the p-value greater than 0.05 means that the level of confidence with which we can say that the two sets of results are significantly different is not high enough to make any concrete conclusions but if the p-value is less than 0.05, we can then consider that there is a significant difference between the two sets of data analysis.

In this part, we compare the results of the 2D display group with fixed viewpoint vs 3D LFD group with fixed viewpoint by *T-test* in order to evaluate whether the only variable between the two groups, i.e. display types, has the significant impact on participants' task performance results. In the same way, we also compare the results of the 3D LFD group with fixed viewpoint vs 3D LFD group with free view to assess whether the

Table 2. *T-test* analysis results of display types to scores and response times

	Display types (Means ± Standard Deviations)		t	p
	2D ($n = 15$)	3D ($n = 15$)		
Scores/50	40.20 ± 3.55	43.07 ± 2.76	− 2.468	0.020*
Average response time per model pair (ms)	4745.09 ± 2272.54	4585.33 ± 1576.70	0.224	0.825

* $p < 0.05$ ** $p < 0.01$

Table 3. *T-test* analysis results of motion parallax information to scores and response times

	Motion parallax (Means ± Standard Deviations)		t	p
	Fixed viewpoint	Free view ($n = 15$)		
Scores	43.07 ± 2.76	45.27 ± 2.46	−2.179	0.038*
Average response time per model pair (ms)	4585.33 ± 1576.70	6061.90 ± 2192.29	−2.118	0.043*

* $p < 0.05$ ** $p < 0.01$

Table 4. *T-test* analysis results of gender to scores and response times in each experimental group

2D Display with Fixed Viewpoint		female ($n = 6$)	male ($n = 9$)	t	p
	Scores/50	39.33 ± 2.34	40.78 ± 4.21	−0.76	0.461
	Response Time per Model Pair(ms)	4319.10 ± 1149.10	5029.08 ± 2825.89	−0.579	0.573
3D LFD with Fixed Viewpoint	Scores/50	female ($n = 5$)	male ($n = 10$)	t	p
		42.00 ± 2.12	43.60 ± 2.99	−1.062	0.308
	Response Time per Model Pair(ms)	5631.23 ± 1965.18	4062.38 ± 1113.14	2.002	0.067
3D LFD with Free View	Scores/50	female ($n = 5$)	male ($n = 10$)	t	p
		43.60 ± 2.70	46.10 ± 1.97	−2.056	0.06
	Response Time per Model Pair(ms)	7099.15 ± 2988.92	5543.27 ± 1615.28	1.331	0.206

* $p < 0.05$ ** $p < 0.01$

information of motion parallax with large viewing angle, has a significant effect on the task performance results. In addition, the genders' effect is also evaluated through comparing male vs female results under the three different experimental conditions by *T-test*, respectively.

(1) Effect of Display Types

In order to evaluate the impact of display types on the task results, the data of 2D group with fixed viewpoint and 3D LFD group with fixed viewpoint are compared and analyzed by *T-test*, whose analysis results are shown in Table 2. As we can see, the p-value for comparing the 2D and 3D LFD scores was 0.02, which means different display types can make significant difference on the result of scores ($t = -2.468, p = 0.02 < 0.05$). Meanwhile, the average scores performance of 3D group (43.07 ± 2.76) has shown its superiority than the 2D group (40.20 ± 3.55), therefore we can make conclusion that display types can significant effect the correct rate of MR tasks and participants on the 3D LFD condition obviously do better than 2D with an improvement of 7.14%.

However, we can't make the same conclusion similar to scores in average response time per model pair, since the p-value for comparing the 2D and 3D LFD response times is 0.825, which is far more than the value of 0.05. Although the average response time of 3D group with fixed viewpoint (4585.33 ± 1576.70) has shown a better performance than 2D (4745.09 ± 2272.54), however with the p-value of 0.825 the difference resulting from display types is not significant enough to make any firm conclusion on the response time aspect ($t = 0.224, p = 0.825 > 0.05$).

(2) Effect of Motion Parallax with Large Viewing Angle

The data of the 3D LFD group with fixed viewpoint and the 3D LFD group with free view are compared and analyzed by *T-test* in order to evaluate whether the motion parallax information can make significant difference on results. The analysis results in Table 3 indicate that there are some benefit in scores from free view group with the participants in this group getting about 5.1% higher scores on average, and the p-value ($t = -2.179$, $p = 0.038 < 0.05$) indeed suggests that the information of motion parallax can make significant difference on the correct rate of MR tasks.

Significant difference can also be observed in average response time per model pair with the p-value of 0.043 ($t = -2.118, p = 0.043 < 0.05$) which indicates that the information of motion parallax can make significant difference on the response time of MR tasks. Considering the average response time per question under 3D LFD with free view is 32.2% longer than 3D LFD with fixed viewpoint, the conclusion can be made that the information of motion parallax with large viewing angle can significantly affect the response time of MR tasks with free view group takes more time than fixed viewpoint group.

(3) Genders Difference on Different Experimental Conditions

The male and female experimental results data is compared and analyzed by *T-test* on each group, respectively. In this way, genders' effect on performance of MR tasks is evaluated. With all p-value greater than 0.05, the *T-test* analysis results in Table 4 have indicated that no matter under the condition of 2D display or 3D LFD, genders can't make significant difference on the task performance of MR. That is, gender has no significant effect on tasks performance when people complete the MR missions.

5 Conclusion

In this paper we have attempted to evaluate the 3D LFD by performing the same MR task and comparing the task performance with the 2D display. In order to investigate the impact of factors like display types, motion parallax information and genders on the task performance, we divide 45 participants evenly into 3 different groups and assign them to complete the MR task under three different experimental conditions respectively, including a 2D display group with fixed viewpoint, a 3D LFD group with fixed viewpoint and a 3D LFD group with free view. The experimental platform records the scores and response times of participants and uses a statistical analysis method called *T-test* to analyze the significant differences between two sets of results between groups. The results have shown a clear trend that the 3D LFD is significantly superior to the 2D display with the 12.61% higher scores under the condition of 3D LFD with free view than the condition of 2D and 7.14% higher under the 3D LFD with fixed viewpoint both than the condition of 2D on correct rate of MR tasks. There is also a significant difference on response times which is resulted from the information of motion parallax with large viewing angle. In this case, we can say that the 3D LFD can dramatically improve the correct rate on MR tasks, but it obviously needs more time to obtain the information of motion parallax by extra movement. In addition, the results also show that no matter the experimental environment is 2D display or 3D light field display with free view or fixed viewpoint, genders can't make significant difference on the task performance.

In the future, the task performance description factors system will be expanded and we will attempt to assess the task performance of 3D LFD on aspects of other spatial ability besides MR. So the task performance of 3D LFD can be evaluated more systematically and comprehensively.

Funding. This work was supported in part by the National Pre-research Project under Grant 41412040304, in part by the National Natural Science Foundation of China under Grant 61905020, in part by the National Natural Science Foundation of China under Grant 61905017, in part by the National Key R&D Program of China under Grant 2017YFB1002900, and in part by the Fundamental Research Funds for the Central Universities under Grant 2019PTB-018.

References

1. Liu, X., Li, H.: The progress of light-field 3-d displays. Inf. Disp. **30**(6), 6–14 (2014)
2. Wetzstein, G., Lanman, D., Hirsch, M., Raskar, R.: Tensor displays. US
3. Song, W., Zhu, Q., Huang, T., Liu, Y., Wang, Y.: Volumetric display based on multiple mini-projectors and a rotating screen. Opt. Eng. **54**(1), 013103 (2015)
4. Chen, D., Sang, X., Yu, X., Zeng, X., Guo, N.: Performance improvement of compressive light field display with the viewing-position-dependent weight distribution. Opt. Express **24**(26), 29781 (2016)
5. Sang, X., et al.: Demonstration of a large-size real-time full-color three-dimensional display. Opt. Lett. **34**(24), 3803–3805 (2009)
6. Sang, X., Fan, F.C., Choi, S., Jiang, C., Yu, C., Yan, B., et al.: Three-dimensional display based on the holographic functional screen. Opt. Eng. **50**(9), 091303–091305 (2011)
7. Liu, B., Sang, X., Yu, X., Gao, X., Du, J.: Time-multiplexed light field display with 120-degree wide viewing angle. Opt. Express **27**(24), 35728–35739 (2019)
8. Lixia, N., Zhenxing, L., Haifeng, L., Xu, L.: 360-degree large-scale multiprojection light-field 3d display system. Appl. Opt. **57**(8), 1817 (2018)
9. Beurden, M.H.P.H.V., Hoey, G.V., Hatzakis, H., Ijsselsteijn, W.A.: Stereoscopic displays in the medical domains: a review of perception and performance effects. In: Human Vision and Electronic Imaging XIV. International Society for Optics and Photonics (2009)

10. Aitsiselmi, Y., Holliman, N.S.: Using mental rotation to evaluate the benefits of stereoscopic displays. In: Proceedings of SPIE - The International Society for Optical Engineering, p. 7237 (2009)
11. Shepard, R.N., Metzler, J.: Mental rotation of three-dimensional objects. Science **171**(3972), 701–703 (1971)
12. Neubauer, A.C., Bergner, S., Schatz, M.: Two- vs. three-dimensional presentation of mental rotation tasks: sex differences and effects of training on performance and brain activation. Intelligence, **38**(5), 529–539) (2010)
13. Ware, C., Franck, G.: Evaluating stereo and motion cues for visualizing information nets in three dimensions. ACM Trans. Graph. **15**(2), 121–140 (1996)
14. Hubona, G.S., Shirah, G.W., Fout, D.G.: The effects of motion and stereopsis on three-dimensional visualization. Int. J. Hum.-Comput. Stud. **47**(5), 609–627 (1997)
15. Drascic, D.: Skill acquisition and task performance in teleoperation using monoscopic and stereoscopic video remote viewing. In: Proceedings of the Human Factors and Ergonomics Society Annual Meeting, vol. 35, no. 19, pp. 1367–1371 (1991)
16. Peinsipp-Byma, E., Rehfeld, N., Eck, R.: Evaluation of stereoscopic 3D displays for image analysis tasks. In: Proceedings of SPIE - Stereoscopic Displays and Applications XX, vol. 7237, no. 72370L (2009)
17. Votanopoulos, K., Brunicardi, F.C., Thornby, J., Bellows, C.F.: Impact of three-dimensional vision in laparoscopic training. World J. Surg. **32**(1), 110–118 (2008)
18. Mckee, S.P., Watamaniuk, S.N.J., Harris, J.M., Smallman, H.S., Taylor, D.G.: Is stereopsis effective in breaking camouflage for moving targets? Vis. Res. **37**(15), 2047–55 (1997)
19. Willemsen, P., Gooch, A.A., Thompson, W.B., Creem-Regehr, S.H.: Effects of stereo viewing conditions on distance perception in virtual environments. Presence **17**(1), 91–101 (2015)
20. Yu, X., et al.: Dynamic three-dimensional light-field display with large viewing angle based on compound lenticular lens array and multi-projectors. Opt. Express **37**(11), 16024–16031 (2019)
21. Okuda, F.C., Wanters, B.S.: Evaluation of the TNO random-dot stereogram. Am. Orthoptic J. **34**, 124–131 (1977)
22. Box, J.F.: Guinness, gosset, fisher, and small samples. Stat. Sci. 2(1), 45–52 (1987)

Large Horizontal Viewing-Angle Three-Dimensional Light Field Display Based on Liquid Crystal Barrier and Time-Division-Multiplexing

Renxiang Dai[1](✉), Xinzhu Sang[1](✉), Shujun Xing[1,2], Xunbo Yu[1], Xin Gao[1], Li Liu[1], Boyang Liu[1], Chao Gao[1], Yuedi Wang[1], and Fan Ge[1]

[1] State Key Laboratory of Information Photonics and Optical Communications, Beijing University of Posts and Telecommunications, P.O. Box 72, Beijing 100876, China
stsdl001@163.com, xzsang@126.com
[2] State Key Laboratory of Precision Measurement Technology and Instruments, Tsinghua University, 100084 Beijing, China

Abstract. Three-dimensional (3D) light field display can reconstruct vector of light field of 3D scene eliminating convergence-adjustment conflict (CAC) with full parallax and nature color cues, however it suffers from its limited viewing-angle, the mediocre display resolution, an insufficient gross of viewing perspectives and the complex setup. Here, a large horizontal viewing-angle 3D light field display with horizontal viewing zone of 70° and vertical viewing zone of 35° without resolution reduction based on liquid crystal barrier (LC-Barrier) and time-division-multiplexing (TDM) is presented. The proposed 3D light field display consists of a holographic functional screen (HFS), a lens array (LA), an LC-Barrier and a 28-inch LCD with resolution of 3840 × 2160. By analyzing the corresponding relationships of rays from elemental image array (EIA), a series of pixel-mapping equations are derived. Moreover, the issue that horizontal resolution will decrease as the horizontal viewing-angle doubles can be addressed by enhancing the resolution utilizing TDM. The fill factor is introduced to evaluate the imaging effect. Experimental results demonstrate that the large horizontal viewing-angle 3D light field display based on LC-Barrier and TDM can present actual 3D stereoscope images with correct occlusion and perception.

Keywords: Light field display · Liquid crystal barrier · Time-division-multiplexing · Lens array · Elemental image array · Fill factor

1 Introduction

Human being perceive real world scene using pupils to obtain binocular parallax both plane and depth-oriented. Common display device is hard to meet the demands of viewer

This work was supported in part by the National Key Research and Development Program (2017YFB1002900), in part by the National Natural Science Foundation of China (61575025, 61705014), and in part by the Fundamental Research Funds for the Central Universities (2018PTB-00-01, 2016ZX01, 2019RC13, 2019PTB-018).

© Springer Nature Singapore Pte Ltd. 2021
W. Song and F. Xu (Eds.): ICVRD 2020, CCIS 1313, pp. 45–55, 2021.
https://doi.org/10.1007/978-981-33-6549-0_5

to observe actual 3D images, so 3D display technology that provides realistic natural scenes has attracted much attention and various 3D innovative techniques have been proposed [1–12]. These methods could implement 3D displays such as holographic display, binocular stereoscopic 3D display and 3D light field display. Holographic display can provide light intensity and phase information of target objects simultaneously. However, the equipment is complex and it is difficult to realize larger-size, full color hint and dynamic display in a few years. Binocular stereoscopic 3D display can provide viewer's pupils with two parallax perspectives synthesized into stereoscopic images in viewer's brain where human is able to sense depth cues of 3D scene. However, it suffers from CAC, a periodic phenomenon of viewing areas and limited viewing-angle. Moreover, the binocular stereoscopic 3D display based on parallax barrier sheet presents low brightness since the barrier blocks most of the light from the display panel. 3D light field display could reconstruct vector of light field of 3D scene and eliminate CAC due to different image forming principle compared to binocular stereoscopic. The projector arrays could project images in multiple directions thus realizing the 360° 3D light field display with high resolution, large viewing-angle and full smooth motion parallax. However, the implementation comes with relatively high costs and complex adjustment due to its large space occupancy, which injures the application of the system.

In recent years, many researchers have devoted to the development of 3D light field display. Jang et al. developed a near-eye light field display via a holographic optical element (HOE) as an image combiner to enhance transparency with this thin structure [13]. Ni et al. proposed a 360° multi-projection 3D light field display system using a cylindrical light field diffusion screen with 1.8 m height and 3 m diameter [6]. Our previous researches overcome the problem of low spatial resolution by introducing HFS [1]. It demonstrates an interactive floating full-parallax 3D light field display with a viewing-angle of 45° and all depth cues. Gao et al. proposed a 3D light field display based on the aspheric substrate Fresnel-lens-array with high brightness [14]. Moreover, a 162-inch large-scale horizontal light field display based on aspheric lens array with a resolution of 3840 × 2160 and a viewing-angle of 40° is proposed [4]. A horizontal dense multi-view light field display based on real-time light field pickup and reconstruction with low crosstalk of less than 7% between micro-pitch viewing zones and the resolution of 1920 × 1080 in the viewing-angle of 70° is proposed [15]. A dynamic 3D light field display based on three projectors and compound lenticular lens array with viewing-angle of 90° is demonstrated [2]. However, there still exist some drawbacks including limited viewing-angle, lack of display resolution, insufficient gross of viewing perspectives, without vertical parallax or complex setup on projectors.

In order to achieve better performance of 3D light field display, a large viewing-angle light field display with horizontal viewing zone of 70° and vertical viewing zone of 35° without resolution reduction based on LC-Barrier and TDM is presented. In order to achieve deeper immersion and higher realism for human being viewer, the horizontal viewing-angle plays a more critical role in improving the quality of the 3D light field display compared to the vertical viewing-angle.

The proposed system adopts TDM technique to provide a double resolution and guarantee the large horizontal viewing-angle of 70° for pupils based on the principle of the persistence of vision. Moreover, the LC-Barrier is necessary to realize the TDM with a maximum scanning frequency of 60 Hz, which will load two types of parallel barrier structures. The mode of the proposed 3D light field display has two timeslot presenting periodically and each timeslot sustains for 12 ms succeeding an interval for 4.6 ms. The proposed system can provide two EIA based on a liquid crystal display (LCD) with pixels of 3840×2160 offering 144×72 viewing perspectives. In this lens-type 3D light field display, the fill factor, defined by the ratio of the active display region compared to the each individual elemental region, is introduced to analyze the quantitative value of the visibility for each elemental viewing area [16]. In the experiment, the 3D light field display based on LC-Barrier and TDM can provide high quality 3D images with horizontal viewing-angle of 70° and vertical viewing-angle of 35°, correct occlusion and authentic perception of 3D object.

2 Experimental Configuration

2.1 Design of the Optical Configuration

Figure 1(a) illustrates the configuration 3D light field display with LC-Barrier. The proposed 3D light field display is constituted by multiple optical components including LCD, LC-Barrier, LA and HFS. To present a high-performance light field of 3D objects,

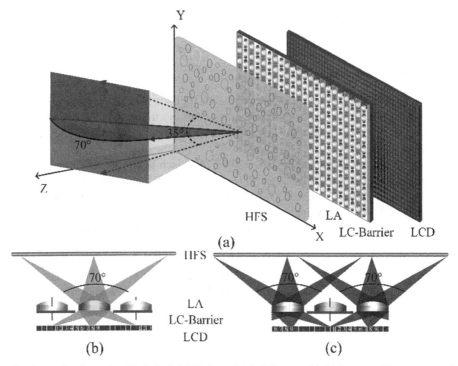

Fig. 1. (a) Configuration 3D light field display with LC-Barrier. (b) Light controlling process of the first timeslot in horizontal. (c) Light controlling process of the second timeslot in horizontal.

the angle of horizontal viewing area should be at least 70° larger than the vertical viewing-angle of 35°. In the practical application situation, multiple viewing perspectives in horizontal direction can provide more comfortable observation experience attributing to that viewer need wider observation area in horizontal to get consecutive motion parallax.

Therefore, two synthetic EIAs containing 144 rows viewing perspectives are loaded on the LCD with pixels of 3840 × 2160 in two timeslots respectively. An LC-Barrier is in the rear of the LA to realize effect of TDM coordinating the LCD. The LC-Barrier keeps refreshing from a periodic barrier-grating pattern to another one with a complementary pattern, which will be demonstrated in Sect. 2.2. To provide enough brightness for viewer, it is necessary to ensure the polarization direction of the lower polarizer of the LC-Barrier same as the polarization direction of the upper one constituting LCD.

The LA is constituted by standard micro-lens of 53 × 30, which is divided into two groups to work in different timeslots. Owing to only half of the micro-lens work in a single timeslot, the period of EIA has doubled in horizontal to offer more positions observing the 3D image, as shown in Fig. 1(b) and (c), hence the viewing-angle is expanded simultaneously. The light ray emitting from LCD carrying information of 3D object from EIA forms 3D light field through modulation of the LC-Barrier and LA. However, the horizontal resolution available declines by half at a viewing position in a single timeslot. The application of TDM can compensate the horizontal resolution available ensuring the resolution does not drop due to expansion of viewing area, which will be elaborated in Sect. 2.2. The light field of the 3D image is reconstructed on the position of the HFS and an available viewing scope is formed, which is a 1.21 m × 0.65 m rectangle at the best viewing position of 1.1 m from the HFS.

2.2 Image Coding and Process of TDM

As described above, the design of the proposed 3D light field display based on LC-Barrier and TDM owns the function to rearrange the rays from the LCD panel forming a high-resolution 3D image with large horizontal viewing-angle of 70° and vertical viewing-angle of 35°.

Figure 2 illustrates the coding process of EIA, which is a process of mapping the pixel of input (PI) and pixel of output (PO), along with the parameters of the proposed optical system. $PO(T, x, y, u, v, R, G, B)$ is a pixel located at (x, y) of viewing perspective totaling $M \times N$. T, x and y are the timeslot and the coordinate of viewing perspective respectively. u, v, R, G and B are the coordinate of the pixel and intensity of colors. $PI(t, i, j, R, G, B)$ is a pixel on the two-dimensional liquid crystal display panel at n timeslot. The six parameters represent the slot time, coordinates, intensity of colors.

The rays containing the information of multiple viewing position converge on the imaging surface of micro lens that is the site of HFS. To simplify the analysis procedure of coding, only one single timeslot is illustrated. According to the geometric relations, the mathematical expression of mapping relationship between PI and PO can be derived as Eq. (1) to (3).

$$\begin{pmatrix} T \\ x \\ y \end{pmatrix} = \frac{1}{2} \begin{pmatrix} 0 \\ M \\ N \end{pmatrix} + \begin{pmatrix} 1 & 0 & 0 \\ 0 & -1 & 0 \\ 0 & 0 & -1 \end{pmatrix} \begin{pmatrix} t \\ i\%M \\ j\%N \end{pmatrix} \tag{1}$$

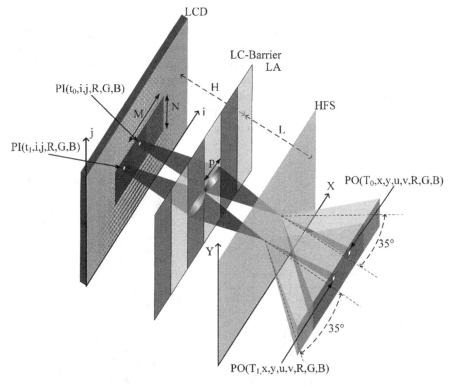

Fig. 2. Coding process of elemental image array.

$$u = \left[\frac{i}{M}\right] \tag{2}$$

$$v = \left[\frac{j}{N}\right] \tag{3}$$

where M denotes the number of pixels of an elemental image in the horizontal direction, N is the number of pixels of an elemental image in the vertical direction, "%" is a modulo operational character and "[]" is an operational character to round down.

As shown in Fig. 2, the spacing of LCD and LC-Barrier and the spacing of LA and HFS are decided by the focal length of micro lens of LA, which conform to the formula as follows.

$$\frac{1}{H} + \frac{1}{L} = \frac{1}{f} \tag{4}$$

Due to the TDM operation is implemented into the proposed light field display, a timeslots synchronized soft-controller (TSSC) is utilized to command LC-Barrier and LCD panel to load proper barrier pattern and synthetic EIA image, which can guarantee no loss of resolution and number of viewing perspectives meanwhile double view-angle. The time sequence diagram of TSSC of the LC-Barrier and LCD panel is depicted in

Fig. 3(a). In one timeslot, an EIA signal and the corresponding barrier pattern work for 12 ms and each cycle has a gap of 4.6 ms. The EIA signal is coded synchronized by TSSC from an array of viewing perspectives collected on corresponding viewing position. The barrier patterns are synthesized according to the structure of LA in advance as shown in Fig. 3(b). The barrier pattern 1 is used to activate the even columns of lens and the barrier pattern 2 is used to activate the odd columns of lens. To avoid the reduction of horizontal resolution, compensation is introduced in the proposed display system originating the pixels from different timeslots, as shown in Fig. 3(c).

Fig. 3. (a) The time sequence diagram of the LCD signal and LC-Barrier pattern. (b) The pattern of the LC-Barrier. (c) The schematic diagram of TDM in the viewing position of center.

2.3 Fill Factor Enhancement by the HFS and Resolution Enhancement by the TDM

The fill factor is deemed as an indispensable evaluation value of the visibility for each elemental viewing-area [17]. In this lens-type 3D light field display, the fill factor is defined as the ratio of the effective viewing-area and the individual elemental area. In the conventional lens-type 3D display, larger viewing-angle would bring about lower fill factor due to the limited size of the aperture. However, the introduction of HFS could break this trade-off through a function of diffusion of HFS, which would greatly increase the fill factor.

Figure 4(a) illustrates the captured display effect of the conventional light field display without HFS, which is a vague image with insufficient fill factor. Moreover, Fig. 4(c) is a detailed diagram of the certain area with a frame as shown in Fig. 4(a). The fill factor formula is given in Eq. (5)

$$r_f = \frac{S_1}{S_0} \tag{5}$$

where the S_0 is the individual elemental area and the S_1 is area of effective viewing-area.

Fig. 4. Comparison of display effects for (a) the conventional light field display without HFS and (b) the proposed light field display with HFS. (c) The effective viewing-area and the individual elemental area of the conventional light field display without HFS (d) The effective viewing-area and the individual elemental area of the proposed light field display with HFS.

Figure 4(b) illustrates the captured display effect of the proposed light field display with HFS, which is a realistic and clear 3D image with a proper fill factor eliminating the border dark stripes. The value of the fill factor is calculated in Eq. (5), as shown in Table 1.

Table 1. Value of fill factor

	S_0/mm^2	S_1/mm^2	r_f
The light field display without HFS	175.56	21.90	0.125
The light field display with HFS	175.56	175.56	1

S_0 comes from an actual measuring result of lens and S_1 comes from a capturing image of a 3D bear-model object in the corresponding 3D light field display. In the proposed light field display system with HFS, it is obvious that the value of fill factor is enhanced just by eight times compared to the conventional light field display without HFS. The introduction of HFS can optimize image quality by increasing fill factor.

Figure 5 shows the comparison of display effect of horizontal resolution for the light field display with horizontal viewing-angle of 70° based on LC-Barrier and TDM method and the conventional 70° light field display without LC-Barrier and TDM method. The horizontal resolution keeps from loss while the horizontal angle increases twice as much due to the introduction of LC-Barrier and TDM method.

(a)   (b)

Fig. 5. Comparison of display horizontal resolution for (a) the light field display with horizontal viewing-angle of 70° based on LC-Barrier and TDM method and (b) the conventional 70° light field display without LC-Barrier and TDM method.

3   Experimental Results

In the demonstrated large horizontal viewing-angle 3D light field display system, the number of lens of LA is 53 × 30. The number of interlaced stripes loaded to the LC-Barrier is 53 in each timeslot. Moreover, the polarization direction of lower polarizer constituting the LC-Barrier is horizontal, which is the same as the polarization direction of upper polarizer of display panel, to provide higher brightness. The distance between LC-Barrier and LA is 3 mm and the distance between the LA and HFS is 200 mm. The EIA is displayed on an LCD with the size of 32 inches and the resolution of 3840 × 2160.

Exhibition of products is an important application of the 3D light field display. By coding 144 × 72 viewpoints perspectives for the demonstrated large horizontal viewing-angle light field display, a 3D fluffy bear image is reconstructed. Different angle views of the 3D model images are shown in Fig. 6. Obviously, the occlusion of multiple angles is correct.

Fig. 6. Different perspectives of the large horizontal viewing-angle 3D light field display.

One of the prominent applications of the proposed large horizontal viewing-angle light field display is for medical analysis and diagnosis. The medical data of human gums is used to demonstrate the feasibility and superiority of our proposed large horizontal viewing-angle light field display. By employing the described method, the demonstrated light field display presents perspectives as shown in Fig. 7.

Fig. 7. Different perspectives of the 3D human gums.

4   Conclusion

A large horizontal viewing area 3D light field display with horizontal viewing-angle of 70° and vertical viewing-angle of 35° is demonstrated. It can provide both correct occlusion and proper perception. In the proposed 3D light field display system, the LC-Barrier is designed to arrange timeslots sequence expanding horizontal viewing-angle and maintaining resolution. A rectangle viewing scope with 1.21 m × 0.65 m at the best viewing position at a distance of 1.1 m from the HFS is formed. The mapping relationship between pixels of EIA and pixels of viewing perspectives is discussed and a series of corresponding equations are derived. Compared with the previous approaches, a crucial indicator of fill factor is introduced to evaluate the imaging effect. Moreover, the proposed light field display doubles the horizontal viewing-angle, enhances fill factor to eight times, keeps the resolution at a satisfactory level and ensures the integrity of vertical viewing-angle compared to traditional methods. In the experiment, the large horizontal viewing-angle 3D light field display based on LC-Barrier and TDM presents multiple perspectives in different directions.

References

1. Sang, X.Z., Gao, X., Yu, X.B., et al.: Interactive floating full-parallax digital three-dimensional light-field display based on wavefront recomposing. Opt. Exp. **26**(7), 8883–8889 (2018)
2. Yu, X.B., Sang, X.Z., Gao, X., et al.: Dynamic three-dimensional light-field display with large viewing angle based on compound lenticular lens array and multi-projectors. Opt. Exp. **27**(11), 16024–16031 (2019)
3. Yang, L., Sang, X.Z., Yu, X.B., et al.: Demonstration of a large-size horizontal light-field display based on the LED panel and the micro-pinhole unit array. Opt. Commun. **414**, 140–145 (2018)
4. Yang, S.W., Sang, X.Z., Yu, X.B., et al.: 162-inch 3D light field display based on aspheric lens array and holographic functional screen. Opt. Exp. **26**(25), 33013–33021 (2018)
5. Yontem, A.O., Li, K., Chu, D.P.: Reciprocal 360-deg 3D light-field image acquisition and display system. J. Opt. Soc. Am. A Opt. Image Sci. Vis. **36**(2), A77–A87 (2019)
6. Ni, L.X., Li, Z.X., Li, H.F.: 360-degree large-scale multiprojection light-field 3D display system. Appl. Opt. **57**(8), 1817–1823 (2018)
7. Choi, G., Jeon, H., Kim, H., et al.: Horizontal-parallax-only light-field display with cylindrical symmetry. In: Advances in Display Technologies VIII, vol. 10556 (2018)
8. Wu, F., Wu, R., Deng, H., et al.: Effect of width of light source on viewing angle of one-dimensional integral imaging display. Optik **157**, 873–876 (2018)
9. Chou, P.Y., Wu, D.Y., Huang, S.H.: Hybrid light field head-mounted display using time-multiplexed liquid crystal lens array for resolution enhancement. Opt. Exp. **27**(2), 1164–1178 (2019)
10. Zeng, X.Y., Zhou, X.T., Guo, T.L., et al.: Crosstalk reduction in large-scale autostereoscopic 3D-LED display based on black-stripe occupation ratio. Opt. Commun. **389**, 159–164 (2017)
11. Xia, X.X., Zhang, X.Y., Zhang, L., et al.: Time-multiplexed multi-view three-dimensional display with projector array and steering screen. Opt. Exp. **26**(12), 15528–15538 (2018)
12. Wan, W.Q., Qiao, W., Huang, W.B., et al.: Multiview holographic 3D dynamic display by combining a nano-grating patterned phase plate and LCD. Opt. Exp. **25**(2), 1114–1122 (2017)
13. Jang, C., Bang, K., Moon, S., et al.: Retinal 3D: augmented reality near-eye display via pupil-tracked light field projection on retina. ACM Trans. Graph. **36**(6), 1–13 (2017)
14. Gao, X., Sang, X.Z., Yu, X.B., et al.: High brightness three-dimensional light field display based on the aspheric substrate Fresnel-lens-array with eccentric pupils. Opt. Commun. **361**, 47–54 (2016)

15. Yang, L., Sang, X.Z., Yu, X.B., et al.: A crosstalk-suppressed dense multi-view light-field display based on real-time light-field pickup and reconstruction. Opt. Exp. **26**(26), 34412–34427 (2018)
16. Choi, S., Takashima, Y., Min, S.W.: Improvement of fill factor in pinhole-type integral imaging display using a retroreflector. Opt. Exp. **25**(26), 33078–33087 (2017)
17. Park, S.G., Song, B.S., Min, S.W.: Analysis of image visibility in projection-type integral imaging system without diffuser. J. Opt. Soc. Korea **14**(2), 121–126 (2010)

Extended-Depth Light Field Display Based on Controlling-Light Structure in Cross Arrangement

Fan Ge and Xinzhu Sang[⊠]

State Key Laboratory of Information Photonics and Optical Communications, Beijing University of Posts and Telecommunications, Beijing 100876, China
xzsang@126.com

Abstract. Despite the light field display with many advantages is considered as one of the most potential three-dimensional display technologies, the limited depth range is common drawback which restricts its applications. Small depth of focus (DOF) caused by diffraction is one of the reasons those limit the display depth range. Here, the proposed method extends the display depth range by enlarging DOF of the lens. In order to verify the feasibility of the method, a 32-inch three-dimensional light-field display system based on the controlling-light structure in cross arrangement and holographic functional screen (HFS) is demonstrated. Two extended DOFs are superposed to form the extended depth due to the controlling-light structure in cross arrangement combined by lenslet array and aperture array. The function of HFS is to modulate and rebuild the light field distribution so as to eliminate the gaps between the adjacent lenslets and increase the fill factor of the controlling-light structure. In terms of contrast experiments, the depth range of the improved display system is extended effectively, which is extended from 6 cm to 13 cm on the premise of the 40° horizontal and vertical viewing angle and acceptable resolution.

Keywords: Light field display · Depth range · Controlling-light structure

1 Introduction

Three-dimensional (3D) display has attracted considerable attention of scientists and engineers because of contribution to providing natural scenes in an intuitive and natural manner. In order to provide the 3D information of 3D objects or natural scenes, many kinds of 3D display have been developed [1–4]. Autostereoscopic display based on binocular parallax with a lenticular lens array or a parallax barrier often causes visual confusion and fatigue induced by inconstancies in the 3D visual information and convergence–accommodation conflict [1]. Volume display based on uses optical scanning with mechanical components constructs 3D images consisting of light points arranged in 3D space [2]. However, due to their limited color reproduction and the scanning range of the optical scanner, it cannot provide completely convincing 3D images. The holographic 3D display has been considered as an alternative to current stereoscopic display, but it's

© Springer Nature Singapore Pte Ltd. 2021
W. Song and F. Xu (Eds.): ICVRD 2020, CCIS 1313, pp. 56–65, 2021.
https://doi.org/10.1007/978-981-33-6549-0_6

still challenging due to unavailable dynamic devices with high information throughput and limited information processing capability [3]. Among these various 3D display techniques, light field display based on integral imaging is an attractive method to obtain a 3D image, which can offer full-parallax and continuous-viewing 3D images without the convergence-accommodation conflict [4]. Unlike traditional 3D display methods based on the binocular disparity, light field display [5] supports all depth cues, which can be treated as the vector light-field, and the light field is distributed with different colors and variable brightness in different directions. If the relative direction and intensity information of light field originated from a 3D scene are recorded, the 3D light-field information of the scene can be recovered by generating the beams with the same relative directions and intensities based on the recorded information. However, the image depth range [7] is one of the main limitations of its applications in medical, military, geographic information and entertainment. There are preceding studies relevant to depths extension [8–11] by the researchers. One of those is synthetic aperture integral imaging (SAII) [8, 9], in which a camera is translated on a 2D grid to obtain multiple perspective images of high resolution. Although the depth range of the SAII system is significantly extended, it is still restricted by the lenses of cameras. Miao Zhang et al. [9] proposed a method to extend the depth range of a SAII system by realizing the image fusion method on the multi-focus elemental images with different perspectives. The depth range can be substantially improved with no deterioration of lateral resolution by proper reduction of the fill factor of pickup microlenses [10]. The method to extend the depth range of the wavefront imaging system through an integrated architecture of a liquid-crystal microlens array powered by electricity and a common photosensitive array was presented [11]. However, those solutions above are with high cost or large volume. Small depth of focus (DOF) caused by diffraction is one of the reasons those limit the display depth range. According to the imaging principle, DOF can be enlarged by decreasing the aperture of lens.

To verify the feasibility of the proposed display method, a 32-inch light field display system with extended depths based on controlling-light structure in cross arrangement is constructed, which is consist of a liquid crystal display (LCD) screen, non-uniform lenslet array (NLA), non-uniform aperture array and holographic function screen (HFS). By introducing an aperture array, light beams are limited thus extending the DOF of lenslet. Two extended DOFs are superposed to form the extended depths thanks to the controlling-light structure combined by NLA and aperture array. The function of HFS is to modulate and rebuild light field distribution so as to eliminate the gaps between the adjacent lenslets [12]. In the contrast experiments, the depth range of the improved display system is extended effectively, which is extended from 6 cm to 13 cm.

2 Configuration

2.1 System Structure

Light-field display system with high quality based on controlling-light structure in cross arrangement as shown in Fig. 1 is proposed, which is composed with the LCD screen, NLA, nun-uniform aperture array and HFS. The LCD screen with a resolution of 3840 × 2160 is used to load on synthetic image through computer processing with the specific algorithm. The controlling-light structure, combined by NLA and non-uniform aperture array, serves to increase the depth range on the premise of ensuring viewing angle and the clarity of the image. HFS is utilized to increase the fill factor of the controlling-light structure.

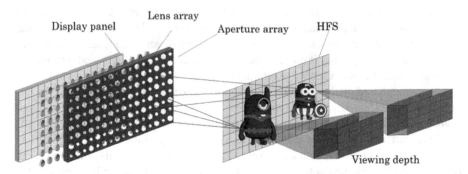

Fig. 1. The configuration of optical field display system based on tunable aperture array.

Different from pixel mapping pixel in planar object imaging, pixel maps voxel in light field display. In Fig. 2, the elemental unit of 3D light field display is magnified, which is composed of an element image and a corresponding lenslet. Because the position of voxels is not necessarily the ideal conjugate image plane, the non-conjugate points in the image space are no longer the point images, but the cross section of some corresponding beams, namely dispersion spots. Considering the minimum angular resolution of human eyes, as long as the size of spot is adequately small, it can be recognized as a clear image point.

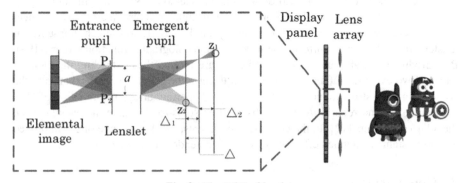

Fig. 2. The DOF of lenslet.

As shown in Fig. 2, from Gauss lens law and corresponding geometric relations, the ideal image plane located at $l = gf/(g-f)$. There are two planes around the ideal image plane A′, which are separated from the ideal image plane by Δ_1 and Δ_2 respectively.

The distance between two planes deviating from the ideal image plane in image space is $\Delta_1 + \Delta_2$, and the DOF Δ is expressed by satisfying the following equation:

$$\Delta = \frac{2zl}{a} \tag{1}$$

where g is the distances between the ideal image plane and the lenslet, f and a are focal length and diameter of lenslet respectively. $z = z_1 = z_2$ represents the minimum diffuse spot size recognized by human eyes, which is set to 0.1 mm. According to the above relationships, Δ increases with a decreasing.

2.2 Pickup and Coding Processes

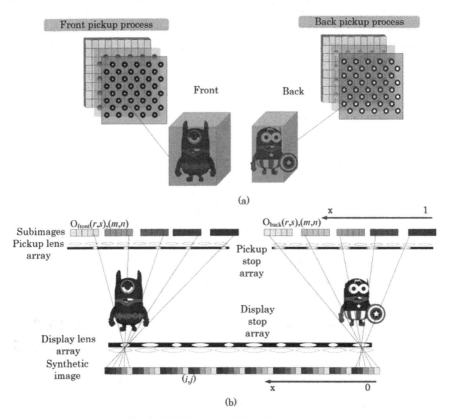

Fig. 3. (a) Pickup and (b) coding process.

Pickup and coding processes are illustrated in Fig. 3. The target model or scene is divided into front and back parts, and then the two parts are pickup processed respectively. The coding process can be summarized as follows:

$$\begin{pmatrix} r \\ s \end{pmatrix} = \begin{pmatrix} R \\ S \end{pmatrix} - \begin{pmatrix} i \\ j \end{pmatrix} \mod (R\,S) \tag{2}$$

$$\begin{pmatrix} m \\ n \\ site \end{pmatrix} = \frac{1}{2} \begin{pmatrix} M - p \\ N - q \\ 0 \end{pmatrix} + \begin{pmatrix} p \\ q \\ p + q \end{pmatrix} \bmod 2 \tag{3}$$

where

$$p = \text{floor}\left(\frac{i}{R}\right) \tag{4}$$

$$q = \text{floor}\left(\frac{j}{S}\right) \tag{5}$$

where Osite(r, s), (m, n) represents the pixel located at row m column n in the rth row and sth column element image. M × N is the number of the lenslets in LA and R × S pixels are covered by a lenslet. The signs "mod" and "floor" represent modulo calculation and rounding down function respectively. When the value of site is 0, the taken pixel Osite(r, s), (m, n) comes from the element images during front pickup process, otherwise from back process (shown in Fig. 3(a)). The coding process is illustrated in Fig. 3(b).

2.3 Reconstruction Process

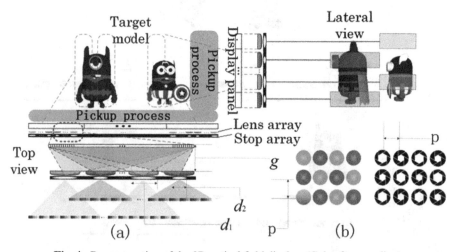

Fig. 4. Reconstruction of the 3D optical field display. (Color figure online)

Figure 4 illustrates the reconstruction process of the light field display. Beams from pixels of synthetic image loaded on the LCD display screen bundle through the corresponding lenslet and aperture and then image at different depth. To simplify the analysis, a part of system is magnified and illustrated top view and lateral view as shown in Fig. 4(a). Figure 4(b) shows the layout of non-uniform lens array and aperture array in cross arrangement. A lenslet with the same color has the same focal length, and a larger focal length is for the purple lenslet whose corresponding diameter of aperture array is also larger. The light in red from the pixels of element image passes through the controlling-light structure to form a farther and narrower DOF, while the lenslet in blue has a smaller focal length, and the aperture in front of it is smaller, and the light in green forms a closer and wider DOF. Equation (6) expresses the total depths of the proposed system, which is added by two extended DOFs. g donates the distance between LCD and lenslet array. f_1 and f_2 are focal lengths of lenslets in NLA. d_1 and d_2 are diameters of apertures in a cross arrangement. The pitch of lenslet array is represented by p.

$$\text{depths} = 2zg\left[\frac{f_1}{d_1(g - f_1)} + \frac{f_2}{d_2(g - f_2)}\right] \tag{6}$$

To simulate the natural 3D vision, a large number of perspectives is necessary to achieve smooth motion parallax. Due to the cross arrangement of the controlling-light structure, the pitch of image points mapped by elemental images at identical depths is enlarged. The formation of continuous smooth parallax is influenced. To solve this problem, HFS is introduced and placed in front of controlling-light structure (in Fig. 1). The continuous and clear 3D scene can be obtained since the fill factor is increased and the gaps between the adjacent lenslets are eliminated due to the HFS. HFS is set to a specific diffusion angle in horizontal and vertical direction respectively, as shown in Fig. 5(b). Our planar HFS is holographically printed with speckle patterns exposed on proper sensitive material. It is easy to control the screen's diffused angle by controlling the shape and size of speckles through making the mask aperture to realize angular distributions of the light beams with the diffused angle close to ω_d or ϕ_d. The fully random speckle structure is wavelength-independent and without chromatic aberration, which enables high transmission efficiency. With this method, a large size HFS [13] can be fabricated easily. The point of the HFS emits multiple light beams of various intensities and colors in different directions in a controlled way, as if they were emitted from the point of the real 3D object at a fixed spatial position.

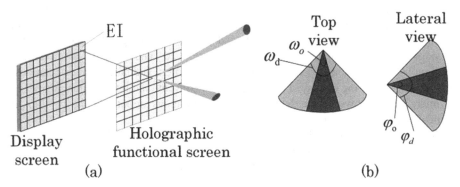

Fig. 5. Function of holographic functional screen.

3 Experiment

To validate the proposed method, the light-field display prototype is constructed, which is composed of a 32-inch LCD panel with a resolution of 3840 × 2160, an NLA, an aperture array in cross arrangement and an HFS. By utilizing the controlling-light structure combined by NLA and aperture array in cross arrangement, a 3D imaging effect with extended depth range is realized. In the experiment, the aperture array is realized with the printed film. In addition, the fill factor is increased and the gaps between the adjacent lenslets are eliminated due to introducing HFS.

Table 1. Experimental parameters

Parameters	Values
Size of LCD panel	32 inches
Resolution of the LCD screen	3840 × 2160
Pitch in LA (p)	1.49 mm
Distance from LCD to LA (g)	2 mm
Diameter of a lenslet in LA (a)	1.2 mm
Viewing angle (θ)	40°
Viewing distance	1.1 m
Larger focus length of lenslet in LA (f_1)	1.989 mm
Smaller focus length of lenslet in LA (f_2)	1.987 mm
The larger diameter of aperture (d_1)	1.1 mm
The smaller diameter of aperture (d_2)	0.9 mm

In our experimental setup, key parameters of the proposed light-field display system are listed in Table 1. Figure 6 illustrates the comparison of the displayed 3D effects produced by the proposed system and conventional system with the same LCD panel and the same number of lenslets. According to Eq. (1) and (6), the calculations of depth range of conventional and proposed display system are 6.03 cm and 13.37 cm respectively for the parameters in Table 1. Figure 6(a) demonstrates 3D light-field display results with 40° horizontal and vertical viewing angle and 13 cm depth range of a 3D image of 2 Minions captured from upper 20°, left 20°, center, right 20°, and lower 20° positions, and continuous smooth motion parallax is observed in vertical and horizontal orientations. Figure 6(b) shows the displayed 3D scene of the conventional integral imaging based on microlens array with 6 cm depth range and continuous smooth motion parallax in vertical and horizontal orientations.

The experiment proves the feasibility of the proposed method. To present the comparison clearly, the regions of the black Minion's yellow belt and the blue Minion's shield in red rectangles are magnified. As illustrated in the magnified picture, as for the black Minion's yellow belt in the front boundary, display quality of the proposed light-field display is much better than that of the conventional integral imaging. For the blue Minion's shield in the middle area, the display quality of both is very clear. Therefore, the depths range is significantly improved in the proposed light-field display. Figure 7 shows the depth information of different parts of the displayed 3D scene and the actual

Fig. 6. 3D light-field display results by (a) the proposed way and (b) the conventional way.

arrangement of the target objects. There are various applications of 3D light-field displays with extended depth based on the controlling-light structure in cross arrangement, such as military exercise, cultural relic demonstration and commercial exhibition. Here, 3D display results of urban terrain and mushrooms with the proposed 3D light field display system are shown in Fig. 8.

Fig. 7. Light-field produced by the designed virtual scene: (a) the EPI analysis of the proposed light-field display and (b) the arrangement of the target objects.

Fig. 8. Video of the experimental results (a) urban terrain (see Visualization1.mp4) and (b) mushrooms (see Visualization2.mp4).

4   Conclusion

In summary, a 32-inch 3D light-field display system based on controlling-light structure in cross arrangement and HFS is demonstrated, which can realize the depth range of 13 cm on the premise of the 40° horizontal and vertical viewing angle and acceptable resolution. The proposed controlling-light structure consist of NLA and aperture array can extend the depth range from 13 cm to 27 cm. The continuous and clear 3D scene can be obtained since the fill factor is increased due to introducing HFS. The proposed extended depth-range light field display reconstructs a 3D scene with an excellent stereoscopic sense applied in military, education, biomedical and commercial exhibition for multiple observers.

Funding. This work was supported by the National Key Research and Development Program (2017YFB1002900); National Natural Science Foundation of China (61575025, 61705014); Fundamental Research Funds for the Central Universities (2018PTB-00-01, 2016ZX01, 2019RC13, 2019PTB-018).

References

1. Yu, X.: Autostereoscopic three-dimensional display with high dense views and the narrow structure pitch. Chin. Opt. Lett. **12**(6), 060008 (2014)
2. Maeda, Y.: Volumetric display using rotating prism sheets arranged in a symmetrical configuration. Opt. Exp. **21**(22), 227074–227086 (2013)
3. Ito, Y.: Wide visual field angle holographic display using compact electro-holographic projectors. Appl. Opt. **58**(34), G135–G142 (2019)
4. Martínez-Corral, M.: Fundamentals of 3D imaging and displays: a tutorial on integral imaging, light-field, and plenoptic systems. Adv. Opt. Photonics **10**(3), 512–566 (2018)
5. Sang, X.: Interactive floating full-parallax digital three-dimensional light-field display based on wavefront recomposing. Opt. Exp. **26**(7), 8883–8889 (2018)
6. Qin, Z.: Resolution-enhanced light field displays by recombining subpixels across elemental images. Opt. Lett. **44**(10), 2438–2441 (2019)
7. Yang, S.: Analysis of the depth of field for integral imaging with consideration of facet braiding. Appl. Opt. **57**(7), 1534–1540 (2018)
8. Piao, Y.: Three-dimensional reconstruction of far and big objects using synthetic aperture integral imaging. Opt. Lasers Eng. **88**, 153–161 (2017)
9. Zhang, M.: Depth-of-field extension in integral imaging using multi-focus elemental images. Appl. Opt. **56**(22), 6059–6064 (2017)
10. Martínez-Cuenca, R.: Enhanced depth of field integral imaging with sensor resolution constraints. Opt. Exp. **12**(21), 5237–5242 (2004)
11. Tong, Q.: Depth of field extension and objective space depth measurement based on wavefront imaging. Opt. Exp. **26**(14), 18368–18385 (2018)
12. Yu, X.: Distortion correction for the elemental images of integral imaging by introducing the directional diffuser. Chin. Opt. Lett. **16**(4), 041001 (2018)
13. Sang, X.: Demonstration of a large-size real-time full-color three-dimensional display. Opt. Lett. **34**(24), 3803–3805 (2009)
14. Yang, L.: Viewing-angle and viewing-resolution enhanced integral imaging based on time-multiplexed lens stitching. Opt. Exp. **27**, 15679–15692 (2019)
15. Yu, X.: Large viewing angle three-dimensional display with smooth motion parallax and accurate depth cues. Opt. Exp. **23**, 25950–25958 (2015)
16. Gao, X.: 360° light field 3D display system based on a triplet lenses array and holographic functional screen. Chin. Opt. Lett. **15**, 121201 (2017)

Stereoscopic 3D Depth Perception Analysis of H.264/AVC Coded Video

Wenfei Wan[1(✉)], Hong Ren Wu[2], Jinjian Wu[1], and Guangming Shi[1]

[1] School of Artificial Intelligence, Xidian University, Xi'an 710071, China
wenfei.wan@stu.xidian.edu.cn
[2] School of Engineer and Computer Science, RMIT University, Melbourne, Australia
henry.wu@rmit.edu.au
https://www.rmit.edu.au/contact/staff-contacts/academic-staff/w/
wu-professor-hong-ren

Abstract. Compared to two single-view videos, stereoscopic three dimensional (S3D) videos provide a single most significant feature and a major difference, i.e. depth perception. However, the compression, transmission, and storage of 3D videos will inevitably introduce spatiotemporal and stereoscopic distortions, which may cause loss and/or variations of depth perception, resulting in visual discomfort to viewers. Nevertheless, the study remains limited of how these distortions affect the depth perception and how the human vision system (HVS) perceives such loss and variations of depth perception in compressed 3D videos. In this paper, a series of subjective experiments have been constructed to investigate the visual impact of video compression by the H.264/AVC standard on 3D depth perception. Especially, different frequency components of the compressed videos were extracted to examine their impact on depth perception. The subjective experiments reveal that the degradation of video quality as a result of compression will cause the loss and reduction of the 3D depth perception. Moreover, the subjective data showed that the HVS response in depth perception varies depending on different frequency components of 3D videos, which may bring about a better understanding of human stereoscopic vision, and coding and quality assessment of 3D videos.

Keywords: Stereoscopic 3d video · Depth perception · Subjective experiments · Frequency components.

1 Introduction

With the development of multimedia and three dimensional (3D) display technologies [1], stereoscopic 3D (S3D) videos that can provide the viewers with more realistic viewing experience and S3D video products and services have become more and more popular in digital media entertainment, consumer electronics and advanced manufacturing industries, such as 3D cinema, VR (virtual reality), and Blu-ray 3D and so on [2,3]. In fact, most of practical applications of

W. Song and F. Xu (Eds.): ICVRD 2020, CCIS 1313, pp. 66–77, 2021.
https://doi.org/10.1007/978-981-33-6549-0_7

digital video enjoyed by billions of people to date are compressed by current video coding standards because the raw or uncompressed video generates tremendous amount data which are too large or uneconomical to be transmitted or stored due to the limitation of network bandwidth and storage space [4–6].

However, video coding will inevitably cause various video coding artefacts, such as blocking effect, blurring, ringing, temporal fluctuation/flickering, and so on [7]. These artefacts not only have impact on the visual quality of each view of 3D videos, but also may cause loss and variations of depth perception. In general, 3D visual perception is very complicated, which includes many factors such as image/video quality, naturalness, depth perception and visual comfort, etc. [8]. Compared with single-view videos, S3D videos provide a single most significant feature and a major difference, i.e. depth perception. Moreover, all S3D videos are ultimately viewed by human eyes and the HVS has its characteristics for depth perception. In short, these distortions in depth perception have been a source of viewing discomfort (e.g., eye strain, visual fatigue, headaches and nausea) which is a technological roadblock which hinders further development and applications of 3D video technology [9].

In recent years, there were related reports on analysis and evaluation of the depth perception of S3D images/videos, which can be divided into two categories. The first category mainly focuses on evaluation of the depth perception of original stereoscopic images/videos as a result of 3D video acquisition [8]. Silva et al. analyzed the sensitivity of human viewers with regard to three different depth cues of 3D scene on S3D displays and proposed a just noticeable difference in depth (JNDD) model, which revealed that the human eyes were more sensitive to depth variations at screen level than those behind or in front of the screen level [10]. Kekkbhofer et al. conducted psychovisual experiments to measure the impact of motion parallax on depth perception, and proposed a joint parallax disparity computational model in depth perception [11]. The other category considers the impact of compression distortions on depth perception. Mikkola et al. found that the compression artifacts degraded the performance of depth perception and were unequal on different depth cues, especially for texture cues at high compression ratios [12]. Zhang et al. conducted a subjective experiment to report that the loss of video details can cause the degradation of the depth perception from the perspectives of monocular and binocular depth cues [2]. In addition, it also explored the depth perceptual degradation of symmetrically and asymmetrically distorted S3D videos.

The aforementioned reports focus on either different depth cues of S3D scene or the impacts of the compression artifacts on depth perception in combination with these depth cues, while having overlooked the HVS's perception and estimation of the depth loss or variations induced by visual signal compression. It is well-known that the HVS has different sensitivities to different frequency contents [13]. A hypothesis was proposed that the HVS's depth perception in S3D vision would respond differently to different spatial frequency contents of 3D video. Several subjective experiments were conducted to explore the visual impact of S3D videos compressed by H.264/AVC standard and to investigate

(a) 3D_02   (b) 3D_14   (c) 3D_15

(d) 3D_17   (e) 3D_28   (f) 3D_46

Fig. 1. The cropped left-view frames of six original S3D videos selected from RMIT3DV database [14]. All sequences are 12 s in length.

the depth perception response of the HVS to stereoscopic video sequences of different spatial frequencies.

According to the analyses of the subjective experimental results, the compressed distortions can cause the losses of depth perception of 3D videos and their frequency components. Furthermore, as the coding artifacts increase, the differences in depth perception between different frequency and components also increase. Moreover, the HVS is more sensitive to HP and BP components of S3D videos than their LP counterparts in terms of depth perception, which is a noticeable difference for the coding designs of single-view and S3D videos where LP components are protected well and redundant high frequency components are discarded for the efficiency and quality of videos.

The remainder of this paper is organized as follows. Section 2 describes in detail the subjective experiments on depth perception of compressed S3D videos and their frequency components. Experimental results and analyses of depth perception are presented in Sect. 3. Finally, conclusions are drawn in Sect. 4.

2 Subjective Experiments on Depth Perception

2.1 S3D Video Test Sequences

To conduct the subjective experiments, six uncompressed full HD (high-definition) S3D videos from the RMIT3DV database [14] are selected. These 3D video sequences have diverse visual contents, including various video scenes (indoor and outdoor, fast and slow motion, smooth and textural visual contents),

(a) Gaussian LPF   (b) Gaussian BPF   (c) Gaussian HPF

(d) LP Component   (e) BP Component   (f) HP Component

Fig. 2. The example of the S3D test video 3D_28, which is decomposed into LP, BP and HP components by Gaussian filters. The top row shows the 2D Gaussian filter functions and the bottom row presents the corresponding decomposition results.

different depths/distances, i.e., close, medium and long distance, and various video contents such as water, trees, people, trams and so on. The original 3D videos were filmed in 1080×1920 HD resolution and recorded in uncompressed 10-bit YCBCR 4:2:2 at 25 fps (frames per second). Due to the limitation of the stereoscopic display screen resolution and the necessity of comparative tests, the original videos are cropped to 360×480 stereoscopic video patches for the references, the first left-view frames of the cropped reference S3D video sequences are shown in Fig. 1.

These reference 3D videos are encoded by an H.264/AVC standard compliant implementation of ffmpeg for each view at four different bitrates (512K, 1M, 2M, 4M), and then decoded to obtain the processed S3D videos with compression distortions. Considering that the sensitivities of the HVS are unequal to different frequency components, the Gaussian filters are used to decompose the S3D videos into low-pass (LP), band-pass (BP) and high-pass (HP) stereoscopic components [15]. An example is shown in Fig. 2.

Before the formal tests, the 3D video 3D_14 was selected as the training sequence to familiarize the subjects with the 3D video viewing and depth perception assessment task. Thus, the subjective experiments have 5 uncompressed reference 3D videos, 20 processed S3D videos with distortions by the H.264/AVC coding, and the corresponding 75 stereoscopic decomposed videos by Gaussian LP, BP and HP filters. In short, there are 100 S3D videos in total prepared for the subjective tests.

Reference S3D video	Processed S3D video
(a)	(b)
Single-view video	Single-view video
(c)	(d)

Fig. 3. Screen display setup based on pair comparison model: (a) the reference S3D video or its corresponding frequency stereoscopic components; (b) the processed S3D video; (c) and (d) the single-view (left-view) reference video shown to both eyes.

2.2 Experimental Setup and Procedure

The subjective experiments mainly consist of two parts: the impact of compression distortions on depth perception, and the depth evaluation of Gaussian decompositions of S3D videos. All S3D test videos are displayed on the True3Di SDM-240 full HD 3D monitor, which is devoted to display the polarized 3D videos with 1080×1920 resolution. Thus, they are displayed in the original resolution and free of scaling or re-targeting distortions. There were 18 subjects (12 males, 6 females) participated in the depth perception experiments. The majority of the subjects are non-experts on compute vision and their average age is 28. Furthermore, they all have functional eyesight or corrected normal vision and passed the color test and random dot depth perception test. The experimental environment conforms to Recommendation ITU-R BT.2021 [16]. The brightness through the polarized glasses is $400 \, cd/m^2$. The viewing distance is set to three times height of the screen, i.e., about 160 dm.

The pair comparison (PC) model with a binary scale is adopted, which is easier for subjects to compare and assess the depth performance [17]. For each test, there are four videos shown on the True3Di display screen at the same time, where the top left is the reference S3D video and the top right is the processed S3D video with left and right views, the bottom two are the corresponding single-view videos displaying only the left-view sequence. The reference S3D video (with the original range of full depth) and the single-view video (with the range of zero depth) serve as anchor points to facilitate the subjects in perceiving the 3D depth and its variations. The display setup based on PC model is shown Fig. 3.

After viewing the test 3D video sequences with polarized 3D glasses, each subject was asked to answer two questions: "Is there any 3D depth in the top right video?" and then "Is the 3D depth of top right different from the top left?". Here, the answer "Yes" is recorded as 1 and "No" as 0. Each test session took no more than 20 min. Each subject had a five minutes break after each test session. It is noted that the answer to the first question is whether the subject can see any depth shown by the test/processed sequence regardless whether its perception is the same or not as that based on the original sequence, while the answer to the second question will bear out if there is loss/distortion/variation of depth perception in processed 3D video compared with the original.

2.3 Subjective Score Processing

The binary score of PC model means the score of each subject is either 0 or 1. Let $d_{i,j,b}$ be the subjective score given by the subject i to sequence j at coding bitrate b. These scores are collected to calculate the proportion of participants who can perceive the 3D depth of the processed videos with regard to the first question, or think that there is not depth loss for the compressed 3D videos compared with the reference 3D videos with regard to the second question. Thus, the proportion $P_{j,b}$ is computed for sequence i coded at bitrate b as a performance measure for depth perception:

$$P_{j,b} = \frac{1}{N} \sum_{i=1}^{N} d_{i,j,b},$$ (1)

where N is the total number of subjects.

With respect to answers to the first question, $P_{j,b}$ is a quality/affirmative measure, i.e., the higher the value, the more viewers observe the presence of depth and the better the performance. With respect to answers to the second question, $P_{j,b}$ is a distortion/non-placet measure, i.e., the higher the value, the more viewers observe the loss or distortions in depth perception compared with the original 3D videos and the worse the performance. The score processes of the depth perception tests for different frequency components with Gaussian filter are similar to the one described above.

In order to analyze the mean depth perception performance of general S3D videos coded at different bitrates and different spatial frequencies. The subjective scores $d_{i,j,b}$ should be averaged over sequence j, i.e. $d_k(i, b)$. Since the number of subjects are not exceed 30, in order to ensure the reliability of the subjective scores of the experiment, here, T-test is necessary. Then, $d_k(i, b)$ is normalized to T-scores for each subject i,

$$T(d_k(i, b)) = \frac{d_k(i, b) - \mu_{i,b}}{\sigma_{i,b}/\sqrt{N-1}},$$ (2)

where $\mu_{i,b}$ is the mean value and $\sigma_{i,b}$ is the standard derivations of the score $d_k(i, b)$. The T-test operation is denoted as $T(\cdot)$.

Unreliable average scores $d_k(i, b)$ is rejected if the $T(d_k(i, b))$ belongs to the rejection region of threshold $\alpha = 0.01$. After the T-test, the average subjective scores $\bar{d}_k(i, b)$ is calculated based on the rest subjective scores of the selected reliable viewers in the subjective experiments. Then, the mean subjective score $P_k(b)$ for general S3D videos coded at bitrate b is measured as,

$$P_k(b) = \frac{1}{N_1} \sum_{i=1}^{N_1} \bar{d}_k(i, b),$$ (3)

where the N_1 is the corresponding number of the $\bar{d}_k(i, b)$ that has passed the T-test.

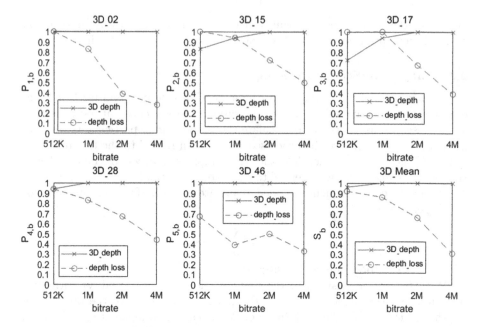

Fig. 4. The normalized proportion of subjects who can perceive the 3D depth of impaired S3D videos and detect the depth loss compared with the reference. The "3D_Mean" is the final average proportion of five test stereoscopic sequences coded by the H.264/AVC at four bitrates. (Color figure online)

3   Experimental Results and Analyses

The subjective experimental results of the depth perception are shown in Fig. 4 using the 3D videos with H.264/AVC compression distortions. In Fig. 4, the blue solid lines represent the percentage of subjects who were able to perceive 3D depth in the impaired 3D videos coded at four coding bitrates. As the bitrate increased, almost all the subjects could perceive the 3D depth, noting that when the bitrate was 512Kbps a small percentage of subjects could not perceive 3D depth, due to the severe deterioration of video quality. An obvious example is sequence 3D_17 which has water wave sloshing and leaves floating. The coding artifacts of the compressed 3D video degrade the textures and details, which has a significant impact on depth perception of 3D vision.

The orange dotted line represents the percentage of viewers in the subjective tests who detected the depth loss incurred in the impaired S3D videos compared with their original counterparts. As the bitrate increases, the downward trend of the orange dotted line for each sequence means that the impact of compressed distortions on 3D depth perception is significantly reduced. From the perspective of monocular and binocular depth cues [18], the different compressed bitrates generate different levels of coding distortions which affect some structural regions and textural details where these depth cues, such as perspective, texture gradi-

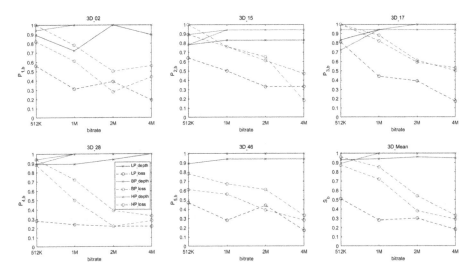

Fig. 5. The normalized proportion of subjects who can perceive the 3D depth of LP, BP and HP components and detect their depth loss compared with the reference 3D videos. The "3D_Mean" is the final average proportion of five S3D test sequences coded at four different bitrates. (Color figure online)

ent, blur, convergence and binocular parallax most likely had various degrees of impact on the depth structure.

The experimental results of the depth perception using Gaussian decompositions of H.264/AVC coded 3D videos are shown in Fig. 5, whereby the 3D depth perception performance is examined of LP, BP and HP components of 3D videos coded at four different bitrates. Generally speaking, whether there is an absence of 3D depth perception or exist differences in depth perception with respect to each frequency component, they all have a consistent trend in terms of the coding bitrates. However, distinctive differences can be observed between LP, BP and HP frequency sequences with regard to their impact on depth perception.

By comparing the solid lines of LP, BP and HP components, it's generally the blue solid lines represent LP components are the lowest percentage of subjects who were able to perceive 3D depth coded at four coding bitrates. Especially, the coding bitrates almost have no effect on the performance of the 3D depth perception with respect to the first question. However, for the dotted lines of LP, BP and HP components, similarly, the LP component has the lowest value and HP component is the largest value which represents the percentage of subjects who detect the depth loss incurred in the impaired S3D videos compared with their original counterparts.

In order to avoid the influence of compounding effects (i.e., distortions) by H.264/AVC compression and to strict the investigation to the impact of LP, BP and HP processing on depth perception of the HVS, additional subjective tests were conducted with 10 subjects selected randomly from the 18 participants.

Reference S3D video	LP component video
(a)	(b)
BP component video	HP component video
(c)	(d)

Fig. 6. Screen display setup of LP, BP and HP components: (a) the reference S3D video; (b), (c) and (d) are the LP, BP and HP component videos with left- and right-view sequences.

The 3D monitor displays four cropped S3D videos, which are the reference video and its LP, BP and HP filtered counterparts from top left to bottom right. The display setup pattern is different from the Fig. 3, which is shown in Fig. 6.

Each subject was asked to compare the visual quality of LP, BP and HP filtered 3D videos with the reference 3D video in terms of depth perception, and sort them by depth perception performance in a descending order. The results are shown in Table 1 using original 3D video as reference, where BP>HP>LP means that visual quality of BP filtered 3D video in terms of depth perception judged by the subject is better than that of its HP filtered counterpart, and in turn depth perception of HP filtered 3D video is deemed better than that of its LP filtered counterpart by the same subject.

Based on results presented in Fig. 5 and Table 1, there is an overwhelming evidence that the depth perception of the HVS is more sensitive to HP and BP components of 3D videos than their LP counterparts. In other words, LP filtering has more significant negative impact on visual quality of S3D video in terms of depth perception, highlighting a noticeable difference in spatiotemporal and stereoscopic psychovisual characteristics of the HVS which underpin coding designs between single-view video and S3D video. While Table 1 also showed that BP filtered 3D videos provided better depth perception than their HP filtered counterparts to the small sample pool of viewers, further investigation is required to model spatiotemporal, orientational and stereoscopic psychovisual response of the HVS for visual quality assessment of S3D video and HVS based S3D coding design.

Table 1. Comparisons of visual quality in terms of depth perception by the HVS using LP, BP and HP filtered 3D videos with reference to their originals.

Subjects	3D_02	3D_15	3D_17	3D_28	3D_46
1	BP>HP>LP	LP>BP>HP	BP>HP>LP	BP>LP>HP	BP>HP>LP
2	BP>LP>HP	HP>BP>LP	BP>HP>LP	HP>LP>BP	BP=HP=LP
3	BP>HP>LP	HP=BP>LP	BP>HP>LP	BP>HP>LP	BP=HP>LP
4	BP>HP>LP	BP=HP>LP	BP>HP>LP	BP>HP>LP	BP>HP>LP
5	BP>HP>LP	HP>BP>LP	HP>BP>LP	HP>BP>LP	HP>BP>LP
6	BP>HP>LP	LP>BP>HP	BP>HP>LP	BP>HP>LP	BP>HP>LP
7	BP>HP>LP	HP>BP>LP	HP>BP>LP	HP>BP>LP	BP>HP>LP
8	BP>HP>LP	HP>BP>LP	HP>BP>LP	BP>HP>LP	BP=HP>LP
9	BP>HP>LP	HP>BP>LP	BP>HP>LP	BP>HP>LP	BP=HP>LP
10	BP>HP>LP	BP=HP>LP	BP>HP>LP	BP>HP>LP	BP=HP>LP
Percentage (BP Vs. HP)	BP>HP 100%	HP>BP 50% BP>HP 20% BP=LP 30%	BP>HP 70% HP>BP 30%	BP>HP 70% HP>BP 30%	BP>HP 40% HP>BP 10% BP=HP 50%
Percentage (LP VS. BP or HP)	HP>LP 90% LP>HP 10% BP>LP 100%	HP>LP 80% BP>LP 80% LP>BP 20% LP>HP 20%	HP>LP 100% BP>LP 100%	HP>LP 90% BP>LP 90% LP>HP 10% LP>BP 10%	BP>LP 90% HP>LP 90% HP=LP 10% BP=LP 10%

4 Conclusion

This paper reported subjective experiments to examine the impact of video coding artifacts on 3D depth perception using compressed stereoscopic 3D video sequences with each view encoded by an H.264/AVC compliant coder at four different bitrates, and to investigate spatiotemporal and psychovisual characteristics of the HVS in 3D depth perception by frequency decomposition of S3D video using Gaussian lowpass, bandpass and highpass filtering. The subjective experimental results reveal that the perceived depth loss of the impaired 3D videos increases significantly as the coding bitrate decreases. There exists an overwhelming evidence that the depth perception of the HVS is more sensitive to HP and BP components of 3D videos than their LP counterparts. While subjective test results obtained using a small sample pool of viewers showed that BP filtered 3D videos provided better depth perception than their HP filtered counterparts, further investigation is required to vertify this phenomenon.

In fact, depth perception of the HVS is not only related with the frequency, but also refers to the orientation, motion and so on with respect to binocular and monocular depth cues. Therefore, it is required to model spatiotemporal, orientational and stereoscopic psychovisual response of the HVS for visual quality assessment of S3D video and HVS based S3D coding system design in the future.

References

1. Kim, T., Kim, J., Kim, S., Cho, S., Lee, S.: Perceptual crosstalk prediction on autostereoscopic 3D display. IEEE Trans. Circ. Syst. Video Technol. **27**(7), 1450–1463 (2017)
2. Zhang, Y., Liu, X., Liu, H., Fan, C.: Depth perceptual quality assessment for symmetrically and asymmetrically distorted stereoscopic 3D videos. Signal Process.: Image Commun. **78**, 293–305 (2019)
3. Li, L., Chen, X., Zhou, Y., Wu, J., Shi, G.: Depth image quality assessment for view synthesis based on weighted edge similarity. In: CVPR Workshops, pp. 17–25 (2019)
4. Wu, H.R., Reibman, A.R., Lin, W., Pereira, F., Hemami, S.S.: Perceptual visual signal compression and transmission. Proc. IEEE **101**(9), 2025–2043 (2013)
5. Zhang, Y., Yang, X., Liu, X., Zhang, Y., Jiang, G., Kwong, S.: High-efficiency 3D depth coding based on perceptual quality of synthesized video. IEEE Trans. Image Process. **25**(12), 5877–5891 (2016)
6. Li, L., Chen, X., Zhou, Y., Wu, J., Shi, G.: Depth image quality assessment for view synthesis based on weighted edge similarity. In: IEEE Conference on Computer Vision and Pattern Recognition (CVPR) Workshops, pp. 17–25, Long Beach, CA, USA, 16–20 June 2019
7. Wu, H.R., Lin, W., Karam, L.J.: An overview of perceptual processing for digital pictures, In: Jian, Z., Dan, S., David, D.F. (eds.) IEEE International Multimedia and Expo Workshops (ICMEW) 2012, Melbourne, Australia, pp. 113–120 (2012). https://doi.org/10.1109/ICMEW.2012.27
8. Carballeira, P., Gutierrez, J., Moran, F., Cabrera, J., Jaureguizar, F., Garcia, N.: Multiview perceptual disparity model for super multiv: multiview perceptual disparity model for super multiview video. IEEE J. Sel. Top. Signal Process. **11**(1), 113–124 (2016)
9. Al Boridi, O.N., Wu, H.R., van Schyndel, R.: Wavelet decomposition-based stereoscopic 3-D video watermarking - a comparative study. In: IEEE ICSPCS 2017, Surfers Paradise, Australia, 13–15 December 2017. https://doi.org/10.1109/ICSPCS.2017.8270458
10. De Silva, V., Fernando, A., Worrall, S., Arachchi, H.K., Kondoz, A.: Sensitivity analysis of the human visual system for depth cues in stereoscopic 3-D displays. IEEE Trans. Multimed. **13**(3), 498–506 (2011)
11. Kellnhofer, P., Didyk, P., Ritschel, T., Masia, B., Myszkowski, K., Seidel, H.P.: Motion parallax in stereo 3D: model and applications. In: International Conference on Computer Graphics and Interactive Techniques, vol. 35, no. 6, p. 176 (2016)
12. Mikkola, M., Jumisko-Pyykko, S., Strohmeier, D., Boev, A., Gotchev, A.: Stereoscopic depth cues outperform monocular ones on autostereoscopic display. IEEE J. Sel. Top. Signal Process. **6**(6), 698–709 (2012)
13. Wu, J., Shi, G., Lin, W., Liu, A., Qi, F.: Just noticeable difference estimation for images with free-energy principle. IEEE Trans. Multimed. **15**(7), 1705–1710 (2013)
14. Cheng, E., Burton, P., Burton, J., Joseski, A., Burnett, I.S.: Rmit3dv: pre-announcement of a creative commons uncompressed HD 3D video database. In: Fourth International Workshop on Quality of Multimedia Experience, Yarra Valley, VIC 2012, pp. 212–217 (2012). https://doi.org/10.1109/QoMEX.2012.6263873
15. Wang, Y., Shi, M., You, S., Xu, C.: DCT inspired feature transform for image retrieval and reconstruction. IEEE Trans. Image Process. **25**(9), 4406–4420 (2016)

16. International Telecommunication Union - Radiocommunication Sector (ITU-R), F.: Subjective methods for the assessment of stereoscopic 3DTV systems, Rec. BT.2021-1, February 2015
17. Shi, G., Wan, W., Wu, J., Xie, X., Dong, W., Wu, H.R.: SISRSET: single image super-resolution subjective evaluation test and objective quality assessment. Neurocomputing **360**, 37–51 (2019)
18. Lebreton, P., Raake, A., Barkowsky, M., Le Callet, P.: Measuring perceived depth in natural images and study of its relation with monocular and binocular depth cues. In: 2014 Proceedings of SPIE Stereoscopic Displays and Applications XXV, San Francisco, California, United States, vol. 9011 (2014). https://doi.org/10.1117/12.2040055

AR Application Research Based on ORB-SLAM

Baihui Tang[1](✉), Zhengyi Liu[1], and Sanxing Cao[2]

[1] State Key Laboratory of Media Convergence and Communication, Communication University of China, Beijing 100024, China
tangbaihuiyt@163.com, zyliu35@cuc.edu.cn

[2] State Key Laboratory of Media Convergence and Communication, Communication University of China, Collaborative Innovation Center, Beijing 100024, China
sxcao@cuc.edu.cn

Abstract. SLAM is a key technology that describes a moving robot that calculates its pose, positioning, and mapping in scenarios where environmental information is unknown. ORB-SLAM uses ORB features to perform real-time tracking, positioning, and mapping tasks, and has good stability. mainly includes three modules: tracking module, local mapping module, and loop closing module. The ORB feature extraction part of the tracking module is time-consuming, In this paper, the feature extraction part of the ORB-SLAM algorithm is optimized and accelerated, and the application research of ORB-SLAM on AR is carried out according to the principle of AR technology.

Keywords: ORB feature · Feature point extraction · Feature point description · Augmented reality

1 Background

Augmented Reality (AR) refers to the superposition of virtual information or objects in real scenes, and the fusion of virtual objects and real scenes, so as to enhance people's perception and interaction with the real environment. It realizes the enrichment and compensation of virtual world to the real world. AR technology has three characteristics: real-time interaction, 3D registration and combination of virtual and real. Its essence is to realize 3D interaction, understanding and perception of the real world through sensor data and image information from the perspective of the real world. Among them, real-time interaction refers to the need for real-time interaction with augmented reality scenes. The combination of virtual and real is the perfect combination of virtual object and real environment. 3D registration is the most important feature in augmented reality. The principle of 3D registration is to accurately integrate virtual objects and real environment by calculating the 3D position correspondence between virtual objects and real environment.

In AR technology, tracking and recognition technology is the key technology to realize virtual and real alignment. There are two main implementation methods of tracking and positioning technology: hardware-based positioning and computer vision based positioning. Inertial tracking and optical tracking can realize positioning based on hardware,

W. Song and F. Xu (Eds.): ICVRD 2020, CCIS 1313, pp. 78–88, 2021.
https://doi.org/10.1007/978-981-33-6549-0_8

such as inertial measurement unit, which can measure the acceleration and angular velocity of the camera. The tracking and positioning based on computer vision is mainly to calculate the camera position and pose through the three-dimensional rigid body motion, and to optimize the tracking accuracy by combining the filter and nonlinear optimization techniques. The advantages are non-contact, low cost and high precision. Among them, the tracking and positioning technology based on computer vision is widely used in AR field and is one of the mainstream technologies of AR.

The tracking and positioning techniques based on computer vision mainly include 2D image positioning, 3D object positioning and 3D environment positioning based on SLAM algorithm. 2D picture positioning refers to the tracking and positioning of two-dimensional planar objects, such as books and cards, which can be widely used in education, medical treatment, tourism and other fields. Its principle is to take two-dimensional plane object as the anchor point of positioning, based on the two-dimensional plane location point, the computer draws images to fuse the virtual object with the real environment. 3D object localization is based on regular 3d object and irregular 3d object, such as specific irregular object face and corresponding face recognition algorithm. 3d environment positioning based on SLAM refers to the acquisition of camera pose (R, t), Point Cloud, Local Map and other information through SLAM technology to realize tracking, positioning and reconstruction of the real world. Due to the limitation of computer hardware speed, there will be some delay in the alignment process between virtual scene and real environment. Therefore, AR application requires that the underlying SLAM algorithm has good real-time performance.

2   ORB-SLAM

SLAM (Simultaneous Localization and Mapping) describes the process by which a robot moves in an unknown location to estimate its own positioning and reconstruct its surroundings. Visual SLAM is a SLAM scheme with the camera as the sensor. The classic Visual SLAM framework is shown in Fig. 1. SLAM consists of four modules: Visual Odometry (VO) module, back-end Optimization module, Loop Closing module and Mapping module. The main working process is as follows: first, read the data of sensors (camera, inertial measurement unit, etc.), then estimate the camera pose between two adjacent images, and establish a local map. Finally, the camera pose and return loop Closing information calculated by the back-end optimization visual odometer module is used to form the global map and track.

ORB-SLAM is a visual SLAM system based on the characteristics of the ORB, which supports monocular, binocular and RGB-D camera modes. It can operate in large-scale, small-scale, indoor and outdoor scenes. It is also robust to ORB-SLAM in scenes of intense movement. The ORB feature is proposed to use an improved FAST corner detection method, add scale and directivity, and to match feature points with an improved BRIEF descriptor with rotation characteristics. The scale characteristics of ORB features are realized by building an eight-layer image pyramid, which is a collection of the same frame image at different resolutions. Feature points need to be extracted layer by layer from the eight-layer image pyramid. The rotation characteristics of the ORB feature are realized by the grayscale centroid method, which is to find the centroid in the image with the grayscale value as the weight.

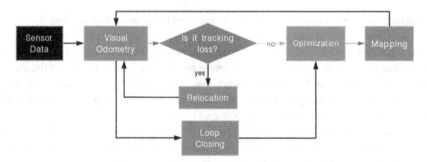

Fig. 1. Classic visual SLAM framework

ORB-SLAM inherits the four modules of the classic visual SLAM framework, while simultaneously using three threads for Tracking, Local Mapping, and Loop Closing. The reason why ORB-SLAM can be tracked and located in real time is the use of sparse feature point method and the simultaneous sparse 3d reconstruction of the scene. Figure 2 shows the overall architecture of ORB-SLAM.

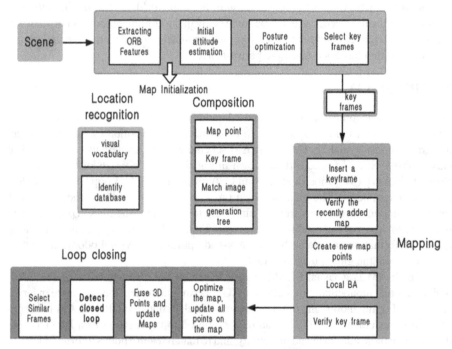

Fig. 2. ORB-SLAM architecture

As can be seen from Fig. 2, the overall architecture of ORB-SLAM is dominated by three major threads. Among them, the tracking thread of ORB-SLAM mainly includes tasks such as the extraction of ORB features, relocation, initial attitude estimation and local map tracking. Local map building thread mainly includes key frame insertion and elimination, redundant map point elimination and new map point creation, local BA optimization and other tasks. The Loop Closing thread mainly includes closed-loop keyframe detection, similarity transformation calculation, closed-loop correction and other tasks. The ORB-SLAM system can track, locate and map in real time. The tracing thread for ORB-SLAM is shown in Fig. 3.

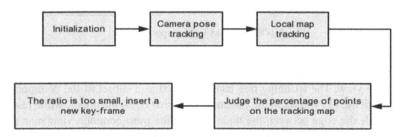

Fig. 3. ORB-SLAM tracing thread

The tracking thread for ORB-SLAM tracks the calculated input image for each frame while optimizing the pose of the current frame. In the tracking thread, ORB-SLAM first constructs an eight-layer image pyramid and then abstractions the FAST feature points layer by layer. The eight-layer image pyramid is an image set with different resolutions of the same image, and its purpose is to ensure the scale invariance of the SLAM algorithm. ORB-SLAM extracted ORB descriptor BRIEF on the basis of FAST feature points. The BRIEF descriptor has stable invariance under different observation angles and different lighting conditions, and the computation speed is much faster than SIFT and SURF. Descriptors need to be calculated layer by layer by feature point on the eight-layer image pyramid, and each feature point needs to calculate 256 dimensional descriptors, which are mainly used for feature point matching and loop detection. The estimation method of the current image frame position attitude is to project the map points calculated in the previous image to the current image frame, then find the matching feature points, and then find enough matching feature points to optimize the solution. In terms of determining whether the current frame is a keyframe, ORB-SLAM requires that the number of match points for the current frame to be less than 90% of the keyframe to consider inserting a new keyframe, because the more intensive the keyframe, the less likely it is to fail to track. The problem with this is that there are redundant keyframes, so by creating a map locally, the extra keyframes are removed to control the complexity of the local BA optimization. The local mapping thread for ORB-SLAM is shown in Fig. 4.

Local map building thread includes three parts: key frame insertion, redundant map points and key frame elimination, and local BA optimization. First, the new keyframe obtained by the trace thread is inserted as a new node into the common view, which describes how many identical map points can be observed by different keyframes. Each keyframe is regarded as a node. If more than 15 identical map points can be observed between the two keyframes, that is, the number of map points in the total view is greater than 15, an edge is established between the nodes corresponding to the two keyframes, and the weight of the edge is the number of observed map points. Next, update the

Fig. 4. ORB-SLAM local mapping thread

adjacent edges and spanning trees of the key frame nodes of Shared map points in the common view. The spanning tree can be viewed as a subset of the common view, containing all the key frames in the common view, that is, all the nodes, while reserving for each node the edge between the node that has the most common view map points. Then, the word bag description BoW of the new keyframe is calculated. On the one hand, it is used to match the feature points and triangulate the new map points. On the other hand, it is used for closed-loop detection. The rule of adding new map points is that 25% of the key frames can observe the map point, and the map point also exists in the key frames with certain probability to observe the point. The mechanism of adding and deleting map points ensures that the map points are accurate and not redundant. The principle of local keyframe elimination is that as long as 90% of the points can be observed by more than 3 keyframes, the frame is considered as redundant. Finally, local BA optimization was carried out. By constructing the reprojection error equation, all observed pixels and map points were projected according to the current estimated camera pose, and the camera pose with the smallest error result was taken as the current optimal camera pose. The closed-loop detection thread for ORB-SLAM is shown in Fig. 5.

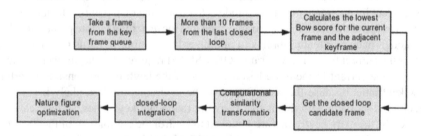

Fig. 5. ORB-SLAM loop closing thread

The map points obtained by camera pose and triangulation will form error accumulation over time. Even if local or global BA optimization is used, the cumulative error will still exist. Closed-loop detection is an effective method to eliminate the accumulation of errors. The optimization of all results based on the closed-loop can make the results more accurate. In the closed-loop detection thread, ORB-SLAM selects the mainstream scheme in visual SLAM, which is to determine the back-loop detection relationship from the similarity between the two images. Firstly, the word bag similarity of the new keyframe and the keyframe connected with it is calculated. Secondly, ORB-SLAM takes the minimum similarity between the new keyframe and the surrounding keyframe as the dynamic threshold, and only if the similarity of other keyframes is greater than this threshold can they be closed-loop keyframes. In the monocular camera mode, due to the scale fuzziness, it is impossible to determine the specific position of map points in triangulation, so it is necessary to calculate the similarity transformation and optimize the map. At last, in the closed-loop fusion stage, the repeated map points are fused first, and new edges are inserted in the common view to connect the closed loop. Then, according to the transformation relationship between the new keyframe and the closed-loop keyframe, the position attitude of the new keyframe and the surrounding keyframe is adjusted to align the closed loop. Then the map points around the closed loop keyframe are projected to the new keyframe and the map points that can be matched are fused. Finally, the position and attitude of all key frames are optimized according to the essence diagram, and the closed-loop error is dispersed to all key frames.

3   Application of ORB-SLAM on AR

From the overall architecture of ORB-SLAM and the specific three threads, we can see the complexity of its algorithm, which requires a lot of calculation. Due to the large number of feature points extraction, the tracking thread takes a lot of time. In this paper, through the optimization process of the extraction of feature points, implementation in the accuracy and robustness are good cases, shortening the time of tracing the thread, the frame rate of the ORB-SLAM is increased, the through the ORB-SLAM the extracted feature points in real-time drawing, and then after the initialization of the ORB-SLAM build world coordinates, to render 3D models, finally realizes the AR effect.

3.1   Principle of AR Technology

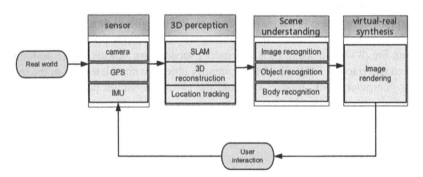

Fig. 6. Typical AR system structure

The typical AR system structure is composed of four parts: sensor, 3D perception, scene understanding and virtual and real combination (as shown in Fig. 6). Firstly, the sensor collects videos or images of real scenes. Secondly, combining with the sensor data, the surrounding environment is analyzed and reconstructed by a specific algorithm, as well as the scene understanding and the recognition of specific objects. Through calculation, the obtained camera attitude and the virtual object that needs to be superimposed are converted into the coordinate system and calculated relative positions, so as to fuse the virtual object into the real scene in the correct position. Finally, combining with computer graphics, rendering out virtual image information, to achieve real-time interaction. At present, AR technology is widely used in robotics, medical care, education, autonomous driving and other fields as a key technology.

3.2 Description of SLAM Feature Points

When the ORB-SLAM is initialized, the image captured by the camera will be converted to grayscale, the ORB feature extraction and matching will be carried out for each image, and the camera pose and triangulation map points will be calculated. The main process for getting feature points is to first load the ORB dictionary file by the system, then call the ORB-SLAM function, get feature points by initialization, ORB feature detection and extraction match, and get all the map point information by polar geometry, triangulation, and so on. In the process of feature points extraction, using OpenMP (Open Multi-Processing) technology based on feature points extraction process was optimized, and parallel computing of eight image pyramid to the serial code optimization for 4 is a thread of parallel code, and then to shorten the time of feature points extraction, improve operational efficiency, realize the feature points extraction under optimal speedup. OpenCV is used to depict feature points. OpenCV USES template class to create a variety of data types, in which the point class can be used to describe feature points, and supports a variety of data types such as int, float, etc., mainly supporting two kinds of templates, two-dimensional point type and three-dimensional point type. In this paper, 2D 32bit floating point data is used to represent the position coordinates of feature points. Firstly, all the map points obtained by triangulation need to be converted into the coordinates of two-dimensional image coordinate system through camera internal parameters and camera external parameters (camera pose), and then the feature point information in the current image frame is depicted through the function in OpenCV library. Figure 7 shows the flow diagram of the feature points.

From Fig. 8 we can see in the small indoor scene, some objects on the desktop are identified and tracked. ORB-SLAM can identify objects with rich texture in the image, such as computer, book, mouse, etc., and the extracted feature points are relatively uniform.

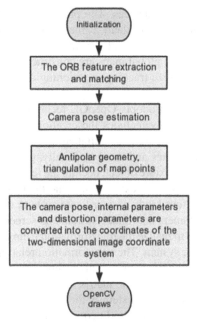

Fig. 7. The flow diagram of the feature points

Fig. 8. Description of feature points in indoor scenes

3.3 3D Model Rendering

In AR technology, SLAM algorithm can be used to calculate the pose of the current camera and the 3D structure information of the internal environment of the image frame. In combination with 3D rendering technology, virtual and real interaction can be realized through mobile phone and other devices. The parameters of SLAM include Camera Pose, Point Cloud and Map. Among them, camera pose is obtained by feature point extraction and matching, map point cloud information is obtained by polar geometry and triangulation, and local and global maps are constructed by back-end optimization of front-end data, so as to realize tracking, positioning and reconstruction of the real world.

The rendering of 3D model adopts OpenGL technology. As the key technology of 3D model rendering, it mainly includes the creation of texture objects. Load texture resources; Create a model class and initialize the parameters of the model such as radius, size, vertex coordinates and number. Finally, get the vertex shader text and fragment shader text, load the texture object, declare the texture coordinates, the number of lines and columns divided by the texture map, bind the texture and start drawing. In OpenGL, there are mainly four kinds of coordinate system: model coordinate system, world coordinate system, camera coordinate system and screen coordinate system. The final model rendering needs to realize the transformation from the model coordinate system to the screen coordinate system. The transformation relation of the four coordinate systems is shown in Fig. 8, which is mainly realized through three matrices: model transformation matrix, camera transformation matrix and projection transformation matrix. Among them, the world coordinate system is the ORB-SLAM initialization after the success to establish the system of the world coordinate system, through the extraction of feature points matching can be calculated at this time the position of the camera (outside), the world coordinate system to the camera coordinate system transformation is accomplished by camera pose matrix of SLAM, the camera pose matrix need through certain transformation can be used. After each successful initialization of ORB-SLAM, the 3D model will be rendered in the world coordinate system created by SLAM and the current camera perspective, so as to achieve the AR effect and perfect fusion of the real world and virtual objects to achieve the effect of virtual and real combination.

As can be seen from Fig. 9, the rendering of the model requires the transformation from the model coordinate system to the screen coordinate system. According to the principle of camera imaging, the transformation from model coordinate system to camera coordinate system is realized by the camera pose matrix calculated by the trackmonocular function of SLAM, and the camera pose matrix can be used as the model view matrix only through certain transformation, that is, the transformation from model coordinate system to camera coordinate system. After successful initialization of ORB-SLAM, the 3D model will be rendered under the current camera perspective to achieve the effect of AR, which perfectly integrates the real world and virtual objects to achieve the effect of virtual reality.

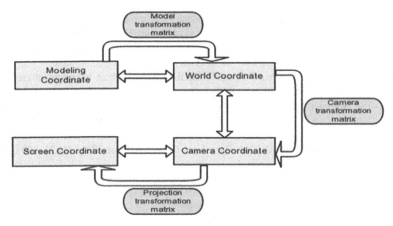

Fig. 9. Four coordinate systems and transformation relations in OpenGL

4   Conclusion

In this paper, combining the visual SLAM technology research and development, under the scope of indoor small scene, choose the speed, accuracy and robustness are better the ORB-SLAM algorithm, through the ORB-SLAM the real-time tracking, positioning and built figure function, calculate the current camera position and environment is the three-dimensional structure of information in the image frames, and following the thread used in OpenMP technology optimization feature points extraction process, and thus enhanced the frame rate of real-time tracking, after finally realize AR applications such as 3D rendering.

Acknowledgements. Supported by the High-quality and Cutting-edge Disciplines Construction Project for Universities in Beijing (Internet Information, Communication University of China).

References

Author, F.: Article title. Journal **2**(5), 99–110 (2016). 高翔张寿视觉SLAM十四讲从理论到实践. 北京: 电子工业出版 (2017)

Silveira, G., Malis, E., Rives, P.: An efficient direct approach to visual SLAM. IEEE Trans. Robot. **24**(5), 969–979 (2008)

Galvez-Lopez, D., Tardos, J.D.: Bags of binary words for fast place recognition in image sequences. IEEE Trans. Robot. **28**(5), 1188–1197 (2012)

Latif, Y., Cadena, C., Neira, J.: Robust loop closing over time for pose graph SLAM. Int. J. Robot. Res. **32**(14), 1611–1626 (2013)

Cadena, C., Carlone, L., Carrillo, H., et al.: Past, present, and future of simultaneous localization and mapping: toward the robust-perception age. IEEE Trans. Robot. **32**(6), 1309–1332 (2016)

Qin, T., Li, P., Shen, S.: Relocalization, global optimization and map merging for monocular visual-inertial SLAM (2018)

Shen, S., Michael, N., Kumar, V.: Tightly-coupled monocular visual-inertial fusion for autonomous flight of rotorcraft MAVs. In: Proceedings - IEEE International Conference on Robotics and Automation, 2015, pp. 5303–5310 (2015)

Yang, Z., Shen, S.: Monocular visual–inertial state estimation with online initialization and camera–IMU extrinsic calibration. IEEE Trans. Autom. Sci. Eng. **14**, 39–51 (2017)

Quan, M., Piao, S., Tan, M., et al.: Accurate monocular visual-inertial SLAM using a map-assisted EKF approach. IEEE Access **7**, 34289–34300 (2017)

Calonder, M., Lepetit, V., Strecha, C., Fua, P.: BRIEF: binary robust independent elementary features. In: Daniilidis, K., Maragos, P., Paragios, N. (eds.) ECCV 2010. LNCS, vol. 6314, pp. 778–792. Springer, Heidelberg (2010). https://doi.org/10.1007/978-3-642-15561-1_56

Hajebi, K., Abbasi-Yadkori, Y., Shahbazi, H., et al.: Fast approximate nearest-neighbor search with k-nearest neighbor graph. In: Proceedings of the 22nd International Joint Conference on Artificial Intelligence, IJCAI 2011, Barcelona, Catalonia, Spain, July 16–22, 2011. DBLP (2011)

Janschek, K., Tkocz, M., et al.: Towards consistent state and covariance initialization for monocular SLAM filters. J. Intell. Robot. Syst. **80**(3–4), 475–489 (2015)

罗秋明, 刘刚, 明仲, 等. OpenMP编译原理及实现技术. 北京清华大学出版社(2012)

周期超. 基于嵌入式系统视觉SLAM算法的优化. 天津职业技术师范大学(2019)

Wang, X., Bai, G., Lang, J.: 3D reconstruction of real-time scene with monocular SLAM. Agric. Equip. Veh. Eng. **56**(10), 57–60 (2018)

Wei, S., Liu, Z., Zhao, J.: A review of indoor 3D reconstruction with SLAM. Sci. Surv. Mapp. **43**(7), 15–26 (2018)

Zhang, J.: Research on 3D Content Generation System Based on Virtual-Real Fusion. Zhejiang University, Zhejiang (2015)

Xu, H., Yu, L., Fei, S.: Large scene dense 3D reconstruction system based on semi-direct SLAM method. Pattern Recogn. Artif. Intell. **31**(5), 477–484 (2018)

Yan, J.: Research on Virtual and Real Scene Fusion of Mobile Augmented Reality Assembly System. School of Electromechanical Engineering Guangdong University of Technology, Guangzhou (2016)

Chen, H.: Monocular Camera based Perception in Augmented Reality Scene. School of Electromechanical Engineering Guangdong University of Technology, Guangzhou (2016)

Virtual Reality App for ASD Child Early Training

Lei Fan[1,2], Wei Cao[3], Yasong Du[4], Jing Chen[4], Jiantao Zhou[2], and Guangtao Zhai[1(✉)]

[1] Shanghai Jiao Tong University, Shanghai 200240, China
zhaiguangtao@sjtu.edu.cn
[2] University of Macau, Macau 999078, China
[3] Shanghai Mingxiang Information Technology Co., Ltd., Shanghai 200241, China
[4] Shanghai Mental Health Center, Shanghai 200030, China

Abstract. Autism spectrum disorder (ASD) is a mental developmental disorder that behaves as communication difficulty, limited interests and activities, repetitive patterns of behavior, etc. ASD is estimated to affect about 1% of people (62.2 million globally) as of 2015. According to the statistics, there are about 70,000,000 globally, and more than 13,000,000 in China, which including 3,000,000 young patients under 14 years, and increasing about 200,000 per year. The early rehabilitation training for child patient could affect the ASD patient's viability improvement and care cost reduction in their later life. A new virtual reality (VR) app, VR-ASD, was developed to reduce the cost and training skill requirements to the trainer, and improve the efficiency and quality of ASD training for child ASD patients. Based on the preliminary study, we state the prime principles, chief framework, and typical functional models of the app, VRASD, with details about operations and skills.

Keywords: Virtual reality · ASD · Autism · Child · Early training

1 Introduction

Autism Spectrum Disorder (ASD) is a mental developmental disorder that behaves as communication difficulty, limited interests and activities, repetitive patterns of behavior, etc. [1, 2]. The current mainstream diagnosis golden standard for mental disorders is the Diagnostic and Statistical Manual of Mental Disorders (DSM) from American Psychiatric Association (APA), which firstly released in 1952 and kept reversing. In 2013, DSM-5 [3] released by APA, as an important event in 2013 recommended by Nature. DSM-5 states 22 kinds of disorders, with one as Neurodevelopmental Disorders, which is about disorders in child development, mainly appearing before school age and harming child's capabilities in personality, social communication, academy or work, with ASD as an important subtype. ASD replaced Pervasive Developmental Disorder (PDD) defined

This work was supported in part by the National Natural Science Foundation of China under Grants 61831015, in part by the Shanghai Municipal Commission of Health and Family Planning under Grant 2018ZHYL0210.

in DSM-4, with the concept of spectrum instead of the previous Autism definition by various symptoms and severities.

Large scale survey showed that the morbidity of ASD was about 1–2% now [4–10], with the median was 0.62–0.70% [11, 12], which was kept increasing in the last tens of years [13–15]. According to the statistics, there are about 70,000,000 globally, and more than 13,000,000 in China, which including 3,000,000 young patients below 14-year-age, and increasing about 200,000 per year. There is no difference of ASD morbidity between China and the western countries [16]: 10–33% ASD patients could not use simple phrases, and require great deal of assistance and help from others [17]. There are 45% of ASD patients with dysgnosia [12], and 32% with intellectual deterioration [18]. 58–78% of adult ASD patients perform poorly or very poorly in independent life, education level, employment and peers relationship [19–21]. However, the mainstream media mainly focused on the high-functioning patients, rather than the low-functioning ones, who really require much more attentions from the public, which leading to even worse social problems associated [22].

2 Motivation

In one hand, there is no reliable treatment for ASD; in another hand, researches showed that the early training against ASD negative performance has high possibility to improve ASD patients' capabilities [23]. Therefore, the early training for ASD patients (e.g. child of 4–8 years) will do great favor to improving the ASD patients' later life qualities, and reducing the family and society cost of nursing [24]. As ASD patients have obvious difference from normal people in perception, they usually are apt to partly processing rather than overall sensation-perception, which could explain ASD patient's high attention towards details, enhanced sensorial perception processing capacity and discriminability, and peculiar sensory reactivity (sensory input over-reaction or under-reaction, or peculiar interest to environmental sensory characteristics) [25, 26].

ASD triangle of ability lack of communication, interaction and imagination [3] just matches Virtual Reality's (VR) 3I components: interactivity, immersion and imagination [27] (Fig. 1). This strong correlation above leaded to the idea to apply VR tech on the applications of ASD early training and the R & D on this direction in recent years by

Fig. 1. ASD triangle & 3I components of VR

Prof. Guangtao Zhai's team in Shanghai Jiao Tong University and Prof. Yasong Du's in Shanghai Mental Health Center, with great assistance from Shanghai Mingxiang Information Technology Co., Ltd.

The overall procedure of the VRASD training includes 4 steps (Fig. 2), resolving ASD child's acceptance of the training interface and system, cognition basis for social contact, social experience and skill training, and merge training for further training in next stage [28].

Fig. 2. VRASD training procedure

Acceptance Training. The most important is the understanding and supporting from the parents, who manage to understand that the key of VRASD startup is to offer ASD children the right not do anything they don't want during VRASD training. We could always wait until they generate interest in VRASD app from inside other than forced from outside. This could help them gain the sense of security, and be willing to the other steps following. And the performance assessment in this step could well percept the style and speed of the later 3 steps of training [29–33].

Cognition Training. Cognition training as the basis of social training offers the ASD children the raw materials for information assimilation and integration later, including the elements of objects, relationships between objects, the procedure how we operate them. In another word, all the information for cognition is well cooked and ready for their capacity.

Social Training. In this key step, with the grounded prepare in previous 2 steps, social training could be much smoother than ever, which used to seem a mass of blackbox without resolution and internal details to the ASD children. All the elements during cognition training are integrated in different scenes for case study and training. VR could provide practices with low cost and high quality controls [3].

Merge Training. Merge means the ability of independence, and reliable relationship with others. Therefore, as the last step for this VR training system, VR would show its great advantages on feedback processing and progress assessing, And as the final target encourage the ASD children the will to leave VR and more active interactions with real people.

3   Approach

3.1   Brief Introduction

The new generation VR app on ASD, VRASD (Fig. 3), was developed and released in 2019, and broadly test in hospitals, schools, and lots of ASD training facilities in several cities including Shanghai [28].

Fig. 3. Main GUI of the app VRASD

This VR app requires hardware and software conditions below:

Proper PC with RTX1060 GPU or above, Mixed Reality Head Mounted Displayer (MR HMD) and controllers supporting Windows Mixed Reality, with Windows 10, STEAMVR and Windows Mixed Reality installed.

This app could be applied on ASD child patients or normal children as controls, with operated by mental health doctors, researchers or teachers in ASD training facilities.

3.2 VR and PC Displayer GUI

Its VR UI in HMD is friendly to the end user of ASD child, convenient to the operator, and all situation concerned obvious to the parent alongside as third-party if applied (Fig. 4). In the operator GUI, operator could watch the first perspective view of the trainee in main screen, and the third perspective view of trainee's head and hands status from the upper-left windows, all the voices from the robotic teacher and cartoon animal roles would be typing in the main screen in white, and the operation prompts just beneath them in yellow. Clock above and level and score indicators at the bottom [31, 32].

Fig. 4. VR UI (left) and operator GUI (right) of the app VRASD

3.3   Character Setting

The training based on the previous VR apps in last several years showed that ASD children with social deficit with normal people were high possible feeling friendly with robotic or cartoon animal characters. Therefore, robotic or cartoon animal characters were taken into consideration and showed very good performance in ASD training (Fig. 5).

Fig. 5. Robotic and cartoon animal characters

3.4   Scene Setting

This app integrated 10 grades of scenes in a virtual large shopping-mall (Fig. 6), which provides large enough space for indoor navigation training and performance assessment. And there are 5–7 levels in each grade, which provides totally 55 levels with enough resolution to locate ASD child's still status and dynamic progress by time. Different

Fig. 6. Scenes integrated in a virtual large shopping-mall

scenes emphasis on different aspects like cognition with 13 levels, music with 10 levels, logic link with 5 levels, reaction with 15 levels, math with 5 levels, social skill with 11 levels (Fig. 7).

Fig. 7. Scene menu, grade 1–10

Balloon Boom. Cognition level 1–7, locate in the game room, startup of the VR app, main purpose to have ASD child accept the VR environment and the internal command system, as well as the cognition of colors, body and space directions, the definition of same and different. The preliminary study showed that ASD group have high rate (more

Fig. 8. Grade 1, balloon boom

than 50%) with touch sensitive, which have them fear or refuse to wear VR HMD. A well designed strategy by our team made it practical to have 90% ASD children accept the HMD within 3 times training (Fig. 8).

Magic Music. Music level 1–5, locate in the music room, primary access to music training, as well as backup startup of the VR app, in case some ASD children are over-sensitive to the sound of balloon booming. This scene provides basis understanding of music includes regular music treatment methods in VR platform (Fig. 9).

Fig. 9. Grade 2, magic music

Food & Feast. Logic link level 1–5, locate in the restaurant, daily life scene integrating specific cognition knowledge accumulation and abstract relationship basis startup in real-time command model. Prepare for later scenes with complex relations judgement (Fig. 10).

Fig. 10. Grade 3, food & feast

Pretty Pet. Reaction level 1–5, and music level 6–10, locate in the music room, music scene with further challenges of reactions, like more short-term memory tasks, basis of melody, higher requirements for speed and practice. Especially, for the first time, this scene request the ASD child trying to simply imagine and percept the next step during a real-time command sequence (Fig. 11).

Fig. 11. Grade 4, pretty pet

Zone of Zoo. Math level 1–5, locate in the music room, primary access to the sense of number and the relationship with real objects, both for objects and parts of objects. All the objects in this scene are animals in dynamic movements, which attract more attentions from ASD child than the still objects do (Fig. 12).

Fig. 12. Grade 5, zone of zoo

Meet Me. Reaction level 6–10, locate in the changing room in clothing shop, the step-by-step training and practice to use the rockers on VR controllers for movement in large scale space, aiming specific target, high-light label, and abstracted navigation on a virtual iPad. The short term memory and simple logic analysis are involved during the game of hide-and-seek. This scene prepare for the later social case training in large scale space (Fig. 13).

Fig. 13. Grade 6, meet me

Face Friend. Social skill level 1–5, locate in the restaurant, basis cognition of expressions on face, using the operation of logic link and relationship with primary case training of imagination, with consideration of face size [32] (Fig. 14).

Fig. 14. Grade 7, face friend

Deli Deliver. Only Cognition level 8–13, locate in the restaurant, as an advanced stage for Grade 3, Food & Feast, with more challenge for short-term memory, abstract meaning understanding, speed and practice, usage of virtual menu and memo on iPad (Fig. 15).

Find Friends. Social skill level 6–11, locate in the game room, with much more complex roles and relationship, long story line and noisy environment in full scale of the

Fig. 15. Grade 8, deli deliver

scene of the shopping-mall space. Dynamic face expression on live characters as a higher level reward mechanism to improve ASD child in this training stage with empathy ability. Reasoning and understanding of information with ambiguity are necessary during the high level task in this scene grade (Fig. 16).

Fig. 16. Grade 9, find friend

Hello Home. Only Reaction level 11–15, locate in the urban street, outsides the shopping mall with the movement mechanism of portal. As the last grade of scene in this app, an exit mechanism is applied to reduce the challenge and complexity in this scene relative to Grade 9 of Find Friend, in order to provider better subjective experience of sense of achievement for ASD children, and encourage them to interact with real people in real world (Fig. 17).

Fig. 17. Grade 10, hello home

4 Conclusion

Autism Spectrum Disorder (ASD) is a mental developmental disorder that challenges traditional mental health treatments and training systems. VR tech showed great advantages in ASD training during the VRASD app development and testing (Fig. 18). Low cost and risk, large scale and high assessment resolution with reliable training quality controls by VRASD app were broadly accepted by almost all concerned.

Fig. 18. Real training and practice with VRASD

The framework extension for the training system and the optimization for the training procedure greatly improve the operability of VRASD training system, and greatly reduced the individual skill requirements towards the training teachers and mental health doctors. The acceptance training resolved the issue of touch sensitive has most of the ASD children take VRASD training as a pleasure game, and the cognition training has most of the parents take it as a better training and education, while the operator would benefit from lower labor load and potential better career development (Fig. 19). These above indicate necessary for more efforts and research on this direction in the future.

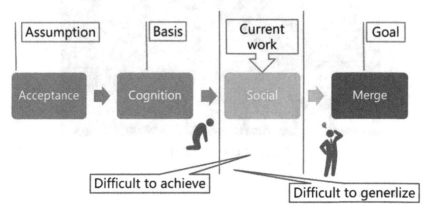

Fig. 19. 4-step training procedure extends the traditional social skill training

References

1. Lord, C., Elsabbagh, M., Baird, G., Veenstra-Vanderweele, J.: Autism spectrum disorder. Lancet **392**(10146), 508–520 (2018)
2. Lai, M.-C., Lombardo, M.V., Baron-Cohen, S.: Autism. Lancet **383**(9920), 896–910 (2014)
3. American Psychiatric Association: Diagnostic and statistical manual of mental disorders (DSM-5®). American Psychiatric Pub (2013)
4. Kim, Y.S., et al.: Prevalence of autism spectrum disorders in a total population sample. Am. J. Psychiatry **168**(9), 904–912 (2011)
5. Baron-Cohen, S., et al.: Prevalence of autism-spectrum conditions: UK school-based population study. Br. J. Psychiatry **194**(6), 500–509 (2009)
6. Hsu, S.-W., Chiang, P.-H., Lin, L.-P., Lin, J.-D.: Disparity in autism spectrum disorder prevalence among Taiwan National Health Insurance enrollees: Age, gender and urbanization effects. Res. Autism Spectr. Disord. **6**(2), 836–841 (2012)
7. Russell, G., Rodgers, L.R., Ukoumunne, O.C., Ford, T.: Prevalence of parent-reported ASD and ADHD in the UK: findings from the Millennium Cohort study. J. Autism Dev. Disord. **44**(1), 31–40 (2014)
8. Saemundsen, E., Magnússon, P., Georgsdóttir, I., Egilsson, E., Rafnsson, V.: Prevalence of autism spectrum disorders in an Icelandic birth cohort. BMJ Open **3**(6), e002748 (2013)
9. Brugha, T., et al.: Autism Spectrum Disorders in Adults Living in Households Throughout England: Report from the Adult Psychiatric Morbidity Survey 2007. The NHS Information Centre for Health and Social Care, Leeds (2009)
10. Mattila, M.L., et al.: Autism spectrum disorders according to DSM-IV-TR and comparison with DSM-5 draft criteria: an epidemiological study. J. Am. Acad. Child Adolesc. Psychiatry **50**(6), 583–592 (2011)
11. Elsabbagh, M., et al.: Global prevalence of autism and other pervasive developmental disorders. Autism Res. **5**(3), 160–179 (2012)

12. Fombonne, E., Quirke, S., Hagen, A.: Epidemiology of pervasive developmental disorders. In: Autism Spectrum Disorders, pp. 90–111 (2011)
13. Wing, L., Gould, J.: Severe impairments of social interaction and associated abnormalities in children: epidemiology and classification. J. Autism Dev. Disord. **9**(1), 11–29 (1979)
14. Newschaffer, C.J.: National autism prevalence trends from United States special education data. Pediatrics **115**(3), e277–e282 (2005)
15. CDC: Prevalence of autism spectrum disorders: autism and developmental disabilities monitoring network, six sites, United States, 2000. MMWR Surveill. Summ. **56**(SS-1), 12–28 (2007)
16. Sun, X., et al.: Autism prevalence in China is comparable to Western prevalence. Mol. Autism **10**, 7 (2019)
17. Happé, F.G., Mansour, H., Barrett, P., Brown, T., Abbott, P., Charlton, R.A.: Demographic and cognitive profile of individuals seeking a diagnosis of autism spectrum disorder in adulthood. J. Autism Dev. Disord. **46**(11), 3469–3480 (2016)
18. Barger, B.D., Campbell, J.M., McDonough, J.D.: Prevalence and onset of regression within autism spectrum disorders: a meta-analytic review. J. Autism Dev. Disord. **43**(4), 817–828 (2013)
19. Howlin, P., Goode, S., Hutton, J., Rutter, M.: Adult outcome for children with autism. J. Child Psychol. Psychiatry **45**(2), 212–229 (2004)
20. Billstedt, E., Gillberg, C., Gillberg, C.: Autism after adolescence: population-based 13-to 22-year follow-up study of 120 individuals with autism diagnosed in childhood. J. Autism Dev. Disord. **35**(3), 351–360 (2005)
21. Howlin, P., Moss, P., Savage, S., Rutter, M.: Social outcomes in mid-to later adulthood among individuals diagnosed with autism and average nonverbal IQ as children. J. Am. Acad. Child Adolesc. Psychiatry **52**(6), 572–581 (2013)
22. Bishop, D.V., Snowling, M.J., Thompson, P.A., Greenhalgh, T.: CATALISE: a multinational and multidisciplinary Delphi consensus study of problems with language development. Phase 2. Terminology. J. Child Psychol. Psychiatry **58**(10), 1068–1080 (2017)
23. Dawson, G.: Early behavioral intervention, brain plasticity, and the prevention of autism spectrum disorder. Dev. Psychopathol. **20**(3), 775–803 (2008)
24. Pickles, A.D., Lord, C.: Heterogeneity and plasticity in the development of language: a 17-year followup of children referred early for possible autism. J. Child Psychol. Psychiatry **55**, 1354–1362 (2014)
25. Baron-Cohen, S., Ashwin, E., Ashwin, C., Tavassoli, T., Chakrabarti, B.: Talent in autism: hypersystemizing, hyper-attention to detail and sensory hypersensitivity. Philos. Trans. R. Soc. B: Biol. Sci. **364**(1522), 1377–1383 (2009)
26. Mottron, L., et al.: Veridical mapping in the development of exceptional autistic abilities. Neurosci. Biobehav. Rev. **37**(2), 209–228 (2013)
27. Richard, P., Burdea, G., Coiffet, P.: Performances Humaines dans des Taches Impliquant des Objets Virtuells avec Retour d'Effort. In: Interface to Real and Virtual Worlds Conference, pp. 229–238, Montpellier (March 1993)
28. Fan, L., Du, Y., Zhai, G.: VR as an adjuvant tool in ASD therapy. Sci. Technol. Rev. **36**(9), 46–56 (2018)
29. Zhai, G., Cai, J., Lin, W., Yang, X., Zhang, W.: Three dimensional scalable video adaptation via user-end perceptual quality assessment. IEEE Trans. Broadcast. **54**(3), 719–727 (2008)
30. Duan, H., Zhai, G., Min, X., Zhu, Y., Sun, W., Yang, X.: Assessment of visually induced motion sickness in immersive videos. In: Zeng, B., Huang, Q., El Saddik, A., Li, H., Jiang, S., Fan, X. (eds.) PCM 2017. LNCS, vol. 10735, pp. 662–672. Springer, Cham (2018). https://doi.org/10.1007/978-3-319-77380-3_63
31. Zhu, Y., Zhai, G., Min, X.: The prediction of head and eye movement for 360 degree images. Signal Process.: Image Commun. **69**, 15–25 (2018)

32. Duan, H., et al.: Learning to predict where the children with ASD look. In: IEEE International Conference on Image Processing (ICIP), pp. 704–708, Athens (2018)
33. Tian, Y., Min, X., Zhai, G., Gao, Z.: Video-based early ASD detection via temporal pyramid networks. In: IEEE International Conference on Multimedia and Expo, pp. 272–277, Shanghai (2019)

Convolutional Neural Networks for Face Illumination Transfer

Zhonglan Li, Xin Jin[✉], Xiaodong Li, and Yannan Li

Beijing Electronic Science and Technology Institute, Beijing, China
jinxinbesti@foxmail.com

Abstract. Face images contain rich and diverse information and have become the focus of research in the field of computer vision. The current research on facial images includes facial recognition, facial image makeup transfer, facial image segmentation, facial image illumination transfer, facial image beautification and rendering. Among them, the illumination of face images is the focus of research. This paper proposes and implements a illumination transfer method combined with a deep neural network to obtain a illumination transfer result that is closer to the real illumination effect. This method mainly implements illumination transfer through illumination model training and illumination classification, illumination matching, and based on the transfer of image style transfer. First, by combining the convolutional neural network to complete the classification of illumination on the face dataset, a model that can classify the illumination of the face image is obtained; then use the model to achieve the illumination matching of a single face image and obtain an image similar to the illumination of a given face image from the face image illumination dataset; finally, through the illumination classification model, the given reference face illumination image is extracted and processed for the relevant illumination features to facilitate the transfer to the input face image so that realizes the illumination transfer to the entire face image, including the neck, etc., and can move the illumination in multiple directions.

Keywords: Convolutional neural network (CNN) · Face image · Illumination transfer

1 Introduction

The illumination effect of images is a research hotspot in the field of computer vision. The effect of illumination and shadow has a wide range of application needs in modern digital film and television production, beautification of portrait photography, advertising and other artistic designs. Face illumination transfer aims to generate target images or videos in one step only by providing ideal illumination effects, without complicated operation methods, saving time, labor and resource costs. This paper studies and implements a CNN-based face illumination transfer method, which migrates the illumination of the reference face

© Springer Nature Singapore Pte Ltd. 2021
W. Song and F. Xu (Eds.): ICVRD 2020, CCIS 1313, pp. 103–120, 2021.
https://doi.org/10.1007/978-981-33-6549-0_10

image to the input face image, while maintaining the facial structure characteristics of the input image. First, by combining convolutional neural networks
[1] VGG19 and VGG16, the illumination classification is completed on the Yale
Face face dataset [2] and the PIE face dataset, and a model that can classify
the face image illumination is obtained. Then using this model, the illumination matching of a single face image is achieved, and the image similar to the
given face image illumination can be obtained from the face image illumination
dataset. Finally, through the illumination classification model, extract and process the relevant illumination features for the given reference face illumination
image, and migrate to the input face image to achieve the overall transfer of the
illumination of a single face image.

The contributions of our method are as follows:

1. This paper implements the illumination transfer of the entire face image,
   including the neck and other parts, and can transfer the illumination in multiple directions, including the positive illumination source, the left illumination
   source, and the right illumination source.
2. This paper uses the VGG network to train the illumination dataset to obtain
   the accuracy rate of the illumination classification model that can classify the
   face image illumination on the Yale Face test data set to 94.375%.
3. This paper proposes a illumination effect matching method based on the illumination classification model. Experiments show that the matching accuracy
   is high.

2   Related Work

2.1   Face Image Illumination Transfer Based on Image Segmentation

Debevec first proposed the illumination transfer in face images. In 2000, he introduced a method of illumination transfer in static scenes. However, this method
does not transfer illumination by segmenting the image to obtain illumination
information, but collects a large amount of face image data to construct a reflection function to represent the value of a pixel in the illumination space and
directly generate a face image of any illumination effect [3]. In 2007, Peers et
al. introduced a real-time transfer of facial image illumination based on quotient images. This method can do illumination transfer for images and videos,
and use two-way optical flow to propagate illumination information from key
frames to the rest of the video, thereby maintaining time consistency. In 2009,
Qing Li [4] et al. introduced a face image illumination transfer method combined
with logarithmic total variation (LTV) model. This method first uses the image
deformation technology based on radial basis functions (RBFs) to align the facial
features of the reference image with the facial features of the input image. Then
use the LTV model to segment the two aligned face images into light-related and
light-independent quantities, respectively. Finally, the amount of the face part
of the input image related to the light is replaced with the amount of the face
part of the reference image related to the light to obtain the resulting image. In

2010, Chen J [5] and others introduced the face-constrained global optimization of face image illumination transfer scheme. Under the fact that the real illumination environment is locally uniform, when global illumination is transformed, adjacent pixels in the image can be combined into small Overlapping windows, applying local constraints. In 2010, Chen X [6] et al. proposed a illumination transfer method migrated the illumination effect of the reference image to the input image through a filter. In 2013, Wu H [7] and others introduced a method of illumination transfer of video images combined with linear interpolation, which transmits the illumination of a single reference video to the input video with uniform illumination.

2.2   Image Transfer Combined with Deep Nerual Network

The rise of deep learning has brought breakthroughs to many studies in the field of computer vision, and style transfer is a typical one of them. There is a certain similarity between style transfer and illumination transfer, both of which transfer information from one image to another. In addition to style transfer, face image makeup transfer [8,9] is also very close to the research topic face image illumination transfer.

In the field of style transfer, in 2015 Gatys [10] et al. proposed a style transfer method Neural Style based on deep convolutional neural networks (Convolutional Neural Networks, CNN). When the convolutional neural network is trained for object recognition, it can gradually extract the required target information in the image. The information is extracted through a specific convolutional layer as the style part in the style transfer. This information retains the image style information while discarding the global information of the image scene. On this basis, two loss functions are defined, representing the content part of the input image and the style part of the reference image, respectively. Define a total loss function to make the resulting image close in content to the input image and close in style to the reference image. In 2017, Liao [11] and others proposed a CNN-based image migration method Deep Image Analogy. All the visual information of the migrated image includes color, hue, texture and style. The migrated object can be a painting image or a real scene. Image. In 2018 Zhu et al. proposed Cycle-GAN [12] without paired images. CycleGAN solves the problem of the need for paired images in traditional GANs, that is, the need for real images in two styles.

In the field of face image makeup migration, in 2016 Liu [13] and others proposed a face makeup migration network based on FCN network that can recommend makeup. In 2017, Chen [14] et al. began by removing the face beautification effect, and proposed a network CRN to remove portrait beautification, that is, blind beautification removal. In the case of unknown beautification algorithm used in the input image, the beautification effect is removed. In the field of image illumination transfer, Tu [15] and others introduced a face illumination transfer scheme based on deep learning and Markov Random Fields (MRF) in 2018. He used paired face data training in the Yale Face dataset to separately construct two datasets with specified illumination effects for the images of the same camera object under the original illumination and reference image illumination effects. First, each image in the dataset is decomposed into illumination components and detailed texture components, and then training to extract illumination features and detailed texture features respectively. Finally, based on the MRF method, the illumination features and the detailed features are synthesized to obtain the result image of the illumination transfer. Papers in the field of style transfer and face makeup transfer are of reference significance to this paper. The use of convolutional neural networks to extract the required image information, cyclic consistency against loss-constrained images etc. are instructive to the work of this paper.

3   Method

Convolutional Neural Networks for Face Illumination Transfer algorithm mainly includes the following steps: (1) Dataset preparation and establishment; (2) Pre-training model preparation; (3) Achieve illumination classification model; (4) Illumination matching based on illumination classification model; (5) Illumination transfer based on illumination classification model.

3.1   Dataset Preparation and Establishment

At present, the more detailed datasets for illumination classification are the Yale Face dataset and the PIE dataset. The Yale Face dataset was originally published in a paper on face classification and recognition published by Yale University in 2001. The Yale Face dataset B contains 10 photographic subjects, 9 males and 1 female, all of which are black and white images. Each camera object contains 9 poses, each pose has 64 kinds of illumination effects, a total of 5760 face illumination images with background. Subsequently, the team expanded the dataset and published the Extended Yale Face dataset B, which contains 28 photographic subjects, both male and female, also black and white images, each photographic subject is also 9×64 kinds of illumination, a total of 16128 background face illumination image. A total of 21888 face images in the two datasets. The nine poses of the Yale Face dataset are shown in Fig. 1.

Among them, postures 2, 3, 4, 5, 6 are about $12°$ away from the optical axis of the camera (that is, distance posture 1), and postures 7, 8, and 9 are about $24°$. As shown in Fig. 1, in order to facilitate the learning of illumination information, this paper uses the illumination image of all faces in pose 1, a total of 2432 pictures. Pose 1 is the pose facing the camera in the front, and the image in this pose has the clearest illumination without interference from other factors. The image of the Yale Face face dataset is named according to the orientation of the light source relative to the camera axis, and the horizontal azimuth angle with the subject as the standard and the elevation angle with the horizon as the standard combine 64 kinds of illumination.

The PIE face dataset is a color face dataset, with a total of 68 photographic objects, including men, women, and all races. Among them, there are 13 poses of

Fig. 1. 9 poses of Yale Face face dataset.

the face illumination image without background lights, and 3 poses of the face illumination image with background lights, as shown in Fig. 2. Each posture contains 21 kinds of light, which are classified by the position of the camera in the x direction, y direction, and z direction. A total of 22,848 images of the human face illumination image part of the dataset, including a background lights and poses facing the camera, a total of 1428 images.

Fig. 2. PIE face dataset with 3 poses including background lights.

Both of the above datasets are relatively small. For the Yale Face face dataset, the face data of 28 photographic subjects are used for training, and the face data of 10 photographic subjects are used for testing. For the PIE face dataset, this section uses the face data of 50 photographic subjects for training and the face data of 18 photographic subjects for testing. The background lights of all images in the PIE dataset that contain background lights are close, which interferes with the learning and classification of face illumination, so the image data is matted. As shown in Fig. 3, it is a comparison of the dataset before the matting and the dataset after the matting.

3.2   Illumination Classification

There are currently two methods for training classification tasks [17]. One is to prepare a sufficient number of datasets and labels, select an appropriate network structure, randomly initialize relevant parameters, and start training from the initial state. The other is transfer learning, which transfers the weights in a network model that can be trained to complete a certain classification task to another brand-new network model for target classification training, rather than starting from the initial state. Transfer learning is usually used when the number

Images classified as 5 before matting

Images classified as 20 before matting

Images classified as 5 after matting

Images classified as 20 after matting

Fig. 3. Image comparison of PIE dataset before and after matting.

of datasets is insufficient or the task target is similar to the existing classification model. Only a few layers of the network can be trained to complete the target classification task. He [18] proved that the models obtained by these two methods have the same effect. There is no transfer learning that is less effective than random initialization training, and on small datasets, the effect of using the pre-trained model transfer learning model is better than random initialization.

The number of images in the PIE face dataset and the Yale Face face dataset are both small, and the classification criteria and number of categories of the two datasets are different. The Yale Face image is a black and white image, and the PIE image is a color image, so the two the dataset needs to be trained separately, and it is completed by fine-tuning the pre-trained model.

For the Yale Face human face dataset, this paper uses the convolutional neural network VGG19, a pre-trained model of the object classification dataset ImageNet provided by Matconvnet. For the PIE face dataset, the convolutional neural network VGG16 and the pre-trained model of the face recognition model Vgg Face provided by Matconvnet are used. ImageNet is a large-scale computer vision recognition project, commonly used is a subset of ImageNet object classification, a total of 1000 categories. Matconvnet is a toolbox for convolutional neural networks that can be used in Matlab. It has a wealth of pre-trained model resources. There are 12 pre-trained models on the ImageNet dataset. The networks used include ResNet, GoogLeNet, VGG-VD, VGG-S,M,F. The ImageNet pre-training model of the VGG19 network is used in Yale Face training.

3.3 Illumination Matching

Illumination matching refers to a given face illumination input image, looking for an image with the same illumination effect as the input image in the face illumination image dataset, and outputting the image with the same illumination. The key to illumination matching is how to calculate the illumination information representing the image. In this paper, the illumination information is obtained from the illumination classification model. The last fully connected layer of the VGG network, the output data dimension is consistent with the number of image categories, and the dimension number corresponding to the maximum value in the output 64-dimensional data is the same as the image category label. Therefore, based on the illumination classification model, the model trained on the Yale Face dataset with high classification accuracy and detailed classification is used to find the correlation between the illumination information and the output of the last fully connected layer of the model. Match the illumination of the face illumination image. The illumination matching algorithm based on the illumination classification model is shown in Fig. 4:

Fig. 4. Illumination matching algorithm.

For the face illumination input image, first obtain the feature data of the image in the last fully connected layer of the network, a total of 64 dimensions, each dimension data represents the possibility that the image is a certain type of illumination, and the larger the number, the image is this type the higher the possibility of illumination. Then look for possible result images from the face illumination image dataset. The maximum value of the feature data of these images in 64 dimensions is in the same dimension as the maximum value of the input image feature data. From these images, find the image with the smallest difference from the maximum value of the input image, and output the image as the illumination matching result image.

3.4 Illumination Transfer

The illumination transfer is based on the illumination classification model, inspired by Neural Style, and combined with the quotient image method of traditional illumination transfer research to complete the end-to-end single face image illumination transfer.

First, prepare the input image and reference image required for illumination transfer. The input image is generally a uniform frontal illumination image, and the reference image is generally an image with obvious illumination and shadow differences. As shown in Fig. 5, there are multiple sets of input and reference images. Input the input image and the reference image into the illumination transfer network (VGG19), get the feature matrix values of the two images, and then solve the illumination and shadow quotient according to the feature matrix values. The illumination and shadow quotient and the desired result image are returned to the transfer network to minimize the transfer loss function, and the result image is output after 1000 iterations.

Fig. 5. Multiple sets of input images and reference images.

The illumination transfer method based on the illumination classification model first calculates the illumination and shadow quotient of the feature matrix of the input image and the reference image at the third convolutional layer, as shown in Eqs. (1), (2).

$$S_l = \frac{F_l\,[E]}{F_l\,[I] + \varepsilon} \tag{1}$$

$$F_l\,[M] = F_l\,[I] \times S_l \tag{2}$$

Where $F_l\,[I]$ is the feature matrix of the input image I at the convolution layer l, and $F_l\,[E]$ is the feature matrix of the reference image E at the convolution layer l. ε is a minimum value of constant, which is set to 0.0001 by experiment to avoid division by zero. The feature matrix value of the reference image is divided by the feature value of the input image to obtain the ratio after VGG network learning, and the input image feature matrix is multiplied by this ratio to obtain the illumination and shadow quotient. The constraints on $F_l\,[M]$ are shown in (3).

$$F_l\,[M] = \begin{bmatrix} r_{11} & \cdots & r_{1i} \\ \cdots & \cdots & \cdots \\ r_{ji} & \cdots & r_{ij} \end{bmatrix}, r_{ij} \in [0.4, 5] \tag{3}$$

Among them, the constraint values 0.4 and 5 are obtained through experiments. Within this constraint range, the illumination information can be transferred well, and the structure and content of the reference image will not be transferred to the input image too much.

The transfer loss function of the illumination transfer method is shown in (4). $F_l\,[O]$ is the desired result image and $F_l\,[OM]$ is the illumination and shadow quotient, calculate the $L2$ distance between the two and continuously narrow the gap between the two to obtain natural illumination transfer.

$$L_{total} = \sum_{l=1}^{L} \left(\alpha_l \frac{1}{2N_l D_l} \sum_{ij} (F_l\,[O] - F_l\,[M])_{ij}^2 \right) \tag{4}$$

4   Experiment Results

4.1   Illumination Classification Model Results and Analysis

To train the illumination classification model, first remove the last fully connected layer of the original network according to the classification task, add a new softmax layer, top1-error layer, and top5-error layer for training, and add a new full connection layer according to the number of categories in the dataset, the Yale Face dataset is 64 categories, and the PIE dataset is 21 categories. Then fine tune the entire network, fine-tune the weights of the first few layers of the network, set the learning rate to 1×10^{-4}, and iterate for 300 epoches to complete the face image illumination classification task. Figure 6 shows the training curve for training two datasets.

The average accuracy rate of the illumination classification model trained by the VGG16 network and the VGG Face pre-training model on the PIE face

Yale Face dataset training curve   PIE Face dataset training curve

Fig. 6. Training curve.

Fig. 7. Accuracy of each category of Chen face illumination-shadow matching algorithm [16].

dataset test set is 62.8571%. The illumination classification model trained by the VGG19 network and the ImageNet pre-training model has an average accuracy rate of 94.375%. On the test set of the Yale Face face dataset, of the 64 types of illumination, 48 types of illumination effects have a classification accuracy of 100%. The accuracy of each category of Chen [16] face illumination and shadow matching algorithm using traditional methods is shown in Fig. 7, and the accuracy of each category of the model in this paper is shown in Fig. 8:

From Fig. 7 and Fig. 8, on the Yale Face face dataset, the illumination classification model combined with the convolutional neural network has higher classification accuracy than the Chen illumination and shadow matching algorithm, and there are more categories with 100% classification accuracy. The reason why the accuracy rate of the PIE face dataset is not high is that the illumination and shadow gap between the images of the dataset is small, and there are data collection errors. Some images with the same illumination category label have different actual illumination effects. As shown in Fig. 9.

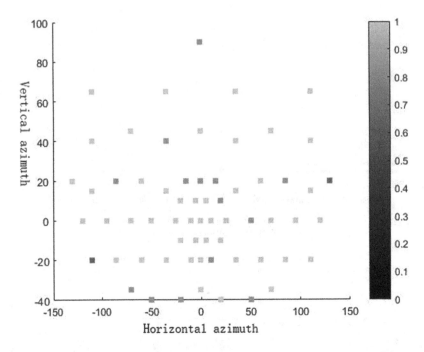

Fig. 8. Accuracy of each category of illumination classification model.

Fig. 9. PIE dataset with the same illumination category label.

4.2   Illumination Matching Results and Analysis

The matching result on the Yale Face face dataset is shown in Fig. 10. The results of the matching experiment in this paper are better than those of Chen [16] face illumination and shadow matching algorithm. The results of Chen's traditional method are shown in Fig. 11.

Input

Matching

Fig. 10. Matching results on Yale Face face dataset.

It can be seen from Fig. 10 that the illumination matching based on the illumination classification model is very good and can distinguish images with large differences in matching illumination. As shown in the figure, the azimuth angle is −85° and the elevation angle is −20°. Strong dichroic image. It can also distinguish images with more complicated illumination differences. As shown in the figure, the azimuth angle is 35° and the elevation angle is 40°. The cheek part has a right triangle illumination and shadow. It can also distinguish images with very insignificant illumination. As shown in the figure, the image with azimuth angle of −10° and elevation angle of −20° is very similar to the image of uniform illumination. There are also four images in Fig. 12. The illumination effects are close but the illumination category labels are different. However, Chen's [16] traditional face illumination-shadow matching algorithm cannot accurately distinguish images with similar illumination effects, and cannot accurately match images with the same azimuth and elevation angles as the input image. In addition, Chen's traditional face illumination-shadow matching algorithm needs to align the faces of the two images for comparison. Various methods compare the illumination information of each part of the face. However, the illumination matching algorithm based on the illumination classification model does not need to align the images. Image illumination matching can be completed.

Fig. 11. Matching results of Chen's face illumination and shadow matching algorithm [16].

4.3   Illumination Transfer Results and Analysis

A illumination transfer was performed on the Yale Face dataset, and the result image and reference image obtained by combining different convolutional layers were compared. According to experiments, the convolutional layers used for illumination transfer are convolutional 1_2 layer and convolutional 2_1 layer. The lower convolutional layer is more sensitive to the content and structural information of the image and can retain the content information of the input image, as shown in Fig. 13.

Azimuth 0, elevation −20   Azimuth −10, elevation 0

Azimuth 0, elevation 20   Azimuth −10, elevation −20

Fig. 12. Figures with different illumination classifications but close to actual illumination.

In Fig. 13, the result image a sets the convolution layer as the convolution layer 1_2 and the convolution layer 2_1; the result image b sets the convolution layer as the convolution layer 1_1 and the convolution layer 1_2; Convolution 1_2 layer. More experimental results are shown in Fig. 14.

From Fig. 14, the illumination transfer method based on the illumination classification model can transfer illumination in multiple directions on the same camera object, including positive light source, left light source, and right light source. It can transfer illumination and the illumination is natural.

Fig. 13. Illumination transfer results of different convolutional layers.

Fig. 14. Experimental results of multiple reference images.

5   Conclusion

In this paper, using the VGG network to train the illumination dataset to obtain a illumination classification model that can classify the face image illumination, the accuracy rate on the Yale Face test dataset reaches 94.375%, and the accuracy on the PIE dataset that is more difficult to classify, reaches 62.8571%, and it also has a good classification effect. On the basis of the illumination classification model, based on the features derived from the model, a illumination effect matching method based on the illumination classification model is proposed, which is more accurate and more accurate than the Chen [16] face illumination and shadow matching algorithm. It can also accurately match illumination on images in non-Yale Face datasets. Furthermore, based on the illumination classification model, a illumination transfer method is proposed. The input and reference figures of the same camera object in the Yale Face dataset can obtain a transitional natural illumination transfer effect.

Acknowledgements. This work is partially supported by the National Natural Science Foundation of China (grant numbers 62072014, 61772047), the Beijing Natural Science Foundation (grant number L192040), the Open Project Program of State Key Laboratory of Virtual Reality Technology and Systems, Beihang University (grant number VRLAB2019C03), the MOE Layout Foundation of Humanities and Social Sciences (grant number 20YJA880056).

References

1. Girshick, R.: Fast R-CNN. In: 2015 IEEE International Conference on Computer Vision (ICCV), Santiago, pp. 1440–1448 (2015)
2. Georghiades, A.S., Belhumeur, P.N., Kriegman, D.J.: From few to many: illumination cone models for face recognition under variable lighting and pose. IEEE Trans. Pattern Anal. Mach. Intell. **23**(6), 643–660 (2001)
3. Debevec, P.E., Hawkins, T., Tchou, C., et al.: Acquiring the reflectance field of a human face. In: Proceedings of the 27th Annual Conference on Computer Graphics and Interactive Techniques, pp. 145–156. ACM Press/Addison-Wesley Publishing Co. (2000)
4. Li, Q., Yin, W., Deng, Z.: Image-Based Face Illumination Transferring Using Logarithmic Total Variation Models. Springer, New York (2009)
5. Chen, J., Su, G., He, J., Ben, S.: Face image relighting using locally constrained global optimization. In: Daniilidis, K., Maragos, P., Paragios, N. (eds.) ECCV 2010. LNCS, vol. 6314, pp. 44–57. Springer, Heidelberg (2010). https://doi.org/10.1007/978-3-642-15561-1_4
6. Chen, X., Chen, M., Jin, X.: Face illumination transfer through edge-preserving filters. In: CVPR, Colorado Springs, CO, USA, pp. 281–287 (2011)
7. Wu, H., Chen, X., Yang, M., et al.: Facial performance illumination transfer from a single video using interpolation in non-skin region. Comput. Anim. Virtual Worlds **24**(3–4), 255–263 (2013)
8. Guo, D., Sim, T.: Digital face makeup by example. In: 2009 IEEE Conference on Computer Vision and Pattern Recognition, Miami, FL, pp. 73–79 (2009)
9. Tong, D., Tang, C.K., Brown, M.S., et al.: Example-based cosmetic transfer. In: 15th Pacific Conference on Computer Graphics and Applications (PG 2007), HI, Maui, pp. 211–218 (2007)
10. Gatys, L.A., Ecker, A.S., Bethge, M.: A neural algorithm of artistic style. Computer Science (2015)
11. Liao, J., Yao, Y., Yuan, L., et al.: Visual attribute transfer through deep image analogy. ACM Trans. Graph. **36**(4), 1–15 (2017)

12. Zhu, J.Y., Park, T., Isola, P., et al.: Unpaired image-to-image translation using cycle-consistent adversarial networks. In: 2017 IEEE International Conference on Computer Vision (ICCV), Venice, pp. 2242–2251 (2017)
13. Liu, S., Ou, X., Qian, R., et al.: Makeup like a superstar: deep localized makeup transfer network. arXiv preprint arXiv:1604.07102 (2016)
14. Chen, Y.C., Shen, X., Jia, J.: Makeup-go: blind reversion of portrait edit. In: 2017 IEEE International Conference on Computer Vision (ICCV), pp. 4511–4519. IEEE Computer Society (2017)
15. Tu, C.T., Chang, C.Y., Chen, Y.C.: Learning-based approach for face image relighting. J. Phys: Conf. Ser. **1061**(1), 012023 (2018)
16. Chen, X., Jin, X., Zhao, Q., et al.: Artistic illumination transfer for portraits. Comput. Graph. Forum **31**(4), 1425–1434 (2012)
17. Pan, S.J., Yang, Q.: A survey on transfer learning. IEEE Trans. Knowl. Data Eng. **22**(10), 1345–1359 (2010)
18. He, K., Girshick, R., Dollár, P.: Rethinking imagenet pre-training. arXiv preprint arXiv:1811.08883 (2018)

Modeling the Self-navigation Behavior of Patients with Alzheimer's Disease in Virtual Reality

Jinghui Jiang, Guangtao Zhai$^{(\boxtimes)}$, and Zheng Jiang

Department of Electronic Engineering, Shanghai Jiao Tong University, Shanghai, China
zhaiguangtao@sjtu.edu.cn

Abstract. Alzheimer's disease is a chronic neurodegenerative disease characterized by the progressive deterioration of memory and cognitive functions. Until 2015, approximately 29.8 million people worldwide suffered from this disease, most of whom were elderly people over 65 years old. Therefore, this has become a new challenge faced by an ageing society. With the development of technologies such as deep learning, virtual reality, and wearable devices, by collecting and analyzing the self-navigation data of patients, the spatial intelligence assessment may become an auxiliary tool for early diagnosis because disorientation is one of the earliest symptoms. Therefore, in this study, through deep reinforcement learning, based on the asynchronous advantage actor-critic algorithm, the agent was trained in the three-dimensional maze environment to imitate the healthy people and Alzheimer's patients on the navigation aspect, respectively. And we established the connection between the neural network and the pathogenesis of Alzheimer's disease. Results show that the navigation model which imitated the patient has worse performance than the "healthy" navigation model in terms of average steps, path efficiency, and decision-making evaluation ability. Finally, we developed a cognitive training program on the Unity platform, which can help patients in the evaluation of navigation ability and cognitive ability training.

Keywords: Deep reinforcement learning · Alzheimer's disease · Spatial navigation

1 Introduction

1.1 Motivation

Alzheimer's disease (AD) is a neurodegenerative disease. A common early symptom is short-term memory decline. As the condition worsens, language disorders, disorientation, and execution disorders will occur [5]. Alzheimer's disease is a common type of dementia. According to "World Alzheimer Report 2015" [1], there are about 46.8 million people worldwide with dementia, of which about 29.8 million people suffer from Alzheimer's disease. Every 20 years the number of patients doubled, and the number is expected to reach 74.7 million until 2030. The incidence rate for people over 65 years

© Springer Nature Singapore Pte Ltd. 2021
W. Song and F. Xu (Eds.): ICVRD 2020, CCIS 1313, pp. 121–136, 2021.
https://doi.org/10.1007/978-981-33-6549-0_11

old is about 6%, but about 4% to 5% of patients will get sick before the age of 65. This has become a new challenge faced by an ageing society.

AD is regarded as a continuous disease process including mild cognitive impairment (MCI) [6], that means, the patient will experience a continuous process of cognitive decline, from the asymptomatic stage to the occurrence of MCI symptoms, eventually to dementia. But there are difficulties in the early diagnosis of AD, especially in developing countries with backward medical standards [2, 3]. Existing clinical diagnosis methods require doctors to talk with patients for a long time, understand the patient's historical cognitive level and conduct relevant cognitive tests, to determine whether there is an abnormal cognitive deterioration. Meanwhile, brain CT, MRI and PET scans can also provide diagnostic evidence, particularly PET scans can show the deposition levels of amyloid and glucose metabolism in the patient's brain at the preclinical stage. However, the cost of PET scanning is too high, so it is not suitable for large-scale early screening. When clinical symptoms appear and the doctor can make a diagnosis, a large number of neurons may have died, and the patient's cognitive ability is impossible to reverse.

In recent years, researchers have begun to introduce technologies such as wearable devices, artificial intelligence (AI), virtual reality (VR) and robots into AD and other dementia studies, offering help in early diagnosis. One way is to use computer vision for the diagnosis of MRI and PET scan images [9], and the other research direction is to collect and analyze potential patients' big data of self-navigation, daily reading, typing and voice message [7, 8].

1.2 Background

The drug maker Eli Lilly together with Apple launched a study [10], by collecting typing, reading speed and other data in smart digital devices, found that participants with symptoms had a slower speed in typing, and showed fewer daily movement. In 2019, Deutsche Telekom collaborated with Alzheimer's Research UK and other universities in UK developed a mobile game called "Sea hero Quest" [11]. The team studied 27,108 players aged between 50 and 75, which is the age group with the highest risk over the next decade. In the game, the player's wayfinding and path integration abilities are tested. Path integration sums the vectors of distance and direction travelled from a start point to estimate current position, and so the path back to the start. At the beginning of the game, the player will be provided with a map which shows the location of the checkpoints. The player must navigate a ship to the checkpoint in the maze without a map to complete the wayfinding task. In addition, to test the player's path integration ability, in some levels, when the player reaches the destination, the player needs to recall the direction of the start point and launch a flare into the air towards the start point. The study found people carrying the specific AD gene ApoE4 will travel longer distances and choose less efficient routes to reach checkpoints. Moreover, the consistency of the navigation behavior in the virtual and the real world is proved [12]. Therefore, spatial intelligence assessment may become an early diagnosis tool for AD, because spatial disorientation is one of the earliest symptoms. And data collection in a virtual environment is convenient, fast, low-cost, large-scale and covers a wider crowd.

In recent years, virtual reality has been used in the diagnosis, cognitive evaluation and training of AD patients [15, 20]. With the use of other daily tools, patients can interact in a secure virtual environment (VE). Duan [43, 44] analyzed and predicted the visual attention of children with Autism Spectrum Disorder (ASD) when looking at human faces in virtual environment. Tarnanas [16] built a virtual museum to study the deficiencies of MCI patients in spatial navigation, prospective memory and executive function. Bellassen [17] compared the short-term memory of AD, MCI patients and healthy people in virtual streets. Rogers [18] found that MCI patients perform worse than the healthy in terms of total time, path distance and success rate in Morris water maze. Besides, Cushman [19] compared people's navigation behavior in both real and virtual environments. The results obtained in the virtual environment are proved to be also effective in the real environment. Howett [21] tested the path integration ability in VR scenes using a triangle trajectory and found that the distance error and the path length of MCI patients will be longer than that of the healthy.

In this article, we used deep reinforcement learning to train agents to complete navigation tasks in a 3D maze environment. We modified the network structure and parameters to simulate the process of cognitive deterioration, we also associated the neural network with the pathogenesis of AD. By completing tasks such as wayfinding, collecting rewards, and finding goals in the maze, it simulates some specific behavior patterns that AD patients displayed in the navigation. And we also developed a maze navigation game in Unity3D used in cognitive training or data collection for subsequent experiments.

2   Related Work

In general reinforcement learning, an agent interacts with an environment according to a policy, collecting rewards at each time-step [27]. The agent wishes to learn a policy which maximizes the expected accumulated rewards from the initial state to T_{max}

$$\overline{R_t} = E_{s_t \sim E, a_t \sim \pi} \left[\sum_{t=0}^{T_{max}} \gamma^t r_{t'} \right] \tag{1}$$

Where the states s_t are sampled from the environment E, the actions a_t are sampled according to the policy π. The action-state value $Q^\pi(s, a) = E[R_t | s_t = s, a_t = a]$ is the expected rewards for selecting action a in state s and following policy π. Similarly, the expected return from state s under policy π is defined as $V^\pi(s) = E[R_t | s_t = s]$.

In the policy-based model-free method [29], it calculates the gradient of the objective function $\nabla_\theta log \pi(a_t | s_t; \theta)(R_t - b(s_t))$, and updates the parameters θ by performing gradient ascent on $E[R_t]$. In the value-based one-step Q-learning [28], the parameters θ of the action-state value function $Q^\pi(s, a; \theta)$ are learned by iteratively minimizing a sequence of loss functions:

$$L_i(\theta_i) = E_{(s,a,r,s')} \left[\left(r + \gamma max_{a'} Q(s', a'; \theta_i^-) - Q(s, a; \theta_i) \right)^2 \right] \tag{2}$$

where s' is the state encountered after state s, and γ is the discount factor. The Asynchronous Advantage Actor-Critic (A3C) algorithm has achieved very good results on Atari games as well as continuous motor control tasks [30, 32]. Combing the policy-based and the value-based method, the Actor-Critic algorithm employs two networks, including a policy network $\pi(a_t|s_t; \theta)$ and a value function network $V(s_t; \theta_v)$, which may share some parameters. Based on the n-steps Q-learning, the network is updated every n steps. The updated gradient can be seen as $\nabla_\theta log \pi(a_t|s_t; \theta) A(s_t, a_t; \theta, \theta_v)$ where $A(s_t, a_t; \theta, \theta_v)$ is the advantage function that equals to $\sum_{i=0}^{k-1} \gamma^i r_{t+i} + \gamma^k V(s_{t+k}, \theta_v) - V(s_t, \theta_v)$ where k is upper-bounded by T_{max}.

Deep RL has recently been used in solving the navigation problem. To deal with the sparsity of rewards and facilitate representation learning, auxiliary tasks are introduced in training [26, 32, 33]. These include pixel control, hidden layer units activation, reward prediction, depth prediction and loop closure task.

Humans have three types of brain cells related to navigation: place cells remember past locations, head direction cells sense movement and direction, grid cells can induce significant neural responses at specific spatial locations when you are navigating an open area, allowing you to understand your position in space by storing and integrating information about location, distance, and direction. There is a hypothesis that the grid cells encode a neural representation of Euclidean space. To train a deep RL agent behaved like a mammal in spatial navigation, Banino [25] used a recurrent network and MLPs to simulate grid cells and trained the network to perform path integration, leading to the emergence of representations resembling grid cells, which are thought to be critical for path integration and planning direct trajectories to goals in the human brain. In addition, to prove the similarity between the neural network navigation and human navigation, some studies attempt to establish the connection between deep reinforcement learning neural networks and human brain in memory and navigation [23, 24], such as associating value functions and network inputs with biological signals in the human brain.

3   Approach

3.1   Architecture

The A3C Architecture. Figure 1 shows the based A3C navigation network structure (GA3C_LSTM) proposed in [32]. It is used to simulate the navigation of healthy people with a normal cognitive level in a 3D maze. The RGB format image x_t is the input of the convolutional layer. The output of the encoder is used as the input of the LSTM layer. The output of the recurrent network includes a policy π, which is the probability distribution of the action space size, and a value function V. In this problem, we set up a discrete, six-dimensional motion space. So that the agent can look around and move in four directions. At the same time, auxiliary inputs are added to the LSTM layer to better process time sequences information, including the reward signal of the previous state r_{t-1}, the current agent's movement speed and rotation speed in the x, y, and z-axis v_t, and the action taken in the previous step a_{t-1}. Reward signal r_{t-1} and convolutional layer output as the input of the first LSTM layer. The speed vector v_t, the previous action a_{t-1}, convolution layer output and the first LSTM layer output are used as the input of the second LSTM layer.

Also, the auxiliary task of depth prediction is added, and the loss function of the depth prediction will be calculated into the overall loss function to accelerate convergence. The depth information can provide the agent with three-dimensional depth information of

(a) GA3C_LSTM   (b) details

Fig. 1. Network architecture (a) the A3C architecture with auxiliary inputs as basic navigation network (b) details on the size of each layer

the environment and help the agent understand key features. Considering the training efficiency and computing power, only 4 × 16 pixels in the middle of the input image is intercepted for prediction, and be regarded as a classification task. The encoder and LSTM are followed by the Multilayer Perceptron (MLP), output the depth prediction map: D_1, D_2.

So now the objective function of the navigation network is:

$$J(\theta) = \sum_{t=0}^{T_{max}-1} -\left(log\pi(a_t|s_t; \theta)(R - V^{\pi_\theta}(s_t; \theta_v)) + \beta H(\pi(s_t; \theta))\right)$$
$$+ \beta_{d_1} H\left(d_1^{s_t}\right) + \beta_{d_2} H\left(d_2^{s_t}\right) + 0.5 * \left(R - V^{\pi_\theta}(s_t; \theta_v)\right)^2 \tag{3}$$

The cumulative reward R in the formula is expressed as:

$$R = \sum_{i=0}^{T_{max}-t-1} \gamma^i r_{t+i} + \gamma^{T_{max}} V^{\pi_\theta}\left(s_{t+T_{max}}\right) \tag{4}$$

The objective function is composed of four parts: the objective function of the policy, the policy entropy, the cross entropy of the two depth predictions, and the loss of the value function. We hope to maximize the policy entropy to encourage the agent to explore the environment, so as to prevent the policy from converging to the local optimum. Parameters are updated every T_{max} steps. We chose RMSProp as optimization function, the principle is as follows:

$$g = \alpha g + (1 - \alpha)\Delta\theta^2;$$
$$\theta \leftarrow \theta - \eta \frac{\Delta\theta}{\sqrt{g+\varepsilon}} \tag{5}$$

We chose GA3C [31], the hybrid CPU-GPU implementation of the A3C algorithm, to train multiple agents using one global model on GPU. The maze environment is obtained from DeepMind Lab, which is an open-source 3D platform for studying the behavior of RL agents in complicated, visual game settings. A rich Python API affords easy communication with the environment. Through the API, the agent can receive observations image and optional depth information, agent velocity information (both translational and rotational), and rewards by collecting objects along the way or reaching destination coordinates.

Pathogenesis. Alzheimer's disease is pathologically characterized by senile plaques (SP) formed by amyloid β-protein (Aβ) deposition, the neurofibrillary tangles (NFTs) caused by tau protein, and the loss of neurons in the cerebral cortex and hippocampus. Although experts are still unclear about the pathogenesis of AD, the β-amyloid cascade hypothesis is the mainstream theory about the pathogenesis of AD, and it is believed that excessive production of β-amyloid in the brain is the main cause of AD [35].

However, with the progress of research, the intracellular deposition of soluble Aβ rather than intercellular plaques are gradually considered to be an important cause of AD neuron damage [36]. They will bind to the surface of nerve cells and change the structure of synapses, thus disrupting the transmission of information between neurons. The neurotoxic effects of Aβ include inducing apoptosis and accelerating abnormal phosphorylation of Tau protein. Studies have shown that the combined effect of Tau protein and Aβ can cause memory loss and behavioral deficits in AD patients [37].

Microtubules are one of the main components of the cytoskeleton and participate in the maintenance of neuronal morphology and the formation of axons and dendrites. Microtubules are composed of tubulin and microtubule-associated proteins. Tau protein is one of the microtubule-associated proteins. Tau protein combines with tubulin to form microtubules, and maintain its stability. The phosphorylation level of AD patients is three to four times higher than that of normal people. The hyperphosphorylated tau protein will fall off from the microtubules, gathering and further twisting to form NFTs. These changes can disrupt microtubules, making cells died and communications between nerve cells ineffective [37, 38].

Therefore, we want to simulate the impairment of information transmission between neurons and the apoptosis of neurons, that happens in MCI and AD patients' brains, by adjusting the network structure and some nodes and parameters, to show their short-term memory impairment and execution obstacle.

Network. As shown in Fig. 2, the noise navigation network (GA3C_Noise) and the de-memory navigation network (GA3C_FF) respectively simulate MCI patients with partially impaired cognitive function and dementia patients who have completely lost short-term memory. In GA3C_Noise, we added random noise to the input and output and disabled some nodes of the hidden layer in the network. By adding random noise to the output action with probability p_o, the dysfunction of output neurons is simulated, corresponding to the patient's executive obstacles and the decline in judgment ability. To simulate the impaired information transmission between neurons and the death of some neurons, we added dropout on the fully connected layer to disable some hidden nodes of the fully connected layer, with a probability p_{drop}. For the auxiliary input-the previous action and reward, add random noise with probability p_i to simulate the short-term memory impairment of the patient. No noise is added to the image input because the patient's vision is not damaged, but the ability to understand visual cues declines, that is, the ability of the encoder to understand features declines. In GA3C_FF, we removed the recurrent network, and simply replaced by a feed-forward network. The network thus loses short-term memory, thereby simulating the apoptosis of neurons in cerebral cortex and hippocampus of AD patients, which leads to complete loss of short-term memory.

(a) GA3C_Noise   (b) GA3C_FF

Fig. 2. The modified navigation network (a) with extra random noise and dropout to simulate MCI patients (b) without LSTM layers to simulate dementia patients

3.2 Route-Based Navigation

In the wayfinding task, humans mainly make strategies based on routes or based on maps. Route-based strategies depend on landmarks and will establish the connection between the landmarks and the moving or turning direction. Each time when navigating from the starting point, they tend to choose the route that they have traveled in the past. In a map-based strategy, the map provides the location information of starting point, destination and landmarks, thereby planning the route.

Research by Anggraini et al. [23] proved that the model-free reinforcement learning model is closer to the route-based strategy, while the model-based model is more like map-based. However, A3C architecture does not need to model the environment map. It's model-free. In the navigation task, the agent is trained to continuously explore the environment, optimize the cumulative reward and the value function to find the shortest path, and also choose the shortest route when departing again, so it is similar to the route-based strategy.

And Anggraini found that the value function used to evaluate the strategy is equivalent to a biological signal, Blood Oxygenation Level Dependent (BOLD) signal, generated in the cerebral cortex during human navigation. The cerebral cortex generally provides visual information and is also rich in grid cells that play an important role in the navigation. However, Sukumar believed the value function is equivalent to the basal ganglia of the human brain [24]. In short, the value function may represent a certain signal in the brain during policy-making and path planning in navigation. Although we do not directly constrain the value function error like Sukumar, by comparing the V (s) output of different navigation networks, we can know there must be some changes in neural signals, and these changes are caused by impaired information transmission or damaged neurons of AD patients. At the same time, comparing depth map outputs can explain the change in the ability to understand visual features.

4 Result

We chose a 5×10 grid size maze as the training environment, and set the parameters in the noise network:$p_o = p_i = 0.1$, $p_{drop} = 0.15$. In the early training period, to maximize the strategy entropy, the action probability is uniformly distributed, and later it will converge to one optimal strategy. The value function plays a role in strategy evaluation and path planning in navigation. The value function curve of the model is supposed to like a sawtooth wave, with low noise, which means that the expected future reward is steadily increasing in each round, which shows that the agent is approaching the target position. Figure 3 compares the value function curves of the three models. The agent can understand the depth of objects in a 3D environment by the depth map. When the agent faces a wall the depth map is closer to black (a larger Z-buffer value), while the agent faces a hallway the depth is closer to white (a smaller Z-buffer value). There may appear some noise in the depth map of GA3C_Noise.

| (a) GA3C_LSTM | (b) GA3C_Noise | (c) GA3C_FF |

Fig. 3. Value function curve (a) a sawtooth wave (b) unstable wave with a louder noise (c) lose the shape entirely and the value approach to zero

We collected 100 rounds of test data for each model separately to obtain the distribution of scores. It can be observed from Fig. 4 and Table 1 that the average scores of the GA3C_LSTM, GA3C_Noise and GA3C_FF network decrease in turn. The median of the GA3C_FF is much smaller than its average score. This is because its passing rate only reaches 32%, most of the data is located less than 3 points.

We first selected three fixed starting points with coordinates: (550, 50), (350, 350), (50, 50). The distance and the total rewards on the road decline in turn. For each starting point, we randomly select 20 effective trajectories of each model and compares the number of steps taken to reach the destination. We also defined the shortest path rate and

Table 1. Statistics of 100 rounds scores

Model	GA3C_LSTM	GA3C_Noise	GA3C_FF
Average score	90.73	57.81	7.94
Median score	90.00	57.00	3.00
Standard deviation	9.64	11.43	8.08
Passing rate	100%	100%	32%

the bias of the selected path from the shortest path. The shortest path rate is the ratio of the number of times the shortest route is selected to the number of all routes:

$$P_{shortest} = \frac{T_{shortest}}{T_{total\_track}} \tag{6}$$

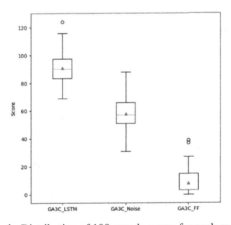

Fig. 4. Distribution of 100 rounds scores for each model

We first find the route with the smallest steps $n_{shortest}$, if the number of steps is less than $1.3 \times n_{shortest}$ and the trajectory is nearly the same, then we take this route as the shortest path. Therefore, the bias is defined as:

$$B_{track} = \frac{n_{track} - n_{shortest}}{n_{max} - n_{shortest}} \tag{7}$$

Where the n_{max} is the largest steps. The closer the bias is to 1, the closer the trajectory is to the longest path, and further away from the shortest path.

As shown in Table 2, wherever the starting point is, GA3C_LSTM has the fewest steps, followed by GA3C_Noise, and finally GA3C_FF has the most. And $P_{shortest}$ of the GA3C_Noise is less than or equal to the GA3C_LSTM at all starting points.

Table 2. Steps, shortest path rate and bias of three different starting point

Model	GA3C_LSTM	GA3C_Noise	GA3C_FF
(a) Starting point: (50, 50)			
$n_{shortest}$	30	37	42
n_{max}	64	76	133
$P_{shortest}$	0.300	0.300	0.250
B_{track}	0.472	0.402	0.630
(b) Starting point: (350, 350)			
Model	GA3C_LSTM	GA3C_Noise	GA3C_FF
$n_{shortest}$	87	96	900
n_{max}	133	223	900
$P_{shortest}$	0.750	0.350	0
B_{track}	0.384	0.419	1
(c) Starting point: (550, 50)			
Model	GA3C_LSTM	GA3C_Noise	GA3C_FF
$n_{shortest}$	170	180	900
n_{max}	220	372	900
$P_{shortest}$	0.800	0.200	0
B_{track}	0.384	0.481	1

Figure 5 compares the shortest path trajectory of each model at each starting point. It is observed that the trajectory of GA3C_Noise (red) and GA3C_LSTM (blue) are almost the same, but the trajectory of GA3C_FF (yellow) is very different from theirs.

Figure 6 compares the trajectory of the shortest path and the non-shortest path. The location of the non-shortest path is closer to the border. At the corner, it will tend to travel in longer triangles than straight lines, so it will bring more steps. GA3C_Noise deviated more from the shortest path than GA3C_LSTM when departed from (350, 350) and (550, 50). But the bias of GA3C_LSTM network increases if (50, 50) is the starting point. Although it is closest to the destination, there is no reward distributed on the road, and the bends are dense, so it is easy to deviate from the shortest path.

From Fig. 7, it can also be observed that the GA3C_FF has the lowest route efficiency. But when the starting point is closer to the goal, its passing rate can also reach 100%, despite its poor performance at further starting points.

In summary, the networks that imitate AD patients have lower scores, while the path length of them is longer and the probability of choosing the shortest path is lower. When the distance between the start point and the destination is longer, the patient networks are more likely to deviate from the shortest path. The result is consistent with the patient's navigational behavior pattern in reality [11, 18, 19, 21].

We also developed a cognitive training program based on Unity and trained simple automatic navigation AI based on the Unity machine learning toolkit, ML-Agents [39,

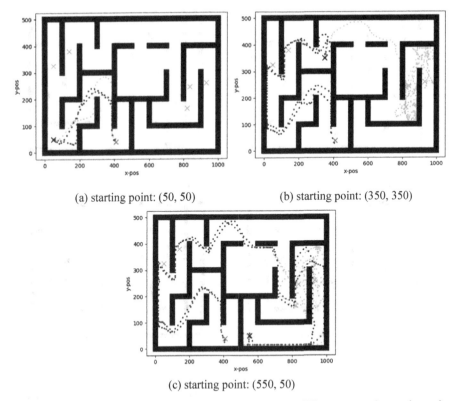

(a) starting point: (50, 50)   (b) starting point: (350, 350)

(c) starting point: (550, 50)

Fig. 5. Shortest path trajectory. The black, orange and green "X" represents the starting point, destination and rewards. The blue line represents the shortest path of GA3C_LSTM, red is GA3C_LSTM, and yellow is GA3C_FF (Color figure online)

40]. We used the off-policy SAC algorithm [34] and curriculum learning which is supported by this plugin to train the AI. We also set auxiliary curiosity reward to encourage the agent to discover more states and actions when solving the sparse reward problem. After several hours of asynchronous training of multiple agents, the agent has been able to find the destination in the square in Fig. 8. However, we found that the agents move in a different way than we expected. It scans the environment by drawing circles, not walking straight to the rewards.

(a) GA3C_Noise, (50, 50)

(b) GA3C_Noise, (350, 350)

(c) GA3C_Noise, (550, 50)

(d) GA3C_LSTM, (550, 50)

Fig. 6. Non-shortest path trajectory. Dark color represents the shortest path, light color represents non-shortest path. And red line is GA3C_Noise model, blue line is GA3C_LSTM (Color figure online)

Fig. 7. Steps distribution with the starting points (50, 50). The passing rate of GA3C_FF can reach 100%

(a) complex 5×10 grid size maze   (b) simple square in curriculum learning

Fig. 8. Maze environment built in Unity

5   Conclusion

In this article, we used deep reinforcement learning agents to simulate AD patients in a 3D labyrinth environment. We have associated the neural network architecture with the beta-amyloid cascade hypothesis, which explains the cause of AD. By collecting and analyzing the navigation data of the three models in the maze, we found that compared with the GA3C_LSTM model, both the GA3C_Noise and GA3C_FF model have a declined ability to extract features from visual input and to evaluate policies. The ratio of choosing the shortest path to the destination is lower, and they are more inclined to choose the path with a long-distance and lower efficiency during navigation. Thus, they take more average steps to reach the end and get fewer points in the same time. When the network has no memory at all, it will even lose the sense of direction, so that it can't reach the goal. Finally, we also introduced a maze environment built in Unity. However, the model still has some problem in generalization, and the navigation network does not perform well in an unfamiliar and complex maze map. Compared with other experiments, our maze has a larger size and a more complex map design. We mainly rely on several rewards to function as the landmarks in the route-based navigation. Although there are particular decorations on the wall as hints, we can't prove that the network can understand and make use of this feature for prediction.

In future work, we can use the 3D or VR cognitive training program to collect navigation data of AD patients and healthy people and establish a database. We can compare the large amount of path data generated by the trained RL model with the data of real players to evaluate the players' cognitive ability. And we can also train the agent to learn the features of the patient's trajectory by imitating learning and compare it with the model proposed in this article.

Acknowledgments. This work was sponsored by the National Natural Science Foundation of China 61831015.

References

1. Prince, M.F.: World Alzheimer Report 2015: the global impact of dementia: an analysis of prevalence, incidence, cost and trends. Alzheimer's Disease International (2015)

2. Patterson, C.F.: World Alzheimer report 2018: the state of the art of dementia research: new frontiers. Alzheimer's Disease International, London, UK (2018)
3. Silberstein, S.F.: MSD Manuals. https://www.msdmanuals.com/. Accessed 25 May 2020
4. Ding, Y.F., Sohn, J.S.: A deep learning model to predict a diagnosis of Alzheimer disease by using 18F-FDG PET of the brain. Radiology 290(2), 456–464 (2019)
5. Alzheimer's Association: 2017 Alzheimer's disease facts and figures. Alzheimer's & Dementia 13(4), 325–373 (2017)
6. Jack Jr., C.R., Albert, M.S., Knopman, D.S.: Introduction to the recommendations from the National Institute on Aging-Alzheimer's Association workgroups on diagnostic guidelines for Alzheimer's disease. Alzheimer's Dementia 7(3), 257–262 (2011)
7. Astell, A.J., Bouranis, N., Hoey, J.: Technology and dementia: the future is now. Dement. Geriatr. Cogn. Disord. 47(3), 131–139 (2019)
8. The Medical Futurist, When Technology Remembers: Digital Health And Alzheimer's Disease. https://medicalfuturist.com/digital-health-and-alzheimers-disease/. Accessed 15 May 2020
9. Liu, M., Cheng, D., Yan, W.: Classification of Alzheimer's disease by combination of convolutional and recurrent neural networks using FDG-PET images. Front. Neuroinform. 12, 35 (2018)
10. Evidation Health And Apple Study Shows Personal Digital Devices May Help In The Identification Of Mild Cognitive Impairment And Mild Alzheimer's Disease Dementia. https://investor.lilly.com/news-releases/news-release-details/lilly-evidation-health-and-apple-study-shows-personal-digital. Accessed 15 May 2020
11. Coughlan, G., Coutrot, A., Khondoker, M.: Toward personalized cognitive diagnostics of at-genetic-risk Alzheimer's disease. Proc. Natl. Acad. Sci. 116(19), 9285–9292 (2019)
12. Coutrot, A., Schmidt, S., Coutrot, L.: Virtual navigation tested on a mobile app is predictive of real-world wayfinding navigation performance. PloS One 14(3) (2019)
13. Hardy, J.L., Nelson, R.A., Thomason, M.E.: Enhancing cognitive abilities with comprehensive training: a large, online, randomized, active-controlled trial. Plos One 10(9) (2015)
14. Optale, G., Urgesi, C., Busato, V.: Controlling memory impairment in elderly adults using virtual reality memory training: a randomized controlled pilot study. Neurorehabil. Neural Repair 24(4), 348–357 (2010)
15. Cogné, M., Taillade, M., N'Kaoua, B.: The contribution of virtual reality to the diagnosis of spatial navigation disorders and to the study of the role of navigational aids: a systematic literature review. Ann. Phys. Rehabil. Med. 60(3), 164–176 (2017)
16. Tarnanas, I., Laskaris, N., Tsolaki, M., Muri, R., Nef, T., Mosimann, U.P.: On the comparison of a novel serious game and electroencephalography biomarkers for early dementia screening. In: Vlamos, P., Alexiou, A. (eds.) GeNeDis 2014. AEMB, vol. 821, pp. 63–77. Springer, Cham (2015). https://doi.org/10.1007/978-3-319-08939-3_11
17. Bellassen, V., Iglói, K., de Souza, L.C.: Temporal order memory assessed during spatiotemporal navigation as a behavioral cognitive marker for differential Alzheimer's disease diagnosis. J. Neurosci. 32(6), 1942–1952 (2012)
18. Rogers, N., SanMartin, C., Ponce, D.: Virtual spatial navigation correlates with the moca score in amnestic mild cognitive impairment patients. J. Neurol. Sci. 381, 116–117 (2017)
19. Cushman, L.A., Stein, K., Duffy, C.J.: Detecting navigational deficits in cognitive aging and Alzheimer disease using virtual reality. Neurology 71(12), 888–895 (2008)
20. García-Betances, R.I., Arredondo, W.M.T., Fico, G.: A succinct overview of virtual reality technology use in Alzheimer's disease. Front. Aging Neurosci. 7, 80 (2015)
21. Howett, D., Castegnaro, A., Krzywicka, K.: Differentiation of mild cognitive impairment using an entorhinal cortex- based test of VR navigation. Brain 142(6), 1751–1766 (2019)

22. Zhu, Y., Mottaghi, R., Kolve, E.: Target-driven visual navigation in indoor scenes using deep reinforcement learning. In: IEEE International Conference on Robotics and Automation (ICRA) 2017, pp. 3357–3364. IEEE (2017)

23. Anggraini, D., Glasauer, S., Wunderlich, K.: Neural signatures of reinforcement learning correlate with strategy adoption during spatial navigation. Sci. Rep. **8**(1), 1–14 (2018)

24. Sukumar, D., Rengaswamy, M., Chakravarthy, V.S.: Modeling the contributions of Basal ganglia and Hippocampus to spatial navigation using reinforcement learning. PloS One **7**(10) (2012)

25. Banino, A., Barry, C., Uria, B.: Vector-based navigation using grid-like representations in artificial agents. Nature **557**(7705), 429–433 (2018)

26. Jaderberg, M., Mnih, V., Czarnecki, W: Reinforcement learning with unsupervised auxiliary tasks. arXiv preprint arXiv:1611.05397 (2016)

27. Sutton, R.S., Barto, A.G.: Reinforcement Learning: An Introduction. MIT Press, Cambridge (2018)

28. Mnih, V., Kavukcuoglu, K., Silver, D.: Human-level control through deep reinforcement learning. Nature **518**(7540), 529–533 (2015)

29. Schulman, J., Wolski, F., Dhariwal, P.: Proximal policy optimization algorithms. arXiv preprint arXiv:1707.06347 (2017)

30. Mnih, V., Badia, A.P., Mirza, M.: Asynchronous methods for deep reinforcement learning. In: International Conference on Machine Learning, pp. 1928–1937 (2016)

31. Babaeizadeh, M., Frosio, I., Tyree, S.: Reinforcement learning through asynchronous advantage actor-critic on a GPU. arXiv preprint arXiv:1611.06256 (2016)

32. Mirowski, P., Pascanu, R., Viola, F.: Learning to navigate in complex environments. arXiv preprint arXiv:1611.03673 (2016)

33. Mirowski, P., Grimes, M., Malinowski, M.: Learning to navigate in cities without a map. In: Advances in Neural Information Processing Systems, pp. 2419–2430 (2018)

34. Haarnoja, T., Zhou, A., Hartikainen, K.: Soft actor-critic algorithms and applications. arXiv preprint arXiv:1812.05905 (2018)

35. Hardy, J.A., Higgins, G.A.: Alzheimer's disease: the amyloid cascade hypothesis. Science **256**(5054), 184–186 (1992)

36. Selkoe, D.J., Hardy, J.: The amyloid hypothesis of Alzheimer's disease at 25 years. EMBO Mol. Med. **8**(6), 595–608 (2016)

37. Paula, V.D.J.R.D., Guimarães, F.M.: Neurobiological pathways to Alzheimer's disease: Amyloid-beta, TAU protein or both? Dementia Neuropsychologia **3**(3), 188–194 (2009)

38. Plouffe, V., Mohamed, N.V., Rivest-McGraw, J.: Hyperphosphorylation and cleavage at D421 enhance tau secretion. PloS One **7**(5) (2012)

39. Introducing: Unity Machine Learning Agents Toolkit. https://blogs.unity3d.com/2017/09/19/introducing-unity-machine-learning-agents/. Accessed 15 May 2020

40. Juliani, A.F., Berges, V.S., Teng, E.T.: Unity: a general platform for intelligent agents. arXiv preprint arXiv:1809.02627 (2018)

41. Zhu, Y., Zhai, G., Min, X.: The prediction of head and eye movement for 360 degree images. Sig. Process. Image Commun. **69**, 15–25 (2018)

42. Sun, W., Min, X., Zhai, G.: MC360IQA: a multi-channel CNN for blind 360-degree image quality assessment. IEEE J. Sel. Top. Signal Process. **14**(1), 64–77 (2019)

43. Duan, H., Zhai, G., Min, X., et al.: A dataset of eye movements for the children with autism spectrum disorder. In: Proceedings of the 10th ACM Multimedia Systems Conference, pp. 255–260, June 2019

44. Duan, H., Min, X., Fang, Y., et al.: Visual attention analysis and prediction on human faces for children with autism spectrum disorder. ACM Trans. Multimed. Comput. Commun. Appl. (TOMM) **15**(3 s), 1–23 (2019)

45. Zhu, Y., Zhai, G., Min, X.: The prediction of saliency map for head and eye movements in 360 degree images. IEEE Trans. Multimed. (2019)
46. Shen, W., Ding, L., Zhai, G.: A QoE-oriented saliency-aware approach for 360-degree video transmission. In: 2019 IEEE Visual Communications and Image Processing (VCIP), pp. 1–4. IEEE, December 2019
47. Yang, J., Zhai, G., Duan, H.: Predicting the visual saliency of the people with VIMS. In: 2019 IEEE Visual Communications and Image Processing (VCIP), pp. 1–4. IEEE, December 2019
48. Zhai, G., Min, X.: Perceptual image quality assessment: a survey. Sci. China Inf. Sci. **63**, 211301:1–211301:52 (2020)

A Large-Scale VR Panoramic Dataset of QR Code and Improved Detecting Algorithm

Zehao Zhu, Guangtao Zhai$^{(\boxtimes)}$, Jiahe Zhang, Jun Jia, and Fuwang Yi

Institute of Image Communication and Network Engineering,
Shanghai Jiao Tong University, Shanghai, China
{zhuzehao,zhaiguangtao,zhangjiahe,jiajun0302,yifuwang}@sjtu.edu.cn

Abstract. With the rapid development of mobile payment and scanning technology, QR code has become widespread in both consumer and enterprise domains. However, there is the lack of corresponding research on detecting QR code in panoramic video due to the lack of high-quality datasets. To fill this gap, in this work we propose a large-scale panoramic QR code dataset to facilitate relevant research. Our dataset includes the following characteristics: (1) It is by far the largest dataset in terms of image quantity. (2) Compared with the existing datasets, ours is closer to the realistic setting and can derive a variety of research problems. In addition to the dataset, we propose a QR code detecting approach in a complex environment based on deep learning improving accuracy of QR code detection.

Keywords: VR video panoramic detection · QR code · Deep learning

1 Introduction

Barcode has become an integral part of life and has played an important role in shopping, advertising, communication, etc. Barcodes were invented in 1949 by Bernard Silver and Norman Woodland [1]. Barcodes can be classified into two different main categories: 1D and 2D barcodes. 1D barcode is a graphic identifier that expresses a set of information by arranging a plurality of black bars and spaces of different widths according to certain coding rules [30–32]. 2D barcode is composed of black and white squares arranged in a certain regular pattern. The common types of the 2D barcode are QR Code, Micro QR Code, Data Matrix, Color Circular Code [27], etc.

QR code is greatly famous and popular in 2D barcodes and has a huge application space in mobile payment, advertising, and many automation scenes [19–21]. For example, Takashi Anezaki invented a robot that can identify QR code to track people [2,25]. In the shopping field, BlindShopping is a piece of assisting equipment designed to help blind people shop in the supermarket. The blind can use the barcode detecting device to get the current location and product

© Springer Nature Singapore Pte Ltd. 2021
W. Song and F. Xu (Eds.): ICVRD 2020, CCIS 1313, pp. 137–148, 2021.
https://doi.org/10.1007/978-981-33-6549-0_12

information [3,24]. Library instruction and content can also be delivered with smartphones by scanning QR codes, which is more reliable than augmented reality [4,23]. QR Code can also be embeddef on digital screen via temporal psychovisual modulation (TPVM) [26]. QR code can be used as "invisible watermark" and "physical hyperlink" [14,35].

Due to the rapid development of machine learning and deep learning, the accuracy of object detection has now been greatly improved. Today's barcodes are usually attached to interesting objects, such as products, express packages, corridors, and the object detection process can be simply replaced with barcode detection, which is easier and more accurate than ordinary object detection. Today, virtual vision has been applied to many fields such as video surveillance [15,22], intelligent cameras [16,28] and wearable vision assistance system [17,29]. The application of QR code detection to the field of virtual vision is very promising [31,33,34].

When decoding these QR codes, the biggest challenge is that adverse environments, barcode such as blurring, high contrast, dark light, etc, will have various adverse effects on the detection of the barcode. How to detect barcode quickly and reliably is still a challenging task, and has become a critical topic in the computer vision community.

As far as we know, several barcode detection approaches have been proposed and the corresponding QR code datasets have been built, such as Melinda Katona [5], Gábor Sörös [6], Gallo [7], Dubská [8] and Zamberletti [9]. All of the above detection approaches have achieved very good detection results on the corresponding datasets. Unfortunately, these approachess are not effective in the detection of QR codes of VR panoramic videos. In addition, these datasets are far from the actual situation in terms of quantity and quality.

This paper builds a large-scale VR panoramic QR code dataset including QR codes and 1D barcodes. The captured environment includes blurring, excessive exposure, deformation, tilted filming angle, etc. (see Fig. 1). Compared with the existing datasets, our dataset is much closer to a realistic scenario. In addtion, an improved detecting algorithm is proposed to detect QR codes. In our approach, we apply region proposal network (RPN) introduced by Faster R-CNN to generate region proposals [12].

The rest of this paper is organized as follows. In Sect. 2, we We introduce the dataset of other authors and the corresponding detection methods. Characteristics of our dataset and evaluation metrics are given in Sect. 3. In Sect. 4, we describe the details of the proposed method. Section 4 concludes this paper and introduces the future work.

2   Related Work

In this part, we review the existing datasets and detection approaches that are relevant to our task.

The Dataset and Detecting Approach of Gábor Sörös. Gábor Sörös's dataset [6] is a 1D barcode and QR code dataset which focuses on testing the

Fig. 1. Several types of low-quality barcodes. (a) blurring QR code; (b) deformed 1D barode; (c) the QR code under the case of high contrast; (d) the barcode under the case of tilted filming angle.

algorithm of detecting blurred 1D barcode and QR code. It includes 328 images (resolution: 720×1280). Gábor Sörös used the saliency map to detect areas with high a concentration of edge structures as well as for areas with high a concentration of corner structures. However, the environment in which the barcode is located is very simple. The detection algorithm obtained from this dataset is not well suited to Panoramic video detection.

The Dataset and Detecting Approach of Dubská. Dubská's dataset [8] is a QR code dataset which focuses on testing the algorithm of detecting QR code. It includes 400 images (resolution: 2560×1440). Most of the images in the database are very clear. Dubská used Hough transformation and parallel coordinates to detect QR code. In actual situations, the QR code may be blurred or deformed in various background. The database and algorithms can only be applied to Panoramic video detection.

The Dataset and Detecting Approach of Zamberletti. Zamberletti's dataset [9] is a 1D barcode dataset. It includes 521 images (resolution: 648×488). Among them, the training set includes 366 images, and the test set includes 155 images. Zamberletti presented a novel method based on a supervised machine learning algorithm that detects 1D barcodes in the twodimensional Hough Transform space. However, the dataset is the same as the two datasets above. The captured environment of this dataset is very simple and is not well suited to

Panoramic video detection. In addition, the localization of barcode is a rectangle with an angle, however, the barcode bounding boxes are not accurate when barcodes are distorted, and the background of their training images is not complex.

The Dataset and Detecting Approach of Hansen. Hansen [10] did not build his own dataset. In the training of 1D Barcodes Zamberletti's dataset was used using the split into train and test as provided by the dataset. For the QR barcodes. the QR database provided by *Gábor Sörös* and the Dubská are used for training. Hansen applied YOLO [13] to detect tect QR code and 1D barcode at the same time. Due to the shortcomings of the data set, the detection results in the actual environment are not ideal.

3   A New Dataset for Detecting QR Code

In this section, we elaborate on the details of the QR code dataset. First, we introduce the characteristics of the dataset. Then, we propose evaluation metrics adopted for detecting QR codes.

3.1   Characteristics of Our Dataset

In this paper, we build QR code dataset to facilitate relevant research. The characteristics of the dataset can be summarized into three aspects.

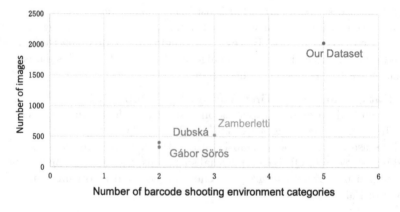

Fig. 2. Comparison with other related datasets in the literature

- **Large-scale:** As shown in Fig. 2, our dataset is the largest dataset so far for QR code detection. To collect this dataset, we capture 2024 images using insta360 ONE X action camera(resolution: 3024×4032). Among them, the training set includes 1300 images, and the test set includes 724 images. This is almost 4 times the size of the category of the previous largest dataset.

- **Multiple environments:** We made the following classifications of the shooting environment in which the images in the database are located. (1) Normal environment; (2) Blurring: The area of QR code is blurred due to inaccurate focus; (3) Excessive exposure: Due to excessive exposure, the black and white data area of the code is not obvious. (4) Deformation: The code on some products will change with the irregular shape of the product. (5) Tilted shooting angle: If the shooting angle is tilted, QR code are stretched at an angle. Their shapes are no longer rectangles, making them undetectable. (6) Shooting light is too dark. As shown in Fig. 2, Our database includes the above six environments. Table 1 shows the number of images in different environments.
- **Close to realistic scene:** The images in our database are all taken in the wild. These QR codes exist in products, advertisements, posters, books, etc. Compared to the single scene of other datasets, our dataset is closed to a realistic scene. The network trained with this data set is more suitable for the detection of the actual environment.

We use the dataset provided by Gábor Sörös and Dubská. These two datasets contain 328 images and 114 images, respectively. We hand-labeled our dataset and the two author's dataset, since they do not provide ground truth. The background of these images is more complex, and some distortions, such as excessive exposure, blur, tilted shooting angle, also exist on images to simulate the real challenging situations. Besides, we also take some images containing small barcodes. We split these 2466 images into a training set and a test set randomly, and the number of the training set is 1742. We evaluate our method on the test set.

Table 1. Comparison with other related datasets in the literature

	Ours	Gábor Sörös	Dubská	Zamberletti
Total number	2024	328	114	521
Normal environment	1304	86	92	450
Blurring	280	242	–	43
Excessive exposure	156	–	–	–
Deformation	110	–	–	–
Tilted filming angle	94	–	12	–
Dark shooting light	80	–	12	28

3.2 Evaluation Metrics

In this section, we use two metrics to evaluate our experiment results.

Intersection Over Union (IoU): IoU is a measure of the accuracy of detecting a corresponding object in a particular dataset. It can reflect whether the predicted bounding box matches the ground truth. IoU can be calculated as follow:

$$IoU(GT, DR) = \frac{GT \cap DR}{GT \cup DR} \tag{1}$$

where GT is ground truth and DR is detection result. In general, if $IoU \geq 0.5$, the result is a good test result. We think the detection result is correct.

Mean Average Precision (mAP): The first metric is mean Average Precision. In the target detection algorithm, mAP is often used as a benchmark to measure the accuracy of the algorithm. The nature of mAP is actually an average of each category of average precision (AP). Average precision is calculated from the precision-recall curve. The precision recall are defined as follow:

$$P = \frac{TP}{TP + FP} \tag{2}$$

$$R = \frac{TP}{TP + FN} \tag{3}$$

Calculate the average precision using the following formula:

$$AP = \sum_{n}(R_n - R_{n-1})P_n \tag{4}$$

where n is rank order, R_n and P_n are precision and recall at rank n. mAP is the average of each class of AP:

$$mAP = \frac{1}{N}\sum_{n}^{N} AP_n \tag{5}$$

where N is the total number of class.

Mean Area Ratio (mAR): The second metric that we propose is mean Area Ratio. In the actual situation, it is not enough to locate only the barcode. The final purpose is to obtain the decoding result of the barcode. The more accurate the prediction bounding box is, the higher the decoding rate will be. In order to evaluate the accuracy of barcode locating, we use mAR as another evaluation metric. The mAR is defined as follows:

$$AR = \begin{cases} \frac{|A_p - A_t|}{A_p} & if IoU > 0.5 \\ 0 & otherwise \end{cases} \tag{6}$$

$$mAR = \frac{1}{N}\sum_{n}^{N} AR_n \tag{7}$$

where A_p is prediction bounding box and A_t the area of barcode in prediction bounding box. AE is the proportion of bar code in the prediction bounding box. N is the number of prediction bounding boxes. For one ground truth, $AE \in [0,1]$, so that if IoU is less than 0.5, we think it is a false prediction and set AE to 0.

4   Our Methodology and Experiment

In this section, we use two metrics to evaluate our experiment results.

4.1   Our Methodology

In this section, we will introduce our approach for barcode detection. Firstly the VR Panoramic video will be divided into video frames(panoramic images), then we will use Faster R-CNN algorithm [10] to detect QR code in the panoramic image, and finally we will stitch the detected images according to the frame rate of the original video. The network structure is shown in Fig. 3. The whole process can be separated into two stages: one is region proposal network (RPN) and another is a classification network and a bounding box regression network.

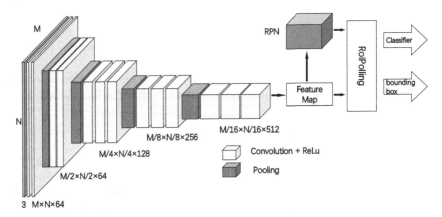

Fig. 3. Network structure. Input image is on the left with size $M \times N \times 3$, and filters are consistent with VGG16 [11]

We also use a classification layer to predict region proposals, and a regression layer to refine region proposals. The shape of region proposals is a horizontal rectangle which simplifies the RoI pooling. The rectangle region proposal comes from the circumscribed rectangle of the quadrilateral.

The network process is as follows. In Convolution Layers, the input is images and the output is the feature maps of the extracted image, which is used as a shared feature of the Region Proposal Network (RPN) and the fully connected layer. In RPN, generate region proposals based on feature maps. Get the ideal proposals by bounding box regression on anchors [12]. In RoI Pooling, the input is feature map and proposals, and the output is the extracted proposal feature maps, which are used for fully connected layer pair category determination. In Classifier, the proposal feature maps are used to calculate the category of the proposal, and the bounding box regression is performed again to get the exact object detection frame position. In the last step, train classification probability

and bounding tree regression using Softmax Loss (Detection classification probability) and Smooth L_1 Loss (Detection border regression). By regressing the
bounding box, we can get the detection frame position of the object. Softmax
Loss is defined as follows.

$$L = \sum_{j=1}^{T} y_j \log S_j \tag{8}$$

L is a loss. S_j is the jth value of the output vector S of softmax. The range of
j is 1 to the number of categories T. y is a $1 \times T$ vector with T values inside, and
only 1 value is 1, and other T−1 values are 0. The flow chart of the algorithm
is shown Table 2.

Smooth L_1 is defined as follows.

$$SmoothL_1 = \begin{cases} 0.5x^2 & |x| < 1 \\ |x| - 0.5 & otherwise \end{cases} \tag{9}$$

$x = f(x_i) - y_i$ is the difference between the true value and the predicted
value

We apply RoIAlign method proposed by He [13] to get each Region of Interest
(RoI), and extract feature from integrated feature map according to each RoI.

4.2   Experimental Details

In our experiments, we use VGG16 [10] network as our base network. The
VGG16 network is initialized with an ImageNet-pre-trained model. For testing and training the same computer has been used with an Intel(R) Xeon(R)
E5-1620 3.50 GHz processor, 16 GB DDR4 memory, 1TB SSD hard drive and
Nvidia GeForce GTX 1080 with Windows 10 as the operating system. Before
the images are fed into the network, we resize the shortest side to 600. We use
four scales: 512, 256, 128 and 64, and three aspect ratio: 1:1, 1:2, and 2:1, for
our anchors. The number of candidate region proposal is 300. We use insta360
ONE X to shoot VR panoramic videos with QR codes. The frame rate of this
video is 30.

Data augmentation techniques are applied to expand the training set in our
experiment. Inspired by Zhang [18], We use image flipping and image rotation
to process our images during the training procedure. Image flipping directions
are horizontal and vertical, image rotation angles are 90, 180 and 270. For each
image, we randomly choose image flipping or image rotation. If image flipping
is chosen, we randomly choose the flipping direction. Similarly, if image rotation
is chosen, we randomly choose the rotation angle.

4.3   Performance

In this section, we evaluate our model. In the first experiment, we compare
our method with others' methods. Henson [10] used a *You Only Look Once*

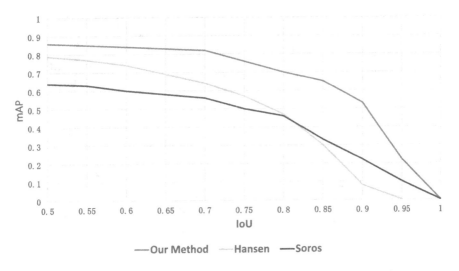

Fig. 4. mAP vs: IoU overlap ratio

Table 2. Comparison with different methods

Method	mAP	mAR
Gábor Sörös [6]	0.538	0.588
Hansen [10]	0.642	0.685
Dubská [8]	0.581	0.601
Our method	**0.886**	**0.811**

network (YOLO) [13] to detect QR codes. Compared to YOLO, although the calculating speed of Faster R-CNN is slower, the accuracy is higher. The methods of Dubská [8] and Zamberletti [9] only detect one barcode category, as show Table 2. Dubská's method relies on Hough Transform to detect lines. But our experimental dataset contains a distorted image, therefore, their line detector cannot detect straight lines effectively. This restricts the performance of their method. Although the method proposed by Gábor Sörös [6] can resist blur, it is less effective in complex environments. In the second experiment, we compare our model with others' models. The result is shown in Fig. 4. The superiority of the proposed method is obvious. With IoU overlap ratio increasing, the mAP of the Faster R-CNN model decreases significantly. The qualitative results can be seen in Fig. 5. we localize the barcodes and classify them. The picture in Fig. 5 represents a certain video frame in the test video. From the results, we can see that the network can detect distorted QR codes such as blur and deformation.

Fig. 5. Example video snippets of object instances

5   Conclusion and Future Work

This paper presents a large-scale VR panoramic QR code dataset. Comparing with the existing datasets, ours is closer to the realistic setting. At the same time, we propose our method for detecting QR codes. After testing, our model is superior to other models. Compared with others, they have certain advantages. In the future, We will expand the number of images of the dataset. In addition, the algorithm will be extended to detect more barcodes.

Acknowledgement. This work was sponsored by e National Natural Science Foundation of China 61831015.

References

1. Tuinstra, T.R.: Reading barcodes from digital imagery. Ph.D. thesis, Cedarville University (2006)
2. Anezaki, T., Eimon, K., Tansuriyavong, S., et al.: Development of a human-tracking robot using QR code recognition. In: 2011 17th Korea-Japan Joint Workshop on Frontiers of Computer Vision (FCV), pp. 1–6. IEEE (2011)
3. López-de-Ipiña, D., Lorido, T., López, U.: BlindShopping: enabling accessible shopping for visually impaired people through mobile technologies. In: Abdulrazak, B., Giroux, S., Bouchard, B., Pigot, H., Mokhtari, M. (eds.) ICOST 2011. LNCS, vol. 6719, pp. 266–270. Springer, Heidelberg (2011). https://doi.org/10.1007/978-3-642-21535-3_39
4. Walsh, A.: QR codes-using mobile phones to deliver library instruction and help at the point of need. J. Inf. Literacy **4**(1), 55–65 (2010)
5. Katona, M., Nyúl, L.G.: Efficient 1D and 2D barcode detection using mathematical morphology. In: Hendriks, C.L.L., Borgefors, G., Strand, R. (eds.) ISMM 2013. LNCS, vol. 7883, pp. 464–475. Springer, Heidelberg (2013). https://doi.org/10.1007/978-3-642-38294-9_39
6. Sörös, G., Flörkemeier, C.: Blur-resistant joint 1D and 2D barcode localization for smartphones. In: Proceedings of the 12th International Conference on Mobile and Ubiquitous Multimedia, pp. 1–8 (2013)
7. Gallo, O., Manduchi, R.: Reading 1D barcodes with mobile phones using deformable templates. IEEE Trans. Pattern Anal. Mach. Intell. **33**(9), 1834–1843 (2011)
8. Dubská, M., Herout, A., Havel, J.: Real-time precise detection of regular grids and matrix codes. J. Real-Time Image Process. **11**(1), 193–200 (2013). https://doi.org/10.1007/s11554-013-0325-6
9. Zamberletti, A., Gallo, I., Albertini, S.: Robust angle invariant 1D barcode detection. In: 2013 2nd IAPR Asian Conference on Pattern Recognition, pp. 160–164. IEEE (2013)
10. Hansen, D.K., Nasrollahi, K., Rasmussen, C.B., et al.: Real-time barcode detection and classification using deep learning. In: IJCCI, pp. 321–327 (2017)
11. Simonyan, K., Zisserman, A.: Very deep convolutional networks for large-scale image recognition. arXiv preprint arXiv:1409.1556 (2014)
12. Ren, S., He, K., Girshick, R., et al.: Faster R-CNN: towards real-time object detection with region proposal networks. In: Advances in Neural Information Processing Systems, pp. 91–99 (2015)
13. He, K., Gkioxari, G., Dollar, P., Girshick, R.: Mask R-CNN. In: Proceedings of the IEEE International Conference on Computer Vision, pp. 2961–2969 (2017)
14. Gao, Z., Zhai, G., Hu, C.: The invisible QR code. In: Proceedings of the 23rd ACM International Conference on Multimedia, pp. 1047–1050 (2015)
15. Qureshi, F.Z., Terzopoulos, D.: Surveillance camera scheduling: a virtual vision approach. Multimed. Syst. **12**(3), 269–283 (2006)
16. Qureshi, F.Z., Terzopoulos, D.: Towards intelligent camera networks: a virtual vision approach. In: 2005 IEEE International Workshop on Visual Surveillance and Performance Evaluation of Tracking and Surveillance, pp. 177–184. IEEE (2005)

17. Jiang, B., Yang, J., Lv, Z., et al.: Wearable vision assistance system based on binocular sensors for visually impaired users. IEEE Internet Things J. **6**(2), 1375–1383 (2018)
18. Zhang, J., Jia, J., Zhu, Z., et al.: Fine detection and classification of multi-class barcode in complex environments. In: 2019 IEEE International Conference on Multimedia Expo Workshops (ICMEW), pp. 306–311. IEEE (2019)
19. Liu, Y., Yang, J., Liu, M.: Recognition of QR Code with mobile phones. In: 2008 Chinese Control and Decision Conference, pp. 203–206. IEEE (2008)
20. DeSoto, D.B., Peskin, M.A.: Login using QR code: U.S. Patent 8,935,777, 13 January 2015
21. Kan, T.W., Teng, C.H., Chou, W.S.: Applying QR code in augmented reality applications. In: Proceedings of the 8th International Conference on Virtual Reality Continuum and its Applications in Industry, pp. 253–257 (2009)
22. Jia, J., Zhai, G., Zhang, J., et al.: EMBDN: an efficient multiclass barcode detection network for complicated environments. IEEE Internet Things J. **6**(6), 9919–9933 (2019)
23. Zhang, J., Li, D., Jia, J., et al.: Protection and hiding algorithm of QR code based on multi-channel visual masking. In: 2019 IEEE Visual Communications and Image Processing (VCIP), pp. 1–4. IEEE (2019)
24. Zhang, J., Min, X., Jia, J., Zhu, Z., Wang, J., Zhai, G.: Fine localization and distortion resistant detection of multi-class barcode in complex environments. Multimed. Tools Appl. 1–20 (2020). https://doi.org/10.1007/s11042-019-08578-x
25. Jia, J., Zhai, G., Ren, P., et al.: Tiny-BDN: an efficient and compact barcode detection network. IEEE J. Sel. Top. Signal Process. **14**, 688–699 (2020)
26. Song, K., Liu, N., Gao, Z., et al.: Deep restoration of invisible QR code from TPVM display. In: 2020 IEEE International Conference on Multimedia & Expo Workshops (ICMEW), pp. 1–6. IEEE (2020)
27. Yi, F., Zhai, G., Zhu, Z.: A robust circular two-dimensional barcode and decoding method. In: 2019 Picture Coding Symposium (PCS), pp. 1–5. IEEE (2019)
28. Zhu, Y., Zhai, G., Min, X.: The prediction of head and eye movement for 360 degree images. Signal Process.: Image Commun. **69**, 15–25 (2018)
29. Zhai, G., Min, X., Liu, N.: Free-energy principle inspired visual quality assessment: an overview. Digital Signal Process. **91**, 11–20 (2019)
30. Sharif, A., Zhai, G., Jia, J., et al.: An accurate and efficient 1D barcode detector for medium of deployment in IoT systems. IEEE Internet Things J. (2020)
31. Zhai, G., Min, X.: Perceptual image quality assessment: a survey. Sci. China Inf. Sci. **63**(11), 211301 (2020)
32. Sun, W., Min, X., Zhai, G., et al.: MC360IQA: a multi-channel CNN for blind 360-degree image quality assessment. IEEE J. Sel. Top. Signal Process. **14**(1), 64–77 (2019)
33. Zhu, Y., Zhai, G., Min, X., et al.: The prediction of saliency map for head and eye movements in 360 degree images. IEEE Trans. Multimed. (2019)
34. Shen, W., Ding, L., Zhai, G., et al.: A QoE-oriented saliency-aware approach for 360-degree video transmission. In: 2019 IEEE Visual Communications and Image Processing (VCIP), pp. 1–4. IEEE (2019)
35. Jia, J., Gao, Z., Chen, K., et al.: Robust Invisible Hyperlinks in Physical Photographs Based on 3D Rendering Attacks. arXiv preprint arXiv:1912.01224 (2019)

Author Index

Cao, Sanxing   78
Cao, Wei   89
Chang, Yang   1
Chen, Duo   33
Chen, Jing   89

Dai, Renxiang   45
Du, Yasong   89

Fan, Lei   89
Fu, Jun   1

Gao, Chao   45
Gao, Xin   45
Ge, Fan   45, 56

Han, Hongxiang   1

Jia, Jun   137
Jiang, Jinghui   121
Jiang, Zheng   121
Jin, Xin   103

Li, Jingwen   33
Li, Shuang   14
Li, Xiaodong   103
Li, Yannan   103
Li, Zhonglan   103
Liu, Boyang   45
Liu, Li   45
Liu, Zhengyi   78

Ning, Zhiwen   1

Qi, Shuai   33

Ren, Hui   14

Sang, Xinzhu   33, 45, 56
Shi, Guangming   66
Song, Limei   21

Tang, Baihui   78

Wan, Wenfei   66
Wang, Peng   33
Wang, Qiong-Hua   14
Wang, Yuedi   45
Wu, Hong Ren   66
Wu, Jinjian   66

Xia, Yun-Peng   14
Xing, Shujun   45
Xing, Yan   14

Yan, Binbin   33
Yang, Yangang   21
Yi, Fuwang   137
You, Yang   21
Yu, Xunbo   45

Zhai, Guangtao   89, 121, 137
Zhang, Jiahe   137
Zhou, Jiantao   89
Zhu, Zehao   137

Printed in the United States
By Bookmasters

GLOBAL DIGITAL DATA GOVERNANCE

This book provides a nuanced exploration of contemporary digital data governance, highlighting the importance of cooperation across sectors and disciplines in order to adapt to a rapidly evolving technological landscape. Most of the theory around global digital data governance remains scattered and focused on specific actors, norms, processes, or disciplinary approaches. This book argues for a polycentric approach, allowing readers to consider the issue across multiple disciplines and scales.

Polycentrism, this book argues, provides a set of lenses that tie together the variety of actors, issues, and processes intertwined in digital data governance at subnational, national, regional, and global levels. Firstly, this approach uncovers the complex array of power centers and connections in digital data governance. Secondly, polycentric perspectives bridge disciplinary divides, challenging assumptions and drawing together a growing range of insights about the complexities of digital data governance. Bringing together a wide range of case studies, this book draws out key insights and policy recommendations for how digital data governance occurs and how it might occur differently.

Written by an international and interdisciplinary team, this book will be of interest to students and scholars in the field of development studies, political science, international relations, global studies, science and technology studies, sociology, and media and communication studies.

Carolina Aguerre is Associate Professor at the Universidad Católica del Uruguay, Honorary Co-Director at the Centro de Estudios en Tecnología y Sociedad (CETYS), Universidad de San Andres, Argentina, and Associate Senior Fellow at the Centre for Global Cooperation Research at the University of Duisburg-Essen, Germany. Her publications have appeared in journals such as *Digital Policy, Regulation and Governance, Information and Culture*, and *Palabra Clave*, as well as book chapters.

Malcolm Campbell-Verduyn is Senior Lecturer in International Political Economy at the Department of International Relations and International Organization, University of Groningen, Netherlands, and Associate Senior Fellow at the Centre for Global Cooperation Research at the University of Duisburg-Essen, Germany. His recent publications have appeared in journals including *Anthropology Today, Environment & Planning C, New Political Economy*, and *Security Dialogue*.

Jan Aart Scholte is Chair of Global Transformations and Governance Challenges at Leiden University, Netherlands, and Co-Director of the Centre for Global Cooperation Research at the University of Duisburg-Essen, Germany. His research covers globalization, governing global affairs, civil society in global politics, global democracy, legitimacy in global governance, and Internet governance. Previously, he co-edited volumes in the Routledge Global Cooperation Series on *Power and Authority in Internet Governance: A Return of the State?* (with Blayne Haggart and Natasha Tusikov) and *Hegemony and World Order: Reimagining Power in Global Politics* (with Piotr Dutkiewicz and Tom Casier).

ROUTLEDGE GLOBAL COOPERATION SERIES

The Routledge Global Cooperation series develops innovative approaches to one of the most pressing questions of our time – how to achieve cooperation in a culturally diverse and politically contested global world?

Many key contemporary problems such as climate change and forced migration require intensified cooperation on a global scale. Accelerated globalisation processes have led to an ever-growing interconnectedness of markets, states, societies and individuals. Many of today's problems cannot be solved by nation states alone and require intensified cooperation at the local, national, regional and global level to tackle current and looming global crises.

Series Editors: **Tobias Debiel, Dirk Messner, Sigrid Quack** and **Jan Aart Scholte** are Co-Directors of the Käte Hamburger Kolleg / Centre for Global Cooperation Research, University of Duisburg-Essen, Germany. Their research areas include climate change and sustainable development, global governance, internet governance and peacebuilding. **Tobias Debiel** is Professor of International Relations and Development Policy at the University of Duisburg-Essen and Director of the Institute for Development and Peace in Duisburg, Germany. **Dirk Messner** is President of the German Environment Agency (Umweltbundesamt – UBA). **Sigrid Quack** is Professor of Sociology at the University of Duisburg-Essen, Germany. **Jan Aart Scholte** is Professor of Global Transformations and Governance Challenges at Leiden University, Netherlands. **Patricia Rinck** is editorial manager of the series at the Centre for Global Cooperation Research.

European Union Communities of Practice
Diplomacy and Boundary Work in Ukraine
Maren Hofius

Global Digital Data Governance
Polycentric Perspectives
Edited by Carolina Aguerre, Malcolm Campbell-Verduyn and Jan Aart Scholte

For more information about this series, please visit: www.routledge.com/Routledge-Global-Cooperation-Series/book-series/RGC

GLOBAL DIGITAL DATA GOVERNANCE

Polycentric Perspectives

Edited by Carolina Aguerre, Malcolm Campbell-Verduyn and Jan Aart Scholte

Centre for
Global Cooperation Research

SPONSORED BY THE

Federal Ministry of Education and Research

Routledge
Taylor & Francis Group
LONDON AND NEW YORK

Designed cover image: © vanillamilk

First published 2024
by Routledge
4 Park Square, Milton Park, Abingdon, Oxon OX14 4RN

and by Routledge
605 Third Avenue, New York, NY 10158

Routledge is an imprint of the Taylor & Francis Group, an informa business

British Library Cataloguing-in-Publication Data
A catalogue record for this book is available from the British Library

ISBN: 978-1-032-48311-5 (hbk)
ISBN: 978-1-032-48310-8 (pbk)
ISBN: 978-1-003-38841-8 (ebk)

DOI: 10.4324/9781003388418

Typeset in Sabon
by Taylor & Francis Books

CONTENTS

List of Figures   *ix*
List of Tables   *x*
List of Contributors   *xi*
Acknowledgments   *xiv*

1 Introduction: Polycentric Perspectives on Digital Data
  Governance   1
  Carolina Aguerre, Malcolm Campbell-Verduyn and
  Jan Aart Scholte

PART I
Perspectives   **19**

2 Nudging the Ostroms' Vision of the Commons on
  Polycentric Governance into the Digital Environment   21
  Anjanette H. Raymond and Scott Shackelford

3 Internet Interoperability and Polycentric Attributes in Global
  Digital Data Ordering   34
  Carolina Aguerre

4 The Challenges of Governance in a Datascape: Theorizing
  the Role of Non-extractive Methodologies in the 2030
  Agenda   51
  Isabel Rocha de Siqueira and Laís Ramalho

5 Grassroots Data Activism and Polycentric Governance:
   Perspectives from the Margins   68
   Daivi Rodima-Taylor

6 Questions as a Device for Data Responsibility: Making Data
   Science Responsible by Formulating Questions in a
   Polycentric Way   88
   Stefaan Verhulst

PART II
Controversies   **103**

7 Decentralized but Coordinated: Probing Polycentricity in EU
   Data Protection Cross-border Enforcement   105
   Wenlong Li and Dan Yang

8 Trade Agreements and Cross-border Disinformation:
   Patchwork or Polycentric?   125
   Susan A. Aaronson

9 Trackers and Chasers: Governance Challenges in
   Disinformation Datafication   148
   Clara Iglesias Keller and Bruna Martins dos Santos

10 Privacy Governance from a Polycentric Perspective   165
    Rotem Medzini and Dmitry Epstein

PART III
Technologies   **185**

11 Global Data Governance by Internet Interconnection   187
    Nathalia Sautchuk Patrício

12 The Distributions of Distributed Governance: Power,
    Instability and Complexity in Polycentric Data Ordering   205
    Malcolm Campbell-Verduyn

13 Polycentric Theory Diffusion and AI Governance   223
    Janet Hui Xue

14 Conclusion: The End of a Beginning   238
    *Carolina Aguerre, Malcolm Campbell-Verduyn and
    Jan Aart Scholte*

Index   244

FIGURES

11.1 Peering agreement between Network A and B. Network A can reach data from Network B directly, and vice versa   190

11.2 One transit agreement between Network A and C, and another between B and C. Network A can reach data from Network B through Network C, and vice versa   190

11.3 Example of network interconnection with peering and transit agreements   191

11.4 Network interconnection through IXP   193

11.5 Network with CDN infrastructure   195

TABLES

6.1 Questions as tool for data responsibility 97

7.1 An overview of the EDPB's initiatives to improve enforcement by and cooperation between the DPAs 111

7.2 Seven investigations by EU DPAs vis-à-vis Clearview AI between 2021 and 2022 116

7.3 The DPA's selected regulatory targets in their investigations 118

11.1 Summary of data governance strategies and practices 197

11.2 Polycentric attributes and Internet interconnection 198

12.1 Polycentricity in blockchain-based global digital data governance 216

13.1 Key attributes of the polycentricity of "personal data" in AI applications 227

CONTRIBUTORS

Susan A. Aaronson is Research Professor and Director of the Digital Trade and Data Governance Hub at George Washington University. She holds further positions at GWU's Institute for International Economic Policy, Institute for International Science and Technology Policy, and Sigur Center for Asian Studies. She is also a Senior Fellow at the Centre for International Governance Innovation (CIGI) in Canada.

Dmitry Epstein is Assistant Professor in the Department of Communication and the Federmann School of Public Policy and Government at the Hebrew University of Jerusalem. He is former chair of the Global Internet Governance Academic Network (GIGANET) and a co-founder of the Comparative Privacy Research Network (CPRN). He studies internet and information governance, privacy, cybersecurity, and the digital divide.

Janet Hui Xue is Associate Senior Fellow at the Centre for Global Cooperation Research at the University of Duisburg-Essen and a Research Associate of the Consumer Rights Beyond Boundaries Programme at the University of Oxford. She is currently researching human-empowered governance of AI. Janet is an editor of the *Journal of International Data Privacy Law*.

Clara Iglesias Keller leads the research group "Technology, Power and Domination" at the Weizenbaum Institute, with the WZB Berlin Social Science Center. She is a Guest Professor at the Brazilian Institute for Education, Development and Research – IDP/Brazil.

Wenlong Li is Postdoctoral Research Fellow in Law, Ethics and Computer Science at the University of Birmingham, LEADS Lab. He also serves as a

Research Affiliate at the Edinburgh Centre for Data, Culture & Society (CDCS) and teaches at the Edinburgh Law School. As a qualified lawyer in China, Wenlong worked for the Tencent Institute and the Media Law Centre at the China University of Political Science and Law, Beijing.

Bruna Martins dos Santos was a Visiting Researcher at the WZB Berlin Social Science Center after which she joined the NGO Digital Action as their Global Campaigns Manager. She is a graduate of the Centro Universitário de Brasília (CEUB) with a Bachelor of Laws (LLB) and former German Chancellor Fellow. Her work addresses digital rights concerns around platform governance and spaces like the Internet Corporation for Assigned Names and Numbers (ICANN) and the Internet Governance Forum (IGF).

Rotem Medzini is a Postdoctoral Research Fellow at the University of Birmingham. He studies data and platform governance, self-regulation via regulatory intermediaries, and new and emerging digital assurance regimes. His research has appeared in prominent journals, including *New Media & Society, Policy & Internet, Internet Policy Review,* and the *Journal of Comparative Policy Analysis.*

Laís Ramalho is a PhD candidate at the Institute of International Relations (IRI) at the Pontifical Catholic University, Rio de Janeiro (PUC-Rio), Brazil. Her PhD research addresses how the language of development, frequently articulated as an instrument of technocracy, has been transformed and challenged by the ongoing data revolution. Ramalho's main research interests are development, governance, emotions, data, cities, spatiality, and urban planning.

Anjanette H. Raymond is Associate Professor of Business Law and Ethics at the Kelley School of Business and an adjunct Associate Professor of Law at the Maurer School of Law at Indiana University, Bloomington, USA. She has written widely about international commercial law, international commercial arbitration, and international secured transactions in such publications as the *American Review of International Arbitration, Harvard Negotiation Law Review,* and *Northwestern Journal of Technology and Intellectual Property.*

Isabel Rocha de Siqueira is Assistant Professor and Director of the Institute of International Relations (IRI) at the Pontifical Catholic University, Rio de Janeiro (PUC-Rio), Brazil. She holds a PhD in International Relations from the Department of War Studies, King's College London. Recent publications include *'Fragile States' in an Unequal World* (2022), reports commissioned by the G7+ and the United Nations Organization South-South Cooperation (UNOSSC), a book by Routledge, edited books by Editora PUC-Rio, as well as articles in *Global Governance, International Political Sociology,* and *Third World Quarterly.*

Daivi Rodima-Taylor is a social anthropologist and researcher at the African Studies Center of the Pardee School of Global Studies, Boston University. Her recent publications include co-edited volumes *Cryptopolitics: Exposure, Concealment, and Digital Media* (2023), *Land and the Mortgage: History, Culture, Belonging* (2022), and special issue "FinTech in Africa" (2022) in the *Journal of Cultural Economy*. Her articles have appeared in *Africa, African Studies Review, Social Analysis, Review of International Political Economy, Geoforum, American Ethnologist, Global Networks,* and *Georgetown Journal of International Affairs*.

Nathalia Sautchuk Patrício was German Chancellor Fellow of the Alexander von Humboldt Foundation in 2020–2022 at the Centre for Global Cooperation Research at the University of Duisburg-Essen in Germany. In 2022 she joined Karlsruhe University of Applied Sciences. Sautchuk Patrício is a computer engineer with an active participation in the Internet Governance community, such as LACNIC, Internet Governance Forum (IGF) and Internet Engineering Task Force (IETF).

Scott Shackelford is the Provost Professor of Business Law and Ethics at the Indiana University Kelley School of Business. He serves as the Executive Director of the Ostrom Workshop and the Center for Applied Cybersecurity Research. Professor Shackelford has written more than 100 articles, book chapters, essays, and op-eds for diverse publications. Both Professor Shackelford's academic work and teaching have been recognized with numerous awards, including a Harvard University Research Fellowship, a Stanford University Hoover Institution National Fellowship, a Notre Dame Institute for Advanced Study Distinguished Fellowship, the 2014 Indiana University Outstanding Junior Faculty Award, the 2015 Elinor Ostrom Award, and the 2022 Poets & Quants Best 40-Under-40 MBA Professors Award.

Stefaan Verhulst is Co-Founder of The GovLab (New York City) and The Data Tank (Brussels). He is a Research Professor at the Tandon School of Engineering, New York University, and editor-in-chief of the journal *Data and Policy*.

Dan Yang is currently Senior Legal Counsel at Great Wall Motor Company Limited, specializing in the regulation of Internet-connected vehicles. She has rich experience of engaging and contributing to policy- and standard-making in China, particularly in the realm of data governance. She graduated from the University of Reading in 2017 and aims to pursue a doctoral degree on the topic of facial recognition technology deployed by law enforcement agencies.

ACKNOWLEDGMENTS

This book would not have been possible without the generous funding, rich networks engaged, and comprehensive administrative support from the Käte Hamburger Kolleg Centre for Global Cooperation Research at the University of Duisburg-Essen in Germany. The Centre brought together contributors to the volume (Medzini, Sautchuk Patrício, Xue) and editors (Aguerre and Campbell-Verduyn) in its Internet Research Group. This group, initiated and led by the Center's Co-Director Jan Aart Scholte met, appropriately perhaps, online during the period of the COVID-19 pandemic, when the Centre funded and hosted two virtual workshops. We acknowledge here the invaluable support of the Centre's Managing Director, Professor Sigrid Quack during these events. We also acknowledge feedback provided at events held by the International Studies Association (ISA), the Society for the Advancement of Socio-Economics (SASE), and the Internet Governance Forum (IGF). In first-name alphabetical order, our sincere thanks for personal feedback go to: Alisson Gillwald, Blayne Haggart, Daniel McCarthy, Lauren Eastwood, Matthias Ecker-Ehrhardt, Rocco Bellanova, and Tony Porter. Finally, we thank the Centre as well as the University of Groningen for funding the Open Access publication of this volume.

1

INTRODUCTION

Polycentric Perspectives on Digital Data Governance

Carolina Aguerre, Malcolm Campbell-Verduyn and Jan Aart Scholte

Introduction

Digital data (that is, information that is encoded electronically in strings of positive [1] and nonpositive [0] values) are pervasive and pivotal in contemporary society. An ongoing "digitization" and "datafication" transpires today with social media, artificial intelligence (AI), blockchain technology, cloud computing, Internet of Things (IoT), Big Data, robotics, virtual reality, and more. Further, these trends unfold on a world scale, involving all countries (to varying degrees) as well as countless connections between them. Digitization is a global transformation that asks for substantial global cooperation and governance.

The datafication of contemporary society has far-reaching implications. For one thing, as just noted, the growing "datasphere" (Rushkoff 1994) reinforces a wider trend of globalization that interconnects people's lives on a planetary scale. In addition, digital data deeply impact the economy, both by creating major new sectors of production (i.e., of relevant hardware as well as the information itself) and by reshaping overall production processes (i.e., in agriculture, manufacturing, finance, health, etc.). Digital data also affect ways of governing, for example, with e-governance and enhanced surveillance capacities (Hansen 2015). Digital data furthermore transform how knowledge is generated, circulated, and applied – now largely virtually. "Datascapes" (Rocha da Siqueira and Ramalho, in this volume) moreover affect how (e.g., through social media) people construct their individual and collective identities, for example, around class, gender, ideology, nationality, race, and sexuality. Digitization and datafication likewise change how politics and power unfold at and across local, national, regional, and global scales.

Digital data pose both opportunities and problems. On the one hand, the contemporary technological revolution with digital networks, AI, and various

DOI: 10.4324/9781003388418-1

hardware devices provides unprecedented quantities and qualities of information, together with unparalleled capacities to process that information. Digital data also offer enormous creative potentials for culture, economics, and politics. On the other hand, digitization also enables invasions of privacy and the spread of mis- and disinformation as never before. In addition, access to (the power of) digital data is highly unequal, and much governance of digital data evades adequate democratic accountability. Both the upsides and the downsides of digital data often transcend state borders with transnational and global reach.

Pressing questions therefore arise about digital data governance. What kinds of rules and regulatory processes apply in this arena? What sorts of policies and politics can maximize the potential benefits and minimize the potential damages of digital data? How can society make and implement rules and regulatory arrangements that channel the production, circulation, and use of digital data in suitably deliberated and democratically controlled ways?

These vital core questions motivate this book. Since digital data pervade contemporary life, how they are governed substantially shapes whether societal problems are resolved or exacerbated; whether politics turn democratic or authoritarian; whether conflicts are handled peacefully or violently; whether the gains and burdens of data are shared justly or unjustly; and whether the ecological implications of a datafied society move towards sustainability or destruction.

Of course, our volume is not the first to address the (global) governance of digital data. Growing scholarship across an expanding range of academic disciplines is exploring rules and regulations that shape the digital processing of information (e.g., Obendiek 2022; Hasselbalch 2021; Leonelli and Tempini 2020; Vavrushka 2020; Bigo et al. 2019; Flyverbom and Murray 2018; Ruppert et al. 2017). How digital data governance can and should be done is increasingly discussed in cultural and media studies, development studies, international relations, law, political economy, and political sociology (Liu 2021; Steedman et al. 2020; Bonina and Eaton 2020; Hintz et al. 2019; Madianou 2019; Ricaurte 2019; Couldry and Mejias 2019; Milan and Treré 2019; Taylor 2017; Mosco 2016).

Yet, theory of (global) digital data governance remains little consolidated. How does one credibly describe, explain, and evaluate the rules and regulatory processes that order the production, circulation, and use of digital data? Different academic fields offer varying accounts, emphasizing different actors, processes, and normative criteria. Moreover, most existing studies are monodisciplinary, for instance, framed for legal or technical practitioners (Abraham et al. 2019). Productive conversation and integration among the varying approaches are wanted. In addition, most books that address digital data governance are limited to a national or local sphere. Little research examines the issue beyond the state, to take in also regional and global scales.

To meet these limitations, this volume harnesses "polycentric" perspectives to develop an interdisciplinary and transscalar approach to understanding digital data governance. Polycentrism, we argue, provides a set of lenses that help tie together the enormous variety of actors, issues, and processes that figure in digital data governance at intertwined subnational, national, regional, and global levels. Two particular insights result.

First, substantively, polycentrism reveals many power centers and connections in digital data governance. This concept covers both formal and informal arrangements, multiple scales (local-to-global), and different sectors (governmental, commercial, civil society, technical, academic). A polycentric perspective brings out a mix of chaos and order in this complex regulation of digital data (Koinova et al. 2021). On the one hand, polycentrism entails diffusion, fluidity, and contradictions in governance constellations. On the other hand, the prima facie confusion of digital data governance on closer inspection shows patterns and complementarities. Hence, the polycentric condition involves both dispersion and structure (Gadinger and Scholte 2023). Polycentrism's emphasis on plurality also encourages creative reflections on how digital data governance *could* and *should* be constituted, including different ways to construct (more) democratic and just arrangements.

Second, methodologically, polycentric perspectives bridge disciplinary divides in the analysis of digital data governance. Discipline-based analyses of AI, cyber security, smart cities, health immunity passes, fake news farms, and other instantiations of digital data all mobilize varying assumptions (typically implicit) of what governance involves. These divergences lead to varying understandings of digital data governance which often remain siloed inside individual scholarly disciplines. In contrast, polycentric perspectives help draw together a growing range of insights from different disciplines about the complexities of digital data governance: how it occurs, how it might occur differently, and how it should occur.

The rest of this introduction further elaborates on the nature of digital data and their governance; what polycentric perspectives on governance entail; and how this set of perspectives offers an empirically grounded and nuanced interdisciplinary understanding of digital data governance. We finish by reviewing the other chapters of this book.

Digital Data and Their Governance

Data are processed information (Beaulieu and Leonelli 2021). They can take the form of numbers, scripts, images, and audio. Digital data more specifically (and in contrast to analog data) consist of strings of binary digits ("bits") each valued as 0 or 1. Bits are grouped (usually in sets of eight) as bytes: hence storage values of digital data in terms of kilobytes (KB, a thousand bytes), megabytes (MB, a thousand kilobytes), gigabytes (GB, a thousand megabytes), and so on.

Digital data have qualities of precision, reproduction, and compression that have made them especially prone to proliferate and pervade all corners of contemporary society. These qualities give digital data degrees of fluidity and interoperability across networks, devices, databases, and software and algorithmic systems that non-digital data do not have. Digital data are translatable in and across different electronic devices. They have the possibility to be simultaneously available in diverse contexts. Digital data also have a degree of non-rivalry: their use by some person or entity does not generally preclude others from using them unless artificial barriers are created for market, security, or other policy purposes. Non-fungible tokens (NFTs) that live on distributed ledgers (Chapter 12 of this volume by Campbell-Verduyn) artificially introduce both scarcity and security by ensuring that digital artwork, for instance, cannot be reproduced. Finally, digital data can be "synthetically created" by computer programs themselves, with relative autonomy from the humans and organizations that originally set up those programs, for example, in AI (Jacobsen 2023).

The digitization of data has occurred with lightning historic speed (Hansen and Porter 2012, 2017; Flyverbom et al. 2019). In the 1980s, less than 1 percent of the world's stored data was in digital format. This proportion grew to more than half by 2002 and 99 percent by 2020 (Hilbert 2020). Some 59 zettabytes (i.e., trillion gigabytes) of digital data were produced across the world in 2020, a figure that is expected to more than triple to 175ZB by 2025 (Vopson 2021). "Big" data, indeed (Cukier and Mayer-Schoenberger 2014)!

Accelerating digitization has often made it difficult to distinguish between digital and non-digital data. We see this confluence with books (like this one) that are digitized before they appear in print. Similarly, automobiles and household appliances are increasingly linked to the Internet. With such interconnections, less and less data in the world is fully non-digital.

The astounding expansion of digital data raises a host of concerns, including several that are highlighted in this volume. For example, aggregated digital data may serve to identify people and potentially compromise their rights to privacy (Chapter 10). Floods of digital data open space for disinformation campaigns (Chapters 8 and 9). Cyberattacks use Internet traffic to topple network infrastructure (Chadd 2018; Shackelford 2014). Specifying and respecting intellectual property rights in the colossal, fast-moving, and transboundary datasphere can likewise pose major challenges (Dulong de Rosnay and Stalder 2020; Frischmann et al. 2014). Large Language Models (which train generative AI systems) use the vast data available on the open Internet with unforeseen consequences and risks (Lim et al. 2023; Greenfield and Bhavnani 2023).

Particularly crucial issues concern the distribution of ownership and benefits related to digital data. The sheer scale of digital data, the speed of their circulation, and their deep penetration across the whole of economy and society place digitization at the heart of contemporary capitalism. Digital data not only facilitate surplus accumulation in other sectors of production (manufacturing, finance, etc.), but they have also become a major commodity (and source of capital) in their own right. In today's digital capitalism (Pace 2018), those who own and control digital data also hold much of the wealth and power in society. Consequently, the (mal)distribution of gains and harms from digital data has far-reaching implications for contemporary social justice.

Currently a handful of transnational platform companies largely control the production, circulation, and distribution of digital data across the planet (Lehdonvirta 2022; Zuboff 2019; Khan 2018). For example, Google held 85 percent market share of the global search engine market at the end of 2022. Amazon Web Services, Microsoft Azure, and Google Cloud together had 65 percent of the global market for cloud infrastructure services at the beginning of 2023. Facebook holds data concerning its 2.98 billion active users as of 2023 (Statista 2023). While these digital platforms have global reach, their operations are largely centered in the United States. In China, tech giants, such as Baidu, Tencent, and Alibaba dominate the market and control social media, e-commerce, and digital services. Several China-based companies, too, are expanding globally (Nanni 2022; Liu 2021).

All of these matters – corporate power, distribution of benefits, intellectual property, human rights, cybersecurity, disinformation, consequences of AI, and more – raise questions of *governance*. By governance we here mean the rules and regulatory processes that operate to bring (greater) order, predictability, and guided change to a field of social action (in this case the datasphere). Such rules can take the form of laws, standards, benchmarks, recommendations, general principles, and norms. The regulatory processes can be formal and/or informal, state and/or nonstate, public and/or private, national and/or international.

Governance thereby has a broader scope than government (Van Eeten and Mueller 2013; Hofmann et al. 2017). To be sure, societal rules in respect of digital data can take the form of statutes and regulations of the nation-state. However, governance can also include directives of the European Union, resolutions of the United Nations, decisions of multistakeholder bodies, benchmarks established by standard-setting agencies, agreements between companies, and more. As chapters in this volume specify, governments (in the sense of territorial states) often figure importantly in digital data governance, but they are far from alone in today's regulatory field (Haggart et al. 2021; Weber 2010; Goldsmith and Wu 2006; Froomkin 2002).

The Internet *Governance* Forum (IGF) is therefore appropriately named. This United Nations initiative goes beyond governments to attract academics, the business sector, civil society, political parties, technical experts, and more (Tjahja et al. 2022). Not surprisingly, the IGF agenda has in recent years given issues around digital data ever greater attention. Multiple IGF sessions now address issues such as AI, anti-trust, content moderation, digital literacy, disinformation, privacy, and rights, as well as the interplay of digitization with the environment, finance, health care, labor conditions, and other fields. Indeed, several chapters of this book were presented at the IGF 2022.

In sum, then, the cultural, ecological, economic, and political stakes around digital data are very high, making questions of governance ever more pressing. How do rules and regulatory processes for the digital sphere operate, and with what consequences? What forces make governance of digital data work as it currently does? What alternative rules and regulatory arrangements for digital data could be possible and desirable? To pursue such questions, one needs a general conception of the dynamics of governance, which we develop in this book around the notion of polycentrism.

What Is Polycentrism?

In general, polycentric governance is taken to involve complex actor constellations operating with multiple institutional arrangements, rationalities, and normative orientations (Gadinger and Scholte 2023). However, as with any key concept, polycentrism has attracted a variety of interpretations, as particular scholars have developed a broad insight in a range of different ways. Here we distinguish three main conceptions that have marked the literature.

Polycentrism as a General Concept

The notion of polycentrism first emerged seventy years ago in the work of Michael Polanyi (1951). Polanyi introduced the term in order to understand the paralysis of cooperation when a single center of power seeks to impose a single direction of action, as in the socialist arrangements of a command-and-control economy that marked his day. For Polanyi, a convinced liberal, the polycentric alternative embedded human freedom, spontaneity, and self-organization into economic, political, and social systems. He observed polycentric dynamics in the practices of science as well as certain species. Yet Polanyi kept the concept at a quite general level and in particular did not specify how power and order operate under conditions of polycentrism.

Polycentrism as Dispersed Governance

From the 1960s onwards, Vincent and Elinor Ostrom brought greater focus to the dynamics of polycentrism by linking the concept directly to governance processes (Ostrom et al. 1961; Ostrom 2005). For the Bloomington School of political economy that developed around the Ostroms' work, polycentrism arises where a governance arrangement has multiple decision-making centers with de jure or de facto autonomy from each other (Aligica and Tarko 2012; Stephan et al. 2019; Thiel 2016). Bloomington School scholars have also explored polycentric governance in relation to other features, including the number of centers involved, dimensions of authority, gatekeeping functions, types of laws and norms, and adjustment mechanisms. Yet, for the Ostroms and subsequent generations of scholarship in this genre, multiple and autonomous decision centers remain the baseline feature of polycentricity as a property of governance.

The Ostrom/Bloomington perspective on polycentrism has been applied to many substantive policy fields, particularly issues that are framed in terms of the commons and collective or public goods (Carlisle and Gruby 2019). Examples include forests (Ostrom and Nagendra 2012), the environment (Berkes

2010), water (Da Silveira and Richards 2013), and information (Chapter 2, Raymond and Shackelford, this volume). The Ostroms' early work mainly examined local government, but in later years they extended ideas of polycentrism also to global (especially environmental) governance (Ostrom 2010).

While the Ostrom/Bloomington conception helpfully developed polycentrism as a way to understand governance, this perspective has remained mostly actor-centric. In other words, it conceives of polycentric regulatory processes as a matter of interactions among self-determining individuals, groups, and organizations, without systematic attention to larger social forces that bring pattern and order to those interactions. For Ostrom/Bloomington accounts, polycentrism is driven by the features, goals, and initiatives of the actors involved, with no autonomous power for social structures.

Polycentrism as "Ordered Chaos"

A third type of perspective on polycentrism foregrounds a social ordering dimension of governance dynamics. This more expansive notion retains the Ostrom/Bloomington stress on a plurality of actors promulgating rules and regulations for a given policy problem, but in addition this approach attends to the influence of social structures. These ordering forces can take the form of norms (such as human rights), embedded practices (such as institutionalized decision-taking procedures or shared narratives), and/or overarching macro structures (such as capitalism or patriarchy) (Azmanova 2018). In this way, polycentrism involves both the "chaos" of multitudinous actors and the "order" of social structures (Koinova et al. 2021; Gadinger and Scholte 2023). This third way of thinking about polycentrism especially informs this book and emphasizes four important properties (both of governance in general and of digital data governance in particular).

First, polycentric governance of a given policy area (such as digital data) is dispersed across multiple scales (local, national, regional, global) and multiple sectors (public, private, and hybrid public-private). Hence, the rules and regulatory processes are "transscalar" and "transsectoral", as governance bodies situated on the different levels and in the different spheres interact with one another in respect of the policy issue at hand. Governance of digital data thereby occurs through a dense network that interlinks a plethora of regulatory actors across the world.

Second, polycentric governance (of digital data) encompasses both formal measures and informal practices. Formal governance occurs with constitutions, statutes, treaties, resolutions, and other explicitly articulated rules. For example, the formal realm includes government legislation on disinformation and board decisions at the Internet Corporation for Assigned Names and Numbers (ICANN). Informal governance occurs with memoranda, habits, routines, discourses, creeds, and other practices that are not officially encoded and enforced – yet still can have governing effects. Targets set by the Group of

Twenty (G20) and pervasive security narratives provide illustrations of informal regulation. Both formal and informal governance transpire within and across the different scales and sectors of a polycentric network.

Third, polycentric governance can involve more systemic ordering of a policy field (e.g., of digital data) through macro structures. Examples of such "deeper" or "overarching" regulatory forces could include (depending upon one's theoretical proclivities) capitalism, a hegemonic state, militarism, patriarchy, and more (Scholte 2018). The power of these larger patterns has the effect of directing governance that seems chaotic (at the level of actor interactions) into relatively predictable channels. Owing to structural power, we can anticipate that, for instance, most rules and regulatory processes for digital data will conform to, and help to enable, capitalist relations of surplus accumulation.

Fourth, complex interrelations among the many regulatory actors and multiple ruling structures can generate considerable dynamism and change in polycentric digital data governance, certainly at the level of actors and their actions. The result is "continual creation and reconstruction" in "quite fluid" governance processes (Koinova et al. 2021, p. 1991). Hence, change comes not only from external shocks, but is also an inherent internal feature of polycentric systems.

In sum, all three above readings of polycentrism share a focus on multiple and autonomous decision centers. The second and third relate this core idea more specifically to governance processes, and the third looks beyond actors to social structures as regulatory forces. We argue in this book that this third, "ordered chaos" perspective is more conducive to productive nuanced interdisciplinary discussions of global digital data governance.

Why Polycentrism?

Having set out several different conceptions of polycentrism that have circulated in contemporary social and political research, why would one want to make this concept pivotal to an analysis of digital data governance? Here we underline two main reasons: an empirical reason related to the complex structured networks that mark digital data governance; and a methodological reason related to the facilitation of interdisciplinary research.

Empirical Evidence

Regarding the empirical reason, the notion of polycentrism fits well with concrete evidence from actually unfolding digital data governance. We observe that rules and regulatory processes for this policy area do indeed come from public, private, and hybrid actors operating across local-to-global scales. We see different types of formal and informal authority across the digital arena. On the one hand, the many players often pursue different (and competing) visions, priorities, and practices vis-à-vis the digital economy and society. On the other hand, complex regulatory networks for the digital field also display unifying patterns, as the plethora of actors speak a similar professional language, follow common dress codes, reproduce social hierarchies, and so on. In short, the concept of polycentrism "works", empirically.

Of course, we could have adopted another vocabulary to convey the complex character of the governance of digital data. For example, other theorists have discussed this phenomenon in terms of "field" (Bourdieu 1993), "new medievalism" (Friedrichs 2000), "multi-level governance" (Hooghe and Marks 2001), "global governmentality" (Larner and Walters 2004), "actor-network" (Latour 2005), "assemblage" (Sassen 2006), "regime complex" (Alter and Meunier 2009), "fragmentation" (Biermann et al. 2009), "intersectionality" (Collins and Bilge 2016), "patchwork" (Pouliot and Thérien 2023), and more. Additional newly invented labels appear pretty much by the year.

Yet, while other vocabularies have their merits, there are good reasons for preferring "polycentrism" (Gadinger and Scholte 2023, pp. 8–10). For one thing, this term is especially effective at evoking a mix of diffusion, diversity, and chaos ("poly") along with pattern, framework, and order ("centers"). In addition, as elaborated below, polycentrism is especially conducive to interdisciplinary dialogue, drawing together legal, institutional, relational, and structural conceptions of governance. The term polycentrism is moreover compact and easily remembered. With such benefits, the idea of polycentrism has attracted increased interest in recent governance research (Scholte 2004, 2017; Black 2008; Ostrom 2010; Mittelman 2013; Jordan et al. 2018; Carlisle and Gruby 2019; Thiel et al. 2019; Faude 2020; Kim 2020; Orsini et al. 2020; Wurzel et al. 2020; Koinova et al. 2021; Gadinger and Scholte 2023).

In invoking the concept of polycentrism we do not necessarily ascribe positive connotations to the idea. To say that polycentrism brings analytical sense to observed governance of digital data is not to say that we normatively endorse this condition. On the contrary, as many chapters in this book show, polycentrism can provide a lens to criticize prevailing governance arrangements and to imagine alternative futures.

Interdisciplinary Methodology

The concept of polycentrism has the further advantage of facilitating interdisciplinary conversations about governance, including rules and regulatory processes around digital data. As noted earlier, Polanyi coined and applied the term in an interdisciplinary sense. More recently, the notion has circulated in interdisciplinary contexts, such as environmental studies, global studies, media and communications studies, and science and technology studies. Other contributors to the present volume herald from anthropology, computer science, international relations, law, political economy, and political science. Polycentrism proves able to circulate in all of these academic quarters and more. Not every scholar is equally comfortable with the notion, but all approaches can and do engage with the idea.

In particular, polycentrism can bring into fruitful conversation different ontologies about governance (Gadinger and Scholte 2023). Some of the contributions to the present volume develop a more organizational perspective on polycentrism: that is, they understand governance to lie with organizations and their interactions with each other (e.g., Chapters 2 and 10). Other chapters in the book take a more juridical approach and see governance as resting with the law and legal processes (e.g., Chapter 7). Further authors pursue a more relational ontology, viewing governance as a set of practices: that is, "ways of doing things", be they behavioral, discursive, institutional, and/or material (e.g., Chapters 6 and 12). Still other conceptions in this volume are more macro-structural, locating governance power more in encompassing social orders, such as embedded inequalities (e.g., Chapters 4 and 5). Hence, framing governance as polycentrism encourages inter-paradigm conversations that are otherwise rare in respect of digital data governance.

Project Execution and Chapter Overview

This project was developed at the Centre for Global Cooperation Research (CGCR) at the University of Duisburg-Essen. CGCR is one of a range of Käte Hamburger Kollegs supported by the German Federal Ministry of Education and Research to promote collaborative international interdisciplinary scholarship on frontline issues of the social sciences and humanities. During its second phase (2018–2024), CGCR has highlighted both the conceptual theme of polycentric governing and the empirical field of Internet governance. Cohorts of research fellows from around the world have worked together in Duisburg with the Centre's core staff, producing several collective publications on these subjects (Haggart et al. 2021; Koinova et al. 2021; Gadinger and Scholte 2023).

The present volume originates from collaboration among Internet governance scholars at CGCR during 2020–2021. Carolina Aguerre and Malcolm Campbell-Verduyn were then Senior Research Fellows at the Centre and devised the project with CGCR Co-Director Jan Aart Scholte and further support from other researchers and administrative staff in Duisburg. As lead organizers of the project, Aguerre and Campbell-Verduyn assembled prospective chapter authors in two workshops, held online in July 2021 and November 2021 amidst restrictions of the COVID-19 pandemic. Heralding from various world regions and academic disciplines, the contributors addressed a wide range of issues around digital data governance. Out of these deliberations has emerged a central contribution of this book: namely, an interdisciplinary conversation around the theme of polycentrism that bridges hitherto largely siloed analyses of digital data governance.

The body of this book is organized into three parts with respective themes of theoretical frameworks, controversies, and technologies. The first part contains five chapters that mainly develop insights around concepts and approaches in the study of digital data governance, including the notion of polycentrism in particular. The second part, with four chapters, highlights controversies in digital data governance around content moderation, disinformation, and privacy. The three chapters of the third part examine digital data governance with greater attention to questions around technology, including protocols, blockchain, and AI.

Part I of this book exemplifies how polycentrism brings into conversation different perspectives on digital data governance. Chapter 2 by Anjanette Raymond and Scott Shackelford nudges the "Ostroms' Vision of the Commons and Polycentric Governance into the Digital Environment". The chapter tackles pressing issues identified in the seminal piece by Charlotte Hess and Elinor Ostrom, *Ideas, Artifacts and Facilities: Information as a Common-Pool Resource* (2003). Raymond and Shackelford in particular reflect on contemporary practices of data localization and notions of cyber sovereignty.

While Chapter 2 develops the Ostrom/Bloomington conception of polycentrism, Chapter 3 by Carolina Aguerre works more in the "ordered chaos" vein distinguished earlier, with a particular focus on the implications of digital data flows across the Internet for global interoperability. The chapter examines the governance of digital data flows in relation to the seven attributes of transscalarity, transsectorality, diffusion, fluidity, overlapping mandates, ambiguous hierarchies, and no final arbiter. These disparate arrangements at the level of governance actors are in addition connected to systemic organizing forces, such as underlying norms, practices, and structures. Data that flow across different networks on the Internet are one of the strongest indicators of interoperability at the infrastructure level.

Chapter 4 by Isabel Rocha de Siqueira and Laís Ramalho addresses structural inequalities that shape the use of digital data in efforts to enact the 2030 Sustainable Development Agenda. De Siqueira and Ramalho draw attention to important but overlooked voids in the contemporary "datascape", especially in relation to marginalized communities and the Global South. This chapter underscores how polycentricity offers routes for advancing normative proposals that challenge existing attempts to enact the 2030 Agenda.

In Chapter 5 Daivi Rodima-Taylor addresses polycentric governance in relation to data activism in Africa. The chapter argues that datafication is both problematic (as it is dominated by large tech corporations) and auspicious (by creating new opportunities for collective action around data access and data rights). Grassroots data activism, Rodima-Taylor argues, reveals possibilities for more democratic and sustainable circulation of digital data for the benefit of marginalized people.

Rounding off Part I is Chapter 6 by Stefaan Verhulst, which examines questions as a governance device in relation to digital data. Verhulst underscores that the questions asked (and not asked) substantially determine what kind of governance is (and is not) developed for digital data. The chapter argues that a polycentric approach to the setting of questions can help to advance a more careful and inclusive governance of the digital arena.

Part II of the book then foregrounds controversies in digital data governance. Chapter 7 by Wenlong Li and Dan Yang zooms in on the European Data Protection Board (EDPB) with a view to improving enforcement of the General Data Protection Regulation (GDPR) and cooperation between national data protection authorities (DPAs). The chapter examines the transnational firm Clearview AI to illustrate current challenges around implementation of the GDPR. Li and Yang show that, while the GDPR regime includes polycentric enforcement and cooperation mechanisms, they are inadequate for effective regulation of cross-border enterprises, such as Clearview AI.

Chapter 8 by Susan Aaronson addresses the problem of disinformation at intertwined domestic and international levels. Aaronson frames disinformation as a wicked problem that cannot be "solved" so much as mitigated by coordinated action between multiple centers of power. The chapter proposes that multilateral trade agreements can handle cross-border disinformation, but not domestically created disinformation. Effective governance of disinformation therefore needs a polycentric approach that interlinks national and international measures.

Chapter 9 by Clara Iglesias Keller and Bruna Martins dos Santos further addresses controversies surrounding efforts at regulating disinformation. They show how debates over how best to counter disinformation frame data in a plurality of manners: both as a problem and a solution; as an instrument; and as a target of regulation. This chapter highlights overlaps between what are often presented as binaries and separate discussions of data governance and disinformation, focusing on statutory regulation in Brazil and India.

Chapter 10 by Rotem Medzini and Dmitry Epstein examines how polycentric governance perspectives can identify the different institutional dynamics that shape privacy practices in different national settings. Various regulatory intermediaries, who are pivotal for interpreting, monitoring, and implementing data policy in organizations, constitute multiple centers of power. While the European GDPR provides the normative grounding for these institutions, the cases expose a diversity of institutional choices and practices.

Part III of the book foregrounds issues of technology that are crucial to digital data governance. Chapter 11 by Nathalia Sautchuk Patrício examines key technical protocols that have underpinned the historical evolution of Internet architecture. Sautchuk Patrício traces how these protocols have affected data flows, as well as polycentric efforts to govern these protocols.

Chapter 12 by Malcolm Campbell-Verduyn examines emerging digital technologies around blockchain and cryptocurrency. He provides a topology of efforts to date to govern this arena. Developing an "ordered chaos" perspective on polycentrism, Campbell-Verduyn outlines key norms, practices, and underlying orders that govern distributed governance. The chapter argues that, despite claims of efficacy, polycentric governance of blockchain reproduces the instabilities and concentration of power that are associated with centralized modalities of governance.

Looking at another emerging technology, Chapter 13 by Janet Hui Xue discusses how polycentricity is both a problem and a solution for governing AI. The chapter clarifies the problem raised by AI technologies in the use of personal data from a polycentric lens as "ordered chaos". Xue relates these underlying orders to more formal forms of regulatory tools, such as codes, laws, and markets in contemplating solutions and ways forward for polycentric digital data governance in the 21st century.

Finally, the concluding chapter by the editors summarizes how, in the light of the foregoing chapters, polycentric perspectives offer a nuanced interdisciplinary understanding of digital data governance. We consolidate three general contributions of the book: namely, concerning the advancement of synthetic knowledge, a focus on questions of power, and the furtherance of creative diversity in policymaking. The conclusion of the book also identifies four avenues for future work, related respectively to multistakeholderism, sociological theory, temporality, and normative concerns.

In sum, this book demonstrates how polycentrism provides a useful heuristic to address the complexities around digital data governance. The insights come from – and will be relevant for – scholars in a broad range of academic disciplines and interdisciplinary fields. As debates around digital data governance develop further in the years to come, notions of polycentrism can clarify how policies unfold – and sometimes have unintended consequences. The book also lays ground for critical discussions about power asymmetries, (global) democracy in the digital realm, and legitimate governance of digital data.

References

Abraham, R., Schneider, J., and vom Brocke, J. (2019). Data Governance: A Conceptual Framework, Structured Review, and Research Agenda. *International Journal of Information Management*, 49, 424–438.

Aligica, P. D., and V. Tarko. (2012). Polycentricity: From Polanyi to Ostrom, and Beyond. *Governance*, 25 (2), 237–262.

Alter, K., and Meunier, S. (2009). The Politics of International Regime Complexity. *Perspectives on Politics*, 7 (1), 13–24.

Azmanova, A. (2018). Relational, Structural and Systemic Forms of Power: The 'Right to Justification' Confronting Three Types of Domination. *Journal of Political Power*, 11 (1), 68–78.

Beaulieu, A., and Leonelli, S. (2021). *Data and Society. A Critical Introduction*. Los Angeles, CA: SAGE Publications Ltd.

Berkes, F. (2010). Devolution of Environment and Resources Governance: Trends and Future. *Environmental Conservation*, 37 (4), 489–500.

Biermann, F., Pattberg, P., van Asselt, H., and Zelli, F. (2009). The Fragmentation of Global Governance Architectures: A Framework for Analysis. *Global Environmental Politics*, 9 (4), 14–40.

Bigo, D., Isin, E., and Ruppert, E. (eds.). (2019). *Data Politics: Worlds, Subjects, Rights*. Abingdon: Routledge.

Black, J. (2008). Constructing and Contesting Legitimacy and Accountability in Polycentric Regulatory Regimes. *Regulation & Governance*, 2 (2), 137–164.

Bonina, C., and Eaton, B. (2020). Cultivating open government data platform ecosystems through governance: Lessons from Buenos Aires, Mexico City and Montevideo. *Government Information Quarterly*, 37 (3), 101479.

Bourdieu, P. (1993). *The Field of Cultural Production*. Cambridge: Polity Press.

Carlisle, K., and Gruby, R. L. (2019). Polycentric Systems of Governance: A Theoretical Model for the Commons. *Policy Studies Journal*, 47 (4), 927–952.

Chadd, A. (2018). DDoS Attacks: Past, Present and Future. *Network Security*, 2018 (7), 13–15.

Collins, P., and Bilge, S. (2016). *Intersectionality*. Malden: Polity Press.

Couldry, N., and Mejias, U. A. (2019). Data Colonialism: Rethinking Big Data's Relation to the Contemporary Subject. *Television and New Media*, 20 (4), 336–349.

Cukier, K., and Mayer-Schoenberger, V. (2014). *The Rise of Big Data: How It's Changing the Way We Think About the World*. Princeton University Press.

Da Silveira, A. R., and Richards, K. S. (2013). The Link Between Polycentrism and Adaptive Capacity in River Basin Governance Systems: Insights from the River Rhine and the Zhujiang (Pearl River) Basin. *Annals of the Association of American Geographers*, 103 (2), 319–329.

Dulong de Rosnay, M., and Stalder, F. (2020). Digital Commons. *Internet Policy Review*, 9 (4), 1–22.

Faude, B. (2020). Global Governance als Polycentric Governance. *Zeitschrift für Internationale Beziehungen*, 27 (1), 151–162.

Flyverbom, M., and Murray, J. (2018). Datastructuring—Organizing and curating digital traces into action. *Big Data & Society*, 5(2), 1–12.

Flyverbom, M., Deibert, R., and Matten, D. (2019). The Governance of Digital Technology, Big Data, and the Internet: New Roles and Responsibilities for Business. *Business & Society*, 58 (1), 3–19.

Friedrichs, J. (2000). The Meaning of New Medievalism. *European Journal of International Relations*, 7 (4), 475–502.

Frischmann, B., Madison, M., and Strandburg, K. (2014). Governing Knowledge Commons – Introduction & Chapter 1. In B. M. Frischmann, M. J. Madison, and K. J. Strandburg (eds.), *Governing Knowledge Commons*. Oxford: Oxford University Press, ix–44.

Froomkin, A. M. (2002). ICANN's 'Uniform Dispute Resolution Policy' – Causes and (Partial) Cures. *Brooklyn Law Review*, 67 (5), 605–718.

Gadinger, F., and Scholte, J. A. (eds.). (2023). *Polycentrism: How Governing Works Today*. Oxford: Oxford University Press.

Goldsmith, J., and Wu, T. (2006). *Who Controls the Internet? Illusions of a Borderless World*. Oxford: Oxford University Press.

Greenfield, D., and Bhavnani, S. (2023). Social Media: Generative AI Could Harm Mental Health. *Nature*, 617 (7962), 676.

Haggart, B., Tusikov, N., and Scholte, J. A. (eds.). (2021). *Power and Authority in Internet Governance: Return of the State?* Abingdon: Routledge.

Hansen, H. K. (2015). Numerical Operations, Transparency Illusions and the Datafication of Governance. *European Journal of Social Theory*, 18 (2), 203–220.

Hansen, H. K., and Porter, T. (2012). What Do Numbers Do in Transnational Governance? *International Political Sociology*, 6 (4), 409–426.

Hansen, H. K., and Porter, T. (2017). What Do Big Data Do in Global Governance. *Global Governance*, 23, 31–42.

Hasselbalch, G. (2021). *Data Ethics of Power*. Edward Elgar Publishing.

Hess, C., and Ostrom, E. (2003). Ideas, Artifacts, and Facilities: Information as a Common-Pool Resource. *Law and Contemporary Problems*, 66 (1/2), 111–145.

Hilbert, M. (2020). Digital Technology and Social Change: The Digital Transformation of Society from a Historical Perspective. *Dialogues in Clinical Neuroscience*, 22 (2), 189–194.

Hintz, A., Dencik, L., and Wahl-Jorgensen, K. (2019). *Digital Citizenship in a Datafied Society*. Cambridge: Polity.

Hofmann, J., Katzenbach, C., and Gollatz, K. (2017). Between Coordination and Regulation: Finding the Governance in Internet Governance. *New Media & Society*, 19 (9), 1406–1423.

Hooghe, L., and Marks, G. (2001). *Multi-Level Governance and European Integration*. Lanham, MD: Rowman & Littlefield.

Jacobsen, B. N. (2023). Machine learning and the politics of synthetic data. *Big Data & Society*, 10 (1). doi:10.1177/20539517221145372.

Jordan, A., Huitema, D., van Asselt, H., and Forster, J. (eds.). (2018). *Governing Climate Change: Polycentricity in Action?* Cambridge: Cambridge University Press.

Khan, Lina. (2018). Sources of Tech Platform Power. *Georgetown Law Technology Review*, 2 (2), 325–334.

Kim, R. E. (2020). Is Global Governance Fragmented, Polycentric, or Complex? The State of the Art of the Network Approach. *International Studies Review*, 22 (4), 903–931.

Koinova, M., Deloffre, M., Gadinger, F., Mencutek, Z., Scholte, J. A., and Steffek, J. (2021). It's Ordered Chaos: What Really Makes Polycentrism Work. *International Studies Review*, 23 (4), 1988–2018.

Larner, W., and Walters, W. (2004). Globalisation as Governmentality. *Alternatives*, 29 (5), 495–514.

Latour, B. (2005). *Reassembling the Social: An Introduction to Actor-Network Theory*. New York: Oxford University Press.

Lehdonvirta, V. (2022). *Cloud Empires: How Digital Platforms Are Overtaking the State and How We Can Regain Control*. Cambridge, MA: MIT Press.

Leonelli, S., and Tempini, N. (2020). *Data Journeys in the Sciences*. Springer Nature.

Lim, W. M., Gunasekara, A., Pallant, J. L., Pallant, J. I., and Pechenkina, E. (2023). Generative AI and the Future of Education: Ragnarök or Reformation? A Paradoxical Perspective from Management Educators. *International Journal of Management Education*, 21 (2). doi:10.1016/j.ijme.2023.100790.

Liu, L. (2021). The Rise of Data Politics: Digital China and the World. *Studies in Comparative International Development*, 56 (1), 45–67.

Madianou, M. (2019). Technocolonialism: Digital Innovation and Data Practices in the Humanitarian Response to Refugee Crises. *Social Media + Society*, 5 (3), 1–13.

Milan, S., and Treré, E. (2019). Big Data from the South(s): Beyond Data Universalism. *Television & New Media*, 20 (4), 319–335.

Mittelman, J. H. (2013). Global Bricolage: Emerging Market Powers and Polycentric Governance. *Third World Quarterly*, 34 (1), 23–37.

Mosco, V. (2016). After the Internet: Cloud Computing, Big Data and the Internet of Things. *Les Enjeux de l'information et de la communication*, 17 (2), 146–155.

Nagendra, H., and Ostrom, E. (2012). Polycentric Governance of Multifunctional Forested Landscapes. *International Journal of the Commons*, 6 (2).

Nanni, R. (2022). Digital Sovereignty and Internet Standards: Normative Implications of Public–Private Relations Among Chinese Stakeholders in the Internet Engineering Task Force. *Information, Communication & Society*, 25 (16), 2342–2362.

Obendiek, A.S. (2022). *Data Governance: Value Orders and Jurisdictional Conflicts.* Oxford: Oxford University Press.

Orsini, A., Prestre, P., Haas, P., Brosig, M., Patterg, P., Widerberg, O., and Gomez-Mera, L. (2020). Forum: Complex Systems and International Governance. *International Studies Review*, 22 (4), 1008–1038.

Ostrom, E. (2005). *Understanding Institutional Diversity.* Princeton, NJ: Princeton University Press.

Ostrom, E. (2010). Beyond Markets and States: Polycentric Governance of Complex Economic Systems. *American Economic Review*, 100 (3), 641–672.

Ostrom, V., Tiebout, C., and Warren, R. (1961). The Organization of Government in Metropolitan Areas: A Theoretical Inquiry. *American Political Science Review*, 55 (4), 831–842.

Pace, J. (2018). The Concept of Digital Capitalism. *Communication Theory*, 28 (3), 254–269.

Polanyi, M. (1951). *The Logic of Liberty.* Chicago, IL: University of Chicago Press.

Pouliot, V., and Thérien, J.-P. (2023). *Global Policymaking: The Patchwork of Global Governance.* Cambridge: Cambridge University Press.

Ricaurte, P. (2019). Data Epistemologies, The Coloniality of Power, and Resistance. *Television & New Media*, 20 (4), 350–365.

Ruppert, E., Isin, E., and Bigo, D. (2017). Data Politics. *Big Data & Society*, 4 (2), 1–7.

Rushkoff, D. (1994). *Media Virus!*New York: Ballantine Books.

Sassen, S. (2006). *Territory, Authority, Rights: From Medieval to Global Assemblages.* Princeton: Princeton University Press.

Scholte, J. A. (2004). *Globalization and Governance: From Statism to Polycentrism.* Warwick University/ESRC Centre for the Study of Globalisation and Regionalisation Working Papers. no. 130/04.

Scholte, J. A. (2017). Polycentrism and Democracy in Internet Governance. In Uta Kohl (ed.), *The Net and the Nation State: Multidisciplinary Perspectives on Internet Governance.* Cambridge: Cambridge University Press, 165–184.

Scholte, J. A. (2018). Social Structure and Global Governance Legitimacy. In J. Tallberg, K. Bäckstrand and J. A. Scholte (eds.), *Legitimacy in Global Governance: Sources, Processes, and Consequences.* Oxford: Oxford University Press, 75–97.

Shackelford, S. (2014). *Managing Cyber Attacks in International Law, Business, and Relations: In Search of Cyber Peace.* Cambridge: Cambridge University Press.

Statista (2023). Facebook. https://www.statista.com/topics/751/facebook/.

Steedman, R., Kennedy, H., and Jones, R. (2020). Complex Ecologies of Trust in Data Practices and Data-Driven Systems. *Information, Communication & Society*, 23 (6), 817–832.

Stephan, M., Marshall, G., and McGinnis, M. (2019). An Introduction to Polycentricity and Governance. In A. Thiel, D. Garrick and W. Blomquist (eds.), *Governing Complexity: Analyzing and Applying Polycentricity.* Cambridge: Cambridge University Press, 21–44.

Taylor, L. (2017). What Is Data Justice? The Case for Connecting Digital Rights and Freedoms Globally. *Big Data & Society*, 4 (2), 1–14.

Thiel, A. (2016). *The Polycentricity Approach and the Research Challenges Confronting Environmental Governance.* THESys Discussion Paper No. 2016–1, 1–27.

Thiel, A., Garrick, D., and Blomquist, W. (eds.). (2019). *Governing Complexity: Analyzing and Applying Polycentricity.* Cambridge: Cambridge University Press.

Tjahja, N., Meyer, T., and Shahin, J. (2022). Who Do You Think You Are? Individual Stakeholder Identification and Mobility at the Internet Governance Forum, *Telecommunications Policy*, 46 (10), Article 102410.

Van Eeten, M. J. G., and Mueller, M. (2013). Where Is the Governance in Internet Governance? *New Media & Society*, 15 (5), 720–736.

Vavrushka, D. (2020). *Empower Nations in a Digital Age: A New Data and Digital Governance Framework for the 21st Century*. Prague: Narodni Agentura.

Vopson, Melvin M. (2021). The World's Data Explained: How Much We're Producing and Where It's All Stored. *The Conversation*, 4 May. Available at: https://theconversation.com/the-worlds-data-explained-how-much-were-producing-and-where-its-all-stored-159964.

Weber, R. H. (2010). *Shaping Internet Governance: Regulatory Challenges*. Zurich: Springer.

Wurzel, R, Liefferink, D., and Torney, D. (eds.). (2020). *Pioneers, Leaders and Followers in Multilevel and Polycentric Climate Governance*. Abingdon: Routledge.

Zuboff, S. (2019). *The Age of Surveillance Capitalism: The Fight for a Human Future at the New Frontier of Power*. London: Public Affairs.

PART I

Perspectives

2

NUDGING THE OSTROMS' VISION OF THE COMMONS ON POLYCENTRIC GOVERNANCE INTO THE DIGITAL ENVIRONMENT

Anjanette H. Raymond and Scott Shackelford

> Information that used to be "free" is now increasingly being privatized, monitored, encrypted, and restricted. The enclosure is caused by the conflicts and contradictions between intellectual property laws and the expanded capacities of new technologies. It leads to speculation that the records of scholarly communication, the foundations of an informed, democratic society, may be at risk.
>
> *(Hess, et al., 2003)*

This chapter goes on to tackle many of the pressing issues that have been identified in the emerging digital environment. Now, almost twenty years later, the time is ripe to return to the ideas laid out in 2003 to see how their cautions surrounding the growth of data localization and cyber sovereignty have played out in our increasingly ubiquitous digital existence. At the forefront of the debate is the governance of data, information, and even knowledge itself, in 2022, and beyond.

This brief survey seeks to set out the background of Elinor and Vincent Ostroms' work in this context, while adding to the conversation the contributions of Charlotte Hess and the many others that have tackled the pressing and critical issue of governance of the Internet, and information.

At the forefront of the emerging questions to be considered: when is digital data capable of being viewed in a manner similar to the property envisioned by the early works of Ostrom and Hess, and when might there need to be additions and alternations to governance frameworks? Or maybe more bluntly, when can we use the property regime as a major attribute, and when is something different necessary?

History

For those relatively new to the topic, the field of polycentric (multi-centered) governance may be considered as a multi-level, multi-purpose, multi-functional,

DOI: 10.4324/9781003388418-3

and multi-sectoral model, which has been championed by a variety of scholars and practitioners since the 1950s, including Nobel laureate Professor Elinor Ostrom and Professor Vincent Ostrom. According to Professor Michael McGinnis, "[t]he basic idea [of polycentric governance] is that any group ... facing some collective problem should be able to address that problem in whatever way they best see fit," which could include adapting existing governance structures or crafting new regimes (McGinnis, 2011, pp.171–72). This conceptual model has been known by many names including adaptive governance, collaborative governance, and even "marble-cake federalism" (Polanyi, 1951). Yet the salient point is that it challenged orthodoxy, such as bigger was always better, or the tragedy of the commons model itself preferencing pure nationalization or privatization as solutions to problems posed by common pool resource regimes by demonstrating both the benefits of self-organization, understood here as networking regulations "at multiple levels," and the extent to which national and private control can coexist with communal management (Ostrom, 2008, pp.1–2). It also posits that, due to the existence of free riders in a multipolar world, "a single governmental unit" is often incapable of managing global collective action problems both online and offline (Shackelford, 2020).

The legal field of polycentric governance in the U.S. context was catalyzed by the work of Professor Michael Polanyi in his 1951 book, *The Logic of Liberty* (Polanyi, 1951). Quickly, the implications of this concept came to be known across multiple disciplines, including law, urban networks, and governance studies more broadly (Fuller, 1978, p.353). Professors Vincent and Elinor Ostrom, though, should be rightly credited as having done much to operationalize the concept and give it "empirical substance" (Aligica et al., 2012, p.240). This process began in the 1970s and 1980s through a series of landmark field studies challenging the prevailing notion that the provision of public services—like policing and education—was made better and more cost-effective by consolidating the number of departments and districts (Ostrom et al., 1978; Hanushek, 1986; Hanushek, 1987; Teske et al., 2013). Instead, they showcased the benefits of competition and public choice in municipal governance (Ostrom et al., 2004, p.105).

Professor Elinor Ostrom went on to dive deeply into whether polycentric governance systems could manage collective action problems associated with the provision of common pool resources, leading to her landmark 1990 book, *Governing the Commons* (Ostrom, 1990). She challenged the conventional theory of collective action, which held that rational actors would not cooperate to achieve a socially optimal outcome in a prisoner's dilemma scenario, which is commonly associated with the tragedy of the commons (Olson, 1965). Proponents of this theory thought that only top-down, state-imposed regulations could create the proper incentives for optimal collective action. However, field studies that Professor Elinor Ostrom and others conducted on the provision of water resources in California, (Ostrom, 1965), the design and maintenance of irrigation systems in Nepal (Shivakoti & Ostrom, 2002), and the protection of forests in Latin America (Ostrom et al., 2015) showed that many individuals will in fact cooperate in the face of collective action problems (Prenkert & Shackelford, 2014, pp.455–67). These observations were consistent with laboratory experiments that found that externally imposed regulations, which were intended to maximize joint returns in the face of collective action problems, actually "crowded out" individuals' voluntary cooperative behavior (Frey & Oberholzer-Gee, 1997).

What is it that makes polycentric systems so special? Among other factors, it is the capacity for spontaneous self-correction (Frey, 1997) self-organization, and interaction among diverse stakeholders (McGinnis et al., 2020). In the words of Professor Elinor Ostrom:

> [A] political system that has multiple centers of power at differing scales provides more opportunity for citizens and their officials to innovate and to intervene so as to correct maldistributions of authority and outcomes. Thus, polycentric systems are more likely than monocentric systems to provide incentives leading to self-organized, self-corrective institutional change.
>
> *(McGinnis et al., 2020, p.246)*

The Ostroms also posited that "the structure and dynamics of a polycentric system is a function of the presence of polycentrism in the governance of the other related and adjoined systems[,]" that is, the degree of polycentricity of governmental arrangements is impacted by the polycentricity of political processes and judicial affairs, and vice versa (McGinnis et al., 2020). As such, "[p]olycentricity is a complex system of powers, incentives, rules, values, and individual attitudes combined in a complex system of relationships at different levels" (McGinnis et al., 2020, p.246). Or perhaps more provocatively, "[a]ny island of polycentric order entails and presses for polycentricism in other areas, creating a tension toward change in its direction" (McGinnis et al., 2020, p.246). This insight has interesting implications in the study of digital environments that both encompass and extend beyond diverse national jurisdictions.

Further, as Professor Fikret Berkes has stated, "Polycentric and multilayered institutions improve the fit between knowledge and action in a social-ecological system in ways that allow societies to respond adaptively to change" (Berkes, 2015, p.129). Indeed, the many benefits of polycentric systems have included promoting resilience to shocks, the effective production and provision of diverse public goods, the sustained capacity for self-governance, distributed leadership, and widespread public entrepreneurship (McGinnis et al., 2020).

Yet such networks can also be "inefficient," and are susceptible to institutional fragmentation and gridlock caused by overlapping authority that must still "meet standards of coherence, effectiveness, [and] ... sustainability" (McGinnis et al., 2020; Keohane & Victor, 2011, p.7). As noted by McGinnis, Baldwin, and Thiel:

The structural foundation may fail to provide sufficiently autonomous decision units with the right kinds of overlappability to encourage regular means of mutual adjustment, processes and procedures may become too complex to be fully understood by the people operating that system, or citizens who end up being deeply confused about which authority is responsible for fixing unsatisfactory policy outcomes may lose sight of the reasons why their predecessors ever built such a complex system in the first place.

(McGinnis et al., 2020)

Self-organization and correction, in particular, may be stymied by a variety of factors including forum and search costs, discussion and analytic costs of identifying shared goals, and coordination and authority costs of implementing collective decisions (McGinnis et al., 2020). Other less appreciated costs identified by Elinor Ostrom to polycentric systems can include local tyrannies, stagnation, conflict, and corruption. (Ostrom, 2005, p.282). Vincent Ostrom, on the other hand, was concerned about stalemates in highly federalized systems, along with a variety of other issues including path dependencies that shape viable public policy options. (McGinnis et al., 2020, p.16). Thus, the benefits and drawbacks of polycentric governance must be critiqued both generally and within the cyber context by relying on the institutional analysis literature, and then translated to the extent feasible and desirable into policy proposals to manage both natural and digital ecosystems (McGinnis et al., 2020, p.18).

Ostroms' and Cyber Infrastructure Governance

Among the many applications of the Ostroms' work on polycentric governance, particularly in the context of common pool resource management, is the extent to which it has informed the field of infrastructure governance, seeding frameworks, such as the *Governing Knowledge Commons* literature, discussed below. Particularly in the context of infrastructure, Professor Brett Frischmann has made the case in *Infrastructure: The Social Value of Shared Resources*, that a concept like "infrastructure," which can be understood as the underlying framework or foundation of a system—or "data" for that matter—does not fit neatly within the goods classifications that we typically rely on in describing property types (private goods, club goods, public goods, etc.) (Frischmann, 2013, pp.4, 25). From healthcare to protecting the grid from cyber-attacks, although the policy arenas vary, at their heart, many of these debates center on questions of controlling and accessing diverse infrastructure resources (Frischmann, 2013, pp.xi–xii).

There is an underappreciated polycentric component to such debates given the extent to which various aspects of our digital infrastructure, including U.S. "critical infrastructure," are in private hands. Consider that more than eighty-five percent of U.S. critical infrastructure providers are private firms, yet they are tasked with core societal tasks, such as keeping the lights on, the water running, and the data flowing (FEMA, 2011). Indeed, over time the definition of what constitutes "critical infrastructure" is expanding to encompass sixteen sectors that together comprise more than fifty-three percent of U.S. GDP (BEA, 2022). Protecting cybersecurity, particularly for these diverse businesses, is a key concern, yet how should scholars, practitioners, and policymakers be thinking about this problem? Is cybersecurity a component of a classic public good, like national security, or a club good? Such debates are animated by ongoing disputes about whether we are experiencing a market failure when it comes to cybersecurity (Dourado, 2012).

Global polycentric attention has been targeted at the issue of protecting civilian critical infrastructure, though interdisciplinary research in this context remains in its infancy. For example, polycentric efforts have included the public-private Paris Call for Trust and Security in Cyberspace, which now boasts eighty-one signatory nations, along with hundreds of academic institutions, civil society groups, and companies (Paris Call, 2018). Among the nine principles in the Paris Call, is the protection of civilian critical infrastructure, a norm that was echoed in the eleven cyber norms that were agreed to by the United Nations through two parallel processes known as the Group of Governmental Experts (GGE) and the Open-Ended Working Group (OEWG) in 2021 (Esterhuysen et al., 2019). Other polycentric, multi-stakeholder efforts are also bearing fruit, such as the Cybersecurity Tech Accord, the Trusted IoT Alliance, and the Siemens' Charter of Trust (Hinck, 2018). As we have argued in the past, a Cyber Peace Accord—building from these multi-stakeholder efforts—could promote the cause of protecting civilian critical infrastructure (Hathaway et al., 2017, p.xx). Further, "outcasting," such as by isolating non-compliant regimes through sanctions, could be leveraged to promote enforcement in such a regime (Hathaway et al., 2017, p.373). This was one reason for the success of the Montreal Protocol, as Professor Oona Hathaway has argued, since "[t]he benefits of membership, and costs of nonmembership, increased as the club got bigger" (Hathaway et al., 2017, p.387). Still, though, protecting critical infrastructure is but one component of the larger debate on data governance, and how polycentricity generally—and the Ostroms' other work in particular—can help us better conceptualize both a research and policy path forward.

Ostrom and Data and Information Governance

The governance of the underlying data, on which infrastructure depends, that serves a business, commercial, or other purpose, may need a different concept lens than those discussed above. Many are calling data conceptualized in this manner as a digital commons (Frischmann et al., 2014). Information—as a good—within a commons first garnered attention in software development. In 1984, open software and open-source communities, such as Apache, developed and were managed as commons (Dulong de Rosnay et al., 2020). As such, the progression of the technology eco-system and their commitment to shared—commons-based—governance has a history that the current discussion builds upon. Yet, a commitment to "building" an infrastructure, as a community, and the management of data that flows, is arguably different, at least in some instances.

Because of the complexity of the data eco-system, it might be important for the data to be considered contextually within the hands of the entity that controls the data at any given moment. For example, data, as a packet of information traveling on the Internet, may be governed at any one time by various actors, in various places, with laws and rules about the actor's behavior—polycentric, as described above. However, the bulk of the actors in this scenario may not be interested in the data itself. Instead, these actors are (or should be) committed to the Internet *infrastructure* as a public good. It is not about the data, per se; it is about ensuring the data flows without obstruction, capture, or other limitation.

There are, however, fundamental questions about the governance of the data itself (Ruhaak, 2021). It is this, that we argue, is a digital data commons—that is, the data in an environment unto itself. As Hess and Ostrom wrote in 2003 in their often-cited work: *Ideas, Artifacts, and Facilities: Information as a Common Pool Resource*:

> In the past five years, law review articles have described an information arms race from various perspectives, with multiple sides battling for larger shares of the global knowledge pool.
>
> (Hess & Ostrom, 2003)

This early work is partially an examination of information, conceptualized as a property right through the lens of access, extraction, management, exclusion, and alienation (Hess & Ostrom, 2003, p.111). The introduction of ubiquitous digital technologies has created an eco-system of distributed digitized information that adds more layers of complexity to the flow of data and the ability to own and organize the data. As such, the data considered within the conversation of digital data governance must be vastly expanded to a nearly infinite series of Action Arenas (to use the IAD vernacular), as data is now gathered in ubiquitous amounts and held by an ever-growing number of actors.

There are two questions that are clearly emerging—when is digital data capable of being viewed in a manner similar to the property envisioned by the early works of Ostrom and Hess, and when might there need to be additions and alternations to governance frameworks? Or maybe more bluntly, when can we use the property regime as a major attribute, and when is something different necessary?

There is of course, a starting point for responding to these fundamental questions—it arises in the examination of the types of goods. As Hess and Ostrom note:

Recognizing the class of goods ... enables scholars to identify the core theoretical problems facing individuals, whenever more than one individual or group utilizes resources for an extended period of time.

(Hess & Ostrom, 2003)

Of course, this leads to discussions surrounding goods considering two main issues: subtractability and exclusion (Hess & Ostrom, 2003, p.120). Private goods, those which are both rivalrous (meaning consumption by one entity prevents simultaneous consumption by another entity) and excludable (can easily keep you out), are difficult or impossible to imagine within the discussion of *digital* data and information as rivalrous (subtractability), since these characteristics are not in line with the way digital data exists (Hess & Ostrom, 2003, p.120). As such, within the Ostrom model, data is a resource to be managed as either a club good (non-rivalrous, yet structured as capable of exclusion), a common good/common pool resource (rivalrous but non-excludable), or a public good (non-rivalrous and non-excludable) (Hess & Ostrom, 2003, p.120).

As the title suggests, Hess and Ostrom viewed information as a common pool resource (Hess & Ostrom, 2003, pp.120–21). Since that original examination, support has grown for this evaluation. As Divya Siddarth and E. Glen Weyl point out:

There is already evidence that a move towards common-pool digital public goods could have widely shared benefits. Parts of the digital world—often the most useful and admired parts—already function as commons: Internet protocols, which are governed by international institutions and open standards, the open-source software that enables these protocols, which are often community-stewarded, and much of the crucial information layer of the Internet, including Wikipedia, the Digital Library of Commons and the range of content under Creative Commons, all of which have their own, commons-inspired governance structures.

(Siddarth & Glen Weyl, 2021)

In fact:

Data lends itself especially well to a commons framework: both inputs and impacts are fundamentally shared, distributing access to these resources provides a foundation for further bottom-up innovation and technological progress, siloing or privatizing these erodes the possibility of stewarding collective benefit. Together, they form a shared layer necessary for economic growth and democratic participation.

(Siddarth & Glen Weyl, 2021)

But the governance of the data itself might be a question that leads to further complexity because the data may be part of a local data environment, or may be thought of as part of a global digital data commons, or a combination of both. *This* may be a major question as it really divides the conversation and might lead to using different governance frameworks, or additions to existing frameworks.

Data as the Focus of the Commons

In terms of governance and the complexity of digital data, it should be recognized that there is a discernable difference between data held or managed in a local or regional commons—such as a data cooperative or trust—and data that is part of a global data complex eco-system.

At its most basic, a data hub is a place to share data with others, but the potential models that can be used to manage the data within the hub are numerous and can never be a one-size-fits-all. Existing data hub models are being researched by the Data Economy Lab (Data Econ. Lab, Data Stewardship Models, 2022). The Lab, an initiative by Aapti Institute is a public research institute that focuses on the intersection of tech and society. The Lab is a dynamic space to think through legal, policy, governance, and technological issues on Data Stewardship. In their research, they have noted several models currently being tested by entities when exploring work in the area of data stewardship: (1) trust (Wylie & McDonald, 2018), (2) marketplace, (3) personal data store, (4) exchange, (5) aggregator, (6) enabler, (7) collaborative, (8) repository, or (9) cooperative (Data Econ. Lab, Data Stewardship Models, 2022). And, as one can imagine, each model has its own mechanism of governance and stewardship.

Under the Ostrom model, data is a resource to be managed as either a club good (non-rivalrous, yet structured as capable of exclusion), a common good/common pool resource (rivalrous but non-excludable), or a public good (non-rivalrous and non-excludable) (Hess & Ostrom, 2003, p.120).

In general, because digital data is most often considered non-rivalrous, the options are limited for the mechanisms of governance and stewardship. This limits the governance models to one capable of exclusion, or one not capable of exclusion. In many ways, local or regional digital data environments that exclude can and should be analyzed within the design principles established in *Governing the Commons* (Ostrom, 1990; McGinnis & Ostrom, 1992; Ostrom, 2000; Ruhaak, 2021). These well-known design principles are: (1) well-defined boundaries, (2) congruence between appropriation and provision rules and local conditions, (3) collective-choice arrangements, (4) monitoring, (5) graduated sanctions, (6) conflict-resolution mechanisms, (7) minimum recognition of rights, and (8) nested enterprises. (Ostrom, 1990).

Some recent research done in collaboration with Mozilla has started to translate Ostrom's design principles into a digital governance model (Ruhaak, 2021; Coyle, 2020). Drawing upon prior work completed by the Ada Lovelace Foundation, the newer framework, the design principles are: (1) clearly defined boundaries; (2) appropriate rules; (3) rule-making processes; (4) monitoring; (5)

sanctions; (6) conflict resolution; (7) right to self-governance; and (8) nestedness/interoperability (Ruhaak, 2021). As readers can see, the Ostrom design principles are clearly within the newer framework, with adjustments made for the digital nature of the goods in question, as envisioned by the Ada Lovelace Foundation's work. Yet even these principles depend on mechanisms of limitations (capable of exclusion).

However, with non-rivalrous *and* non-excludable characteristics, it might be time to embrace the global digital commons. To examine this area more closely, we can turn to lessons in natural resource governance. Within natural resource governance, it is generally agreed that the global commons are areas that lie beyond national jurisdiction. For example: the atmosphere, the high seas, and outer space. In comparison, Stern

> compares different types of commons, based on geographic scale, the number of resource users, salience, the distribution of interests and power, the level of cultural and institutional homogeneity, and the feasibility of 'learning' as a management strategy.
>
> *(Berge et al., 2011)*

Yet, the use of natural resource governance leaves some areas of concern as natural resources are, in fact, rivalrous. So, how should the global digital data commons be managed (Cole et al., 2019)? It is here where departure from the Ostrom model may be necessary. As described above, the Internet, as infrastructure, can certainly be thought of as a commons. Yet, this focuses on the infrastructure as the necessary area of governance. Can it also encapsulate the data itself, as an asset carried by the infrastructure? The answer is most likely "no," as the absence of rivalrousness, with the inability to exclude, is the hallmark of open data. Yet, when focusing on the data and not the infrastructure—how might this data within a global digital data commons be managed? At least one model would be to use the governance and stewardship of a knowledge commons.

The term "knowledge commons" refers to information, data, and content that is collectively owned and managed by a community of users, particularly over the Internet. Of course, as previously described, what distinguishes a knowledge commons is that digital resources are non-subtractable (Hess & Ostrom, 2007, pp.12–13). As a shared social-ecological system, a knowledge commons needs to remain committed to guarding against enclosure or other activities that place too high of a burden on entry. Of course, much of our scientific research and libraries are to be thought of as knowledge commons. As such, that does not eliminate property rights, per se, but commits property rights to be exercised in a manner that respects the commitment to non-enclosure. Moreover, at least some argue knowledge commons will be part of the long-term attempt to address some of our most pressing social issues—environment, medicine, and education, as knowledge commons are currently primarily considered within research and other intellectual communities.

In a somewhat contrasting position, Susan Aaronson, who leads the Digital Trade and Data Governance Hub, calls for policymakers to "explore the new means of digital cooperation" on a global level (Data Governance Hub, 2022). The Hub's recent work

> designed a new evidence-based metric to characterize a comprehensive approach to data governance at both the national and international levels. We divided data governance into six attributes (the dimensions in which nations act as they govern data) and subdivided these six into 26 indicators specific evidence of action. We then used the metric to assess 51 countries plus the European Union.
>
> *(Data Governance Hub, 2022)*

The metric, built after an initial survey of law, is an attempt to "weave strategies, ethical frameworks, technological challenges to governance (such as algorithmic discrimination), structural change (how government institutions are adapting and organizing to these new responsibilities), and participation/feedback processes into our framework" (Aaronson et al., 2022, p.6). The attributes: strategic, regulatory, responsible, structural, participatory, and international, are further subdivided into specific measures that are designed to allow for a broader assessment of data governance of a given country. Released in late 2021, it will undoubtedly lead to further research into the evolution of data governance on a global level.

Conclusion

The push to leverage insights of polycentric governance to better understand and protect critical infrastructure is, in many ways, just beginning. As the United States rolls out record-breaking infrastructure investments domestically, as the world battles the dueling global collective action challenges of climate change and cybersecurity, there is a need from both a theoretical and practical perspective to apply lessons from polycentricity to empower diverse multi-stakeholder communities. As we have seen, communication—and coordination—are essential elements in polycentric systems to avoid the associated pitfalls. These pitfalls are precursors to the trust and confidence-building mechanisms that are vital as the international community pivots to move from discussing cyber norms to operationalizing and verifying compliance with them.

In the area of data as the focus of a commons governance model, research into the mechanism of governance and stewardship necessary and sustainable for digital data needs to be undertaken. There are a growing number of mechanisms that appear as promising models. Of course, more work is needed, but certainly, the groundwork has been laid. Most promising are the efforts that are occurring to nudge the Ostrom models in key ways, never losing the fundamental underpinnings of the original model. Yet, innovation—as created by human beings working in tandem to produce, use, and share data in a cooperative manner—is an important long-term commitment to our global digital resources.

Yet, we have barely been able to scratch the surface of all the data governance and infrastructure topics and research questions that deserve further exploration using the analytical tools laid out by the Ostroms and their many collaborators. But we are likewise thankful that this edited volume tackles some of these issues and develops case studies to help further this analysis.

References

Aligica, Paul D., & Vlad Tarko, Polycentricity: From Polanyi to Ostrom, and Beyond, 25*Governance* 237–262 (2012).

Aaronson, Susan, Thomas Struett, & Adam Zable, DataGovHub Paradigm for a Comprehensive Approach to Data Governance: Year 1 Report 6 (2022), https://data govhub.letsnod.com/images/DataGov/Year%20one%20report%20final.pdf.

BEA, GDP by Industry, https://www.bea.gov/data/gdp/gdp-industry (Jan. 5, 2022).

Berge, Erling, & Frank van Laerhoven, Governing the Commons for Two Decades: A Complex Story, 5*Int'l J. Commons* 160–187 (2011) (summarizing Paul C. Stern, *Design Principles for Global Commons: Natural Resources and Emerging Technologies,* 5 Int'l J. Commons 213 (2011)).

Berkes, Fikret, *Coasts for People: Interdisciplinary Approaches to Coastal and Marine Resource Management.* Routledge (2015).

Cole, Daniel H., Graham Epstein, & Michael D. McGinnis, Combining the IAD and SES Frameworks, 13*Int'l J. Commons* 1 (2019), https://www.repository.law.indiana. edu/facpub/2741.

Coyle, Diane, Common Governance of Data: Appropriate Models for Collective and Individual Rights, Ada Lovelace Inst. (Oct. 30, 2020), https://www.adalovelacein stitute.org/blog/common-governance-of-data/.

Cyber Tech Accord, https://cybertechaccord.org/ (last visited Feb. 12, 2022).

Data Stewardship Models, Data Econ. Lab, https://tool.thedataeconomylab.com/our-da ta-models (last visited Feb. 12, 2022).

Digital Trade & Governance Hub, https://datagovhub.letsnod.com/ (last visited Feb. 12, 2022).

Dourado, Eli, *Is There a Cybersecurity Market Failure?* (George Mason Univ. Mercatus Ctr., Working Paper No. 12–05, 2012), http://mercatus.org/publication/there-cybersecurity-market-failure-0.

Dulong de Rosnay, Mélanie, & FrancescaMusiani, Alternatives for the Internet: A Journey into Decentralised Network Architectures and Information Commons, 18*Triple C Communism, Capitalism & Critique: Journal for a Global Sustainable Information Society*2 (2020), https://doi.org/10.31269/triplec.v18i2.1201.

Esterhuysen, Anriette, Deborah Brown, & Sheetal Kumar, *Unpacking the GGE's Framework on Responsible State Behaviour: Cyber Norms,* Ass'n Progressive Commc'ns & Glob. Partners Digit. (Dec. 20, 2019), https://www.gp-digital.org/wp-content/uploa ds/2019/12/unpacking_gge_cyber-norms.pdf.

FEMA, Critical Infrastructure: Long-term Trends and Drivers and Their Implications for Emergency Management, FEMA 2 (June2011), https://www.fema.gov/pdf/about/p rograms/oppa/critical_infrastructure_paper.pdf.

Frey, B., *Not Just for the Money: An Economic Theory of Personal Motivation.* Cheltenham: Elgar (2007).

Frey, Bruno S., & Felix Oberholzer-Gee, The Cost of Price Incentives: An Empirical Analysis of Motivation Crowding-Out, 87*Am. Econ. Rev.* 746–755 (1997).

Frischmann, Brett M., *Infrastructure: The Social Value of Shared Resources*. Oxford University Press (2013).

Frischmann, Brett M., Michael J. Madison, & Katherine J. Strandburg, Human-Focused Turing Tests: A Framework for Judging Nudging and Techno-Social Engineering of Human Beings, Cardozo Legal Studies Research Paper No. 441 (2014), https://papers.ssrn.com/sol3/papers.cfm?abstract_id=2499760.

Fuller, Lon, L., The Forms and Limits of Adjudication, 92*Harv. L. Rev.* 353–408 (1978).

Hanushek, Eric A., The Economics of Schooling: Production and Efficiency in Public Schools, 24*Journal of Economic Literature*31141–1177 (1986).

Hanushek, Eric A., Non-Labor-Supply Responses to the Income Maintenance Experiments, *Lessons from the Income Maintenance Experiments* 106–121 (1987).

Hathaway, Oona A., & Scott J. Shapiro, *The Internationalists: How a Radical Plan to Outlaw War Remade the World*. Simon & Schuster (2017).

Hess, Charlotte, & Elinor Ostrom, Ideas, Artifacts, and Facilities: Information as a Common Pool Resource, 66*L. & Contemp. Probs.* 111–145 (2003).

Hess, Charlotte, & Elinor Ostrom, eds., *Understanding Knowledge as a Commons: From Theory to Practice*. The MIT Press (2007).

Hinck, Garrett, Private-Sector Initiatives for Cyber Norms: A Summary, *Lawfare* (June 25, 2018), https://www.lawfareblog.com/private-sector-initiatives-cyber-norms-summary.

Keohane, Robert O., & David G. Victor, The Regime Complex for Climate Change, 9*Persps. Pol.* 1, 7–23 (2011).

McGinnis, Michael D., An Introduction to IAD and the Language of the Ostrom Workshop: A Simple Guide to a Complex Framework, 39*Pol'y Stud. J.* 1, 169–183 (2011).

McGinnis, Michael D., & Elinor Ostrom, Institutional Analysis and Global Climate Change: Design Principles for Robust International Regimes. In M. Rice, J. Snow, & H. Jacobson (eds.), *Global Climate Change: Social and Economic Research Issues*. Proceedings of a conference held at Argonne National Laboratory, Chicago, IL, 45–85 (1992).

McGinnis, Michael D., Elizabeth B. Baldwin, & Andreas Thiel, When Is Polycentric Governance Sustainable? Using Institutional Theory to Identify Endogenous Sources of Dysfunctional Dynamics (Sept. 14, 2020) (unpublished paper), https://ostromworkshop.indiana.edu/pdf/seriespapers/2020fall-colloq/mcginnis.pdf.

Olson, Mancur, *The Logic of Collective Action: Public Goods and the Theory of Groups*. Cambridge, MA: Harvard University Press (1965).

Ostrom, Elinor, Public Entrepreneurship: A Case Study in Ground Water Basin Management (1965), Ph.D. dissertation, University of California, Los Angeles, https://dlc.dlib.indiana.edu/dlc/handle/10535/3581. doi:10535/3581.

Ostrom, Elinor, R. B. Parks, & G. P. Whitaker, *Patterns of Metropolitan Policing*. Cambridge, MA: Ballinger Publishing Company (1978).

Ostrom, Elinor, *Governing the Commons: The Evolution of Institutions for Collective Action*. Cambridge University Press (1990).

Ostrom, Elinor, Collective Action and the Evolution of Social Norms, 14*Journal of Economic Perspectives*3, 137–158 (2000).

Ostrom, Elinor, *Understanding Institutional Diversity*. Princeton University Press (2005).

Ostrom, Elinor, Polycentric Systems as One Approach for Solving Collective-Action Problems 1–2 (Ind. Univ. Workshop in Pol. Theory and Pol'y Analysis, Working Paper No. 8–6, 2008), http://dlc.dlib.indiana.edu/dlc/bitstream/handle/10535/4417/W08-6_Ostrom_DLC.pdf.

Ostrom, Elinor, & Vincent Ostrom, The Quest for Meaning in Public Choice, 63*Am. J. Econ. & Socio.* 105–147 (2004), http://www.jstor.org/stable/3488034.

Ostrom, Elinor, & Harini Nagendra, Insights on Linking Forests, Trees, and People from the Air, on the Ground, and in the Laboratory, 103*Proc. Nat'l Acad. Scis. U.S. Am.* 51, 19224–19231 (2006).

Paris Call, Paris Call: For Trust and Security in Cyberspace (Nov. 12, 2018), https://pariscall.international/en/.

Polanyi, Michael, *The Logic of Liberty: Reflections and Rejoinders.* Liberty Fund (1951).

Prenkert, Jamie D., & Scott J. Shackelford, Business, Human Rights, and the Promise of Polycentricity, 47*Vand. J. Transnat'l L.* 451–500 (2014).

Ruhaak, Anouk, The *Governance* in Data Governance, Mozilla (Nov. 5, 2021), https://foundation.mozilla.org/en/blog/the-governance-in-data-governance/.

Shackelford, Scott J., *Governing New Frontiers in the Information Age: Toward Cyber Peace*, Cambridge University Press (2020).

Shivakoti, Ganesh, & Elinor Ostrom, eds., *Improving Irrigation Governance and Management in Nepal.* Oakland, CA: ICS Press (2002).

Siddarth, Divya, & E. Glen Weyl, *The Case for the Digital Commons*, World Econ. F. (June 2, 2021), https://www.weforum.org/agenda/2021/06/the-case-for-the-digital-commons/.

Teske, P., Mark Schneider, Michael Mintrom, & Samuel Best, Establishing The Micro Foundations of a Macro Theory: Information, Movers, and the Competitive Local Market for Public Goods, 87*American Political Science Review*3 (2013).

Trusted IoT Alliance, https://www.iiconsortium.org/ (last visited Feb. 12, 2022).

Wylie, Bianca, & Sean Martin McDonald, What Is a Data Trust, Ctr. Int'l Governance Innovation (Oct. 9, 2018), https://www.cigionline.org/articles/what-data-trust/.

3

INTERNET INTEROPERABILITY AND POLYCENTRIC ATTRIBUTES IN GLOBAL DIGITAL DATA ORDERING

Carolina Aguerre

1 Introduction: The Internet and Data Governance

While most major controversies concerning the governance of the Internet in its first years were over protocols and organizations involved in the coordination and management to ensure global interoperability and reach, many of the tensions that have surfaced since the early 2010s are predominantly on the content (as "digital data", see Chapter 1) that travels across these different networks. Even though the oversight of Internet protocols and their underlying infrastructure are still key sources of dispute in the governing of the digital space, the ability to control 'Internet data' and its flows implies unprecedented political, economic, and cultural power. As developed by Raymond and Shackelford (Chapter 2), a large portion of the actors involved in the data packets traveling on the Internet may or may not be interested in the data itself. In addition, business models on the Internet have shifted over the last decade and Internet traffic has become a relevant source of revenue for different players in the Internet value chain, from digital content platforms to network infrastructure providers (Van Couvering, 2011).

Against this political-economic backdrop, the chapter aims to bring in a more nuanced formulation of the issue of Internet fragmentation and digital data governance. It does so by exploring the relationship between the governance of Internet data flows and their effects on interoperability from a polycentric perspective. The work focuses on the elements that constitute Internet data as a phenomenon (Goertz, 2005) that may enable its distinction from other Internet governance contentions. This exercise is undertaken to bring some legibility to the currently (seemingly) disconnected array of themes, actors, and levels using data flows to affect the Internet's interoperability, consciously or unconsciously. Another objective of the work is to critically examine the attributes of

DOI: 10.4324/9781003388418-4

polycentric governance as developed by Scholte (2017) and Koinova et al. (2021) and how they enable or hinder explanations about the unfolding of data governance flows.

There are many pathways for Internet fragmentation based on data governance practices. The layer of content and applications involves the use of data and is contingent on a different set of political and commercial incentives (Drake et al., 2016). It is increasingly regulated by national authorities in the areas of competition, data protection, elections, intellectual property, law enforcement, and human rights, to name just a few of the different centres of authority, yet with limited power over the scope, scale, and capacity to enforce these measures. It is also subject to international and regional bodies, which are concerned with the uses of data for development purposes (World Bank, 2021), economic opportunity (EU Data Governance Act), but also for cybersecurity reasons (Group of Governmental Experts). The Internet's private sector has also engaged with data governance bodies with global implications, such as the Facebook Oversight Board for content moderation controversies over the platform. While the content layer or data layer have historically challenged the norms and practices that have driven global Internet interoperability, its unity, and the central normative component of the Internet protocol suite (TCP/IP), these two have coexisted and struggled with this network's characteristics (Goldsmith & Wu, 2006; Mueller, 2019).

This chapter develops the concept of polycentrism as a distinct formulation on the issue of digital data governance based on the international polycentric lenses developed in the introduction of the volume. The chapter is next organized into four sections: the first addresses the debates between the Internet's architecture and data flows; the second explores the attributes of polycentrism as applied to data governance, with a focus on those issues that affect the Internet's global interoperability; the third part addresses the systemic organizing forces of polycentric governance. In the conclusion, a short discussion addresses the status of these polycentric arrangements and how they enable novel conceptualizations of Internet governance norms and infrastructure.

2 Architectural Principles of the Internet and Data Policies

There is a vast repertoire of strategies being pursued by different state and non-state actors to achieve control over Internet data – based on data sovereignty, privacy, commercial interests, or other concerns, and using measures that range from the development of cloud infrastructure to forced data localization. IR scholarship touched upon the polycentric quality of communications networks and the Internet as an arrangement that lacks one central point of control (Scholte, 2021; Carr, 2015; Nye, 2014). There is a growing literature related to tensions emerging from data-driven platforms and how they shape the Internet, and vice versa (Claffy & Clark, 2014; Constantinides et al., 2018). Yet, there are still theoretical, as well as empirical gaps concerning how limitations to the flow of data, for economic, political, or other reasons, may impact in different ways the Internet's architectural principles and its broader normativity (ten Oever, 2021).

The Internet can be conceptualized as an infrastructure for innovation (van Schewick, 2016), that is, one that fosters different uses and applications. These possibilities for having multiple uses and actors are based on its architectural design principles or the 'tradition' of networking (Carpenter, 1996) of the Internet engineering community. While the architectural principles of the Internet have been debated and contested for three decades (Clark, 1988; Carpenter, 1996; van Schewick, 2016; DeNardis, 2014) and there is not one single version or consensus of what those principles were and how they have evolved, the Internet is still a relatively interoperable and open set of relations between human and non-human actors (Musiani, 2020).

In the introduction of the volume, the different traditions of polycentric theorizing were mapped considering their epistemological approach, analytical focus, and central levels of analysis. In this chapter, I am following the more global approach of polycentrism 3.0 based on Koinova et al. (2021) (and expanded in the Introduction of this volume) to address how the practices and policies concerning the restriction of data flows may shape and affect Internet interoperability, potentially leading to changes in the Internet protocols themselves. The perspective of interoperability in this work is broader than the protocols, to encompass technologies and data

> without the ability to understand and process what is being transmitted, it is insufficient for technological systems to have the capacity to pass bits from one system to another. The data layer is the ability of interconnected systems to understand each other.
>
> *(Gasser, 2015, p. 3)*

At the same time, the perspective that is chosen in this study for the purposes of scope and feasibility excludes other dimensions of interoperability, such as the human and institutional, which have been considered in other literature and policies (Gasser, 2015; European Commission, 2023). The approaches of interoperability beyond technical systems and protocols that have pervaded in the recent literature and technological policies are also addressing the polycentric characteristic of this dimension.

The next part of the chapter addresses a selection of cases and examples and is not a comprehensive compendium of all the policies and practices involved in data governance flows. Rather a selection of data/traffic policies that have effects on the Internet's interoperability and global reach are discussed. This study applies a broad conceptualization of data flows on the Internet and is complementary to Sautchuk's contribution in this volume, in Chapter 11, on data at the interconnection layer of the network stack.

3 Polycentric Attributes of Digital Data Governance

This first section unpacks seven attributes of polycentric governance. These are relevant to characterize when an issue is polycentric from the revised notion of polycentricity as "ordered chaos". Attributes are intrinsic parts or characteristics of an entity (Oxford English Dictionary). These polycentric attributes were originally identified for the governance arrangements concerning Internet resources and identifiers (Scholte, 2017). Here they are reconsidered to unpack how the bits and bytes of 'Internet data' and its governance affect the Internet's interoperability. The attributes that will be examined are *transscalar, transsectoral, diffusion, fluidity, overlapping mandates, ambiguous hierarchies*, and *no final arbiters*.

Transscalar

The attribute of transscalarity refers to the quality of transcending geographical boundaries. It is thanks to the Internet's global reach as a network that digital data faces much lower technical barriers to travel across different territories, provided there is a network infrastructure, including servers and devices, and interoperable communications protocols. When compared to non-digital data, data over the Internet travels at a greater speed, with all the power connotations entailed by enhanced acceleration (Virilio, 1996). Capturing, processing, storing and ultimately the transformation of data are part of the governance tensions as they rely on interconnected devices and networks controlled by different actors.

As data needs to "travel" across both space and time for many of its current uses (with the existing networked architecture and the economies of scale of business models that rely on different providers of digital) it is harder to bind than non-digital data. At the same time, cloud-based services which have revolutionized the infrastructure of the Internet over the last decade have generated greater centralization and less polycentricity from an infrastructure perspective (Mosco, 2016). Transscalarity is a key feature for the development of 'global markets' and 'global audiences' for digital services: entertainment and information based on data. While transscalarity may be achieved at an infrastructure level, it is being increasingly tampered by, to mention a few of the tensions, differences in copyright across jurisdictions, sovereignty concerns, and data protection regimes.

This transscalar quality of infrastructures for transporting and processing data is one of the challenges that have surfaced more commonly for law enforcement agencies, for data protection and copyright, security, or sovereign interpretations, which have tried to address transscalar data flows of the Internet with different measures and varying degrees of success.

While data flows were taken for granted as a 'global' commodity during the early years of the expansion of the Internet, the sources of any data point tend to originate with a person, an object, an organization/institution, and a jurisdiction/space. The data origins have not varied so greatly in the last century, what has changed is the capacity to capture, store, and process such vast amounts and obtain profits from them. The temporal dimension mentioned earlier emerges as a distinct feature of digital data when compared with non-digital data. With the Internet as the backdrop of transscalar data flows, there is a spatial and temporal lens that changes the characteristics of the problem around data governance. An example is the measures taken by The Christchurch Call. After a terrorist attack in two mosques in New Zealand in 2019 that live-streamed 50 deaths on social media over 17 minutes, this initiative backed by a few dozen governments and major platforms and civil society organizations released a 25-point commitment to curb the diffusion of terrorist content on the web. One of these actions is to 'accelerate research into and development of technical solutions to prevent the upload of and to detect and immediately remove terrorist and violent extremist content online'. There are many ways in which this can be approached, which include the inspection of data flows and highlight both the concerns of the geographical breadth and the speed in which this data may be uploaded, and thus the need to also respond hastily.

Transsectoral

The transsectoral arrangements of polycentric approaches capture the different actors involved in the process of setting rules, organizing and attaching a moral, ideological, or a market value to data, and the *assetization* of data (Birch et al., 2021). Because data can serve multiple purposes and be oriented at serving markets and consumers for scientific discovery, for advocacy, for the public interest, for government services, or for a combination of all, there are many different types of actors involved who hail from different sectors and that have different interests.

Typically, the Internet governance literature has referred to transsectoral aspects as multistakeholder (DeNardis & Raymond, 2013). Yet, when concerning data governance and its effects on global Internet interoperability, I propose that there are three major actors that have been traditionally involved in these arrangements: states, companies, and the technical Internet community. States have been particularly conspicuous in regulating data flows for the same reasons mentioned for the first attribute – sovereignty, security, privacy, copyright. In the case of companies, as data is at the heart of their business models, some have increased incentives to intervene not only to achieve greater control of content (as data) but even to shape Internet traffic through protocols. A case in point is QUIC.

The QUIC protocol began to be developed by Google around 2012. It was only presented at the Internet Engineering Task Force a few years later while it was being de facto applied by Chrome users all over the world. QUIC's main aim was to reduce latency, a characteristic whereby 'the delay before a transfer of data begins following an instruction for its transfer' (Oxford Learner's

Dictionaries, n.d.). This protocol was later taken up by engineers at the IETF, which have improved the Google version of QUIC (also labelled gQUIC) to what is known as QUIC "for clients to send data immediately" (RFC 9000). QUIC also enables better security and efficiency of Internet traffic. This is a case in point of how private sector motivations to enhance Internet traffic transfers affect the Internet's interoperability. As mentioned by Huston (2019) about QUIC, "there is a price to pay for this new-found agility, and that price is broad interoperability". QUIC is both an example of efficiency concerns in traffic/data which not only affects network infrastructure but is also a case of user experience and costs with implications and the involvement of several actors, underscoring the polycentric character of the problem and its solutions.

Diffusion of Authority

Diffusion entails scattered authority conceived in both power and legitimacy across different levels and includes diverse sectors as a marker of polycentricity. There are several examples of how this diffusion is manifested, depending on the digital data issue at stake. Internet shutdowns represent one of the most conspicuous and possibly counter-intuitive examples of the diffusion of authority concerning data flows. The counter-example is the Internet's cloud design, which marks a centralized approach.

Internet shutdowns have been as the "intentional disruption of Internet or electronic communications, rendering them inaccessible or effectively unusable, for a specific population or within a location often to exert control over the flow of information" (Internet Society, 2019). Shutdowns take several forms, among the most extreme is the cutting off of all types of connectivity (mobile, broadband, satellite) to prevent access to the Internet as such. A softer approach, which may be combined with the first, entails content-blocking techniques to restrict access to websites and communications apps.

Who has authority to order Internet blackouts or shutdowns? Governments. Usually, but not always in hybrid or authoritarian political systems (Feldstein, 2022; Vargas-Leon, 2016). Yet, while governments may have power to force Internet Service Providers (ISPs) and other Internet communications providers, they do not have sufficient authority nor legitimacy to effectively address a complete shutdown, as there are many ways in which users and connectivity providers may still not abide by the orders for a full shutdown. Companies such as Meta, which in some countries represent "the Internet", are also drawn into the debate of shutdowns when its platforms collapse or remain inaccessible.

The diffusion of authority in Internet blackouts may be exemplified by the Russian government's attempts on this matter, which have spiralled since its invasion of Ukraine in 2022. Even within the policies of a state that has been imposing greater restrictions on data flows, particularly since 2013 and the ensuing sanctions after the annexation of Crimea, it is unable to fully stop data flows coming in and out of its territory. Citizen strategies, civil society, and international firms do not abide by or comply with these rules not only because they can be protected (if they are operating outside of the territory) but also, and more fundamentally, they can also afford not to comply with political orders as they are backed by a decentralized infrastructure and cryptography, which somehow allows them to 'conceal for freedom' (Ermoshina & Musiani, 2022).

Despite this diffusion, there is a difference in the power coming from governments (Haggart et al., 2021), vis-à-vis other stakeholders when addressing Internet shutdowns. While the power might not be concentrated, a state actor can use existing norms and regulatory power to affect communications infrastructure with a greater effect than other private sector or civic actors.

As to hierarchical control to countervail polycentric arguments in this attribute, cloud infrastructure represents a clear centralization of the Internet (Mosco, 2016; Jaeger et al., 2008). The development of cloud infrastructure is intrinsically woven with interests connected with data processing capacity and efficiency. Many of the largest cloud providers are the firms that have become large Internet content platforms, such as Google, Amazon, and Microsoft.

Fluidity

Fluidity refers to the quality of non-stable, in-motion shapes of data governance mechanisms on the Internet. In other words, markers of this attribute for data governance are the continual appearance of new organizations, working groups, regulatory frameworks, and practices. The examples developed for the previous attributes are 'fluid' motions of this data governance on the Internet. The Christchurch Call was convened in less than two months after the attack to activate a multistakeholder community to eliminate terrorist and violent extremist content online and has become a reference point with its "25 commitments" for governments, large platforms, and civil society. The QUIC protocol evolved from a Google-lead initiative and deployed first as a de facto standard to address latency problems with Internet traffic without initial involvement from other sectors to become part of the IETF and as a networking standard codified as RFC 9000. Finally, the practice of Internet shutdowns has evolved over the last years, and while there are still attempts at total disconnection from the Internet at the infrastructure layer, there are now more initiatives focused on blocking content from specific applications (Feldstein, 2022).

The three examples show different tempos around the mechanisms, from the problem definition to the concurrence around a measure. Additionally, these cases show the repertoire of initiatives that may unfold in this fluid attribute: from sociotechnical instruments, such as the QUIC protocol, to governmental policies – and the concomitant practices of resistance from those opposing Internet blackouts – and also to multistakeholder platforms, such as The Christchurch Call. The temporal dimension is again a key to the understanding of a polycentric governance attribute.

Overlapping Mandates

As with the Internet's technical architecture, polycentric governance in digital data implies overlapping jurisdictions "where multiple agencies can claim competence over a given regulatory circumstance" (Scholte, 2017: 171). From an empirical perspective, overlapping mandates can be seen in many different sectors, from finance, to trade, to climate. In Scholte's previous analysis there were also overlaps emerging from the Internet governance regime (Nye, 2014).

The case of digital data poses cross-cutting challenges concerning mandates and overlaps with other sectors facing the same issues. One first example where data governance is being crucially discussed with effects on the Internet's interoperability is the handling of cross-border data flows and cybersecurity issues at the World Trade Organization (WTO). The treatment of these issues within the WTO brings in advocates for working within these institutional boundaries and arguing that it falls within the work scope of this organization, other opinions promote the establishment of new organizations. There is uncertainty concerning whether current WTO rules (written in the pre-Internet era) apply or not to digital trade issues (Panday & Malcolm, 2018). There is even a discussion as to whether data localization policies violate member countries' WTO obligations.

Another example emerges from the Court of Justice of the European Union which in 2015 restricted data flows from Europe to the United States because of concerns about the absence of sufficient privacy protections in the United States through the Schrems Case, which was followed in 2020 with another injunction.[1] While an initial reading of the case would suggest that it was concerned with privacy, there is a trade component as the data between European citizens and U.S. Internet firms was protected through a legal agreement (the Privacy Shield) which was a trade instrument. In recent years and with digital trade negotiations taking place, the European Union has taken a different approach to the United States in dealing with privacy issues in trade agreements, promoting an exclusion of privacy from trade agreements and addressing them in a separate legal arrangement under the General Data Protection Regulation (GDPR) called an "adequacy agreement", to allow for data exchange with the European Union (Sacks & Sherman, 2022). These are attempts to organize and circumscribe the issue as there is not a clear institutional focal point.

While there is a perception and past evidence that the proliferation of International Governmental Organizations (IGOs) generates overlapping mandates, new studies reflect that these overlaps are receding (Reinsberg & Westerwinter, 2023). The regulation of data flows over the Internet is still a hotly contested issue. But I argue that this is not because the organizations are poorly designed to address the problem of cross-border data flow regulation. Rather, it is that data flows are not for one purpose and that they change depending on what type of data it is (personal, proprietary, confidential) and who will be responsible for such uses. Instead of claiming that overlapping mandates riddle the domain of data governance, this attribute also showcases the institutional and regulatory vacuums and misfits around an issue whose constitutive elements are extremely elusive to pin down. This will be addressed in the next attribute of ambiguous hierarchies.

Ambiguous Hierarchies

Different instruments such as laws, conventions, frameworks, norms, and technical protocols for data have been in place for decades and it is implicitly or explicitly wrapped up in existing governance mechanisms around privacy, digital trade/e-commerce, and human rights law. This blurring of instruments and issues has had profound effects on the hierarchy of institutions to address many of these and with an impact on how the networked ecosystem is arranged. Cross-border data flows over the Internet provide once again a relevant example as the discussion about which institution should be responsible for their governance is one of the most contested and with a heavy reliance on the technical governance of the Internet.

As noted in the attribute of overlapping mandates, cross-border data flows can be framed as a trade-related issue, which has been supported by the U.S. government (not by the European Union), and that would entail trade rules and the WTO. This definition is being contested as data flows have other implications and could fall into other organizations' mandates if framed from a human rights or development perspective, or even from an Internet governance paradigm which has favoured a multistakeholder, bottom-up, and open model (Aguerre, 2019). For example, only for the theme of cross-border data flows the following issues have been identified as part of the tensions concerning their regulation: data protection and privacy legislation; national strategies to reap economic and developmental gains, while at the same time respecting HR; capacity-building activities and participatory approaches that foster developing countries to have a seat at the table (Ferracane & Lee-Makiyama, 2018; UNCTAD, 2021).

In the context of ambiguity in both the hierarchy and the mandates, these attributes of polycentric governance are being catalogued as 'weaknesses' of the current arrangements. A case in point is the recommendation by Digital Economy Report (UNCTAD, 2021) that proposes the creation of a new institutional development to meet the "global data governance challenge", with *the appropriate mix of multilateral, multistakeholder, and multidisciplinary engagement* (UNCTAD, 2021: 224). While data is still governed by different centres of authority and through various mechanisms, this is a call for centralization rather than polycentricity.

No Final Arbiter

The attribute of "no final arbiter" is a recursive device that cuts across the previous six. As portrayed by the analysis concerning the first attributes, there is not one single point of authority to address the different concerns emerging from the governance of data flows on the Internet and their effects on the network's interoperability. There is no such thing as one type of universal data which may be regulated or governed hierarchically, as it cuts across sectors and fulfils different objectives. It depends on the type of data involved, its uses, and the different types of institutional actors and instruments that will be employed. While data protection may have an ultimate decision point in national agencies, the issue is different for other uses concerning innovation, research (including Artificial Intelligence technologies), and economic development. There are difficulties in implementing data protection beyond a certain jurisdiction unless there is a more comprehensive approach that also brings in infrastructural control. National security and sovereignty concerns promote centralized control of data flows, but they are not enough to promote their centralization. In theory, all these different purposes and policies affect which types of data are allowed to be transferred and to cross a jurisdictional border. In practice that control is more chaotic and fluid. While the control of data flows for any of the above reasons may not necessarily affect interoperability at the protocol level, they impose additional points of control or centres of authority, that is, chokepoints which could potentially increase more centralized governance arrangements.

4 Systemic Ordering Forces

The seven attributes developed earlier were an exercise to understand how Internet data unfolds or not in a polycentric governance characterization. These attributes interacted with each other in a highly reflexive way, and it was not always straightforward to neatly unpack and match either the governance of data flows or the tensions concerning the support of a globally interoperable Internet. The systemic ordering forces that will be addressed in this section provide a chance to bring more cohesiveness to the analysis and characterization of the attributes. Other chapters in this volume from Sautchuk and Campbell-Verduyn (Chapter 11 and 12 respectively) also bring in the ordering forces to their respective analysis since these provide a relevant heuristic device to organize the seemingly unconnected and disorganized issues. The three systemic ordering forces are *norms*, *practices*, and *underlying structures* and they allow us to move beyond an ontological characterization of data governance through a lens of polycentric attributes, to one where the relations between these three forces and their interconnections are rendered. It helps to move beyond a structural approach concerning issues and institutions, as well as from dissecting the different drivers in isolation (Scholte, 2021).

Norms

> Norms are general articulated principles that inform the process of governing [...] The notion is that certain guiding ideas of the good and the correct become embedded in the conduct of world politics, such that they acquire a force of their own, separate from the actors who enact them.
>
> *(Scholte, 2021: 43)*

Norms become part of the organizing vectors of institutional approaches. In this chapter, a basic underlying norm that is being examined is that of Internet interoperability, as its desirability is taken for granted and that is a normative condition. But in addition, there is a relationship that is being explored on the extent of the 'damage' to the global Internet interoperability that emerges from the tensions derived to control the data flows. Are polycentric governance approaches to data a cause, a consequence, or even a precondition derived from previous processes of datafication, digitalization, and enhanced computer networking capabilities over the Internet? There is not one single answer to these questions, but it underscores how there are multiple norms involved in the issue.

In the first place, normativity is embedded in the technical infrastructure that is not manifested as a written rule, nor as an aspirational guide, but as a condition for certain behaviours, practices, and imaginaries. An open, interoperable Internet may favour integration and cooperation, but some of the governance of the traffic may be following other interests, such as cyberattacks or Internet blackouts.

In the second place, there are long-standing norms and a tradition of State involvement and regulation concerning data and content, even before the Internet and digitization. This normativity has always been present in Internet governance debates and has left States as the actors with the greatest stakes to stop global data flows over the Internet for content regulation purposes (which may imply different issues, from copyright protection to censorship of forbidden material, to the protection of private and sensitive data and to national security).

We have been able to identify different types of norms for this issue and they become a marker of polycentricity as they share many of the polycentric attributes developed earlier. Yet, norms on their own do not explain the unfolding of these preferences and behaviours.

Practices

There is even more diversity in the practices surrounding data governance. This is a second type of structure in polycentric governance that falls into the "practice turn" approach of International Relations.

> Whereas norms refer to what people believe in, practices relate to what people do. While norms are explicitly articulated, practices are often tacit and even unconscious.
>
> (Scholte, 2021: 70)

Recent explorations on polycentric governing from this perspective include the regulating effects of everyday routines (Mencutek, 2021; Bueger & Gadinger, 2018). The way "things are done" in the world of the Internet has incorporated some degree of order (which ultimately reflects a technocratic approach) through practices that relate to functional, running programs, such as "code is law" (Lessig, 1999) or the "culture of innovation" that is present in many of the data-driven Internet corporations.

As mentioned previously in the attributes section, practices that have been identified concerning data flows over the Internet have different purposes and instruments. The Christchurch Call platform or the efforts to generate Internet shutdowns are different kinds of practices: the first institutionalized and responsive to a global demand to curb the spread of terrorist content, the second as part of the repertoire of possibilities employed by governments to contain domestic pressure. The control of Internet data flows is the symptom of more profound causes for socio-political discontent.

Underlying (Infra) Structures

Finally, the last systemic ordering force to be analyzed from a polycentric perspective concerns the underlying structures, defined as

> macro structures that underpin – and manifest themselves through – norms and practices, as well as actor motivations and decisions. Underlying orders are systemic: they permeate – and integrate – all locations and connections in a polycentric regime.
>
> *(Scholte, 2021: 75)*

Underlying structures are the most invisible and deeply embedded approaches that ultimately shape much of the conscious adoption of norms and practices in a polycentric arrangement. The governance of data flows on the Internet is a contested point of underlying orders that depend on the actors, purposes, and uses of the data and its types, as mentioned in the Introduction of this volume.

International Internet connectivity can be conceptualized as a global public good (Canazza, 2018, Raymond, 2012), based on the interconnection of over 70,000 networks where data packets are running through them with the Internet Protocol (TCP/IP). This conceptualization resonates with the Internet as an 'information commons' (Raymond and Shackleford in Chapter 2) with many centers of power, authority, and control. The control of this interconnection of networks that allow for these data flows remains one of the most distributed approaches to communications that challenge centralized controls. This has been a systemic underlying structure that has been openly sustained and supported in different fora for the last three decades by many different actors, from the technical community, civil society, companies, and a large majority of governments that have explicitly supported this global model of interconnectivity. "Internet connectivity means anyone with access can use the Internet to communicate. This means aggressors and opponents alike. Unlike most historical communication methods, the Internet is astonishingly resilient when conditions for connection are bad. It's not magic. It won't end wars or invasions. But it is a great tool for humans to use against their oppressors" were the words of the

Internet Society's director in March 2022 as the war in Ukraine unfolded with cries from many sectors to shut down the Internet for Russia as part of the sanctions package. The sole idea of one institutional actor having the power to disconnect, unplug, or cut off a country from the Internet has been anathema from the sociotechnical imaginaries (Abbate, 1999) that are underlying orders of this network.

The Internet enables the transport of this data that is shared and consumed as "content" by Internet users. The fundamental underlying order of the Internet as this network of networks, polycentric by design, and the values that stem from this open, end-to-end architecture are key principles that sustain the underlying structure of global digital data ordering. While these ordering forces may seem taken for granted and as global values, this socio-technical imaginary over the Internet architecture by protocols hovers between "a technological dream and an economic reality" (ten Oever, 2021: 346) where centralization rather than polycentricity begins to prevail. The critical approaches to contemporary capitalism and its failures to redress imbalances in users' data stemming from digital platforms (Mazzucato, 2018), which benefitted from the original public funding that developed the initial Internet protocols and the architecture that sustains these imaginaries underscore the role of large technological corporations.

Adding to ten Oever's (2021) and Mazzucato's (2018) critique on the role of economic forces that shape the Internet environment, there is also a political reality that challenges protocol interoperability and openness with non-Western actors, as especially China is developing Internet protocols that promote greater centralization and state control of the Internet (Taylor et al., 2022). Economic and political power are centralizing, rather than diversifying the limited repertoire of governance opportunities for the control of Internet infrastructure and their data flows. Actors' constraints emerge from the different political and economic tensions which are rarely monolithic, and also with respect to the open interoperable infrastructure where these rules try to become embedded.

Concluding Remarks

This chapter has used polycentrism as a conceptual lens for understanding the governance of data flows over the Internet and its effects on the global interoperability of this infrastructure. The study has shown that the governance of data flows is inextricably linked to the Internet's centres of power.

It first discussed the turn of Internet governance debates, originally centred on identifiers, resources, and institutions to bring order and authority over these issues in the 1990s, to a more cross-cutting dimension of Internet governance concerning the data flows which are contemporary sources of political and economic power, and which are recursively affecting the same open and interoperable infrastructure that initially empowered many of these interests.

The theoretical attributes developed in Section 3 helped to identify different types of dependencies between data flows and Internet infrastructure, as well as difficulties in dissecting each attribute as independent from the other. Attribute analysis has also exposed the many interpretations and consequences that emerge from different practices concerning Internet data flows. Attributes have also exposed the multiplicity of actors, levels, issues, and spaces, as well as the temporal dimension as one which is crucial, not only to better understand the unfolding of these governance processes (Virilio, 1996) but also because time itself is part of the data flow problem and is still looking for both questions and answers.

While at first glance it may seem that large technological corporations have the biggest share of data and this ownership may imply that they can unilaterally define the rules about its governance and that of the Internet, polycentric theorizing based on attributes and underlying orders in Section 4 challenge some of the inexorable trends towards centralization. Governments have been traditionally invested with the power to protect national interests and legitimate concerns related to the protection of fundamental human rights. These actors aim to re-centralize that power from big tech and may undermine diversity and the polycentric governance of data flows. Yet, this chapter has also shown that despite these efforts, their power has limitations when examining these arrangements with a polycentric lens. Data flow governance may be characterized as a polycentric configuration, considering its embeddedness in the technical and institutional features of the Internet. Polycentric theorizing allows us to unpack the tensions and contestations that emerge in the politics and practices around the efforts to upkeep an interoperable Internet.

Note

1 In 2013 the Austrian citizen Maximilian Schrems filed a complaint against Facebook Ireland Ltd with the Irish Data Protection Commissioner, as it was the country where Facebook has its European Headquarters. The complaint was aimed at prohibiting Facebook from further transferring data from Ireland to the United States, given the alleged involvement of Facebook USA in the PRISM mass surveillance program. This was followed by complaints in 2018–2019 over non-compliance with the GDPR by that company and several other U.S. tech corporations which led to an invalidation of the "Privacy Shield" by the European Court of Justice.

References

Abbate, J. (1999). *Inventing the internet*. MIT Press.

Aguerre, C. (2019). Digital trade in Latin America: Mapping issues and approaches. *Digital Policy, Regulation and Governance*, 21(4). https://doi.org/10.1108/DPRG-11-2018-0063.

Birch, K., Cochrane, D., & Ward, C. (2021). Data as asset? The measurement, governance, and valuation of digital personal data by Big Tech. *Big Data & Society*, 8(1). https://doi.org/10.1177/20539517211017308.

Bueger, C., & Gadinger, F. (2018). Situating practice in social theory and international relations. In C. Bueger & F. Gadinger (Eds.), *International practice theory* (pp. 13–33). Springer International Publishing. https://doi.org/10.1007/978-3-319-73350-0_2.

Canazza, M. R. (2018). The Internet as a global public good and the role of governments and multilateral organizations in global internet governance. *Meridiano 47 – Journal of Global Studies*, 19. doi:10.20889/M47e19007.

Carpenter, B. E. (1996). *Architectural principles of the Internet* (Request for Comments RFC 1958). Internet Engineering Task Force. https://doi.org/10.17487/RFC1958.

Carr, M. (2015). Power plays in global internet governance. *Millennium*, 43(2), 640–659. https://doi.org/10.1177/0305829814562655.

Claffy, K., & Clark, D. (2014). Platform models for sustainable internet regulation. *Journal of Information Policy*, 4, 463–488.

Clark, D. (1988). The design philosophy of the DARPA (Defense Advanced Research Projects Agency) internet protocols. *Symposium Proceedings on Communications Architectures and Protocols – SIGCOMM '88*, 106–114. https://doi.org/10.1145/52324.52336.

Constantinides, P., Henfridsson, O., & Parker, G. G. (2018). Introduction—Platforms and infrastructures in the Digital Age. *Information Systems Research*, 29(2), 381–400.

DeNardis, Laura. (2014). *Protocol politics*. MIT Press.

DeNardis, L., & Raymond, M. (2013). Thinking clearly about multistakeholder internet governance (SSRN Scholarly Paper No. 2354377). https://doi.org/10.2139/ssrn.2354377.

Drake, W. J., Vinton G. Cerf, & Wolfgang Kleinwächter. (2016). *Internet fragmentation: An overview*. Geneva: The World Economic Forum. https://www3.weforum.org/docs/WEF_FII_Internet_Fragmentation_An_Overview_2016.pdf.

Ermoshina, K., & Musiani, F. (2022). *Concealing for freedom*. Mattering Press.

European Commission. (2023). The European Interoperability Framework in detail. *Joinup*. https://joinup.ec.europa.eu/collection/nifo-national-interoperability-framework-observatory/european-interoperability-framework-detail.

Feldstein, S. (2022). *Government internet shutdowns are changing: How should citizens and democracies respond?*Carnegie Endowment for International Peace. Retrieved 29 March 2023 from https://carnegieendowment.org/2022/03/31/government-internet-shutdowns-are-changing.-how-should-citizens-and-democracies-respond-pub-86687.

Ferracane, M. F., & Lee-Makiyama, H. (2018). *Digital Trade Restrictiveness Index*. ECIPE. https://globalgovernanceprogramme.eui.eu/wp-content/uploads/2019/09/Digital-Trade-Restrictiveness-Index.pdf.

Gasser, Urs. (2015). Interoperability in the digital ecosystem. Berkman Klein Center for Internet and Society Research Publication No. 2015–13. http://dx.doi.org/10.2139/ssrn.2639210.

Goertz, Gary. (2005). *Social science concepts*. Princeton University Press.

Goldsmith, J., & Wu, T. (2006). *Who controls the Internet? Illusions of a borderless world*. Oxford University Press.

Haggart, B., Tusikov, N., & Scholte, J. A. (Eds.). (2021). *Power and authority in internet governance: Return of the State?*Routledge. https://doi.org/10.4324/9781003008309.

Huston, Geoff. (2019). A quick look at QUIC. *The Internet Protocol Journal*, 22(1), 2–12.

Internet Society. (2019). *Internet shutdowns: An internet society public policy briefing*. https://www.internetsociety.org/wp-content/uploads/2020/02/ISOC-PolicyBrief-Shutdowns-2019.pdf.

Jaeger, P. T., Lin, J., & Grimes, J. M. (2008). Cloud computing and information policy: Computing in a policy cloud? *Journal of Information Technology & Politics*, 5(3), 269–283. https://doi.org/10.1080/19331680802425479.

Koinova, M., Deloffre, M. Z., Gadinger, F., Mencutek, Z. S., Scholte, J. A., & Steffek, J. (2021). It's ordered chaos: What really makes polycentrism work. *International Studies Review*, 23(4), 1988–2018. https://doi.org/10.1093/isr/viab030.

Lessig, L. (1999). *Code and other laws of cyberspace*. Basic Books, Inc.

Mazzucato, Mariana. (2018). *Let's make private data into a public good*. MIT Technology Review. https://www.technologyreview.com/2018/06/27/141776/lets-make-private-data-into-a-public-good/.

Mencutek, Z. S. (2021). Techniques in the polycentric governing of irregular migration. Part of Koinova, M., Deloffre, M. Z., Gadinger, F., Mencutek, Z. S., Scholte, J. A., & Steffek, J. (2021). It's ordered chaos: What really makes polycentrism work. *International Studies Review*, 23(4), 1988–2018. https://doi.org/10.1093/isr/viab030.

Mosco, V. (2016). After the Internet: Cloud computing, Big Data and the Internet of Things. *Les Enjeux de l'information et de la communication*, 17(2), 146–155. https://doi.org/10.3917/enic.021.0145.

Mueller, M. L. (2019). Against sovereignty in cyberspace. *International Studies Review*, 22(4), 779–801. https://doi.org/10.1093/isr/viz044.

Musiani, F. (2020). Science and technology studies approaches to internet governance: Controversies and infrastructures as internet politics. In L. DeNardis, D. Cogburn, N. Levinson, & F. Musiani (Eds.), *Researching internet governance: Methods, frameworks, futures*. MIT Press. https://doi.org/10.7551/mitpress/12400.003.0005.

Nye, J. (2014). The regime complex for managing complex Cyber Activities. Global Commission on Internet Governance. Chatham House: CIGI (Centre for International Governance Innovation). https://www.cigionline.org/static/documents/gcig_paper_no1.pdf.

Oxford Learner's Dictionaries. (n.d.). Latency. https://www.oxfordlearnersdictionaries.com/us/definition/english/latency?q=latency.

Panday, Jyoti, & Malcolm, Jeremy. (2018). The political economy of data localization. *Partecipazione e Conflitto*, 11(2), 511–527.

Raymond, Mark. (2012, October 26). *The Internet as a global commons?* CIGI (Centre for International Governance Innovation). https://www.cigionline.org/publications/internet-global-commons/.

Reinsberg, B., & Westerwinter, O. (2023). Institutional overlap in global governance and the design of intergovernmental organizations. *The Review of International Organizations*. https://doi.org/10.1007/s11558-023-09488-2.

Sacks, S., & Sherman, J. (2022). *Global data governance. concepts, obstacles, and prospects*. New America.

Scholte, Jan Aart. (2021). Structuring polycentrism: Norms, practices and underlying orders in internet governance. Part of Koinova, M., Deloffre, M. Z., Gadinger, F., Mencutek, Z. S., Scholte, J. A., & Steffek, J. (2021), It's ordered chaos: What really makes polycentrism work. *International Studies Review*, 23(4), 1988–2018. https://doi.org/10.1093/isr/viab030.

Scholte, Jan Aart. (2021). Structuring polycentrism: Norms, practices and underlying orders in internet governance. In M. Koinova, M. Z. Deloffre, F. Gadinger, Z. S. Mencutek, J. A. Scholte, & J. Steffek (Eds.), It's ordered chaos: What really makes polycentrism work. *International Studies Review*, 23(4), 1988–2018. https://doi.org/10.1093/isr/viab030.

Taylor, Emily, McFadden, Mark, & Caeiro, Carolina. (2022). *Standards: The new frontier for the free and open internet*. Oxford: DNS (Domain Name System) Research Federation. https://dnsrf.org/blog/standards–the-new-frontier-for-the-free-and-open-internet/index.html.

Taylor, L. (2017). What is data justice? The case for connecting digital rights and freedoms globally. *Big Data & Society*, 4 (2). doi:10.1177/2053951717736335.

ten Oever, N. (2021). "This is not how we imagined it": Technological affordances, economic drivers, and the Internet architecture imaginary. *New Media & Society*, 23 (2), 344–362. https://doi.org/10.1177/1461444820929320.

UNCTAD. (2021). *Digital Economy Report 2021. Cross-border data flows and development: For whom the data flow*. Geneva: United Nations. https://unctad.org/publication/digital-economy-report-2021.

van Schewick, B. (2016). Internet architecture and innovation in applications. In Barbara van Schewick (Ed.), *Handbook on the Economics of the Internet* (pp. 288–322). https://econpapers.repec.org/bookchap/elgeechap/14700_5f14.htm.

Van Couvering, Elizabeth. (2011). Navigational media: The political economy of online traffic. In D. Winseck & D. Y. Jin (Eds.), *The Political economies of media: The transformation of the global media industries*. Bloomsbury Academic. https://doi.org/10.5040/9781849664264.

Vargas-Leon, P. (2016). Tracking internet shutdown practices: Democracies and hybrid regimes. In F. Musiani, D. L. Cogburn, L. DeNardis & N. S. Levinson (Eds.), *The turn to infrastructure in internet governance* (pp. 167–188). Palgrave Macmillan US. https://doi.org/10.1057/9781137483591_9.

Virilio, P. (1996). *Speed and politics*. MIT Press.

World Bank. (2021). World Development Report 2021: Data for Better Lives. https://wdr2021.worldbank.org.

4

THE CHALLENGES OF GOVERNANCE IN A DATASCAPE

Theorizing the Role of Non-extractive Methodologies in the 2030 Agenda

Isabel Rocha de Siqueira and Laís Ramalho

If we have been datafied beings for a while, the UN 2030 Agenda, with its set of 17 Sustainable Development Goals (SDGs), 169 targets, and 232 indicators, has made that point irrevocable. This fact is demonstrated by the several philanthropic, private, and public initiatives created to provide quantitative data that the United Nations and partner agencies suggest we need in order to 'build back' from the COVID-19 pandemic. However, a key issue the chapter wants to highlight is that data needed for monitoring social issues are not always data that are driving action on the ground. This means that global data governance should not be driven to produce data for data's sake. With that in mind, we suggest that there is a need for efficient polycentric and multiscale governance that is guided by a more profound understanding of how data governance and governance by data can in fact contribute to a social justice agenda.

This chapter highlights the inequalities that populate what we call the *datascape*, of which we take the datafying practices around the 2030 Agenda as proxy. We call a *datascape* the fluidity of perspectives on data we find in the different datasets and the varied modes of engagement that form the vast landscape of datafied beings and things. The *datascape* can encompass different themes at different times and how we approach it depends on our own situatedness. Thus, the notion allows us to move from the determinism of a technology-centred data governance to a more situated and embodied perspective.

We start, in the following section, precisely with Appadurai's idea of a fractioned and irregular global system and his work on the different disjointed landscapes that compose the global economy. We move then to de Sousa Santos's notion of non-extractive methodologies so we can establish some basis for a discussion on justice. That discussion takes place through various insights derived from our empirical engagement with situated and embodied knowledges in citizen-generated data (CGD) projects focused on the SDGs in Rio de

DOI: 10.4324/9781003388418-5

Janeiro, Brazil. The chapter aims to arrive at a multifaceted notion for thinking polycentricity in global digital data governance.

By looking at citizen-generated data (CGD), we learned that the lack of data about certain communities or of data usability in certain contexts is not necessarily a side-effect of the *datascape*, but its ontological necessity. So long as a lack of (reusable) data seems a challenge from the past that technology and modern governance can fix, more and better (in the infrastructural sense) data will remain the future and most logical (only) response. Analyzing what CGD can offer, instead, is one way to show that not all data in the world can compensate for inequalities on the ground. Making data governance 'work' should be as much about the data produced as about how production takes place, who is involved, and how stories that make a difference are being told with the help of data.

Such observations lead us to argue for attention to political matters, that is, a careful look at what should not be considered merely technical but is instead central to the democratic debate: while infrastructural issues of interoperability tend to be emphasized, we argue for a more central role to issues of *relationality*, that is, how data enacts diffuse agency, impacting subjectivities, identities, and political truths. We suggest polycentric data governance should prioritize mutual learning, safeguard space for experimentation by people living the reality of social issues on the ground, and incentivize innovation not only in terms of material technologies but of social processes as well.

The chapter stresses the importance of both seeing *with* data and of thinking of who is made visible in the *datascape*. That way, data governance is about technical capacity and 'bits and bytes' as much as it is about community, and the latter needs to be made a crucial part of any new global political propositions.

The 2030 Agenda as a *Datascape*

In April 2021, a report by the UN Secretary-General on the progress towards the Sustainable Development Goals (SDGs) exposed the immense challenges we face as societies, all of which have been compounded by the pandemic of COVID-19. The tragedy of more than 6 million lives lost (Ritchie et al., 2020) is combined with the on-going health, economic, and social crises everywhere. As part of the envisaged responses, the mentioned report suggested '[t]he ability of governments to respond effectively and achieve a better recovery will also depend on the availability of data' (United Nations, 2021b, p. 3). The document lists how the many targets established by the UN 2030 Agenda are showing distressing signs: around 199 to 124 million additional people became poor in 2020, the extreme poverty rate is increasing for the first time in a generation, and 8 out of 10 'new poor' are in middle-income countries and territories (United Nations, 2021b, p. 4).

Although officially approved by the member states of the United Nations in September 2015, the 2030 Agenda was born from a polycentric process. It took several actors (governments, international organizations and agencies, the private sector, civil society organizations, scholars, and individuals) and several fora (the United Nations Conference on Sustainable Development (Rio+20), the Addis Ababa Action Agenda on Financing for Development, and even online public consultations) to build the complex system we now call the 2030 Agenda. Its execution also can only be achieved through a polycentric strategy: the system relies on flows of information, resources, and practices traveling in all directions. An example of a bottom-up flow is often found in local data being integrated into the global monitoring of the SDGs while a top-down flow example is the efforts of the United Nations to build monitoring capacity of national and local statistics institutions (United Nations, 2021a).

As a complex dashboard, if data are to be produced on all themes of the 2030 Agenda, we would have the most complete informational system of all times and, following the rallying call of the SGDs, it seems reasonable to imagine we would 'leave no one behind'. However, 'data driving action might not be the same as data evidencing progress on the indicators' (Jameson et al., 2018, p. 12).

Therefore, if differentiating between data for monitoring and data for action might be needed in certain contexts, it is also crucial to understand and theorize about how working across scales and with different forms of data collection present enormous challenges to data governance and politics (Idem). Critical voices in data studies have been emphasizing the role of the local in datafication. Loukissas (2019), for instance, claims that, in many ways, 'all data are local', a notion that aligns with the view expressed above that action is a crucial goal of datafication and it often happens on the ground, that is, in situated contexts. Nevertheless, much of the decision-making processes about the data infrastructure being built around and through the SDGs are not able to take the *local* into account with the same theoretical, not to mention political, weight. The issue with this is that relations of power are born and maintained through such decisions, which frame, construct, and intervene in global agendas.

Power in the *Datascape*

Collaborating in another project that approaches the 2030 Agenda as an 'epistemic infrastructure' (Tichenor et al., 2022), we argued the SDGs can be perceived as an epistemic representation of the cumulative effects of datafying practices (Rocha de Siqueira & Ramalho, 2022). In this sense, the Agenda historically accumulates the discourses and practices imbricated in power relations around knowledge production, while also representing the Western scientific overreliance on technological solutions to solve problems often created by this very reasoning. We want to unpack this idea in order to set the scene to discuss the different relations of power/knowledge implicated in the SDGs *datascape*.

Saying that there is an overreliance on technological solutions in the SDGs *datascape* means that many technological fixes are being explored to generate and analyze data for monitoring the SDGs. Big Data is a case in point, along with its 'ecosystem[s] of new data, new tools and new actors', which Letouzé

(2015) has called the '3Cs': 'crumbs, capacities and community' (p. 4). The 'crumbs' have to do with Deleuze's (2017) notion that we have become 'dividuals', that is, 'the decomposition of individuals into data clouds subject to automated integration and disintegration' (Terranova, 2004, p. 34). When Big Data is advanced as a possible complementary solution to producing data – in this case, about the SDGs – the idea is to be able to recombine our 'microstate' data (web use and behaviour data, for instance), as necessary for different purposes, into 'macrostates' (categories, 'measurable types') that are not necessarily equal or restricted to the ones we consider we 'politically own' (Cheney-Lippold, 2017, p. 26). It is in that sense that we can say that 'we are temporary members of different emergent categories' (Cheney-Lippold, 2017, p. 11): 'there is no single, static sense of us but rather an untold number of competing, modulating interpretations of data that make up who we are' (Cheney-Lippold, 2017, p. 27). At play, therefore, are matters of power over the means and the know-how to intervene and govern such modulating interpretations.

In terms of capacities and community, Letouzé (2015) highlights the importance of considering 'Big Data is not just big data – but also tools and techniques that are largely developed and mastered outside the reach and realm of traditional policymaking' (p. 6). Big Data, nevertheless, is but one possibility; there are various data sources. A document elaborated by GIZ and the Global Partnership for Sustainable Development Data proposes four categories: geospatial data, citizen-generated data, privately-held data, and administrative data.[1] Big Data can cross all of them. The case in point is that the *existence* of data ('*availability*' is relative) has been commensurate with the diagnosed need for more: the more data are generated, the more data seem to be required. However, as suggested above, all the data types in the world cannot compensate for politics on the ground and the structural inequalities we witness taking shape in everyday life. This is, perhaps, why '[i]nevitably, then, today's explosion of data, a by-product of the computer revolution, has created new conjunctions between numbers and norms' (Jasanoff, 2017, p. 1) as the data explosion has evidenced and created new disjunctures as well.

After all, if data required for monitoring are not always data required for action, then a series of key questions needs to be at the forefront of global data governance, such as 'how many resources are being diverted for producing data that are not for action?' And 'if the tools and techniques employed are or can be largely outside of the realm of traditional policymaking, who is validating decisions about what data are generated and how?' These are reflexive questions about governance that should permeate legal frameworks, legislative processes, and accountability practices that seek to address inequalities in the international system.

We propose to address these questions by thinking in terms of a *datascape* that is inspired by Appadurai's work on global cultural flows. In a 1990 article that took stock of the many changes in a world that was becoming rapidly globalized with the help of technologies, Appadurai talks about ethnoscapes, mediascapes, technoscapes, financescapes, and ideoscapes, and justifies the use of the suffix by saying that these are 'highly perspectival constructs', marked by 'historical, linguistic and political situatedness'. Moreover, he adds, these are the *'building blocks'* of 'imagined worlds', a term which perhaps does not help make his more important argument that these landscapes are 'fluid' and 'irregular' (Jasanoff, 2017, p. 1). We will not dwell on the particularities of each landscape; it suffices to say that thinking about the landscape of digital data today as *datascape* can help us account for both issues of *interoperability*, that is, in a loose definition, the matter of making data reusable, which is related to standardization, semantics, and infrastructure (Morales & Orell, 2018), and issues of *relationality*, which, at an ontological level, regards the diffuse agency enacted by data in becoming the macrostates mentioned above, that is, subjectivities, identities and, political truths.[2] If interoperability directs one to think of material processes, techniques, and structures, relationality leads to the realization that all these *and* the political truths of "self" and "other" are constantly moving, in fluid and irregular flows. This is so that the fact of establishing a procedure, creating a dataset, or deriving conclusions from data needs to be accompanied by the notion that any such constructions are situated. The absence of this reflexivity might just reinforce inequalities instead of addressing them, no matter how sophisticated data governance processes are designed to be, technologically speaking.

Again, following Appadurai (1990), we can say *datascape* is about the 'deeply disjunctive and profoundly unpredictable' landscape of digital data (p. 298). As a part of this datascape, the informational system that is now the 2030 Agenda 'simultaneously represent[s] the world "out there", the organizational context of their application ... and the political and social roots of that context' (Bowker & Star, 2000, p. 61). That means that it is not enough that new forms of global digital data governance are developed to address seemingly technical infrastructural issues of interoperability so that datafying systems are able to *count* more effectively. It is vital to take into account the ethical and political issues that reside in the construction and functioning of these systems, meaning that they need to go beyond *counting* towards *accounting* for the prioritization in data production and circulation and for the historical injustices in knowledge production – the epistemic violences that are central components of this *datascape*,[3] as we will discuss next, by looking into how counting and accounting practices relate on the ground.

Data Governance Without Data Extractivism: The Role of Citizen-Generated Data

We live in a world that currently abounds with data and their correlations (Jasanoff, 2017). Some argue little is achieved in contrast to all the information that is produced. Big Data and other elements of an epistemic reconfiguration have been 'credited' with the 'death of theory' – all we need is correlations

(Anderson, 2008). In this explosion of correlations, we can lose sight of why any of them are important at all. Enter the narratives. Indeed, it is instructive to relate narratives and the abundance of numerical digital data.

It has been in the territories, in the municipalities – on the ground, so to say, that the narratives for rights, quality of life, and democracy have been stronger, in comparison to global-level institutions. There is where there is clear resistance to life as mere numbers and to the loss of stories in people-less agendas. There is also where there is resistance to extractivist methodologies that extract those numbers without care, that is, without accounting for the justice that they demand in terms of very material consequences. 'Reasons, concepts, thoughts, analyses, or arguments' need to be 'soaked in emotions, affections, and feelings' in order to be actionable, as Jasanoff (2017, p. 97) puts it. In methodological terms, for that matter, to be in the territory is not enough without being a part of it. And being part of that 'somewhere' is a vital piece in the way citizen-data methodologies can be non-extractivist. In order to not merely extract, one needs to know what the other would value receiving or feeling and account for that, becoming imbricated with the consequences of life in the territory.

Of course, when we talk of a global policy framework such as the 2030 Agenda, we need much more than alternative or financially inexpensive methodologies: we need baseline data, homogenized methods for data collection, frequent data reporting, and so on. But nowhere does that mean we do not need, nor should we equally value, systematize, and theorize about embodied, localized, and non-extractivist ways of producing and envisioning data.

However, in the 2030 Agenda datascape, issues of interoperability rather than relationality tend to be prioritized. There have been several reports published by not only the UN but also other specialized and non-specialized organizations on the challenges of integrating and reusing alternative data types. In that sense, much is being done to think of the legal frameworks, technological fixes, and policy-oriented tools that can help make the most of the data that might serve the purposes of monitoring the SDGs (United Nations, 2020; World Bank, 2021; Sachs et al., 2021; Peach et al., 2021; GTSC Agenda 2030, 2020). Nonetheless, if we are to 'leave no one behind' – the 2030 Agenda's motto – and in order, therefore, to make sure data are not produced for data's sake, then, at a minimum, actionable data needs to be considered as relevant as data that are used for monitoring the implementation of the SDGs. Moreover, investments, both of material resources and political will, would need to be calibrated accordingly. These are issues of power and inequality to the extent that the advances in this 'data revolution' have so far been far away from revolutionary.

To begin with, an issue of rather common knowledge, if digital data collection is essential to achieving the SDGs and to 'build back' from the pandemic, discussions on data governance need to consider the fact that almost half of the world's population does not have access to the Internet. According to the UN '2020 Sustainable Development Goals Report', by the end of 2019, only 53.6% of the planet had Internet access. Of course, this number is colored with 'wide regional disparities': approximately 80% in Europe against approximately 20% in sub-Saharan Africa. In addition, 141 countries reported the existence of a national statistical plan, but not all of them were fully funded (United Nations, 2020, p. 59). In response to this, the international community has been exploring new possibilities for concerted efforts.

In the broader *datascape*, that is, going beyond the SDGs *datascape*, a well-established international initiative already existed to support mostly the development of official statistics in low- and lower-middle-income countries, the PARIS21, founded in 1999. In 2021, two other projects were inaugurated that seek to track SDGs data: the Clearinghouse for Financing Development Data,[4] an initiative of the Bern Network on Financing Data for Development; and the World Bank's Global Data Facility, created to fund and support more efficient data statistical production globally.[5]

At the background of such concerns about efficiency, therefore, is an acknowledgement of a basic global inequality in statistical capacity.[6] Recent investments in new data sources and systems envision ways of pursuing a worldwide monitoring system based on other data sources, such as Big Data, as mentioned. Nevertheless, beyond the challenges posed to even the most conventional and, thus, usually more fully supported data types, it is clear there is a set of complex issues alternative data sources must also face in this *datascape*. Diverse actors interacting in overlapping multiple scales, producing and engaging with different kinds of datasets, including informally, and the dynamism of the connections between diverse centers and their modes of production compose a complex puzzle of polycentric governance (see Chapter 1, Aguerre, Campbell-Verduyn and Scholte, 2024, p. 4). The fluidity of perspectives in the -*scape* means there are not only diverse actors involved in data production and analysis but also that the way knowledge is constructed and mobilized for action varies enormously. What norms, values, and standards are followed in which context is a constitutive matter of political communities, something, therefore, of which datafication is an essential part. The issue of what centers should engage in data production in the *datascape* and how they should engage are questions that are at the very core of governance thinking and practice.

If there are investments being mobilized to produce more data, for instance, what methodologies should be prioritized? What data should be produced and how? In addition, how should actors communicate about needs and lessons learned? How can these pieces of information navigate in the *datascape* so as to produce knowledge at a higher level about results on the ground? How can diverse systems guarantee data can be translated from one to another, without loss of important particularities? As Ostrom (2009) originally proposed, such challenges need to be investigated empirically; polycentricity is *not* necessarily better because it in theory includes more actors and modes of engagement. To our minds, not only is there enormous value in better understanding how the implementation of the SDGs can help in the promotion of rights and social justice, but theoretically, an empirical investigation of the various data sources being mobilized in the 2030 Agenda, the power relations around their production and use, and the way interactions and the relationality among these sources feed into the polycentric governance in this *datascape* are all vital insights on our way to a future of even more datafication. If polycentric governance implies somewhat an 'ordered chaos', we need an 'examination of how social ties are built, maintained, and disrupted through norms, practices, techniques, informality, and underlying macro-orders' (Koinova et al, 2021, p. 1992).

Challenges of Alternative Data Sources to Polycentric Governance

There should be no room for extractivist methodologies in polycentric governance. By definition, in our view, polycentricity is 'an opportunity for learning about what works best in different domains' (Jordan et al., 2018, p. 6). To make sure enough emphasis is placed here: it is an *opportunity*, which by definition is not a guarantee. Therefore, a system of governance that does not inscribe within its operations, guidelines, practices, and discourses that encourage mutual learning is still a highly hierarchical one, probably more monocentric in practice. To tease out this notion further and prepare the ground for our empirical investigation, we want to depart from two propositions elaborated by Jordan et al. (2018) as part of a set of core features of polycentric governance systems around which authors generally find themselves agreeing or disagreeing (p. 11).

One of these propositions regards *experimentation*. Jordan et al. (2018) suggest, following this proposition, that analysts should constantly search for what experimentations are taking place, but this knowledge about experiments needs to be able to circulate, so learning is not constrained to very limited spaces. In the authors' view, the problem is that few conceptual frameworks have been advanced that look into how translation takes place between discrete experiments and general innovation (Idem). This is true for the 2030 Agenda, not least because the agenda is quite new and highly complex. In this sense, we question: how much of this datascape is geared towards mutual learning and innovation?

The other proposition regards the *overarching rules*. Most important to our purposes here is that in polycentric governance, such rules represent '"an opportunity structure" through which actors seek to effect change' (Tosun & Schonefeld apud Jordan et al., 2018, p. 17). It seems that the SDGs *datascape* offers important leverage to local initiatives, which may seek to link up to such an informational infrastructure as the 2030 Agenda, with its powerful technical, political, and diplomatic engines.

In what follows, we would like to mobilize the guidelines regarding experimentation and the notion of 'an opportunity structure' to think with initiatives of citizen-generated data (CGD) in Rio de Janeiro, Brazil. The goal is to analyze the role of such non-extractivist methodologies in potentially strengthening the positive features of polycentric governance in the *datascape*.

The Absence in Abundance: Voids in the Datascape

The Nigerian-American artist and researcher Mimi Onuoha makes a point clear in her mixed-media installation called 'The Library of Missing Datasets (2016)': there are telling voids in any *datascape*. Onuoha's artwork seeks to expose the complexity of power relations in an increasingly datafied world. In a physical file cabinet, Onuoha, who is a Visiting Arts Professor at NYU Tisch, reunites empty folders that should guard what she calls the 'missing data sets' which she defines as the 'blank spots that exist in spaces that are otherwise data-saturated'. Some of the folders are reserved for 'number of mosques surveilled by FBI', 'white children adopted by POC', 'ways crime-predicting software produces bias in judges', and 'all extinct languages'. Mimi Onuoha's perspective emphasizes the political implications of these blank spaces. Problematizing the idea that the absences are *mere coincidence*, the artist sets a debate around the fact that 'that which we ignore reveals more than what we give our attention to. It's in these things that we find cultural and colloquial hints of what is deemed important. Spots that we've left blank reveal our hidden social biases and indifferences' (2021). The most important act, then, is understanding that what is missing was not accidentally forgotten, but purposefully hidden. Highlighting and filling out the blanks, then, seems like a useful strategy in the fight for social justice. This practice has been a flagship of citizen-generated data.

Citizen-generated data, or CGD, can be defined as a kind of data that is 'actively created by citizens and their organizations' and that 'is produced to monitor, demand or drive change around issues that are important to them, often collected on the ground and in local contexts' (Jameson et al., 2018). CGD has been gaining momentum with the 2030 Agenda. Usually mentioned as a method capable of 'filling the gaps' of official data, CGD is normally recognized as a means to build a collective intelligence around the SDGs. It is also seen as a strategy to populate official knowledge assemblages with different perspectives. As says the UNDP, 'involving marginalized communities in generating, analyzing and using data' is an opportunity to 'stop replicating existing prejudices and inequalities' (Peach et al., 2021, p. 14).

Data_labe, an activist lab located at the Complexo da Maré, a gathering of 16 favelas in the North Zone of Rio de Janeiro, offers one such example as it tackles what they call a 'desert of news' in what regards their territory. Its strategy of territorializing and racializing all data intends to highlight what has been hidden by traditional data collection methodologies. Data_labe combines the authority of numbers with down-to-earth and emotion-driven narratives establishing an intimate conversation with the surrounding community and humanizing statistics by counting and accounting for inequalities and injustices.

CGD projects usually adopt two main strategies: focusing on the production of new datasets (especially when dedicated to topics that tend to be ignored by the state or traditional research institutes) or analyzing official datasets under the light of peripheral experiences. The latter becomes clear in a data_labe's piece called 'Mental violence' (Roza, 2021) that combines quantitative data and narratives to suggest a correlation between the rates of violence and that of psychiatric hospitalizations. Numbers are presented side by side with personal stories that address the impact of the violent deaths of young black men on their families. This is an effort that translates aseptic dataset figures into tangible stories in which each of those numbers acquires meaning by being traced back to reality in the territory.

The 13th episode of Data Lábia (Marques et al., 2019), data_labe's podcast, is also dedicated to the discussion of what they call 'absent data'. As the data_labe's team comments on the political implications of data invisibility, one of the participants attests that 'when there is no data on something, it is as if that thing does not exist'. They defend the need to ask questions such as: 'who is benefitting from these voids? What are the political and economic interests behind these?'.

In episode #13, the lack of peripheral perspectives in official data collection and analysis is pointed out by the group as a clear case of state negligence. They illustrate this by commenting on the underreporting of acts of violence practiced against Brazilian transsexual people and argue that a great part of this problem starts with the absence of members of this minority group in research and academic institutions: 'It is hard to think of experiences that are not our own', we hear in the podcast. Moreover, commenting on the National Household Sample Survey (PNAD) organized by the Brazilian Institute of Geography and Statistics (IBGE), data_labe researchers highlight how the points of view of those elaborating a research project directly affect its outcomes: the categories established by the survey to characterize family composition, they say, indirectly reinforce women's responsibility for raising children, since there is no option like 'fathers with children' (Sacco & Marques, 2019).

In this regard, the Census of the Maré, organized by the local organizations Redes da Maré and Observatório de Favelas, was designed to look at the specificities of Complexo da Maré. Since 2011, the Census of the Maré maps 'cartographic, economic and demographic' aspects of the territory and its population. The project aimed to tackle the 'misrepresentations and misbeliefs' about the inhabitants of Complexo da Maré producing a 'broad diagnosis' capable of helping public policy intended to meet the social demands of the 'biggest set of favelas in the city of Rio de Janeiro'. The initiative originated from the understanding that the official Brazilian National Census, also organized by the aforementioned IBGE, fails to paint an accurate portrait of the favela for several reasons. According to the 2019 report of the Census of the Maré, favelas suffer from under-registration by official institutions.

First, there is the problem of the 'dissonance of cartographic bases' and the 'reality of the territory' derived from the non-linear, cacophonous space of the favela (Redes da Maré, 2019, p. 11). Second, the biases also affect this kind of survey: the same report attests that the under-registration is also a result of 'the stigmatization of the favela as a locus of violence, barbarism, deprivation and lack of hygiene' (Idem).

Data_labe's team defends that just as data collection has been used to support public policy, we must now ask for public policies capable of fostering data collection among peripheral social groups. As they say, there are many groups that are not even participating in this conversation because they were never introduced into this universe.

Therefore, we imagine how much the 2030 Agenda could gain from incorporating the perspectives of communities for whom hunger and poverty are not concepts in a book but everyday life. On the other hand, we also believe that it is indispensable to bear in mind that CGD is not a panacea. Just as we can recognize how this movement is an exciting and transformative way of developing a sense of community, participation, and democracy, we are also aware of the fact that there is no outside to the broader *datascape*.

To Exist Is More Than Becoming Data

We believe that the CGD movement is highly supported by two main ideas: the first being that data is the lingua franca for 21st-century public policy, that is, a common ground in which different actors can interact; the second being that it is possible for marginalized groups to take a chair at the negotiation table as long as they learn how to communicate in this language. However, things are not that easy. There are also two main issues that integrate what we call a *violent datafication*. The first one is the highly diffused idea that something or someone must be datafied if they want to be even considered to exist. There is a logical appeal to the fact that data can be used to support decisions, but we should not forget that data have for a long time been used to exert power and control over societies through what Halkort (2019) defines as 'disquieting continuities with colonial logics of extraction, exploitation, and enclosure' (p. 318).

As liberating as a polycentric data governance might seem, it is crucial to understand that for some communities, producing or sharing data about themselves is also a risky business. Halkort (2019) presents the case of Palestinian refugees whose 'colonial dispossession and displacement' were orchestrated through the use of 'new methods of counting and measuring space and populations, most notably the census, private property, and cadastral maps' (p. 320).

The second issue of violent datafication affects those groups that are willing to join the conversation. Jonathan Cinnamon (2020) analyzes the case of social audits in South Africa in which data activism is 'pursued as a "credible" strategy to add weight to struggles for service delivery, as a way to situate demands on a rational and scientific plane rather than the emotional or adversarial levels of "people power"' (Cinnamon, 2020, p. 7). By choosing to speak the lingua franca of data, CGD organizations try to '"force" governments to pay attention' to their claims. Not coincidentally, many CGD reports can even be 'mistaken for official planning documents produced by a technocratically minded municipal government' (Cinnamon, 2020, p. 7). In these reports, 'quantitative data are supplemented with experiential accounts and personal testimonies', says Cinnamon. However, most governments decide to "attack the data" (Cinnamon, 2020, p. 8). Inadequacy, inconsistency, and convenience are some of the excuses these political authorities present in order to contest the data, methodology, or objectivity of these reports. That is, even making an effort to learn the 'language', marginalized social groups end up having their work disqualified by the state as 'not good enough'.

Democratizing data science requires more than an uninterested commitment to diversity. The logics of the system are that to which we should pay attention. Without a profound transformation, marginalized groups are bound to get seats at the table only to observe the disparities of the *datascape* from a different angle.

Linking Polycentricism and Non-Extractivist Methodologies by Way of Citizen-Generated Data

While the *datascape* has been peppered by initiatives to fund and otherwise support innovation in data production, analysis, and use, polycentric governance systems such as those put in place with the 2030 Agenda need to actually walk the line. They would do so by (a) promoting actual mutual learning among the diverse actors in the system; (b) making sure experimentation turns into action both on the ground and within the system itself, through organizational learning, adjustments in protocols and practices; and (c) making innovative actors visible within that very system as legitimate promoters of the global agenda and authoritative practitioners in their fields. In addition, if the *datascape* represented here by the SDGs is to be 'an opportunity structure' on which local initiatives can rely to advance rights and social justice agendas, then non-extractivist methodologies need to be further theorized and brought to the forefront of the debates; after all, if the *datascape* is not to exist for data's sake, those practices that are able to benefit people and planet should be at its core. Non-extractivist methodologies would strengthen the relationality of such governance systems by making sure data are not dissociated from context, experience, or the possible consequences to people who already suffer.

For our case in hand, for instance, the danger is in approaching CGD and other alternative and potentially critical data types as only another set of practices that need to be governed without considering that at issue is the need to address them at an ontological level, recentring questions of ethics and politics.

As Ruppert et al. (2017) suggest, it is important to observe 'how the vast amounts of data collected through the Internet and devices continues yet reconfigures colonial logics and objects of knowledge' (p. 207). Just as botanical knowledge once 'ninguneó' ('nobodied') indigenous knowledges (Rivera Cusicanqui, 2018, p. 28), the mere technological or technical take on the matter of governing the datascape incurs the risk of sweeping ontological, ethical, and political questions under the rug for the benefit of usability. But *whose* usability?

We argue the data governance debate needs to urgently bring to the fore and equally prioritize the problem of epistemic extractivism – in this case, directed at digital data (Grosfoguel, 2016; Rivera Cusicanqui, 2018). After decades working within the US aid system, Natsios (2010) recalls 'a central principle of development theory – that those development programs that are most precisely and easily measured are the least transformational, and those programs that are most transformational are the least measurable' (p. 3). To recentre issues of ethics and politics in the current *datascape*, at least in what regards the 2030 Agenda, would mean to make sure data generation and governance serve the purposes of positive social transformation, not the other way around.

It is not that data should not be generated for one or another case where they are missing, especially when invisibility might lead to tragic silences in public policy, but that we should make it an equally important concern to understand what these absences represent and how the 'desert of news' or 'deserts of data' are perceived by those who are supposed to benefit from data generation. In other words, we should learn from the absence of data as data and also learn with those who are innovatively attempting to fill these blanks guided by first-hand experiences and concerns.

In addition, just as poverty is part of the wealth produced in modern capitalism and, thus, not part of its past and something that will be overcome (Blaney & Inayatullah, 2010), the lack of data or even data usability is not necessarily a side-effect of the *datascape*, but an ontological necessity of its existence as such.

To take these points into account for our case here is to think, as seen, that poverty of data, in every sense, is rarely accidental. While the costs are not at all to be undervalued as a key component of decision-making in this area, at the international level within informational systems such as the 2030 Agenda, funding is not always the first absence on the list: many CGD initiatives are being developed in the territories with little funding, for instance. Yet whose 'experts' sit at the table of the advisory committees, who attends consulting sessions at the UN headquarters, and whose manuals are widely circulated are questions made secondary at best. What de Sousa Santos (2012) calls a 'sociology of absences' is precisely his attempt to recover those 'ninguneados' ('nobodied'), that is, those who were not accidentally absent but whose absence is an intimate part of how certain logics and objects of knowledge came to be historically configured. As Rivera Cusicanqui (2018) cautions, however, nothing of what is being argued here means 'a refusal of the basic ideas and principles of the Northern epistème, but of how these are adopted' (p. 29).

In turn, Jasanoff (2017) proposes a thinking *with* situated knowledges, or knowledges 'from somewhere', as she calls it: 'In short, if a data set is to elicit a social response, knowledge of something that matters and principles for understanding why it matters must be generated together, or coproduced' (p. 2). What she terms 'practices of authorized seeing' (Idem), in this sense, are about seeing with data and about what practices of organized seeing are acknowledged in the *datascape*. To this, we add the need to also question who, among those datafying actors, is made visible in the *datascape*.

Conclusion

In February 2022, in a short speech at the event 'Partnering to strengthen Citizen Generated Data: learning from the experiences of National Statistical Offices (NSOs)', Papa Seck, Chief at the Research and Data Section at UN Women said that, a few years ago, CGD existed almost as a barren land: representatives of NSOs would say to CGD activists that 'their data was not good enough', something to which they would reply with 'and yours are not useful enough'. Now, according to Seck, the conversation is far beyond this point.

It is important to bear in mind that several limitations still exist in these dynamics such as the fact that CGD 'is rarely immediately usable for monitoring individual SDG indicators' (Jameson et al., 2018). However, CGD has been proven important as it 'provides partial data which has to be complemented by additional data', 'offers contextual information around indicators', and 'can be applied to several targets and indicators tackling issues more holistically' (Idem).

In the same event, Liliana Suchodolska, from PARIS21, gave the audience a simple but powerful perspective to envisage the power of CGD. In her words, 'it's about the journey, not the destination'. CGD does not have to solve all the issues of the SDGs datascape. CGD's strength lies in its singular ability to point out what is missing from the traditional point of view. In this regard, it also illustrates the importance of polycentric governance in the SDGs *datascape* but offers as many questions as answers at this point. Perhaps the opportunity for real transformation does not depend on filling the blank spaces of the *datascape* as often conceived in 'infrastructural thinking', but in diversifying and circulating perspectives that challenge this mainstream technology-centered logic, its excesses, and voids. This can be done by combining different centers, modes of engagement, and priorities into a polycentric data governance that is more oriented towards social justice. In this sense, we can learn to make ethical and political questions into key parts of data collection methodologies by safeguarding spaces for experimentation in the datascape that have the power to improve democracy, participation, solidarity, and belonging.

Notes

1 See The 2030 Agenda's Data Challenge, p. 5.
2 On political truths, see Hacking (1986).
3 See Jasanoff (2017) on counting/accounting.
4 See https://smartdatafinance.org/about-us.
5 See www.worldbank.org/en/programs/global-data-facility.
6 In this case, we can consider the 17.19.2 b indicator. The Secretary General SDG Report of 2021 attests, in its Statistical Annex, that only 59.6% of countries have "birth registration data that are at least 90 per cent complete", p. 219.

References

Anderson, C. (2008). The end of theory: The data deluge makes the scientific method obsolete. *Wired*, 16(7). https://www.wired.com/2008/06/pb-theory/.

Appadurai, A. (1990). Disjuncture and difference in the global cultural economy. *Theory, Culture & Society*, 7(2–3), 295–310.

Blaney, D. L., & Inayatullah, N. (2010). *Savage economics: Wealth, poverty and the temporal walls of capitalism*. Routledge.

Bowker, G. C., & Star, S. L. (2000). *Sorting things out: Classification and its consequences*. MIT Press.

Cheney-Lippold, J. (2017). *We are data: In we are data*. New York University Press.

Cinnamon, J. (2020). Attack the data: Agency, power, and technopolitics in South African data activism. *Annals of the American Association of Geographers*, 110(3), 623–639. https://doi.org/10.1080/24694452.2019.1644991.

de Sousa Santos, B. (2012). Public sphere and epistemologies of the South. *Africa Development*, 37(1), 43–67.

Deleuze, G. (2017). Postscript on the societies of control. In Wilson D., & Norris, C. (Eds.), *Surveillance, crime and social control* (pp. 35–39). Routledge.

GIZ & Global Partnership for Sustainable Development Data. (2020). The 2030 Agenda's data challenge: Approaches to alternative and digital data collection and use. https://www.data4sdgs.org/sites/default/files/file_uploads/2030AgendasDataChallenge.pdf.

González Morales, L. G., & Orrell, T. (2018). *Data interoperability: A practitioner's guide to joining up data in the development sector*. Global Partnership for Sustainable Development Data (GPSDD). https://www.data4sdgs.org/sites/default/files/services_files/Interoperability%20-%20A%20practitioner's%20guide%20to%20joining-up%20data%20in%20the%20development%20sector.pdf.

Grosfoguel, R. (2016). Del extractivismo económico al extractivismo epistémico y ontológico. *Revista Internacional de Comunicación y Desarrollo (RICD)*, 4, 33–45.

GTSC Agenda 2030 (Grupo de Trabalho da Sociedade Civil para a Agenda 2030). (2020). *Relatório Luz da Sociedade Civil da Agenda 2030 de Desenvolvimento Sustentável Brasil*. https://brasilnaagenda2030.files.wordpress.com/2020/08/por_rl_2020_web-1.pdf.

Hacking, I. (2013). Making up people. In Stein, E. (Ed.), *Forms of desire*, 69–88. Routledge.

Halkort, M. (2019). Decolonizing data relations: On the moral economy of data sharing in Palestinian refugee camps. *Canadian Journal of Communication*, 44(3), 317–329. https://cjc.utpjournals.press/doi/pdf/10.22230/cjc.2019v44n3a3457.

Isin, E., & Ruppert, E. (2019). Data's empire: Postcolonial data politics. In Bigo, D., Isin, E., & Ruppert, E. (Eds.), *Data Politics*, 207–227. Routledge.

Jameson, S., Lämmerhirt, D., & Prasetyo, E. (2018, January). Acting locally, monitoring globally? How to link citizen-generated data to SDG monitoring. https://papers.ssrn.com/sol3/papers.cfm?abstract_id=3229753.

Jasanoff, S. (2017). Virtual, visible, and actionable: Data assemblages and the sightlines of justice. *Big Data & Society*, 4(2), doi:2053951717724477.

Jordan, A., Huitema, D., Van Asselt, H., & Forster, J. (Eds.). (2018). *Governing climate change: Polycentricity in action?* Cambridge University Press. doi:10.1017/9781108284646.

Koinova, M., Deloffre, M. Z., Gadinger, F., Mencutek, Z. S., Scholte, J. A., & Steffek, J. (2021). It's ordered chaos: What really makes polycentrism work. *International Studies Review*, 23(4), 1988–2018. https://academic.oup.com/isr/article/23/4/1988/6403480.

Letouzé, E. (2015). *Reflections on Big Data & the Sustainable Development Goals: Measuring & achieving development progress in the Big Data era*. Data-Pop Alliance

Working Note. http://datapopalliance.org/wp-content/uploads/2016/03/NoteBigData SDGsGlobalSustDevReportELetouze2015.pdf.

Loukissas, Y. A. (2019). *All data are local: Thinking critically in a data-driven society.* MIT Press.

Marques, J. et al. (Hosts). (2019, August 28). Dados Ausentes. (No. 13) [Audio podcast episode]. data_labe. https://datalabe.org/dados-ausentes/.

Natsios, A. (2010). *The Clash of the counter-bureaucracy and development.* Center for Global Development. https://www.cgdev.org/publication/clash-counter-bureaucracy-a nd-development.

Ostrom, E. (2009). *A polycentric approach for coping with climate change.* World Bank Policy Research Working Paper No. 5095. World Bank. https://documents1.worldba nk.org/curated/en/480171468315567893/pdf/WPS5095.pdf.

Peach, K., Berditchevskaia, A., Mulgan, G., Lucarelli, G., & Ebelshaeuser, M. (2021). *Collective intelligence for sustainable development: Getting smarter together.* United Nations Development Programme & Nesta Center for Collective Intelligence Design. https://www.undp.org/acceleratorlabs/publications/collective-intelligence-sustainable- development-getting-smarter-together.

Redes da Maré. (2019). *Censo populacional da Maré.* https://www.redesdamare.org.br/m edia/downloads/arquivos/CensoMare_WEB_04MAI.pdf.

Ritchie, H., Mathieu, E., Rodés-Guirao, L., Appel, C., Giattino, C., Ortiz-Ospina, E., Hasell, J., Macdonald, B., Beltekian, D., & Roser, M. (2020) Coronavirus pandemic (COVID-19). Our World in Data. https://ourworldindata.org/coronavirus.

Rivera Cusicanqui, S. (2018) *Un mundo ch'ixi es posible: Ensayos desde un presente en crisis. Buenos Aires: Tinta Limón.* https://tintalimon.com.ar/public/s7loyv7qkqkfy9 tlizbaucrk6z67/pdf_978-987-3687-36-5.pdf.

Rocha de Siqueira, I., & Ramalho, L. (2022). Participatory methodologies and caring about numbers in the 2030 Sustainable Development Goals agenda. *Policy and Society*, 41(4), 486–497.

Roza, G. (2021). Violência Mental. data_labe. https://datalabe.org/violencia-mental/.

Ruppert, E., Isin, E., & Bigo, D. (2017). Data politics. *Big Data & Society*, 4(2).

Sacco, C., & Marques, J. (2019). O IBGE na produção do data_dabe e o debate sobre sados no Brasil. *Revista Brasileira de Geografia*, 64(1), 109–121.

Sachs, J., Kroll, C., Lafortune, G., Fuller, G., & Woelm, F. (2021). *Sustainable Development Report 2021.* Cambridge University Press. doi:10.1017/9781009106559.

Silva, F. (2020). Mas o que é geração cidadã de dados? *Medium.* https://medium.com/da ta-labe/mas-o-que-é-geração-cidadã-de-dados-fdac93c8fd70.

Terranova, T. (2004). *Network culture: Politics for the information age.* London: Pluto.

Tichenor, M., Merry, S. E., Grek, S., & Bandola-Gill, J. (2022). Global public policy in a quantified world: Sustainable Development Goals as epistemic infrastructures. *Policy and Society*, 41(4), 431–444.

UN Global Pulse. (2020). Annual Report. https://www.unglobalpulse.org/document/ un-global-pulse-annual-report-2020/.

United Nations. (2020). The Sustainable Development Goals Report. https://unstats.un. org/sdgs/report/2020/The-Sustainable-Development-Goals-Report-2020.pdf.

United Nations. (2021a). The Sustainable Development Goals Report. https://unstats.un. org/sdgs/report/2021/The-Sustainable-Development-Goals-Report-2021.pdf.

United Nations (2021b). Progress towards the Sustainable Development Goals: Report of the Secretary-General. https://digitallibrary.un.org/record/3930067#record-files-collap se-header.

United Nations. (2021c). Progress towards the Sustainable Development Goals: Report of the Secretary-General – Statistical Annex. https://digitallibrary.un.org/record/3930067#record-files-collapse-header.

United Nations Development Programme & Nesta Center for Collective Intelligence Design. (2019). https://www.undp.org/acceleratorlabs/publications/collective-intelligence-sustainable-development-getting-smarter-together.

World Bank. (2021). World Development Report 2021: Data for better lives. https://www.worldbank.org/en/publication/wdr2021.

5

GRASSROOTS DATA ACTIVISM AND POLYCENTRIC GOVERNANCE

Perspectives from the Margins

Daivi Rodima-Taylor

The chapters in this collaborative volume discuss the opportunities and challenges for democratic governance that are entailed in the global expansion of digital data and the growth of the Internet. My chapter explores grassroots data activism that is emerging with the growing centrality of social media platforms and electronically mediated finance in everyday life. It explores new opportunities that these practices from the margins offer for collaborative and sustainable data governance. While the era of Big Data and machine learning brings along fundamental changes in how knowledge is produced and governance enacted, it also enables opaque data use by corporate and state actors that can undermine accountability and civil liberties.

I suggest that studying grassroots data activism helps us identify more democratic and sustainable ways of circulating digital data for the benefit of larger groups of people. It also provides much-needed insights into the plurality of existing frameworks, actors, and technologies around data sharing and governance. These issues are relevant for the study of polycentrism in data governance, as they cast light on the politics and processes that can realize the potential benefits and bypass potential challenges of expanding digital data (see Chapter 1, Aguerre, Campbell-Verduyn, and Scholte, 2024). The polycentric governance concept advanced in this volume illuminates the multiple power centers and connectivities that bring together formal and informal attempts to govern data at different levels of activity and across sectors. These actor constellations operate with multiple overlapping rationalities, normative and ethical orientations, technologies, and institutional arrangements (Gadinger and Scholte, 2022).

The origins of the concept of polycentric governance lie in theories of common-pool resource governance. Ostrom (2008) suggests that governance systems that evolve around common-pool resources are able to effectively manage collective action and are capable of self-correction and self-

DOI: 10.4324/9781003388418-6

organization. Such governance systems with multiple centers of power at different scales enable more opportunities for the stakeholders to participate in governance processes and contribute in innovative ways. Ostrom also raised the question about the extent to which national and private controls can co-exist with communal management. These issues are increasingly relevant to the current state of digital data governance. My chapter examines the expansion of digital technologies for financial inclusion and economic development that has been particularly significant in the Global South. The current market-based approach to financial inclusion has loosened protective regulations and broadened the set of stakeholders that include national governments, international development agencies, financial and technology companies, and mobile network operators (see Mader, 2018; Torkelson, 2020). The evolving electronic payments industry increasingly draws on customer transactional data as a source of value (Maurer, 2015). Many countries of the Global South have large numbers of unbanked people who rely on new forms of electronic finance for their daily needs.

Technology platforms and alternative finance are therefore central to the lives of many inhabitants in the Global South, as well as in the low-income communities of the Global North. Platforms collect and circulate immense volumes of data about people's transactions and daily lives, processing these through algorithms (Van Dijck et al., 2018). Building on network effects and multi-sided value creation, they can consolidate market structures towards evolving oligopolies (Langley and Leyshon, 2020, 2017). In addition to dedicated FinTech platforms, social media platforms have become central in people's social lives.[1] This all creates an immense potential of data extraction for the profit of the technology firms.

Hess and Ostrom (2003) characterize the situation around the growing appropriation of data as 'intellectual land grabs,' where enclosures and private controls have entered the digital environment. The burgeoning restrictions to information access accentuate power asymmetries and conflict with the original structure of the Internet as a decentralized, digitally networked ecosystem (see Chapter 3 of this volume, Aguerre). This resonates with recent calls to situate contemporary data practices within the broader global histories of dispossession. Practices of data appropriation may constitute a new type of resource extraction that builds on and expands the coloniality earlier associated with land appropriation (Couldry and Mejias, 2021). Mohamed et al. suggest the term 'algorithmic coloniality' to highlight the discriminatory legacies that are affecting algorithmic decision-making within broader geopolitical power dynamics (2020: 665). This can facilitate the reproduction of the 'hierarchies of race, gender and geopolitics' that served to actuate colonial control (Maldonado-Torres, 2007). Data-centric epistemologies can therefore marginalize human beings from the social order and deny the 'existence of alternative worlds and epistemologies' (Ricaurte, 2019).

Decolonial knowledge-making rejects universalism, instead drawing on localization and pluriversality (see also Mignolo, 2012; Escobar, 2018). In their call for a 'de-Westernization of critical data studies,' Milan and Trere (2019) suggest that 'the South' should be viewed as a plural entity that entails diverse marginalities and invisibilities. More attention is needed on the agency of digital media users and multiple meanings produced and exchanged. An analytical shift from datafication to data activism and data justice would entail an exploration of 'diverse ways through which citizens and the organized civil society in the Souths engage in bottom-up data practices' (Milan and Trere, 2019: 328). Beraldo and Milan (2019) introduce the concept of 'contentious politics of data' that focuses on 'bottom-up, transformative initiatives' that interfere with dominant processes and power structures around datafication (Beraldo and Milan, 2019: 1). That would entail bringing into dialogue social movement studies that focus on the meaning-making practices of social struggles and grassroots agency, with the materiality of datafication as expressed through technological infrastructures, software tools, and data ecosystems (Beraldo and Milan, 2019: 2). For a better understanding of polycentric data governance, it is therefore important to investigate how these activist practices are shaped by new technologies and digital platforms that people are able to access.

My chapter contends that the value of grassroots data activism for the study of polycentric governance is in showing how power and norms are questioned and redefined by local agency and ground-up practices of data sharing. Such bottom-up data activism does not always lead to greater inclusion of the marginal in formal institutions and policy-making, but rather facilitates the formation of alternative civic spaces, discourses, and subject consciousness. Fakhoury and Icaza (2023) point out that the discussions of polycentric governance may sometimes remain rooted in genealogies originating from the Global North and shaped by Western notions of governance and institutional development. My chapter suggests a focus on the practices of grassroots data activism and the ways that they affect knowledge-making processes around data rights, data commons, and data privacy. It inquires about the engagements that people on the margins have with data sharing and joint interpreting, and explores the strategies and narratives that local activists draw upon to challenge top-down regulatory and policy initiatives.

In the first section of the chapter, I explore the peculiarities of grassroots data activism in the era of Big Data, arguing that data activism practices enable novel avenues for citizen data sharing and digital commons. At the example of cases from Africa, Latin America, and disadvantaged communities in the United States, the section shows that these practices that often remain fragmented and small-scale, can nevertheless make a difference even in the context of Big Data and the significant power asymmetries it entails. The chapter then proceeds to examine data policy debates that center on two conflicting issues: data privacy and protection, and the movement towards open finance in the Global South.

The section illustrates these topics with the example of material from Africa. The last section synthesizes the findings and offers pluriversal perspectives on grassroots data activism and its contributions to polycentric data governance.

From Datafication to Data Activism in the Era of Big Data

The increasing centrality of digitized information in society is bringing along new forms of civic engagement and political action. 'Data activism' signifies similar forms of engagement by civil society actors with the kinds of massive data collection and interpretation that have long been seen as the near-exclusive purview of governments and corporations. Data activism includes both data-based advocacy and other forms of 'affirmative engagement with data,' and resistance tactics to massive data collection, such as encryption practices (Milan and van der Velden, 2016: 1).

The intensifying turn to Big Data in framing social issues creates specific opportunities and challenges for data activism. Datafication of, or the act of rendering in data form, many aspects of the world that have not been quantified before (Cukier and Mayer-Schoenberger, 2013) can contribute to increasing surveillance and suppression of citizens by states, but importantly, can also offer new avenues for grassroots contestation (Milan and Gutierrez, 2018). These new forms of grassroots data agency are particularly relevant for conceptualizing polycentric data governance. Data activism can be defined as 'new social practices rooted in technology, which take a critical view towards datafication and use it politically for meaning-making, coordination and change' (Gutierrez, 2018: 1). It incorporates elements of collective action, communicative practices, and citizens' media and journalism (Milan and Gutierrez, 2018: 1). Data activism infrastructures combine data, technology, and communicative practices, seeking to create unconventional narratives and alternative solutions to social problems. Such technopolitical practices[2] can help bypass power asymmetries and enable individuals at the margins of society to communicate and collaborate around challenging socio-economic issues (Milan and Gutierrez, 2018).

Big Data can be employed for social change. More than a matter of volume, Big Data is about complexity, as it is continuously generated and scalable (Kitchin, 2014). It is processed through software-empowered machine learning that mines data and builds predictive models. Data in itself is not factual or informative—it becomes information 'in the process of being transformed for use' (Gutierrez, 2018: 6; see also Boellstorff, 2013). The actors central to these processes are technology firms and governments, while non-experts are much less likely to participate in code writing that defines the type of produced data. Big Data infrastructures that enable massive data gathering and analysis are thus not transparent to a non-specialist, and because of the involvement of technology companies, can foster convergence of corporate and political interests (Gutierrez, 2018: 5). The digital, income, and knowledge divides make it difficult for the marginal to extract value from data as that could entail 'statistical calculation, code writing, storytelling and visual thinking' (Gutierrez, 2018: 11). Big Data is inherently political – 'gathered and produced in a concrete social and political context, acquired with a particular method from a specific source or sources, cleaned, managed, stored and analyzed with a given approach, and framed by a set of underlying politics and ideology' (Gutierrez, 2018: 12).

Big Data can thus provide new insights and knowledge, but also foster biases and inequalities. It has important epistemic consequences, suggest Milan and van der Velden (2016), as it affects how information and knowledge are generated and presented. Data activism offers grassroots perspectives on these processes and enables us to contest them. It aims to decenter the expert-focused epistemology of Big Data that frames knowledge as computationally generated and mediated. By involving new, previously marginalized actors in critical engagement with data, data activism can promote broader democratic participation in knowledge creation. Big Data can therefore hold an emancipatory potential, offering alternative strategies for contesting dominant narratives through user-generated reports and critical engagement with data, and facilitating novel debates and alternative public spaces (Milan and Gutierrez, 2018: 12). Such movement towards data agency from the ground up can also shift the understanding of the governance centers in polycentrism to include the less obvious ones.

Grassroots Data Practices in the Global South

More attention is needed towards the diverse ways in which people in the Global South use and generate data for social change. Activism can be defined as an 'endeavour, individual or collective, designed to foster or guide political, socioeconomic or environmental change, with the intention of making improvements in society or correcting social injustice' (Gutierrez, 2018: 14). The rise of digital media offers advantages, such as cheaper coordination of activism practices and easier collaboration across distances. The users of digital activism platforms hail from a variety of backgrounds, including users of social media, community activists, journalists, humanitarian workers, geoactivists using interactive cartography, and ICT specialists.

These collective endeavors can bring together people from various geographies, creating linkages between local and global. Digital activism frequently contributes to the rise of social movements, which can be defined as 'organisations and diffuse actors with common interests, organised, yet informal and horizontal,' sharing a collective identity and goal of social change (Gutierrez, 2018: 58). There is usually minimal coordination between diverse groups engaged in these practices. In the digital era, social movements frequently define their identities around their technological options (Gutierrez, 2018: 59; see also Milan, 2013). Specific social media platforms and chat apps that people can access can therefore be instrumental in determining the form of data activism in those communities.

The Contested, Partial, and Socially Embedded Nature of Grassroots Data Activism

Case studies from the Global South show that while grassroots data activism often remains contested and partial, these small-scale collective actions matter for a better conceptualization of polycentric governance even in the era of Big Data. Most activists work with 'small data' that is expressed in formats that are usable by humans (Gutierrez, 2018). 'Small data' can be derived from sets of Big Data or collected through various sensing and crowdsourcing platforms. Crowdsourcing of both data and its analysis can be particularly important in the settings of environmental or political crises, as it can build on valuable local knowledge and expertise.

One of the earliest and best-known instances of grassroots data activism originates from Kenya's post-election violence of 2007 when activists established the platform Ushahidi[3] to contest mainstream news media narratives. 'Ushahidi' means 'testimony' in Swahili, and it was created to submit electoral violence reports and map incidents. The crowdsourcing platform combines data and communication infrastructures and geographic overlay systems, incorporating the data of mobile phones, databases, emails, and online cartography. It was soon expanded for use in other regions of crisis, including geolocating earthquake victims in Haiti, and reporting the violence during the Arab Spring (Rotich, 2017). Such digital activism platforms can provide important alternatives to the highly formalized management structures of official relief agencies, challenging state monopoly on data gathering and mobilizing information generated by citizen networks (Gutierrez, 2018: 121). The users of the platform were diverse, including civil society organizations and community-based organizations, media, activists and citizens, researchers and academics (Rotich, 2017).

Ushahidi utilized existing commercial communication platforms, including Twitter. The primary source of income for the platform comes from private foundation grant funding that includes Omidyar Network, MacArthur, Google, Cisco, Rockefeller, and Ford (Hersman, 2012). This shows the significant extent of BigTech funding and commercial platforms even in many grassroots experiences of data activism.

The benefits of grassroots data activism can be diverse and include building critical awareness and collective action in marginalized communities. Although the public visibility of the efforts is important, outcomes are not necessarily defined by inclusion in formal policy-making processes. Exploring the community-collected data practices of an affordable housing activism group in Atlanta, United States, Meng and DiSalvo (2018) show that while data was a strategic asset that people used when making claims to the municipal government, empowerment was a broader process that occurred through relationship-building and changes in critical consciousness. Rather than leading to an improved inclusion in already existing institutional structures and discourses, the counter-data practices of the housing activists resulted in 'greater self-reliance and new subjectivities' through collective action. The multi-institutional approach to social movements (Armstrong and Bernstein, 2008) argues that power and oppression inhibit a wider variety of organizational and cultural sites that go beyond the administrative processes of states. The struggles of social movements involve not only the distribution of resources but also broader variables, such as identity, race, and culture. Marginal groups can therefore draw upon a variety of institutions for leverage and partnership. In this case, counter-data action was rooted in the legacies of Black activism and scholarship in the community (Meng and DiSalvo, 2018: 8).

Furthermore, data activist endeavors are impacted by the imaginaries arising from broader, historical legacies of oppression and inequality. Particularly in the Global South, these continue to define the contested nature of grassroots data activism. Through an empirical study of service provision audits in Johannesburg and Cape Town, Cinnamon (2020) explores how politics and technology were co-constituted through normative discourses on citizenship and justice. Social injustice in South Africa is often understood in spatial terms, drawing attention to the ways in which economic and racial inequalities are geographically patterned. Local activism strives to make visible these spatial patterns of inequality that are often underrepresented in official data sources, hoping to make them actionable by the government (Cinnamon, 2020: 4). South African grassroots organizations are developing data-driven approaches to combat inequities in infrastructure and services. Local data activists view quantitative evidence as central to contemporary governance in the country with profound legacies of inequality. Data are seen as a powerful mediator that can stabilize relationships between oppositional stakeholders. The study calls attention to the fragility of this data imaginary through resistance strategies employed by government officials. The activist ideas about what the data were and what they could do were exploited by the government for its own political ends. Data agency should therefore be seen as 'relational, partial, and provisional,' co-constituted by people, technologies, and political discourses (Cinnamon, 2020: 14).

The importance of considering the disjunctures and limitations of grassroots data practices in polycentric data governance is also highlighted in some contributions to the current volume. For example, Chapter 4 by Siqueira and Ramalho (2024) explored the power inequalities entailed in the datafying practices around the United Nations 2030 Agenda in Brazil, introducing an innovative 'datascape' concept to analyze the unpredictable data flows that are embedded in local activism and its constraints.

The Ambiguous Partnerships with BigTech Platforms

The dependency of grassroots data activists on technology platforms is particularly evident in the Global South where commercial social media platforms such as Facebook and Twitter, and encrypted messaging apps such as WhatsApp and Signal, offer connectivity and safe spaces. In Mexico, grassroots data activists crowdsource data to report local crimes and share information to enhance public safety on the Facebook platform (Garcia and Le Dantec, 2018). These activities exhibit strong online-offline connections, with platform administrators soliciting contributions from the inhabitants of affected neighborhoods. Garcia and Le Dantec show how social media can enable political action in settings where people are not being served by existing institutions, especially with high levels of distrust of formal authorities (see also Aguerre and Tarullo, 2021, on the evolution of the resistance practices of Latin American Civil Society Organizations). Social media facilitated the discussion of issues that were ignored by the authorities and regular media. Users curated data that had been suppressed in other sites and official databases and built online communities for alternative action. This case illustrated the 'pragmatic reality that commercial social media platforms will continue to dictate many of the terms of social engagement, even at a local level' (Garcia and Le Dantec, 2018: 16).

My own recent research suggests that the popularity of social media-based chat apps in Africa presents an intriguing paradox: while they are part of the BigTech dynamic of global data capture by increasingly monopolistic service providers, they are also important to mediating informal livelihood endeavors and collectivities (Rodima-Taylor, 2023). WhatsApp, a digital messaging and voice call service, can work on low-cost phones with limited bandwidth and has become the most widely used chat platform in Africa (Metz, 2016). Differently from publicly visible social media platforms, communication on WhatsApp can be seen only by a designated group of people. The platform is used for political mobilization in many countries where freedom of public speech is restricted (Milan and Trere, 2019). WhatsApp has been seen as facilitating the rise of a new type of political subject whose engagement with public issues emerges gradually in an informal context (Milan and Barbosa, 2020; Pang and Woo, 2020).

The importance of WhatsApp in the daily lives of many Africans has skyrocketed during the COVID-19 pandemic. Banks and other businesses are moving their services on WhatsApp, abandoning physical branches (Kivuva, 2021; Kimega, 2021). Facebook and WhatsApp help people to keep in contact with their overseas families and mobilize remittances (see also Rodima-Taylor, 2022a). Increasingly, WhatsApp is used for pooling money in rotating savings-credit arrangements that are a mainstay in many informal economies in Africa (see Rodima-Taylor, 2022c). The implications of these novel pathways of digital mutuality are ambiguous: while the virtual savings groups build on vernacular organizational templates and facilitate alternatives to formalized versions of financial inclusion, they also lead to scams and Ponzi schemes. Stories of failures and fraudulent activities of online savings groups abound in the media of South Africa and Kenya (see Mavundza, 2020; Moodley, 2019; Pijoos, 2019). Despite the frequent scams, the chat platform features as an informal alternative to digital group accounts offered by commercial banks and FinTech platforms, and to dedicated crowdfunding services that in Africa are still dominated by Western-owned companies.

WhatsApp was acquired by Facebook in 2014 and its spread in Africa is facilitated by Facebook's Free Basics service[4] that provides access free of data charges to a variety of local information and news. The popularity of the service has positioned Facebook as the 'gateway to the Internet for mobile users across the Global South' (Nothias, 2020). Its operation has faced opposition in several countries where it has been critiqued for insufficient transparency in selecting services available on the app with adverse effects on local startups. (Such adverse effects led to a regulatory ban of Free Basics in India in 2016 on the grounds of net neutrality which stipulates that internet service providers should treat all internet traffic equally.) Facebook has focused its recent strategy towards more systematic engagement with civil society organizations—through partnering with local NGOs to onboard social organizations to the Free Basics platform, interacting more closely with local data rights activists on issues such as misinformation and online safety, and assisting local software developers.[5] This engagement with civil society activists is also shaped by the general political and regulatory context on the continent where governments increasingly turn towards limiting digital freedoms to counteract social protests—such as social media taxes, internet shutdowns, and cybersecurity laws that violate privacy (Nothias, 2020). The collaboration of local activists with the platform has therefore contributed to facilitating free speech and political protest in a number of African countries.

The Precarious Balance of Data Privacy and Open Data

Digital Finance and Data Privacy in Africa

There are increasing concerns that the platform-based business model of the rapidly spreading digital economies in Africa is exposing people to privacy risks. This section examines the tension between the growing movement towards open finance and open data, and the need for data privacy and protection, to safeguard the needs of the poorest. Many low-income people in African states are unbanked, and the continent has witnessed extensive growth in diverse forms of electronic finance. A distinguishing feature of financial technology in Africa is the widespread reliance on mobile phones for sending, storing, and spending money, particularly among low-income groups (see also Langley and Rodima-Taylor, 2022). Africa is the largest adopter of mobile money globally and as of 2021, accounts for half of the world's registered mobile money accounts and 70 percent of the global mobile money transaction value (GSMA, 2022). Telecommunications companies and FinTech firms are therefore central to financial access in Africa. This can facilitate the accumulation of consumer data into the hands of corporations and governments.

There is an increasing lack of trust in the digital space of the continent, not only due to spreading cybercrime and identity theft but also surveillance and censorship of the citizens by African states (Adeniran, 2022). Over the past decade, the number of African countries with data privacy laws has tripled. Challenges remain, however. Sharp disparities across income levels and rural-urban divides impede digital development (Goh and Goslar, 2022). Due to the low capacity of institutional frameworks around data governance, implementation of data privacy regulations remains uneven. These challenges are exacerbated by asymmetries of power and knowledge between large financial technology multinationals and resource-constrained African governments. There is a growing recognition, however, that monopoly in data governance, either by states or private companies, is not conducive to sustainable livelihoods (Goh and Goslar, 2022).

Effective data privacy governance is also hampered by the lack of adequate regional and multilateral initiatives, with more progress being made on national levels. As of Fall 2023, fifteen African countries have ratified the Malabo Convention. This African Union Convention on Cyber Security and Personal Data Protection (2014) is a regionally led approach for data protection and fighting cybercrime.[6] Evidence from other parts of the world indicates that regional approaches to data protection policies may encourage fruitful conversations about citizens' data rights between civil society, technology corporations, and governments. In many regions of Europe, the 2018 adoption of the General Data Protection Regulation (GDPR) of the European Union provided that impetus.[7] Calzada and Almirall (2019) describe how the 'data commons' initiative in Barcelona opened up debates and collaboration between diverse stakeholders. Reaching beyond the customary public-private divide, it facilitated a multi-stakeholder network that included the municipal government, technology corporations, academic and nongovernmental institutions, and social entrepreneurs and activists.

Well-functioning data privacy regulations are relevant as data can be seen as an ever-increasing source of power in economic governance. As Mann (2018) points out, the Data for Development projects, often initiated in the Global North, facilitate the creation of data of 'immense value' that can constitute an incentive for foreign corporations to participate in development initiatives (Mann, 2018: 28). These multinational companies frequently fail to disclose to their users the value of their data or the terms of its use, while financial inclusion initiatives push for a broader reliance on FinTech products among poorer and less informed groups. Mann suggests that African governments and civil society actors need to exercise more oversight regarding the data-extractive activities of BigTech corporations. More attention is needed to the distribution of commercial benefits as well as regulations that enable public oversight of data systems in African countries—reminding us about the significant role of the states in polycentric data governance. At present, most African citizens are extremely limited in their ability to govern their data for the benefit of their livelihoods.

Kenya—a country in Africa with one of the most developed FinTech sectors—passed the Data Protection Act in 2019, which is legislation that governs the collection and processing of personal data and defines the rights of data subjects and obligations of data controllers. Data Protection Regulations governing the processing of personal data by civil registration entities were enacted in 2020. The legislation sets out restrictions on the handling, storage, and sharing of personally identifiable data as it is obtained by private companies and government entities. While it is comprehensive and expected to have a significant impact on how companies process people's data, implementation has been somewhat uneven so far: according to a recent survey by a software company, around 36% of Kenyan businesses were not even aware of the rules, and many were uncertain how to comply (McDowall, 2022).

Credit Data and Financial Exclusion in Kenya

Kenya's mobile money service M-Pesa has over 51 million users across seven countries in Africa and is currently the continent's largest FinTech platform (Vodafone, n.d.). While nearly 80 percent of Kenya's population are registered mobile money account holders, only 30 percent of households have access to banking. The reliance on mobile phones for financial management also creates particular challenges for data privacy and activism.

For example, the ubiquitous mobile phones and widespread mobile money have brought along a rapid expansion of digital credit in the country in recent years. In 2017, over a third of Kenya's adult mobile phone-owning population had used digital credit (Gubbins and Totolo, 2018). Various app-based lenders often use alternative methods for credit scoring—extracting and analyzing data from mobile call logs and social media. Such apps are particularly widespread among consumers who do not qualify for formal bank loans and work in the 'informal sector,' and frequently lead to over-borrowing and vicious cycles of debt (Johnen et al., 2021). Digital credit has resulted in extensive blacklisting of defaulting borrowers in Kenya, leading to their long-term exclusion from formal sector credit: by 2017, 2.7 million digital borrowers had been reported to the credit reference bureaus for defaulting (Johnen et al., 2021: 1–2).

Experiments in alternative credit scoring rely on machine learning models and may render people governable in specific ways (Aitken, 2017). These data practices that seek to make the unbanked visible may actually entail 'segmentation' where people are defined as transitory populations to be absorbed in formalized credit networks, or as a category 'too risky to carry value' (Aitken, 2017: 292). Thus, while visibility within formal credit practices can improve a person's access to resources, in other cases it can further constrain one's options, deepening credit denial and confirming exclusion. The exclusionary practices around alternative credit scoring in app-based digital credit therefore highlight the importance of consumers' access to their transaction data and the terms of its use.

Evolving 'Open Data' Approaches in the Digital Finance Space

In the Global South, there is an emerging discussion around 'open finance'—an arrangement where banks and financial service providers would be required to share consumer data among themselves and with third-party providers. These include FinTech companies that are developing new financial tools based on consumer data. 'Open data' therefore constitutes the 'exchange of consumer data between private-sector institutions—including financial institutions and nonbank financial institutions, such as mobile money issuers, utility providers, and telecoms … with customer consent' (Medine and Plaitakis, 2023: 3). If open finance succeeds, this could potentially set a path for 'broader exchanges of data in nonfinancial sectors of the economy' (Medine and Plaitakis, 2023: 5).[8] Open banking or sharing third-party access to financial data through the use of application programming interfaces (API) is seen as boosting Africa's electronic payments and e-commerce sectors by expanding financial service provisioning across borders (Ngila, 2022). Banks, on the other hand, are using open APIs to entrench services, like WhatsApp banking, that enable customers to send money and perform other transactions through their WhatsApp chat window (Kimeria, 2022).

There are numerous benefits as well as drawbacks to open finance in the Global South, as the recent CGAP Technical Report points out. On one hand, such data sharing would offer consumers access to financial products from multiple channels at lower costs and allow remote customer onboarding. Open finance also enables unbanked consumers to transfer data from 'nontraditional' financial sources, such as mobile money accounts, to regular financial institutions (Medine and Plaitakis, 2023: 2–3). The data to be shared includes customers' transaction data as well as personal data required for account opening and Know-Your-Customer compliance. While in some cases, data transfer occurs directly from the data holder, in other cases the transfer involves data intermediaries who handle customer requests. Depending on the jurisdiction, these include various account aggregators and account information service providers. The involvement of a multitude of parties who are able to access customer information constitutes new risks to privacy. Customer data could be mismanaged, and the liabilities may not be clear in this diverse chain of actors. The adoption of open finance should therefore be accompanied by a comprehensive data protection framework that is particularly important for protecting low-income consumers (Medine and Plaitakis, 2023: 5).

Setting up a regulatory framework for consumer data protection in the open finance regime is a complex process, however, and depends on the involvement of multiple parties, such as the central bank, competition authority, and data protection authority. There is also a need to consider socio-cultural and gender-based norms of financial management and information sharing in different countries, as these too can impact the adoption of open data regimes. This highlights the relevance of considering state and industry actors as important stakeholders in facilitating enabling environments for more open and transparent data practices around the financial lives of low-income consumers. For polycentric theorizing, it is important to consider the profound inequalities between these actors and foreground the urgency of seeking ways to establish a constructive dialogue. The next section explores further the need to engage marginalized communities through advocacy and activism in the era of Big Data.

Collective Action for Algorithmic Transparency

Promoting algorithmic transparency is emerging as an important area of data activism as biased algorithms disproportionately discriminate against those who have been relegated to the margins of society. Such pursuits are complicated by the proprietary nature of software and the complexity of machine learning where bias can emerge in the course of data analysis—but may also offer new opportunities for grassroots activism and advocacy. Machine learning can help to better predict consumer behavior by integrating and analyzing relationships between elements from large data sets, but can also create discriminatory proxies for protected categories: for example, school attended or geographical location can be correlated with race and ethnicity (Courchane and Ross, 2019). The combination of alternative data sources with machine learning may perpetuate historical biases inherent in those sources (see also Rodima-Taylor, 2022b for FinTech-mediated mortgage lending). Algorithmic decision-making is not neutral but reflects the values and intentions of the designer, institutionalizing them in code (Mittelstadt et al., 2016: 7). Algorithmic bias arises from preexisting social values, technological constraints and errors, and newly emerging use contexts in the decision-making architecture (Mittelstadt et al., 2016: 7).

The limited ability of humans to interfere highlights the difficulties of applying traditional notions of responsibility to algorithm-empowered decision-making. Calls are increasing for new regulatory and epistemic solutions. Debates on ethical consumer finance increasingly focus on the ways that data activism can actively counter the discriminatory patterns reproduced by algorithms. Innerarity (2021) calls for a strategy to construct comprehensibility of algorithms that is grounded in collective and relational approaches. Auditing algorithms should not be viewed as an individual right, but as a matter of public responsibility, he suggests algorithmic transparency needs to be conceptualized as a relational good, supported by systems of accountability. That entails attention to the 'strategies of non-transparency' by those exercising power, as well as designing new 'architectures of control' for a critical review of artificial systems that focus on concrete actions, settings, and consequences (Innerarity, 2021, p. 7).

There is an increasing recognition that the issues of algorithmic transparency are rooted in everyday biased legacies and discriminatory practices and do not reside just in the virtual realm. Solutions could reside in practices such as 'algorithmic affirmative action' that seek to design algorithms in 'race- and gender-conscious ways,' to counter-act the bias hidden in data (Chander, 2017: 1025). Data activism to promote algorithmic transparency would entail joint engagement between community members and activists, regulatory authorities and planners, as well as new forms of partnerships between FinTech lenders and disadvantaged communities (see Allen, 2019; Velasquez, 2020). Policy reforms may be required in areas such as intellectual property, data protection, and internet law, facilitating disclosures regarding algorithmic decision-making

(Allen, 2019: 262). These issues remain poignant for low-income consumers in the Global South as well as the North.

As the new algorithm-empowered products and services may thus contain an inherent element of unfairness and discrimination, it is evident that while data privacy regulations are important, they alone cannot guarantee a fair and equitable treatment of all customers. Exploring new solutions based on collective action to enhance the accountability of algorithms has therefore emerged as an important project for polycentric data governance.

Grassroots Data Activism and Polycentric Governance in a Pluriversal Perspective

This chapter argued that grassroots data activism can offer important new perspectives on polycentric data governance in the era of Big Data, with the growing centrality of mass-scale, quantitative information in regulating society. While datafication can contribute to state surveillance and data appropriation by technology firms, it also enables new avenues for citizen data sharing. Ground-up data activism increasingly engages with collecting and interpreting massive data that has long remained the purview of technology corporations and governments.

Big Data is not neutral—it is gathered, interpreted, and framed within specific power hierarchies and ideologies. Data activism can offer alternative strategies for contesting dominant narratives through user-generated reports and critical engagement. As the cases from Kenya and Mexico showed, digital activism platforms can be particularly helpful for crowdsourcing local data in the settings of environmental disasters and violent conflicts, as well as for mobilizing local information to enhance public security. This can create novel 'knowledge commons' and enhance global polycentric data governance.

The cases from the Global South also demonstrated that small-scale collective actions of data activism matter even in the era of Big Data. While most grassroots activists do not have the capacity to employ complex computer software for statistical calculations or visual exhibits, it is the local knowledge and expertise that makes a difference. Social media platforms can enhance the visibility of these actions and expand the opportunities for advocacy and support. Furthermore, as we can see, while data activism adds important public visibility, its benefits are not necessarily defined by inclusion in formal policymaking: they can be more diverse and indirect, such as facilitating critical awareness and group-building in marginalized communities.

Data agency thus remains contested and partial, particularly as grassroots data activism is dependent on the very limited technological options available to low-income population. Often this results in uneasy partnerships of grassroots activists with commercial social media platforms originating from the Global North or East. As the case studies of the chapter showed, data agency at the margins is often particularly dependent on global BigTech platforms. While this may contribute to data extractivism, collaboration of local activists with social media platforms has also facilitated civic action and political protest in oppressive states. In polycentric governance theorizing, more attention is therefore needed to the evolving structures of digital activism as complex sociotechnical assemblages that bring together diverse formal and informal, online and offline elements (see also Rodima-Taylor and Grimes, 2019).

Ongoing data policy debates in the Global South focus on two somewhat conflicting issues: data privacy and protection, and the movement towards open finance and other forms of institutionalized data sharing. These issues are particularly poignant in Africa where large parts of the population are unbanked, while depending on their mobile phones for financial management through a multitude of digital finance apps. The rapidly growing role of digital finance in people's livelihoods has created specific challenges for data management, as it leaves people's personal and transaction data vulnerable to exploitation. As data constitutes an ever-increasing source of economic power, data privacy regulations are relevant for offering consumers better control over their information. As the chapter outlined, widespread digital finance apps with their alternative credit-scoring techniques have brought along a rapid expansion of digital credit in countries such as Kenya, resulting in the blacklisting of many low-income borrowers from formal sector opportunities.

The adoption and implementation of data privacy regulations in African countries remain uneven. Data privacy governance is also impeded by the lack of adequate multilateral frameworks across the continent. There is thus room for exploring common regional approaches to data protection and knowledge commons that in other parts of the world have catalyzed conversations about citizens' data rights between civil society, technology corporations, and governments. That is particularly relevant with the emerging debates around open finance in the Global South, which offers consumers more options but also involves new risks to privacy and transparency. The adoption of open finance has to be accompanied by comprehensive data protection frameworks, as a focal point of authority, that are especially important for securing the data rights of low-income consumers.

Another emerging area for data activism is promoting algorithmic transparency and countering bias, which may require novel regulatory and epistemic solutions that rely on the principle of polycentrism. These include joint engagements between community members and activists, regulatory authorities and planners, and new forms of partnerships between financial actors and disadvantaged communities. Algorithmic transparency should thus be seen as a matter of public responsibility and as supported by institutionalized structures of accountability. That entails renewed attention to power differentials and ways to support grassroots data agency.

The elements of grassroots data activism that matter for a fuller understanding of polycentric governance include the fragmented and partial nature of data sharing and collective interpreting. These practices are not always aimed at greater inclusion in institutionalized policy-making but involve creating new, albeit fragmented, civic spaces, and forming uncertain and shifting partnerships with the formal sector. Informal data activism practices do not necessarily get absorbed by the formal. Rather, they reinterpret existing norms and institutions and insert alternative viewpoints and processes, expressed through local insights, narratives, and modes of sharing advanced through crowdsourcing and other digital techniques. Connections to offline modes of collaboration remain important in these endeavors. Further investigation is needed into these rapidly growing expressions of local data agency for a fuller, pluriversal understanding of the emerging multiscalar global data governance.

Notes

1 In many African countries, for example, Facebook has become synonymous with the Internet through its Free Basics service that provides access free of data charges to Facebook and several other websites using a SIM card from a qualifying mobile operator.
2 The notion of technopolitics refers to 'technology-enhanced politics' that revolves around the ability to enact political goals by means of technical artefacts (Gagliardone, 2014, in Milan and Gutierrez, 2018).
3 www.ushahidi.com.
4 www.facebook.com/freebasics/.
5 It has also engaged with more general infrastructural projects that include the Express WI-FI initiative in Ghana, Kenya, Nigeria, Tanzania, South Africa, Senegal, and Malawi; fiber optic cables in South Africa, Uganda, and Nigeria; and plans to build an undersea fiber optic cable surrounding the African continent (Nothias, 2020).
6 https://au.int/en/treaties/african-union-convention-cyber-security-and-personal-data-protection.
7 See also Chapter 10 by Medzini and Epstein, and Chapter 7 by Wenlong Li and Dan Yang, this volume.
8 Similar developments have occurred somewhat earlier in Europe, where large data-driven companies (such as social media platforms) have been striving to embed payment functionalities in their platforms with banks increasingly required by regulators to provide access to their customers' transactional data (see Westermeier, 2020).

References

Adeniran, Adedeji. (2022). Developing an effective data governance framework to deliver African digital potentials. In: Foresight Africa 22 Report. The Brookings Institution. Retrieved 16 October 2023 from https://www.brookings.edu/articles/developing-an-effective-data-governance-framework-to-deliver-african-digital-potentials/.
Aguerre, Carolina, and Tarullo, Raquel. (2021). Unravelling resistance: Data activism configurations in Latin American civil society. *Palabra Clave*, 24(3), e2435.
Aitken, Rob. (2017). 'All data is credit data': Constituting the unbanked. *Competition & Change*, 21(4), 274–300.
Allen, James. (2019). The color of algorithms: An analysis and proposed research agenda for deterring algorithmic redlining. *Fordham Urban Law Journal*, 46(2), 219–270.
Armstrong, Elizabeth, and Bernstein, Mary. (2008). Culture, power, and institutions: A multi-institutional politics approach to social movements. *Sociological Theory*, 26(1), 74–99.

Beraldo, Davide, and Milan, Stefania. (2019). From data politics to the contentious politics of data. *Big Data & Society*, July–December, 1–11.

Boellstorff, Tom. (2013). Making big data, in theory. *First Monday*, 18(10). doi:10.25969/mediarep/14020.

Calzada, Igor, and Almirall, Esteve. (2019). *Barcelona's grassroots-led urban experimentation: deciphering the 'data commons' policy scheme.* Zenodo. doi:10.5281/zenodo.2604618. Conference Data for Policy 2019, London (UK), 11–12 June.

Chander, Anupam. (2017). The racist algorithm. *Michigan Law Review*, 115(6), 1023–1046.

Chenou, Jean-Marie, and Cepeda-Másmela, Carolina. (2019). #NiUnaMenos: Data activism from the Global South. *Television & New Media*, 20(4), 396–411. doi:10.1177/1527476419828995.

Cinnamon, Jonathan. (2020). Attack the data: Agency, power, and technopolitics in South African data activism. *Annals of the American Association of Geographers*, 110 (3), 623–639.

Couldry, Nick, and Mejias, Ulises. (2021). The decolonial turn in data and technology research: What is at stake and where is it heading? *Information, Communication & Society*, 26(4), 786–802. doi:10.1080/1369118X.2021.1986102.

Courchane, Marsha, and Ross, Stephen. (2019). Evidence and actions on mortgage market disparities: Research, fair lending enforcement, and consumer protection. *Housing Policy Debate*, 29(5), 769–794.

Cukier, Kenneth, and Mayer-Schoenberger, Viktor. (2013). The rise of Big Data: How it's changing the way we think about the world. *Foreign Affairs*, 92(3), 28–40.

van Dijck, Jose, Poell, Thomas, and de Waal, Martjin. (2018). *The platform society: Public values in a connective world.* New York: Oxford University Press.

Escobar, Arturo. (2018). *Designs for the Pluriverse. Radical interdependence, autonomy, and the making of worlds.* Durham: Duke University Press.

Fakhoury, Tamirace, and Icaza, Rosalba. (2023). Undoing coloniality: Polycentric governing and refugee spaces. In Frank Gadinger, and Jan Aart Scholte (Eds.), *Polycentrism: How governing works today* (pp. 47–70). Oxford University Press.

Gadinger, Frank, and Scholte, Jan Aart. (2023). *Polycentrism: How governing works today.* Oxford University Press.

Garcia, Adriana, and Le Dantec, Christopher. (2018). Quotidian report: Grassroots data practices to address public safety. Proceedings of the ACM on Human-Computer Interaction. Volume 2 Issue CSCW Article No.: 17, 1–18.

Goh, Lesly, and Goslar, Buhle. (2022). The private sector must do its part on data governance in Africa. In: Foresight Africa 22 Report. The Brookings Institution. Retrieved 16 October 2023 from https://www.brookings.edu/articles/the-private-sector-must-do-its-part-on-data-governance-in-africa/.

GSMA. (2022). State of the industry report on mobile money 2022. https://www.gsma.com/sotir/wp-content/uploads/2022/03/GSMA_State_of_the_Industry_2022_English.pdf.

Gubbins, P., and Totolo, E. (2018). Digital credit in Kenya: Evidence from demand side-surveys. Financial Sector Deepening (FSD) Kenya. https://www.fsdkenya.org/research-and-publications/datasets/digital-credit-in-kenya-evidence-from-demand-side-surveys/.

Gutierrez, Miren. (2018). *Data activism and social change.* Palgrave Pivot Cham.

Hersman, Erik. (2012). What's next for Ushahidi and its platform?Mediashift. Retrieved 15 March 2023 from https://mediashift.org/2012/08/whats-next-for-ushahidi-and-its-platform226/.

Hess, Charlotte, and Ostrom, Elinor. (2003). Ideas, artifacts, and facilities: Information as a common-pool resource. *Law and Contemporary Problems*, 66(1/2), 111–145.

Innerarity, Daniel. (2021). Making the black box society transparent. *AI & Society*. https://doi.org/10.1007/s00146-020-01130-8.

Johnen, Constantin, Parlasca, Martin, and Mußhoff, Oliver. (2021). Promises and pitfalls of digital credit: Empirical evidence from Kenya. *PLoS ONE*, 16(7), e0255215.

Kimega, Godfrey. (2021). Kenyans behaving badly on WhatsApp groups. *The Star*. Retrieved 5 October 2022 from https://www.the-star.co.ke/sasa/lifestyle/2021-08-29-kenyans-behaving-badly-on-whatsapp-groups/.

Kimeria, Ciku. (2022). The era of WhatsApp banking is with us. Quartz. Retrieved 16 March 2023 from https://qz.com/emails/africa-weekly-brief/2184332/the-era-of-whatsapp-banking-is-with-us.

Kitchin, Rob. (2014). Big data, new epistemologies and paradigm shifts. *Big Data & Society*, April–June, 1–12.

Kivuva, Elizabeth. (2021). Zamara targets WhatsApp users with digital pension plan. Business Daily Africa. Retrieved 5 October 2022 from https://www.businessdailyafrica.com/bd/markets/capital-markets/zamara-targets-whatsapp-users-with-digital-pensions-plan-3644884.

Langley, Paul, and Leyshon, Andrew. (2017). Platform capitalism: The intermediation and capitalization of digital economic circulation. *Finance and Society*, 2(1), 11–31.

Langley, Paul, and Leyshon, Andrew. (2020). The platform political economy of FinTech: Reintermediation, consolidation and capitalisation. *New Polit. Econ.*, 26(3), 376–388.

Langley, Paul, and Rodima-Taylor, Daivi. (2022). FinTech in Africa: An editorial introduction. *Journal of Cultural Economy*, 15(4), 387–400.

Mader, Philip. (2018). Contesting financial inclusion. *Development and Change*, 49(2), 461–483.

Maldonado-Torres, Nelson. (2007). On the coloniality of being: Contributions to the development of a concept. *Cultural Studies*, 21(2–3),240–270.

Malik, Nesrine. (2022). How Facebook took over the internet in Africa—and changed everything. *The Guardian*. Retrieved 1 March 2022 from https://www.theguardian.com/technology/2022/jan/20/facebook-second-life-the-unstoppable-rise-of-the-tech-company-in-africa.

Mann, Laura. (2018). Left to other peoples' devices? A political economy perspective on the big data revolution in development. *Development and Change*, 49, 3–36.

Maurer, Bill. (2015). Data mining for development? Poverty, payment, and platform. In A. Roy (Ed.), *Territories of poverty*, 126–143. University of Georgia Press.

Mavundza, Bombi. (2020). WhatsApp stokvels are back and you're probably being scammed. *Business Insider*. Retrieved 5 October 2022 from https://www.businessinsider.co.za/whatsapp-stokvel-scams-2020-6.

McDowall, Tom (2022, July 7). Kenya's data protection laws are now in effect: how to comply. *Fitts*. Retrieved 16 October 2023 from https://www.fitts.io/kenyas-data-protection-lws-are-now-in-effect-how-to-comply/.

Medine, David, and Plaitakis, Ariadne. (2023). Combining open finance and data protection for low-income consumers. CGAP Technical Note. The World Bank.

Meng, Amanda, and DiSalvo, Carl. (2018). Grassroots resource mobilization through counter-data action. *Big Data & Society*, 5(2). https://doi.org/10.1177/2053951718796862.

Metz, Cade. (2016). Forget Apple vs. the FBI: WhatsApp just switched on encryption for a billion people. *Wired*. Retrieved 1 March 2022 from https://www.wired.com/2016/04/forget-apple-vs-fbi-whatsapp-just-switched-encryption-billion-people/.

Mignolo, Walter D. (2012). *Local histories/global designs: Coloniality, subaltern knowledges, and border thinking*. Princeton: Princeton University Press.

Milan, Stefania, and van der Velden, Lonneke. (2016). The alternative epistemologies of data activism. *Digital Culture & Society*, 2(2), 57–74.

Milan, Stefania, and Gutierrez, Miren. (2018). Technopolitics in the age of Big Data. In F. Caballero, and T. Gravante (Eds.), *Networks, movements and technopolitics in Latin America*. Global Transformations in Media and Communication Research. Cham: Palgrave Macmillan. https://doi.org/10.1007/978-3-319-65560-4_5.

Milan, Stefania, and Trere, Emilio. (2019). Big Data from the South(s): Beyond data universalism. *Television & New Media*, 20(4), 319–335.

Milan, Stefania, and Barbosa, Sergio. (2020). Enter the WhatsApper: Reinventing digital activism at the time of chat apps. *First Monday*, 25(1). https://doi.org/10.5210/fm. v25i12.10414.

Mittelstadt, Brent, Allo, Patric, Taddeo, Mariarosaria, Wachter, Sandra, and Floridi, Luciano. (2016). The ethics of algorithms: Mapping the debate. *Big Data & Society*, July–December, 1–21.

Mohamed, Shakir, Marie-Therese Png, and William Isaac. (2020). Decolonial AI: Decolonial theory as sociotechnical foresight in artificial intelligence. *Philosophy & Technology*, 33, 659–684.

Moodley, Clinton. (2019). How WhatsApp groups are ruining the travel stokvel's reputation. *Independent Online*. Retrieved 5 October 2022 from https://www.iol.co.za/travel/travel-news/how-whatsapp-groups-are-ruining-the-travel-stokvels-reputation-35772880.

Ngila, Faustine. (2022). Open banking could be what Africa needs to deepen financial inclusion. *Beechamber News*. Retrieved 16 March 2023 from https://www.bee.co.za/post/open-banking-could-be-what-africa-needs-to-deepen-financial-inclusion.

Nothias, Toussaint. (2020). Access granted: Facebook's Free Basics in Africa. *Media, Culture & Society*, 42(3), 329–348.

Ostrom, Elinor. (2008). Institutions and the environment. *Economic Affairs*, 28, 24–31.

Pang, Natalie, and Yue Ting Woo. (2020). What about WhatsApp? A systematic review of WhatsApp and its role in civic and political engagement. *First Monday*, 25(12). https://doi.org/10.5210/fm.v25i12.10417.

Pijoos, Iavan. (2019). Don't fall for the R200 WhatsApp stokvels scam, Association warns. *Times Live*. Retrieved 1 March 2022 from https://www.timeslive.co.za/news/south-africa/2019-10-09-dont-fall-for-the-r200-whatsapp-stokvels-scam-association-warns/.

Ricaurte, Paola. (2019). Data epistemologies, the coloniality of power, and resistance. *Television & New Media*, 20(4), 350–365.

Rodima-Taylor, Daivi. (2022a). Sending money home in conflict settings: Revisiting migrant remittances. *Georgetown Journal of International Affairs*, 23(1), 43–51.

Rodima-Taylor, Daivi. (2022b). Land, finance, technology: Perspectives on mortgage lending. In Daivi Rodima-Taylor, and Parker Shipton (Eds.), *Land and the mortgage: History, culture, belonging*, 1–34. Berghahn Books.

Rodima-Taylor, Daivi. (2022c). Platformizing Ubuntu? FinTech, inclusion, and mutual help in Africa. *Journal of Cultural Economy*, 15(4), 416–435.

Rodima-Taylor, Daivi. (2023). The cryptopolitics of digital mutuality. In V. Bernal, K. Pype, and D. Rodima-Taylor (Eds.), *Cryptopolitics: Exposure, concealment, and digital media*, 156–183. Berghahn Books.

Rodima-Taylor, Daivi, and Grimes, William. (2019). International remittance rails as infrastructures: Embeddedness, innovation and financial access in developing economies. *Review of International Political Economy*, 26(5), 839–862.

Rotich, Juliana. (2017). Ushahidi: Empowering citizens through crowdsourcing and digital data collection. *Field Actions Science Reports* [Online], Special Issue 16. Retrieved 16 October 2023 from https://journals.openedition.org/factsreports/4316.

Scholte, J. A. (2017). Polycentrism and democracy in internet governance. In U. Kohl (Ed.), *The net and the nation state: Multidisciplinary perspectives on internet governance*, 165–184. Cambridge University Press. doi:10.1017/9781316534168.012.

Siqueira, Isabel, and Ramalho, Laís. (2024). The challenges of governance in a datascape: Theorizing the role of non-extractive methodologies in the 2030 Agenda. In Carolina Aguerre, Malcolm Campbell-Verduyn, and Jan Aart Scholte (Eds.), *Global digital data governance: Polycentric perspectives*. Routledge.

Torkelson, Erin. (2020). Collateral damages: Cash transfer and debt transfer in South Africa. *World Development*, 126, 1–11.

Van Dijck, J., Poell, T., and De Waal, M. (2019). *The platform society*. New York: Oxford University Press.

Velasquez, Sharon. (2020). FinTech: Means to inclusive economic development? *Harvard Kennedy School Journal of Hispanic Policy*, 32, 32–40.

Vodafone. (n.d.). M-Pesa. Retrieved18 October 2023fromhttps://www.vodafone.com/about-vodafone/what-we-do/consumer-products-and-services/m-pesa.

Westermeier, Carola. (2020). Money is data – The platformization of financial transactions. *Information, Communication & Society*, 23(14), 2047–2063.

6

QUESTIONS AS A DEVICE FOR DATA RESPONSIBILITY

Making Data Science Responsible by Formulating Questions in a Polycentric Way

Stefaan Verhulst

Introduction

We are living through an unprecedented transformation in our society, economy, and polity: the datafication of virtually every aspect of our lives (Gray, 2016). From the moment we awake—and often during our sleep too—our devices, the platforms we use, and the transactions we engage in leave an elaborate digital trail. This digital trail (sometimes referred to as "digital exhaust") carries both risk and opportunity (Mergel et al., 2016). From a social sciences perspective, the emergent data surplus has the potential to transform how we generate (and subsequently use) insights, allowing researchers to wean our dependency on what people *tell* us and turn instead to more reliable records of what people actually *do* (Stephens-Davidowitz, 2017).

Yet quantity doesn't necessarily translate into quality. As a string of recent failures in data handling design and mounting public anxieties around data collection practices have shown, the current data age is also marked by a variety of limitations, challenges, and concerns that greatly limit data's capacity to generate insights or effect positive social transformation within existing structures (Ghafur et al., 2020). Many of these challenges reflect existing socioeconomic and political divides (Vartanova & Gladkova, 2019). They include unequal access to data and its insights, asymmetries in technical skills and expertise, the rise of what Shoshana Zuboff has famously called "surveillance capitalism," which refers to the exploitation of data for corporate profit, as well as issues of misinformation, threats to privacy and other individual and collective rights—and much more (Zuboff, 2019; Tisne, 2021; Shafer et al., 2001).

Considered together, these challenges point to the failures of technical design and data governance. Moreover, with the consolidation and commercialization of data-driven or data-generating tools like artificial intelligence, the Internet of

DOI: 10.4324/9781003388418-7

Things, and distributed ledger technologies, these difficulties of data governance are likely to be exacerbated in the coming years. As so often happens, technology risks leaping ahead of our existing institutions and laws, rendering existing policy models obsolete and ineffective at solving the problems of tomorrow.

A number of efforts exist that are seeking to reinvent data responsibility and construct models better suited to twenty-first-century realities. In a previous paper, I argued for ten innovations toward re-imagined models for data responsibility (Verhulst, 2021). Some scholars have further explored approaches that incorporate "privacy by design," while others have suggested the need for new governance models or to expand our notions of user rights by adopting a process known as "contextual consent" (Cavoukian, 2010; Barkhuus, 2012; Micheli et al., 2020). Others have pressed for a revamping of traditional models of antitrust regulation (Khan, 2017) to change business models that support "surveillance capitalism" (Zuboff, 2019). Each of these approaches has its merits. Yet overall, the notion of data responsibility remains a work in progress, with officials and other stakeholders—including the public—still casting about for viable solutions. Society—including public officials, civil society, and community representatives—is today at an inflection point in its search to responsibly handle data so as to maximize the public good while limiting both private and public risks.

This paper argues that *questions* should also be given more consideration as a mechanism for modern data responsibility. Traditionally, questions have typically been seen solely as a device or method for inquiry (De Ruiter, 2016). We suggest, however, that designing a process for asking the *right questions* can support and enhance a polycentric perspective and play an important role in ensuring that data are used responsibly, and with maximum positive social impact. Specifically, we argue that adopting a crowdsourced approach to questions can complement polycentric values, such as multi-leveled governance, diversity and pluralism, and more fluidity. Such an approach, in turn, can help achieve a variety of key data responsibility goals, including data minimization and proportionality, increasing participation, and enhancing accountability. Therefore, in addition to "data science," we need to invest in creating a new kind of polycentric "question science" that can contribute to data responsibility.

In making these arguments, we build on two bodies of knowledge—one conceptual and the other more practical. The former consists of an existing corpus of literature around the importance of questions. In Part I, we briefly explore this research, much of it derived from the social sciences and management theory, and point to some areas of intersection with theories and values of polycentrism. This conceptual discussion is supplemented by the author's own practical experience as founder and lead of "The 100 Questions Initiative," an effort to help determine the most important questions across a variety of fields that could be answered if data were made more readily available to trusted parties. This initiative, which provides valuable insights and lessons into building a new "science of questions," is also briefly described in Part I. In Part

II, we build on this theoretical and practical knowledge to outline a set of benefits of using questions for data responsibility. Part III, the Conclusion, describes some elements of a proposed science of questions, one that can build on and extend existing polycentric governance practices and ensure a more participatory and equitable approach to how data is managed and deployed in society.

I In the Beginning, There Were Questions…

1 The Importance of Problem Definition and Formulating Questions

"If I were given one hour to save the planet, I would spend 55 minutes defining the problem and 5 minutes resolving it," Albert Einstein reportedly said. Yet despite general recognition that *good solutions* flow from *good questions*, social scientists, policymakers, and other decision-makers often overlook the importance of using questions to define and prioritize problems that need addressing. This leads to inefficient, ineffective, and risky initiatives, which in turn increase costs and erode public trust in research (and, increasingly, data) initiatives.

Recent years have, however, witnessed something of a course correction. Perhaps driven by the current surfeit in data and the often-bewildering array of options it presents, there has been a renewed interest in using questions to better design research projects and more effectively target policy interventions. Some of this literature flows from management theory, where scholars speak of the need for "a new Socratic method" to drive efficiency and innovation (Brooks et al., 2018). Social scientists likewise highlight the need for "method-driven questions"—i.e., a new method or science of questions that can circumscribe the limits of research projects, ensuring their relevance and feasibility (Hagel, 2021; Alvesson et al., 2013).

One noteworthy strand that has developed within this literature concerns the potential of opening up who *defines* and *provides input* into the types of questions asked and investigated. Recent years have seen an increase in researchers turning to not only expert opinions but also views from the public. While many projects have sourced informed residents during the empirical stages of the research process, there has been a marked increase in the number of researchers involving crowds in conceptual stages, particularly in formulating questions that research should address (Beck et al., 2022). These projects have explored the significance of *crowdsourcing as a means of defining questions* and helping define the contours of a "new science-based knowledge" (Brassuer et al., 2019).

One study, undertaken by Franzoni et al. (2021), showed that crowdsourcing can help "generate high-quality research questions" and yield important benefits when it comes to increasing efficiency and democratization. Other scholarship has shown the efficiency and potential of crowdsourcing in "building a holistic understanding of unprecedented and ill-defined problems" (Wahl et al., 2022). As we discuss further below, such approaches have much in common with polycentrism, perhaps most obviously—but not only—in their ability to widen the pool to create multiple levels of expertise, offer new avenues for "co-production," and create conditions for multi-stakeholder data governance.

Crowdsourcing, along with other means to widen the pool of expertise, offers a tremendous opportunity to not only define more democratic research processes but also to discover and help solve problems that are truly relevant to a larger section of the population. In addition, a more collaborative and transparent way of formulating questions can also accelerate and mainstream open science practices. Open science aims to ensure the free availability and usability of data that result from scholarly research, as well as the methodologies used to generate the data.

2 Questions, Crowdsourcing, and Polycentricism

The use of questions as a device for widening and making data governance more efficient and responsible shares much in common with polycentric approaches to governance, particularly when combined with crowdsourcing. Of course, the particular areas of overlap depend on how specific questions are used (and sourced), which can take many manifestations. Here, we outline three broad areas of commonality or intersection, based on our experience with the 100 Questions Initiative described further below.

- **Multi-leveled and Diffuse:** As noted by Scholte, polycentrism is characterized by "multi-layered and diffuse" sites of authority. A questions-based approach to data similarly widens the aperture of governance, conceptually by challenging existing norms and principles, but more fundamentally by increasing the number and types of stakeholders with seats at the governance table. This widening is characterized not only by greater numbers of participants but also by greater diversity in the types of stakeholders and their relative positions (or "levels") in existing governance hierarchies. In particular, a process of crowdsourcing can bring together expert opinions alongside citizens and citizen groups to create a "thicker" approach to governance, and to the questions that are asked, investigated, and ultimately acted upon.
- **Equity, Diversity, and Pluralism:** Polycentrism is an essentially pluralistic approach. In much the same way, the use of crowdsourced questions can bring traditionally marginalized and excluded voices into the process of data governance. This pluralistic approach itself operates at multiple levels and jurisdictions. It may involve demarginalizing formerly excluded voices within a specific community (or town); equally, it may operate at the supra-national level, for example allowing citizens or other stakeholders from developing countries who are directly impacted by a policy or governance issue to help reshape the underlying assumptions and hypotheses that currently guide data governance. Such a commitment to equity can ultimately result in more effective governance—mechanisms that are more attuned to local conditions and context, and capable of iterative self-improvement.

- **Fluidity:** The process of challenging existing hypotheses and asking new questions is essentially one of breaking down existing structures, assumptions, and rigidities. Instead, a polycentric questions-based approach replaces traditional methods of governance with a new set of often more informal and fluid approaches. Indeed, one of the underlying motivations for a questions-based approach is an understanding that existing ("legacy") approaches to data governance are somewhat stultified and inadequate for the pace of technical innovation. In addition, by bringing together experts and non-experts from a wide range of disciplines, there is both an understanding that law (and regulation) may be a blunt instrument and a desire to replace it with a more fluid combination of formal and informal (e.g., norm-based) approaches to data governance. As described below, the process of using questions is fundamentally "deliberative," opening up space for more informal approaches to data responsibility.

3 The 100 Questions Initiative

Driven in part by an awareness of this new interest in a science of questions, The GovLab, an action research center I co-founded at New York University's Tandon School of Engineering, launched the 100 Questions Initiative in 2019. This initiative uses a unique participatory methodology to identify the world's 100 most pressing, high-impact questions across a variety of domains—including migration, gender inequality, air quality, the future of work, disinformation, food sustainability, and governance—that could be answered by unlocking datasets and other resources. The approach is based upon the premise that truly has social, political, and economic impact, we need to start with collectively formulating the questions that can define our greatest challenges rather than simply focusing on the available data. Avoiding a regression to the data mean, the 100 Questions Initiative transitions question creation from a supply-driven to a demand-driven approach.

The unique methodology used by the 100 Questions Initiative is one of its defining features. Driven by recent research demonstrating the positive impact of crowdsourcing in science, the initiative is participatory, maximally transparent across all stages, and iterative by design (Beck et al., 2022; Wahl et al., 2022). It seeks input from a wide variety of stakeholders—domain experts, partner organizations, average users, and citizens—to help map topic areas, identify pressing questions, and then vote on and prioritize these questions. The initiative follows a four-step process.

1. **Sourcing 'bilinguals':** A key role in this process is played by so-called bilinguals'—individuals who are both domain experts and data science experts. Their braintrust serves as the linchpin of the question generation process. This melding of context-specific and data expertise ensures that the questions selected are both relevant to the field and answerable by

data. Bilinguals help guide topic-mapping direction and draft first-stage questions. Their participation is fundamentally inter-disciplinary and cuts across policy and professional domains, once again emphasizing the poly-centric potential of a new science of questions.

2. **Topic mapping:** Following stakeholder input, the initiative organizes issues and questions raised by the bilinguals into a topic map. This map serves as a springboard for the creation of data-actionable questions that have practical and/or scientific impact and are novel, feasible, and of high quality. Bilinguals use the topic map to put forward informed questions. This practice of crowdsourcing questions from a variety of experts draws on an experiment conducted in 2012 by Cambridge University's Department of Zoology to determine 100 fundamental ecological questions (Sutherland et al., 2012). Through input from 388 academic participants, 754 questions were submitted and narrowed down to a final 100 through a process of open discussion and voting. This initiative successfully provided a "substantial enhancement in understanding" of the discipline of ecology to steer the agenda for further research in that field.

3. **Clustering and reformulation:** The questions generated by the bilinguals are then grouped and reformulated thematically. By taking stock of the questions posited by experts, the 100 Questions Initiative is fundamentally deliberative and embodies its participatory and collective design values. Also, this practice introduces nuanced and multifaceted perspectives to the conceptual stage of a research project by leveraging different points of view that result in the creation of unique research questions. The bilinguals then vote on the most important questions, of which the top ten questions are published for prioritization voting by the public. This combination of expert curation with public prioritization is a good instance of the multi-leveled, polycentric potential of questions discussed above.

4. **Creating Data Collaboratives:** The end of question deliberation and selection marks the beginning of *policy action*. Equipped with expert and public inputs of which questions are the most pressing, the project brings stakeholders together to examine the top three issue areas and find avenues to build purpose-driven data collaboratives. For example, the Migration Domain led to the creation of the Big Data for Migration Alliance, the first-ever network of stakeholders furthering data collaboration for migration and human mobility policymaking.

The 100 Questions Initiative is a rigorous and time-intensive process—but it leads to a big payoff. Not only does it identify the global and cross-sectoral research areas but it also ensures that policies are actually addressing issues that are considered to be key problems. By building a strong, research- and stake-holder-backed foundation for the problems at hand, the proposed interventions are better equipped to serve communities and steer the creation (and governance) of common goods. Also, working with the public at the early stages of policymaking increases overall engagement throughout the project lifecycle because people are placed in the center, not at the margins, of action.

II Questions as Tools for Data Responsibility

Although these efforts to transform the way we define questions are ongoing, they have already begun to yield valuable insights into the potential of questions to enhance data responsibility, and more generally, into the possibilities offered by a new science of questions for polycentric policymaking. Based on the research conducted thus far, as well as the theoretical context, we believe that an updated science of questions can play an important role in enabling practitioners to develop fit-for-purpose data responsibility strategies and identify and address any gaps in their approaches for responsibly handling information across the data lifecycle. Specifically, questions can help to advance three main values or principles that are key to enhanced data responsibility. These include:

1. Data Minimization and Proportionality
2. Participation (Democratization)
3. Accountability

1. Data Minimization and Proportionality

Driven partly—though not only—by the European Union's General Data Protection Regulation (GDPR) requirement that data collection should be "adequate, relevant and not excessive," data minimization and the related concept of proportionality are integral to data responsibility and remain a key pillar of the Fair Information Practice Principles (FIPPs) (Biega et al., 2020; Antignac et al., 2014; Hartzog, 2017). Data minimization can be defined as the practice of collecting and storing only personal information that is directly relevant (i.e., proportional) to a given task or purpose (i.e., purpose specification).

Asking the right questions can advance the pursuit of data minimization in several ways. First, questions can serve as *devices to frame problems more effectively*. Any initiative that collects or uses data can begin by asking what public problems the data is intended to solve. Too often, data is collected simply because it exists. Indeed, while this practice is data rich, it is information poor. As noted previously, the current *supply-driven* approach to data-driven policymaking is better replaced by a *demand-driven* approach that understands the true nature of social, political, economic, cultural, or other public needs that can be served by the data.

Relatedly, questions can help *determine the purpose for data collection and reuse*. Determining the purpose of data closely follows from the broader task of problem definition. Understanding a problem may alter or limit the types or extent of data collected, and the ways in which it is subsequently stored or used. These are all vital steps in ensuring data proportionality and minimization across the data value chain.

Questions can also help organizations *determine data retention policies*. A key principle of data minimization is that not all data available (within or external to an organization) are required at all times. Asking the right questions about what data are needed and what problems they are intended to solve can help determine if any data should be discarded, or at least archived.

Finally, questions can encourage data minimization by allowing organizations to *develop an overall data strategy*. Such a strategy would clearly identify top-level priorities and force data-holding organizations to focus on high-value problems and seek out the low-hanging fruit—the readily actionable issues—to ensure that data has the maximum impact in a responsible way. A prioritized data strategy discourages the creation of general data platforms or repositories and leads to a more tailored use of data that advances several related causes: data minimization, individual privacy, and more efficient allocation of resources.

2 Participation (Democratization)

As noted, the participatory, inclusive potential of questions has significant overlap with multi-stakeholder and more specifically polycentric approaches to governance (Kalfagianni & Pattberg, 2013; Matasick, 2017; Reggi, 2020). Recently, questions about inclusiveness and equity have moved to the core of conversations surrounding data responsibility as the focus has shifted to the re-use of data collected for one initial purpose to address other questions. Many of these conversations involve opening up data and its potential to spur transparency and democratization but they apply more widely to how all forms of data are collected, used, and re-used (Reggi, 2020). Our research suggests that asking the right questions can play a critical role in increasing democratization and participation by giving average people, who are usually the end-target of resulting policy interventions, a say in the design and direction of public programming. Furthermore, research has shown that increasing communication between users and producers of knowledge is essential to cultivate relevant and credible institutional and technological solutions to some of today's most pressing issues (Sutherland et al., 2011).

These consultations can also provide the needed social license for the re-use of data. These benefits can be achieved in at least four ways. As the example of the 100 Questions Initiative suggests, *questions can themselves be formulated in a participatory manner* by crowdsourcing opinions and priorities from citizens. This sets the foundations for a more inclusive and democratic approach to data governance and data re-use, whereby those most affected are part of the agenda-setting and conversation from the very beginning. This idea is not based on the notion that scientists lack questions, but that involving a broader range of actors can help leverage unique perspectives that result in more well-rounded (and well-received) research questions (Beck et al., 2022). This can be thought of as ensuring *participation by design*, and it also ensures transparency in the question-setting process (i.e., how the questions came to be is traceable and justifiable).

Questions also offer a *more sophisticated way for researchers, policymakers, and data holders to engage with the public* than many other commonly used approaches. They offer a way to create more cohesion between stakeholders in the government, academic, private, and civil society sectors of society and foster greater collaboration. In particular, they are a more nuanced and interactive method than standard consent forms with checkboxes that present users with binary questions and offer little opportunity for laypeople to shape an agenda. This approach puts forward a more polycentric approach to problem-solving by encouraging greater discussion on some of the world's biggest research priorities by stakeholders across levels, domains, and jurisdictions.

At their broadest level, questions offer a mechanism to *foster a more inclusive public debate* on the issues that really matter to society. The benefits go beyond participation or democracy (though these are valuable ends too). A more inclusive, and less ideological, debate leads to more efficient allocation of resources, and helps ensure that a wider pool of expertise is tapped into, thus opening up new solutions and avenues for innovation. It is important to recognize, though, that in order for the debate to be truly inclusive, the questions must themselves be subject to questioning, and in particular, be closely examined for their own implicit biases. Formulating questions in a participatory manner (see above) can help in this regard.

Among the many pressing areas where questions offer potential for better public conversation and debate across fields, few are as vital as the need to *acquire social license for re-using data beyond initial consent*, a key element of data responsibility. Such a license is vital to achieving the critical balance between risk and opportunity offered by data, and to unlocking innovative and unexpected public goods from privately held data.

3 Accountability

The third way in which questions can contribute to data responsibility is by enhancing accountability. Accountability can be captured in various ways. Broadly, it refers to the ability of a system or initiative to self-correct in response to impact or to the measured opinions and feedback expressed by those most affected. In this way, accountability is inextricably linked to the previous value: more participation and inclusiveness create virtuous feedback loops that, when filtered through a responsible data framework, will enhance responsiveness.

Questions can begin to establish accountability by forcing data stewards and other stakeholders to ask who has been impacted by a data project, and who has benefited from its insights (Verhulst, 2018). By identifying demographic groups and subpopulations, questions allow policymakers to *identify and engage with key stakeholders*, a vital initial step in creating feedback loops, reclaiming agency for marginalized populations, and encouraging a more open, polycentric approach to responsible data governance. Importantly, questions can also help identify experts and domain specialists who might otherwise be overlooked in such initiatives.

When filtered through a responsive system or framework, feedback loops create the ability to *fine-tune and iterate on initial versions of projects*. In this way, questions create the conditions not only for accountability but also for improvement and enhanced impact via internal, rapid beta-tests of project directions and ideas. By pinpointing the relevant issues and risks of a problem, questions also create *incentives for data holders (e.g., large technology companies) to share data and participate* in initiatives. This also helps build accountability by allowing data holders to identify potential uses (and misuses) of information, thus building in more adequate safeguards into the way data is used and re-used.

Finally, questions can enhance accountability by helping project holders *anticipate and measure impact and risk*, as shown in Table 6.1. Any self-correcting system relies on adequate inputs in order to fine-tune and iterate. Developing and collecting appropriate metrics is a vital part of ensuring accountability, allowing all stakeholders (including society at large) to maximize the possible benefits of data use and re-use while minimizing its harms.

TABLE 6.1 Questions as tool for data responsibility

Questions as a tool for data minimization and proportionality	*Questions as a tool for participation (democratization)*	*Questions as a tool for accountability*
Questions, developed in a polycentric way, can enable actors to:	Questions, developed in a polycentric way, can:	Questions, developed in a polycentric way, can enable actors to:
• Determine the purpose for data collection and re-use; • Determine data retention policies; • Develop an overall data strategy.	• Offer a more sophisticated way for researchers, policymakers, and data holders to engage with the public; • Foster a more inclusive public debate; • Enable data users acquire a social license for re-using data beyond initial consent.	• Identify and engage with key stakeholders; • Create feedback loops to fine-tune and iterate on initial versions of projects; • Create incentives for data holders to share data and participate in data sharing activities; • Enhance accountability by helping project holders anticipate and measure impact and risk.

III Conclusion: Toward a New Movement and Science of Questions

Current debates about data and its use (and re-use) generally stem from the supply side. Researchers and policymakers examine the data that is most readily available and ask which questions or problems it can address. This paper has argued for a different approach—one that brings a more polycentric perspective that begins from the demand side of the equation. This approach begins by asking questions about what really matters to identify and consider true societal needs. At its core, this is a deeply humanistic approach, one that prioritizes society and its members—and the diversity of their needs—above data. Ultimately, data is a means, not an end. This approach also provides an additional component by fostering enhanced data responsibility. This paper is a call for a new science of questions that would complement many values of polycentrism (specifically, multi-leveled governance, pluralism and diversity, and fluidity), in the process creating a new governance device and more inclusive conditions for data collaboration and re-use. As we have outlined above, this science of questions would help to advance the following three principles:

- **Data Minimization:** Questions serve as a *device to frame problems more effectively* by defining the challenges that data scientists and policymakers seek to address to establish a *gestalt* of the problem space. Taking stock of the organization of data collection, use, and re-use helps *determine the purpose for these practices* and advances the vital goal of reducing the amount of data collected frivolously.
- **Increased Participation and Democratization:** Through crowdsourcing techniques, bringing together domain experts, beneficiaries (including those among the public), and policymakers who will ultimately be tasked with implementing any recommendations or actions generated by the questions can develop richer questions. Increasing the awareness and agency of citizens can herald a more participatory, multi-leveled, and trusted policy-making environment.
- **Increased Accountability:** Finally, a *science of questions must include rigorous methods of (open) assessment* to audit the types of questions put forward, the data available, and the impact of any data use and re-use that results from question-driven initiatives. In essence, we need to be able to question the questions' provenance and action steps. Opening policy conversations from intervention inception can create virtuous feedback loops that enhance responsible data frameworks and produce meaningful expert and citizen responsiveness, advancing the science of open question generation.

We are in the very incipient stages of developing this science of questions. In the coming months and years, our methods will be fine-tuned and improved, always in as participatory a manner as possible. Already, though, we can confidently say that questions are no longer simply devices for inquiry. Their potential impact is much bigger. Questions are living, active devices to ensure data responsibility—and even more, to generate positive social impact. They are fluid tools that can be used to collectively define the borders of common goods—and thus enablers for polycentric governance.

References

The 100 Questions Initiative. (n.d.) Accessed June 29, 2021. https://the100questions.org.

Alvesson, Mats, & Sandberg Jörgen. (2013). *Constructing Research Questions: Doing Interesting Research*. London, UK: SAGE Publications.

Antignac, Thibaud, & Daniel Le Métayer. (2014). Privacy Architectures: Reasoning about Data Minimisation and Integrity. *Security and Trust Management*, 8743, 17–32. doi:10.1007/978-3-319-11851-2_2.

Barkhuus, Louise. (2012). *The Mismeasurement of Privacy: Using Contextual Integrity to Reconsider Privacy in HCI*. CHI '12: Proceedings of the SIGCHI Conference on Human Factors in Computing Systems, 367–376. doi:10.1145/2207676.2207727.

Beck, Susanne, Brasseur, Tiare, Poetz, Marion, & Sauermann, Henry. (2022). What is the Problem? Crowdsourcing Research Questions in Science. *SSRN Electronic Journal*. doi:10.2139/ssrn.3598181.

Biega, Asia J., Peter Potash, Hal Daumé, Fernando Diaz, & Michèle Finck. (2020). *Operationalizing the Legal Principle of Data Minimization for Personalization*. SIGIR '20: Proceedings of the 43rd International ACM SIGIR Conference on Research and Development in Information Retrieval, 399–408. https://doi.org/10.1145/3397271.3401034.

Brasseur, Tiare-Maria, Susanne Beck, Henry Sauermann, & Marion Poetz. (2019). *Crowdsourcing Research Questions? Leveraging the Crowd's Experiential Knowledge for Problem Finding*. Academy of Management Annual Meeting Proceedings, no. 1. https://doi.org/10.5465/AMBPP.2019.115.

Brooks, Alison Wood, & Leslie K. John. (2018). The Surprising Power of Questions. *Harvard Business Review*. https://hbr.org/2018/05/the-surprising-power-of-questions.

Cavoukian, Ann. (2010). Privacy by Design: The Definitive Workshop. *Identity in the Information Society*, 3 (2), 247–251.

Franzoni, Chiara, Marion Poetz, & Henry Sauermann. (2022). Crowds, Citizens, and Science: A Multi-dimensional Framework and Agenda for Future Research. *Industry and Innovation*, 29 (2), 251–284.

Ghafur, Saira, Jackie Van Dael, Melanie Leis, Ara Darzi, & Aziz Sheikh. (2020). Public Perceptions on Data Sharing: Comparing Attitudes in the US and UK. *SSRN Electronic Journal*, 2 (9). doi:10.2139/ssrn.3586711.

Gray, Jonathan. (2016). Datafication and Democracy: Recalibrating Digital Information Systems to Address Societal Interests. *Juncture*, 23 (3), 197–201. doi:10.1111/newe.12013.

Hagel, John. (2021). Good Leadership Is About Asking Good Questions. *Harvard Business Review*. https://hbr.org/2021/01/good-leadership-is-about-asking-good-questions.

Hartzog, Woodrow. (2017) The Inadequate, Invaluable Fair Information Practices. *Maryland Law Review*, 76 (952). https://ssrn.com/abstract=3017312.

Kalfagianni, Agni, & Philipp Pattberg. (2013). Participation and Inclusiveness in Private Rule-Setting Organizations: Does It Matter for Effectiveness? *Innovation: The European Journal of Social Science Research*, 26 (3), 231–250. doi:10.1080/13511610.2013.771888.

Khan, Lina M. (2017). Amazon's Antitrust Paradox. *The Yale Law Journal*, 126 (3), 564–907.

Kingsmill, Sylvia, & Ann Cavoukian. (2016). Privacy by Design: Setting a New Standard for Privacy Certification. Deloitte. https://www2.deloitte.com/content/dam/Deloitte/ca/Documents/risk/ca-en-ers-privacy-by-design-brochure.pdf.

Koenig-Archibugi, Mathias, & Zürn Michael. (2006). *New Modes of Governance in the Global System: Exploring Publicness, Delegation and Inclusiveness*. Basingstoke, England: Palgrave Macmillan.

Matasick, Craig. (2017). Open Government: How Transparency and Inclusiveness Can Reshape Public Trust. In Rolf Alter (ed.), *Trust and Public Policy: How Better Governance Can Help Rebuild Public Trust*, 105–122. Paris: OECD.

Mergel, Ines, R. Karl Rethemeyer, & Kimberley Isett. (2016). Big Data in Public Affairs. *Public Administration Review*, 76 (6), 928–937. doi:10.1111/puar.12625.

Micheli, Marina, Marisa Ponti, Max Craglia, & Anna Berti Suman. (2020). Emerging Models of Data Governance in the Age of Datafication. *Big Data & Society*, 7 (2). doi:10.1177/2053951720948087.

National Academies of Sciences, Engineering, and Medicine. (2018). *Open Science by Design: Realizing a Vision for 21st Century Research*. Washington, DC:The National Academies Press. https://doi.org/10.17226/25116.

Rodima-Taylor, Daivi. (2023). The cryptopolitics of digital mutuality. In V. Bernal, K. Pype, and D. Rodima-Taylor (Eds.), *Cryptopolitics: Exposure, Concealment, and Digital Media*, 156–183. Berghahn Books.

de Ruiter, Jan-Peter. (2016). *Questions: Formal, Functional and Interactional Perspectives*. Cambridge, UK: Cambridge University Press.

Shafer, Steven, Coral Celeste, Paul DiMaggio, & Eszter Hargittai. (2001). From Unequal Access to Differentiated Use: A Literature Review and Agenda for Research on Digital Inequality. *The Russell Sage Foundation Journal of the Social Sciences*. https://www.russellsage.org/research/reports/dimaggio.

Spradlin, Dwayne. (2012). Are You Solving the Right Problem? *Harvard Business Review*. https://hbr.org/2012/09/are-you-solving-the-right-problem.

Stephens-Davidowitz, Seth. (2017). *Everybody Lies: Big Data, New Data, and What the Internet Can Tell Us About Who We Really Are*. HarperCollins.

Sutherland, W. J., Fleishman, E., Mascia, M. B., Pretty, J., & Rudd, M. A. (2011). Methods for Collaboratively Identifying Research Priorities and Emerging Issues in Science and Policy. *Methods in Ecology and Evolution*, 2 (3), 238–247. doi:10.1111/j.2041-210x.2010.00083.x.

Sutherland, W. J., Freckleton, R. P., Godfray, H. C., Beissinger, S. R., Benton, T., Cameron, D. D., Carmel, Y., Coomes, D. A., Coulson, T., Emmerson, M. C., Hails, R. S., Hays, G. C., Hodgson, D. J., Hutchings, M. J., Johnson, D., Jones, J. P., Keeling, M. J., Kokko, H., Kunin, W. E., … Wiegand, T. (2012). Identification of 100 Fundamental Ecological Questions. *Journal of Ecology*, 101 (1), 58–67. doi:10.1111/1365-2745.12025.

Tisne, Martin. (2021). Collective Data Rights Can Stop Big Tech from Obliterating Privacy. *MIT Technology Review*. https://www.technologyreview.com/2021/05/25/1025297/collective-data-rights-big-tech-privacy/.

Vartanova, Elena, & Anna Gladkova. (2019). New Forms of the Digital Divide. In Josef Trappel (ed.), *Digital Media Inequalities: Policies Against Divides, Distrust and Discrimination*, 193–213. Gothenburg: University of Gothenburg.

Verhulst, Stefaan G. (2018). The Three Goals and Five Functions of Data Stewards. *Data Stewards*. https://medium.com/data-stewards-network/the-three-goals-and-five-functions-of-data-stewar ds-60242449f378.

Verhulst, Stefaan G. (2021). Reimagining Data Responsibility: 10 New Approaches toward a Culture of Trust in Re-Using Data to Address Critical Public Needs. *Data & Policy*. doi:10.1017/dap.2021.4.

Wahl, J., Füller, J., & Hutter, K. (2022). What's the Problem? How Crowdsourcing and Text Mining May Contribute to the Understanding of Unprecedented Problems Such as Covid-19. *R&D Management*. https://doi.org/10.1111/radm.12526.

Zuboff, Shoshana. (2019). *The Age of Surveillance Capitalism: The Fight for a Human Future at the New Frontier of Power*. New York, NY: PublicAffairs.

PART II

Controversies

7

DECENTRALIZED BUT COORDINATED

Probing Polycentricity in EU Data Protection Cross-border Enforcement

Wenlong Li and Dan Yang

Introduction

The concept of polycentricity or polycentric governance is rarely used in data protection scholarship, despite some work that addresses polycentric systems of various sorts in relation to the GDPR without reference to this concept. For instance, Bennett and Raab (2006, p. 233) contend that the governance of data protection is 'a complex regime which includes multiple actors and structures and many tools', with DPAs acting simultaneously as 'advocates, ombudspersons, and administrative authorities'. Jóri (2015, p. 134) contends the two functions of DPA – that is, shaping (as a privacy advocate) and applying (as a mediator) data protection law – are not equally written within the data protection law explicitly. Consensus started to emerge on the basis that data protection enforcement is not monocentric, static, and technical. Rather, it is inherently political, dynamic, and polycentric, taking into account social interactions between national authorities, EU bodies, and other stakeholders, particularly in the case of cross-border enforcement. With a detailed comparison between *CNIL* (French DPA) and *Garante* (Italian DPA), Righettini (2011) shows that local enforcement of the GDPR is hierarchical and court-centered in France, but polycentric in Italy, in the sense that Garante shares responsibilities and competences with courts. Vranaki's (2016, p. 265) surveys of cloud investigations conducted by several data protection authorities (DPAs) in the EU suggest that, unlike the usual image of enforcer or advocate, DPAs subscribe to what she calls 'bargaining enforcement', i.e., regular bargaining with cloud service providers with either sticks or carrots. In addition, some empirical works are undertaken on data breaches of a cross-border nature (Kloza & Mościbroda, 2014; Malatras et al., 2017) with enforcement challenges facing DPAs identified, such as language barriers, lack of a single point of contact, lack of (sensitive) information exchange, and divergence in the interpretation of the law.

DOI: 10.4324/9781003388418-9

There are generally two ways in which the GDPR enforcement can be viewed as a polycentric system. First, the fact that each data protection authority retains 'absolute independence' from their equivalents in other Member States as well as from the EU authority (i.e., the EDPB) to investigate, issue fines, and take other enforcement measures aligns with the principles of polycentric governance. Second, the GDPR is characterized by its extraterritorial reach which extends an enforcement landscape beyond the EU and occasionally involves international cooperation and coordination schemes (such as bilateral Memoranda of Understanding) or on an *ad hoc* basis. Yet, this form of coordination and collaboration corresponds more to networked governance rather than polycentric governance.

This chapter primarily addresses the first aspect, characterizing the EU's handling of cross-border enforcement under the GDPR as a polycentric system, with a particular reference to the relevance and impact of coordination. The creation of a polycentric system for the handling of cross-border enforcement stems from the EU's fear of centralization of power (Franchino, 2007), but the enforcement powers conferred upon the EDPB are limited to the instance of strict necessity. As such, the board's coordinating role is crucial in fulfilling the practical goal of ending fragmentation in the Directive era while ensuring a consistent enforcement landscape.

This chapter presents case studies the compromises and intricacies of the current polycentric system for data protection enforcement. On the one hand, the GDPR (enforcement) overlooks, somewhat intentionally, borderless and 'establishment-less' practices that fall outside the scope of the one-stop-shop (OSS). This leads to significant fragmentation and inconsistency in several aspects of the GDPR application, including the identification of the controller/processor (particularly in the context of public–private partnership), the types of violation across the GDPR provisions, and the types of impositions. On the other, the fine line between the EDPB serving in its dispute resolution role only in circumstances of utmost necessity and the EU entity overstepping its remits and projecting itself as a higher hierarchy is difficult, if not impossible, to draw. We further illustrate that the latest various endeavors, respectively by the EDPB and the European Commission, in improving the cooperation and coordination between the DPAs are not intended to address these structural issues.

The chapter has four parts. After the Introduction, Section II provides a primer to polycentric governance that provides contexts for the following analysis. Section III situates data protection enforcement within the context of polycentric governance, examining in particular the role of the EDPB in both sustaining and threatening the system. The endeavors made by the EDPB in addressing this issue are briefly mapped and analyzed as well. Section IV provides two case studies – respectively on Clearview AI and Meta – which illustrate the two contrasting problems concerning GDPR enforcement as a polycentric system. Whereas the EU investigations into Clearview AI reveal the critical loophole intentionally left by the EU legislators to deal with processing by establishment-less undertakings,

Meta shows the intricacy of coordination and conflict between national DPAs and the EDPB. The chapter ends in Section IV with reflections on these two case studies and polycentric governance more generally. A caveat of the chapter is that it focuses only on the interplay between data protection authorities, as well as that between DPAs and the EDPB. Other relationships across realms (e.g., courts and arbitrators) and across fields of law (competition and consumer authorities) are not within the scope of this chapter.

II Polycentric Governance: A Primer

Polycentric governance refers to a normative framework that involves multiple centers of authority and decision-making (Ostrom, 2010; Carlisle & Gruby, 2017; Bruns, 2019). It is decentralized in nature in the sense that each actor has its own rules, powers, and responsibilities. Yet, a certain degree of cooperation and coordination is necessary to make the system sustainable and fulfilling. The idea behind it is that it allows for flexibility, diversity, and adaptability, while encouraging the integration of diverse perspectives and knowledge, with a view to improving overall effectiveness and resilience (Gasser & Alemeida, 2017).

Polycentric governance is employed often in complex and interconnected systems, such as environmental management (Jordan, 2018; Nagendra & Ostrom, 2012; Morrison, 2017), resource allocation (Baldwin et al., 2016), and commons (Carlisle & Gruby, 2019). In the legal realm, it is discussed in decentralized architecture (Gasser & Almeida, 2017), adjudication and justice (King 2008, 2012; Shawoo & McDermott, 2020), as well as early discussions on internet/cyberspace governance (Reidenberg, 2000).

There are some related concepts, such as 'networked governance' (Caplan, 2022), 'nested governance' (Shackelford & Dockery, 2019), or multi-level governance (Stephenson, 2013), which share some similarities with polycentric governance. In brief, polycentric governance features the existence of multiple centers of authority, whereas networked governance emphasizes the interconnectedness and collaboration among actors. Multi-level governance concerns how authority is distributed *vertically* among different levels of government (central, regional, and local), while polycentric governance involves a *horizontal* distribution of power across a diverse range of entities, including non-government actors, communities, and organizations.

In sum, several common parameters can be used to describe or evaluate the overall quality and effectiveness of a polycentric system, including decentralization (distribution of decision-making authority among multiple centers), subsidiarity (empowerment of local and regional institutions), coordination (e.g., presence of communication channels, collaborative mechanisms, and shared goals), adaptability (to changing circumstances), equity and inclusiveness, efficiency and effectiveness, and legitimacy (determined by the transparency, accountability, and fairness of the decision-making processes).

III Cross-border Enforcement as a Polycentric System

The ways in which data protection authorities interact and cooperate with each other with a view to reaching a consensus on a decision correspond approximately to a polycentric system. It is a complex, layered regulatory landscape in which each DPA has, in principle, 'absolute independence'. A number of decision-making centers operate autonomously and yet somewhat coordinated and under cooperation through a number of mechanisms. On the one hand, DPAs compete in a subtle and even arguable manner. The fact that they have varying approaches to enforcement (e.g., the level of activism, the trade-off between action and guidance) could create a perception of competition among DPAs, but not necessarily intentional or harmful. The perceived competition is a by-product of their efforts to achieve effective enforcement. On the other hand, DPAs are also obliged to cooperate, primarily in the case of cross-border processing, with a view to achieving the so-called one-stop shop mechanism (OSS).

1 GDPR and its Predecessor

Prior to the GDPR, the EU data protection laws were enforced by each data protection authority for each individual country. Supranational undertakings that operate across borders therefore must engage with multiple DPAs for the same subject matter. As the CIPL rightly points out, this was 'unmanageable for companies … and an inefficient waste of resources for regulators' (CIPL, 2021, p. 7). The Directive witnessed a fragmented, decentralized enforcement model (Lynskey, 2017), where each DPA was competent to enforce data protection rules in their own territory, with the Art. 29 Working Party (A29WP) lacking power or agency to coordinate. This purely decentralized model emphasizes the independence and autonomy of authorities in accordance with the EU's principles of subsidiarity (Hartley, 2004), and hence aligns with the principles of polycentric governance. Yet, due to the lack of cooperation and coordination marked as one of the primary enforcement problems in need of reform, it is debatable whether the Directive's enforcement corresponds to a polycentric system.

This issue of consistency and coordination is explicitly addressed by the new GDPR. Its enforcement is operated in a decentralized manner in which each DPA has competence to independently perform their tasks or exercise powers on their own territory. For data processing taking place or, having effects on data subjects, in multiple countries, the GDPR provides a system of cooperation called 'one-stop shop' (OSS), within which DPAs cooperate in order to reach consensus. The OSS is devised to reduce the administrative burdens for controllers or processors who would otherwise have to engage multiple authorities on the same matter, and to make it simpler for individuals to exercise their rights from their own country, without needing to engage with other authorities even in cross-border cases. The OSS operates principally as follows: a lead supervisory authority (LEAs) is determined on the basis of the main or single establishment of the controller or processor concerned. LEA is in a position to coordinate with concerned supervisory authorities (CSA) by drafting and tabling a decision for deliberation and approval. CSAs may raise 'relevant and reasoned objections' that LEA shall have due regard. In that case, a LEA may either accept the objection(s), thereby revising the draft decision accordingly, or refuse to do so, hence referring the case to the EDPB. The EU body is in that case obliged to make a binding decision that shall be adopted by the LEA. Under the OSS, the DPAs are obliged to assist each other (Art. 61), including but not limited to information exchange and, where possible, conduct joint operations (Art. 62).

Unlike the A29WP that serves only in an advisory capacity, the EDPB is granted with limited powers to sustain a polycentric decision-making process while in the meantime ensuring consistent and coherent application of the law.

It serves two main roles in OSS: it *first* maintains the polycentric system by facilitating consensus-building so that decisions can be made collectively and effectively. It promotes consistency primarily by offering guidelines, recommendations, and binding decisions on matters relating to the protection of personal data. Second, in the case of a dispute between DPAs that cannot be resolved with best efforts, the EDPB is placed in a position to make a binding decision.

When the EDPB promotes cooperation between DPAs, it does not replace DPAs or affect their enforcement powers by any means. DPAs retain their autonomy and decision-making powers, capable of delivering regulatory actions independently. The coordinating role of the EDPB is designed only to sustain the decentralized decision-making structure, and hence the OSS may be viewed as a polycentric system. Hence, the polycentric nature of data protection enforcement is deeply rooted in the emphasis on independence of various forms explicitly stated in the GDPR, and further consolidated by the Court of Justice of the European Union. In certain circumstances, the engagement of the EDPB may deviate from a polycentric approach to enforcement, as there is a centralization of decision-making power within the EDPB in some circumstances. As Lynskey (2017) rightly points out, the ways in which the EDPB's activities de facto reduce the DPA's independence could cause problems of subsidiarity and national identity. However, polycentric governance does not necessarily exclude all forms of coordination. Quite the opposite, it characteristically requires some degree of coordination, particularly in complex systems involving interdependences and shared objectives. In the context of data protection, coordination facilitated by the EDPB is a critical way to ensure consistency in GDPR enforcement, particularly in the cases of a cross-border nature.

There is one critical weakness of the OSS, which might be deliberately designed, that may affect the polycentric nature of EU data protection enforcement. The OSS is predicated on the fact that the controllers/processors involved have an *establishment* in the EU, interpreted by the EDPB (2020, p. 6, echoing recital 22) as 'effective and real exercise of activity through stable arrangement'.

As the EDPB explains, the threshold for 'stable arrangement' can be quite low, and the presence of one single employee or agent of a non-EU entity in the Union 'acting with a sufficient degree of stability' would suffice. While the EDPB claims (2022c, p. 7) that OSS applies to cooperation between DPAs 'in all cases based on cross-border processing', the omission of those who don't have an establishment are intentionally left to engage separately with all the EU authorities where relevant, without any sense of cooperation or collaboration. As the A29WP states, in its guidelines on the identification of a leading supervisory authority (2017, p. 10), 'the mere presence of a representative in a Member State does not trigger the one-stop-shop mechanism ... [and] controllers must deal with local supervisory authorities in every Member State they are active in, through their local representative'. Similarly, in the EDPB's guidelines on the GDPR's territorial scope (2019, pp. 6–7), the notion of establishment is read as 'broad [but] not without limits'; the mere fact that the undertaking's website is accessible in the Union is not adequate to conclude that the non-EU entity has an establishment. As the EU's incentive for companies overseas to establish within the EU and contribute to its digital economy is obvious, the lack of arrangement can be understandably viewed, not as a blind spot, but as an intentional design. As we will show in the case study on Clearview AI, however, the lack of any coordinating arrangement for 'establishmentless' undertakings is neither negligible nor justifiable, particularly when they are capable of exerting cross-border impacts.

2 Controversy and Reform

Despite the carefully crafted mechanisms of consistency and cooperation, DPAs still confront practical challenges in cooperation with each other. As revealed in a recent report prepared for the EDPB (Herveg et al., 2023), multiple factors affect effective cooperation and coordination, including looming deadlines, varying thresholds for admissibility, inconsistent procedures, and so on.

Since early 2020, the EDPB has made multiple attempts to improve enforcement and cooperation between DPAs. Some of the attempts are clearly stated within the GDPR (such as dispute resolution, urgency procedures, and joint operations), and the EDPB is committed to operationalizing them in a more effective manner. Others do not have explicit legislative backing and hence rest upon the EDPB's broad powers stipulated in Art. 66 GDPR. It appears that the EDPB attends not just to some typical agendas, such as information sharing, but also to resources that may be better pooled and shared, including academic expertise and resource support from each Member State. The EDPB's reform culminated in the two-day meeting held in Vienna in April 2022, with a statement adopted (known as the Vienna Declaration) reflecting the consensus reached about a diversity of methods to improve enforcement cooperation (EDPB, 2022b) (see Table 7.1).

TABLE 7.1 An overview of the EDPB's initiatives to improve enforcement by and cooperation between the DPAs

Starting date	Name	Nature	Objective (original quote from the EDPB)	Measures taken
28/04/ 2022	Enforcement Cooperation (Vienna Meeting)	State- ment	To express the agreement by the EDPB members achieved in the Vienna Meeting	Document on the Selection of the Cases of Strategic Importance
20/10/ 2020	Coordinated Enforcement Framework (CEF)	Project	To allow DPAs to pursue joint actions in a flexible but coordinated manner	Carried out on an annual basis to define topics of common interest (e.g., use of cloud-based services by the public sector in 2022, and the DPO's role in 2023)
15/12/ 2020	Pool of Expert (PoE)	Project	To provide material sup- port to EDPB members in the form of expertise that is useful for investigations and enforcement activities	Call for expression of interest in February 2022 Document on the Terms of Reference of the EDPB Support Pool of Experts
2023	Joint Investi- gations (Art. 62)	Project	To provide an operational platform (taskforces) for cases requiring coopera- tion on enforcement matters	The cookie Banner Taskforce (lead by CNIL)'s report adop- ted by the EDPB on 17 January 2023 ChatGPT taskforce
10/10/ 2022	Harmoniza- tion of pro- cedural rules in relation to the GDPR enforcement	Project	To iron out the differ- ences in administrative procedures and practices which may have a detri- mental impact on cross- border cooperation	Letter to Commis- sioner Reynders Possible Opinion (as indicated in the Work Programme 2023–2024) on the EC draft propo- sal for legislation ("Wishlist") Best practices
2023– 2024	Mutual Assistance (Art. 61)	Guide- lines	To further operationalize the mechanisms of mutual assistance per Art. 61 GDPR by offering gui- dance and details	Work Programme 2023–2024
2023– 2024	Urgency Procedure (Art. 66)	Guide- lines	To further operationalize the mechanisms of urgency procedure per Art. 66 GDPR by offering guidance and details	Work Programme 2023–2024

Starting date	Name	Nature	Objective (original quote from the EDPB)	Measures taken
05/08/ 2021	Resources support	Report	To respond to the request from the Committee on Civil Liberties, Justice and Home Affairs (LIBE Committee) of the European Parliament to share some statistics on resources made available by Member States to the supervisory authorities	Document on the Resources made available by the Member States
14/03/ 2022	International Cooperation	Report	To provide adequate safeguards for personal data transferred to a third country in case of international enforcement cooperation	Document on the Toolbox for International Enforcement Cooperation

Almost all the cooperation mechanisms established by the GDPR now have a bearing on the EDPB's coordinating role, with subtle implications for the current polycentric model of enforcement. Whereas an 'action plan' is expected to be created at the EDPB level (albeit initiated by the LEA) to ensure efficient cooperation through the OSS mechanism, taskforces would be created (as are shown in the case of cookie banners and ChatGPT) to stimulate joint operations (EDPB, 2023). Notably, despite that Art. 62 GDPR does not explicitly engage the EDPB, a new unofficial role is created by the EDPB itself in summoning taskforces, in response to the realities that DPAs may 'not engage as actively as expected, thereby incurring delay, conflict and stifled progress' (EDPB, 2022a). A common enforcement framework would be established at the EDPB level, on an annual basis, in which the DPAs exchange national enforcement strategies at the EDPB with a view to setting joint priorities. Further, the EDPB is explicitly committed to streamlining dispute resolution and urgency procedures, possibly via guidelines, while consolidating joint operations and consistency mechanisms. DPAs are also expected to overcome institutional barriers via unofficial and unformal methods, such as 'rapid informal consensus building', and 'alignment-stimulating' regular internal workshops (organized by the EDPB).

Apart from institutional and organizational arrangements, the EDPB has a notable indication of its enforcement strategies or orientations. Gwendal Le Grand, Head of Activity for Enforcement Support and Coordination, contends that the primary objective of the EDPB's reform is distinct from the focal point of media attention and public debate, that is, actions against tech giants, particularly from the LEAs (Bracy, 2022). A concept of 'case of strategic importance' is thus proposed, with no relevant references to the GDPR provisions. The EDPB does not provide a clear definition but proposes a range of criteria, quantitative and qualitative, such as a large (but undefined) number of data subjects affected, existence of a 'structural or recurring problem' in several member states, and the interplay between data protection and other areas of law (e.g., digital competition). What falls within the scope of strategic importance remains to be contextually assessed.

Since 2020, the EDPB has been initiating discussions on the improvement of cooperation between DPAs in cross-border cases. In its statement on enforcement cooperation in April 2022, the EDPB made a 'wish list' for procedural aspects that can be brought to consistency across the EU. The commission responded by legislating a GDPR Procedural Regulation in July 2023, which intends to harmonize several aspects of the GDPR enforcement, including the form, the structure and procedure of a complaint, and the right of the parties under investigation to be heard (European Commission, 2023). However, the procedural regulation intends to complement, rather than revise, the GDPR. No clarity is provided on either the scope of cross-border processing or the remit of the EDPB's enforcement powers.

In conclusion, the latest developments appear to initiate a shift from the polycentric model established by the GDPR, with the decentralized decision-making structure reserved but more coordinated by the EDPB via a wide array of methods. These initiatives and regulations, considered as a whole, would empower the EDPB in its role of organization, coordination, and dispute resolution, herding the DPAs towards more coordinated course of action. Yet, in the meantime, it consolidates the de facto powers of the EDPB to intervene with coordinated, direct, and even set agendas, which may reconfigure the polycentric model in a way that raises legitimacy concerns. The more it drives enforcement away from a polycentric governance model that stresses the importance of the horizontal distribution of decision-making power, the more it encounters concerns of legitimacy, subsidiarity, and constitutionality. There is an inherent intention deeply embedded in the EU legal order: polycentricity as underpinned by the EU legal principles remains at the core of the legal order, but is increasingly contested by the dynamic, complex, and out-of-bounds technological landscape.

III Case Studies

This section further provides two case studies, respectively, on Clearview AI and Meta, that illustrate the compromises and intricacies of the handling of cross-border enforcement cases as a polycentric system.

1 Clearview AI

Clearview AI was founded in 2017 by Richard Schwartz and now-CEO Hoan Ton-That with financial support from Peter Thiel and Naval Ravikant, among other investors. (Tarantola, 2020) Claiming to be a 'web search for faces'

(Stevens & Brandusescu, 2021), it scraped facial images and voice recordings tagged with people's names and identities (without consent) from Facebook, Instagram, Twitter, Venmo, YouTube, and elsewhere on the internet. The company publicly regarded these data to be up for grabs despite multiple cease-and-desist letters sent to the company. Clearview AI had existed as an inconspicuous and unknown start-up until early 2020, when a database of over three billion images was reported to have been massed by Clearview AI and used to market surveillance tools to law enforcement agencies and to several private entities (including Walmart, AT&T, the NBA, Bank of America, and Best Buy) for security purposes (Spivack & Garvie, 2020, p. 87). Originated from the United States, Clearview AI is said to have engaged over 600 law enforcement agencies since 2019 (Rezende, 2020), and its global expansion as rapid as a pandemic, reaching over twenty countries around the world, including a few having been accused of committing human rights abuses or experiencing social and political strife (Tarantola, 2020). Clearview AI is not the only company specializing in this contentious venture. PimEyes, for instance, markets a database of over 900 million images scraped from the internet and allows anyone to find matching photos online (Laufer & Meineck, 2020). Another instance is FindFace app, launched by NtechLab in 2016 but is no longer available, allowing for facial matching on the Russian social network VK (Roussi, 2020).

Clearview AI's practices are legally contested on multiple grounds. In the EU, a number of data protection authorities have engaged either Clearview AI or its public sector partners, yet the multiple regulatory actions are uncoordinated due to the fact that the company does not have a European headquarters or other forms of stable arrangement whatsoever. For instance, the Swedish Authority for Privacy Protection (*Integritetsskyddsmyndigheten*, IMY hereinafter) initiated an investigation against the Swedish Police Authority for using Clearview AI's services to process personal data for identification purposes (Chiusi et al., 2020, p. 249). An administrative fine of SEK 2,500,000 (approximately €250,000) was imposed, along with mandatory training and education to employees, disclosure of information about the impact on individuals, as well as deletion of all personal data that had been transferred to Clearview AI (IMY, 2021). In Hamburg, Germany, the local authority *Hamburgische Beauftragte für Datenschutz und Informationsfreiheit* (HmbBfDI) reacted to a complaint brought by Matthias Marx, who claimed 'a right to face' and asked his personal data to be deleted. Marx has an explicit intention of initiating a pan-Europe effect, yet contrary to this, the HmbBfDI limited the impact of its decisions to Marx's case only, and demanded the deletion of mathematical hash values only, instead of his personal data (noyb, 2021). The UK's Information Commissioner's Office also intervened before Brexit, in collaboration with the Office of the Australian Information Commissioner (OAIC). This international cooperation was based on the Global Privacy Assembly's Global Cross Border Enforcement Cooperation Arrangement, as well as the Memorandum of Understanding between the two authorities. Yet, the cooperation is restricted to the investigation stage, with two separate different decisions made later. At the time of writing, a total of seven DPAs in the EU have engaged with Clearview AI but mostly on their own accord, with little or no cooperation known between them. The ways in which DPAs investigated and acted were apparently uncoordinated, heterogenous, and caught in controversy for failing to produce a pan-European consistent impact (noyb, 2021). Clearview AI has been challenged elsewhere in the world, such as the United States (primarily litigations) and Canada, but these actions fall outside the scope of this chapter.

The case of Clearview AI shows how regulatory actions and outcomes can be highly heterogenous and fragmented (see Table 7.2), due to the inapplicability of the coordination and consistency mechanism set out by the EU data protection law. First, there is *discretion* in choosing the regulatory target and the legal frameworks in the case of the public–private partnership (PPP). For instance, the Scandinavian countries (Sweden and Finland) approached the public–private partnership by examining the processing of personal data by law enforcement agencies. Conversely, authorities from other jurisdictions engaged Clearview AI solely. The decision on which sector to scrutinize seems within the DPA's discretion, and none of the intervening authorities have acted upon both sectors. Whichever party is engaged initially, the legality of the activities conducted by the other party is left unaddressed. Purtova (2018, p. 53) captures this intricacy by pointing out that the two contexts can 'cross-contaminate', that is, the powers of the public sector authority may 'radiate' onto the private sector, and the public–private engagement may ultimately pose a threat to public values. Similarly, Taylor (2021) warns against the case of 'public actors without public value', which neither business ethics nor private law are able to properly address.

Second, despite the direct application of the GDPR across the EU, there are significant disparities in the types of violations identified, and outcomes imposed, by the authority on the same set of practices of Clearview AI. A variety of grounds have been identified on which Clearview AI's practices are deemed unlawful (see Table 7.3). The lack of consent appears the most commonly used, but some referred to accountability. Only a handful of authorities scrutinized the existence and adequacy of Clearview AI's data protection impact assessment (DPIA). From a global perspective, disparities can be even greater. The European DPA stressed the importance of lawfulness and data subject rights, but Canadian commissioners attended primarily to legitimate purposes (Scassa, 2021). The Australian OAIC, despite the collaboration with the UK's ICO, had to identify violations in accordance with its domestic laws that are not necessarily aligned with the GDPR (OAIC, 2021).

2 Meta

Meta (formerly Facebook) is, as a matter of fact, the most scrutinized US-based undertaking on grounds of data protection. Meta found itself in multiple investigations and lawsuits relating to cross-border transfer, combining different

TABLE 7.2 Seven investigations by EU DPAs vis-à-vis Clearview AI between 2021 and 2022

Date of entry	Jurisdiction	Authority	Starting date	Status	Legal basis and provisions	Behavioral remedies	Fines
19/07/2022	UK	ICO	2020-7-9	Challenged in court [2023] UKFTT 00819 (GRC)	Fairness and transparency (reasonable expectation); lawful basis; indefinite retention (storage limitation); unlawful biometric data processing; obstruction to the right of access (additional information i.e., Photos required)	Stop obtaining and using UK data; delete the existing UK data	£7,552,800
19/07/2022	Hamburg, Germany	HmbBfDI	2020-7	Closed	Unlawful biometric processing; right to be forgotten	Delete hash value mathematically generated by Clearview AI for the complainant Matthias Marx and confirm the deletion to the HmbBfDI	No fines
19/07/2022	Sweden	IMY	2019-aut	Closed	Accountability; unlawful biometric processing; DPIA lacking	Implement sufficient training and organizational measures as per Chapter 3 § 2 CDA; inform the affected data subjects as per Chapter 4 § 2 CDA; delete all data from the Clearview AI app	€248,218
19/07/2022	France	CNIL	2020-05	Closed	Unlawful (biometric) processing; data rights (Art. 12, 15, 17)	Cease the collection and use of data; facilitate the exercise of data rights; deletion upon requests	No fines upon compliance

Date of entry	Jurisdiction	Authority	Starting date	Status	Legal basis and provisions	Behavioral remedies	Fines
19/07/2022	Italy	Garante	2021-3-9	Closed	Fairness, transparency and lawfulness; storage limitation; purpose limitation; lawful basis (Art. 6); unlawful biometric processing; data rights (Art. 12–15); lack of representative (Art. 27)	Prohibition of further processing; deletion of data already collected; designation of a representative	€20,000,000
19/07/2022	Finland	Tietosuojavaltuutetun toimisto	2021-4-7	Closed	Unlawful processing "any prior controls or safeguards"; breach notification	Bring processing into compliance; notify identifiable data subjects of the breach	No fines
19/07/2022	Greece	HDPA	2021-5	Closed	Transparency and unlawfulness (Art. 5, 6, 9, 12, 14, 15); representatives (Art. 17)	Compliance with data access request; prohibition on collection and processing; data deletion	€20,000,000

TABLE 7.3 The DPA's selected regulatory targets in their investigations

Jurisdiction	Regulatory target	Outcome
Sweden	The Swedish Police Authority (IMY) (public)	An administrative fine of SEK 2,500,000 (approximately €250,000); training and education of its employees; notification to the affected data subjects; data erasure
Finland	Finish Central Criminal Police (CCP) (public)	To bring the processing into compliance (if not done already) and to notify the affected data subjects about the breach. No fine was issued to the CPP
France (upon individual complaints)	Clearview AI (private)	(1) Cease processing of biometric data; (2) exercise of data rights, and the right to erasure in particular
Austria (Max Schrems's complaint)	Clearview AI (private)	Deletion of the mathematical hash value representing the biometric profile (but not the photos)
Canada	Clearview AI (private)	(1) Cease offering of services; (2) cease processing of biometric data; (3) delete all the biometric data along with other information
Australia/UK	Clearview AI (private)	£17 million fine by the ICO; cease the processing of biometric data collected; data erasure

sources of data, and lawful grounds of processing (consent). Of the top ten administrative fines ever imposed at the time of writing, half of them relate to Meta platforms. DPAs manifest significantly contrasting views in these cases to the extent that consensus can barely be achieved. As such, the EDPB is often engaged to reach a binding decision. In one of these cases, Meta was pursued by Max Schrems, a leading data protection activist, for the fact that the US company changed its Terms of Services at the dawn of the GDPR in Austria, resulting in the shift of lawful basis from that of consent to that of the performance of contract under Art. 6 GDPR. This means that Meta can process personal data without consent, and Schrems challenged this as a violation of the GDPR.

Unlike Clearview AI, Meta had its European headquarters established in Ireland. Due to the likelihood that Meta's practices significantly affect data subjects in more than one member state, thereby constituting 'cross-border processing', the OSS was triggered. *Datenschutzbehörde* (DSB), the Austrian DPA had first received the complaint, transferred it to the Irish Data Protection Commission (DPC). The latter was identified as the Lead Supervisory Authority (LEA) which was expected to initiate an investigation and deliver a draft decision. The DPC's draft decision, submitted on 18 October 2021, received general support but was not unanimously held by the Supervisory Authorities concerned (CSA). Some contend that the fines should be increased, and others proposed objections about Facebook's reliance on performance of contract for processing personal data for advertising purposes. Without any chance of consensus building, the case was referred to the EDPB for dispute resolution, resulting in a binding decision adopted on 5 December 2022. In that decision, apart from questions raised by the DPC's draft as well as the objections raised by the CSAs, the EDPB required the DPC to 'carry out a new investigation [...] to determine if Meta [Ireland] processes special categories of personal data (Art. 9 GDPR) in a compliant manner and then issue a new draft decision' (EDPB 2022, para 487).

In their pleas to the CJEU, the DPC argues that the EDPB has misinterpreted Art. 4(24) and Art. 65(1)(a) as conferring a competence to instruct a supervisory authority to carry out a new investigation and, on that basis, issue a new draft decision. A literary reading of the provisions leads to the conclusion that Art. 65(1)(a) requires the decision to be adequately responsive to the objection(s) raised but is largely silent on the nature and contents of the decision. This argument is likely to hold, in our view, as neither Art. 4(24) nor Art. 65(1)(a) has conferred powers on the DPA to act, except to adopt a binding decision in case of unresolvable disputes between the LEA and the CSAs. The EDPB is not envisaged to oversee the DPAs' decisions, nor does it have a hierarchical advantage over national DPAs. This requirement was, from the outset, unconventional and contested. The DPC criticizes in a public release that the EDPB's demand was 'open-ended, speculative, and jurisdictionally problematic' (DPC, 2023). The former has referred the case to the Court of Justice of the European Union (T70/23; T84/23; T-111/23) on the grounds that the EDPB 'does not have a general supervision role akin to national courts in respect of national independent authorities', thereby constituting an overreaching of its coordinating powers. These cases before the CJEU are, at the time of writing, pending and under review.

IV Reflections and Conclusion

Polycentricity lies at the heart of EU data protection law enforcement but, for political and practical reasons, it is not in an optimal state and is promptly being challenged by new socio-technological momentums as indicated in the case studies of this chapter. The Clearview AI case indicates a loophole, which the EU legislators might have deliberately designed to nudge or promote establishment within the EU territory, that has seriously backfired and caused problems for data protection authorities handling cross-border processing. This loophole, somewhat intentionally left by the legislators to discriminate against controllers without a stable presence in the EU, is not negligible and inconsequential. As shown in the Clearview AI investigations, the enforcement landscape was shockingly dispersed and inconsistent, particularly in circumstances where stakes are reasonably high due to the processing of sensitive data and the consequential use cases in relation to law enforcement. The fact that OSS is built upon the concept of 'establishment' has a practical reason that the distribution of competence and power in cross-border cases would be fairly difficult, or impossible, without reference to their operational presence. One might argue, however, that there can be an alternative or complementary set of rules to be developed in the reform of the GDPR that covers establishment-less undertakings.

The Meta case is a snapshot of how difficult consensus can be achieved, or how a polycentric system can be maintained, thereby facilitating the EDPB's ambition in promoting consistent application of the law *ultra vires*. According to the EDPB's latest annual report, only eight binding decisions have been made by the EDPB (2023) since its inception in 2018, with three of them in a series against Meta platforms (Facebook, Instagram, and WhatsApp respectively). It is on very rare occasions that the conflict between DPAs ends up with a referral to the EDPB for dispute resolution. In most cases, these conflicts are resolved via continuous, back-and-forth negotiations between DPAs. That said, in the case of a resolvable conflict, the scope and nature of the final adjudicating power of the EDPB remains elusive and broad. With the best efforts already undertaken by the authorities, the fulfillment of the objectives pursued might justify a reduced level of autonomy from the polycentric governance point of view. However, the concern for the legitimacy of the EDPB's direct directive to the DPAs stands. This might potentially make the polycentric governance structure, characterized by a horizontal distribution of decision-making power, shift to a hierarchical one. While the coordinating presence is justifiable within a polycentric nature, its adaptation into a dictating presence is not, even if such dictation is likely to align with the objectives concerned. It is without doubt that the initiatives being undertaken by the EDPB, such as rapid consensus-building, taskforces, and expert pools, would be jointly instrumental in reducing conflicts between DPAs in the mid- or long term. However, these latest efforts are mostly pragmatic and realistic, leaving the fundamental issue concerning the relevance of polycentricity, and the trade-off between it and the stated objectives mostly unaddressed. We argue that this fundamental issue should be urgently brought to the surface as a basis for structural reform in the near future.

The current layout of GDPR enforcement is sub-optimal in the sense that DPAs do not cooperate by default, as required by the GDPR, in cases where there is no establishment within the EU. Remedial mechanisms are being established by the GDPR but, again, on an ad hoc basis, which may or may not effectively address the threats posed by Clearview AI and the like. Moreover, the inability to reach consensus among CSAs, which is commonly seen in complex and controversial major decisions against tech giants, places the EDPB in an awkward position to promote consistent application. As the EDPB and DPAs are not in a strictly hierarchical relationship, any politicized DPA could exploit this structural deficit in impeding any attempts to touch upon critical and controversial legal matters of significant impact.

It is pivotal to recognize that the path towards consistent and effective enforcement is fraught with tension and paradoxes. The cases of Clearview AI and Meta not only underscore the existing fissures within the polycentric system but highlight the imperious need for a recalibration of the GDPR's foundational concepts, principles, and mechanisms in relation to application and coordination. As the EU stands at the juncture to consider the reform of the GDPR, it must do so with the wisdom that the strength of a polycentric approach lies in its fluidity and its capacity to adapt without losing its essence. This short chapter ends with a reflective pause, inviting the reader to gaze beyond the immediacy of legal challenges posed by tech giants while considering polycentricity as a useful concept to deal with such paradoxes.

References

Aligica, P. D., & Tarko, V. (2012). Polycentricity: from Polanyi to Ostrom, and beyond. *Governance*, 25(2), 237–262. https://doi.org/10.1111/j.1468-0491.2011.01550.x.

Baldwin, E., Washington-Ottombre, C., Dell'Angelo, J., Cole, D., & Evans, T. (2016). Polycentric governance and irrigation reform in Kenya. *Governance*, 29(2), 207–225. https://doi.org/10.1111/gove.12160.

Bennett, C. J., & Raab, C. D. (2017). *The governance of privacy: Policy instruments in global perspective*. Routledge.

Bracy, J. (2022). A look behind the EDPB's move to enhance enforcement cooperation. *IAPP*. Retrieved from https://iapp.org/news/a/a-look-behind-the-edpbs-move-to-enhance-enforcement-cooperation/.

Bruns, B. (2019). Practising polycentric governance. In A. Thiel, W.A. Blomquist, D.E. Garrick (eds.), *Governing complexity: Analyzing and applying polycentricity*. Cambridge University Press, 237–255.

Caplan, R. (2023). Networked governance. *Yale Journal of Law & Technology*, 24, 541–533.

Carlisle, K., & Gruby, R. L. (2017). Polycentric systems of governance: A theoretical model for the commons. *Policy Studies Journal*, 47(4), 927–952. https://doi.org/10.1111/psj.12212.

Chander, A., & Schwartz, P. (2023). Privacy and/or trade. *The University of Chicago Law Review*, 90(49). https://papers.ssrn.com/sol3/papers.cfm?abstract_id=4038531.

Chiusi, F., Fischer, S., Kayser-Bril, N., & Spielkamp, M. (2020). Automating Society Report 2020, *Algorithm Watch*. Retrieved from https://automatingsociety.algorithmwatch.org/.

Cihon, P., Maas, M. M., & Kemp, L. (2020). Fragmentation and the future: Investigating architectures for international AI governance. *Global Policy* 11, 545–556. https://doi.org/10.1111/1758-5899.12890.

CIPL. (2021). GDPR enforcement cooperation and the one-stop-shop learning from the first three years. Retrieved from https://www.informationpolicycentre.com/uploads/5/7/1/0/57104281/cipl_discussion_paper_-_gdpr_enforcement_cooperation_and_the_one-stop-shop__23_sept_2021_.pdf.

CNIL. (2023). EDPB adopts final report of outcome of the cookie banner task force. Retrieved from https://www.cnil.fr/en/edpb-adopts-final-report-outcome-cookie-banner-task-force.

DPC. (2023). Data Protection Commission announces conclusion of two inquiries into Meta Ireland. Retrieved from https://www.dataprotection.ie/en/news-media/data-protection-commission-announces-conclusion-two-inquiries-meta-ireland.

EDPB. (2020). Guidelines 3/2018 on the territorial scope of the GDPR (Article 3). Retrieved from https://edpb.europa.eu/sites/default/files/files/file1/edpb_guidelines_3_2018_territorial_scope_after_public_consultation_en_0.pdf.

EDPB. (2022a). DPAs decide on closer cooperation for strategic files. Retrieved from http s://edpb.europa.eu/news/news/2022/dpas-decide-closer-cooperation-strategic-files_en.

EDPB. (2022b). Statement on enforcement cooperation. Retrieved from https://edpb.europa. eu/our-work-tools/our-documents/statements/statement-enforcement-cooperation_en.

EDPB. (2022c). Guidelines 02/2022 on the application of Article 60 GDPR. Retrieved from https://edpb.europa.eu/system/files/2022-03/guidelines_202202_on_the_application_of_a rticle_60_gdpr_en.pdf.

EDPB. (2023). EDPB resolves dispute on transfers by Meta and creates task force on Chat GPT. Retrieved from https://edpb.europa.eu/news/news/2023/edpb-resolves-disp ute-transfers-meta-and-creates-task-force-chat-gpt_en.

EDPS. (2022). EDPS conference 2022: A pan-European approach is going to be necessary for effective enforcement. Retrieved from https://edps.europa.eu/press-publications/p ress-news/press-releases/2022/edps-conference-2022-pan-european-approach-going_en.

European Commission. (2023). Data protection: Commission adopts new rules to ensure stronger enforcement of the GDPR in cross-border cases. Retrieved from https://ec. europa.eu/commission/presscorner/detail/en/ip_23_3609.

Franchino, F. (2007). *The powers of the Union: Delegation in the EU*. Cambridge: Cambridge University Press.

Gasser, U., & Almeida, V. A. F. (2017). A layered model for AI governance. *IEEE Internet Computing*, 21, 58–62. doi:10.1109/MIC.2017.4180835.

Hartley, T. C. (2004). *European Union law in a global context: Text, cases and materials*. Cambridge: Cambridge University Press.

Herveg, J. (2023). Study on the national administrative rules impacting the cooperation duties for the national supervisory authorities, *EDPB*. Retrieved from https://edpb. europa.eu/system/files/2023-04/call_7_final_report_07012021.pdf.

ICO. (2020). The Office of the Australian Information Commissioner and the UK's Information Commissioner's Office open joint investigation into Clearview AI Inc. Retrieved from https://www.privacy365.eu/en/by-the-british-data-protection-authority-the-office-of-the-australian-information-commissioner-and-the-uks-information-comm issioners-office-open-joint-investigation-into-clearview-a/.

IMY. (2021). Beslut efter tillsyn enligt brottsdatalagen – Polismyndighetens användning av Clearview AI. Retrieved from https://www.imy.se/globalassets/dokument/beslut/ beslut-tillsyn-polismyndigheten-cvai.pdf.

Jelinek, T., Kerimi, D., & Wallach, W. (2012). Policy brief: Coordinating committee for the governance of artificial intelligence. *AI and Ethics*, 1, 141–150. https://doi.org/10. 1007/s43681-020-00019-y.

Jordan, A. (2018). Governing climate change polycentrically. In A. Jordan, D. Huitema, H. van Asselt, Johanna Forster (eds.), *Governing climate change: Polycentricity in action?* [Online]. Cambridge University Press. https://doi.org/10.1017/9781108284646.

Jóri, A. (2015). Shaping vs applying data protection law: Two core functions of data protection authorities. *International Data Privacy Law*, 5(2), 133–143. https://doi.org/ 10.1093/idpl/ipv006.

Kim, R. E. (2020). Is global governance fragmented, polycentric, or complex? The state of the art of the network approach. *International Studies Review* 22, 903–931. https:// doi.org/10.1093/isr/viz052.

King, J. (2008). The pervasiveness of polycentricity. *Public Law*, 101–124. https://papers. ssrn.com/sol3/papers.cfm?abstract_id=1027625.

King, J. (2012). *Judging social rights*. Cambridge: Cambridge University Press.

Kloza, D., & Mościbroda, A. (2014). Making the case for enhanced enforcement cooperation between data protection authorities: Insights from competition law. *International Data Privacy Law*, 4(2), 120–138. https://doi.org/10.1093/idpl/ipu010.

Kuner, C. (2009). An international legal framework for data protection: Issues and prospects. *Computer Law and Security Review*, 25, 307–317. https://papers.ssrn.com/sol3/papers.cfm?abstract_id=1443802.

Kuner, C. (2014). The European Union and the search for an international data protection framework. *Groningen Journal of International Law*, 2, 55–71. https://dx.doi.org/10.2139/ssrn.2495273.

Laufer, D., & Meineck, S.A Polish company is abolishing our anonymity. *Netzpolitik*. Retrieved from https://netzpolitik.org/2020/pimeyes-face-search-company-is-abolishing-our-anonymity/.

Lynskey, O. (2017). The 'europeanisation' of data protection law. *Cambridge Yearbook of European Legal Studies*, 19, 252–286. https://doi.org/10.1017/cel.2016.15.

Lynskey, O. (2019). Grappling with 'Data Power': Normative nudges from data protection and privacy. *Theoretical Inquiries in Law*, 20, 189–220. https://doi.org/10.1515/til-2019-0007.

Malatras, A., Sanchez, I., Beslay, L., Coisel, I., Vakalis, I., D'Acquisto, G., … & Zorkadis, V. (2017). Pan-European personal data breaches: Mapping of current practices and recommendations to facilitate cooperation among Data Protection Authorities. *Computer Law & Security Review*, 33(4), 458–469. https://doi.org/10.1016/j.clsr.2017.03.013.

McGinnis, M. D. (2011). Networks of adjacent action situations in polycentric governance. *Policy Studies Journal*, 39, 51–78. https://doi.org/10.1111/j.1541-0072.2010.00396.x.

McGinnis, M. D. (2013). Costs and challenges of polycentric governance: An equilibrium concept and examples from U.S. Health Care. https://papers.ssrn.com/sol3/papers.cfm?abstract_id=2206980.

Morrison, T. H. (2017). Evolving polycentric governance of the Great Barrier Reef. *Proceedings of the National Academy of Sciences of the United States of America*, 114, E3013. https://doi.org/10.1073/pnas.1620830114.

Morrison, T. H., (2019). The black box of power in polycentric environmental governance. *Global Environmental Change*, 57, 101934. https://doi.org/10.1016/j.gloenvcha.2019.101934.

Nagendra, H., & Ostrom, E. (2012). Polycentric governance of multifunctional forested landscapes. *International Journal of the Commons* 6, 104–133. doi:10.18352/ijc.321.

noyb. (2021). Clearview AI deemed illegal in the EU. *noyb*. Retrieved from https://noyb.eu/en/clearview-ai-deemed-illegal-eu.

noyb. (n.d.). Forced consent & consent bypass. Retrieved from https://noyb.eu/en/project/forced-consent-dpas-austria-belgium-france-germany-and-ireland.

OAIC. (2021). OAIC and ICO conclude joint investigation into Clearview AI. Retrieved from https://www.oaic.gov.au/newsroom/oaic-and-ico-conclude-joint-investigation-into-clearview-ai.

OPC (Canada). Clearview AI ceases offering its facial recognition technology in Canada. https://www.priv.gc.ca/en/opc-news/news-and-announcements/2020/nr-c_200706/.

Ostrom, E. (2010). Beyond markets and states: polycentric governance of complex economic systems. *American Economic Review*, 100(3), 641–672. doi:10.1257/aer.100.3.641.

Purtova, N. (2018). Between the GDPR and the police directive: Navigating through the maze of information sharing in public–private partnerships. *International Data Privacy Law*, 8(1), 52–68. https://doi.org/10.1093/idpl/ipx021.

Raab, C., & Koops, B. J. (2009). Privacy actors, performances and the future of privacy protection. In Serge Gutwirth, Yves Poullet, Paul Hert, Cécile Terwangne, Sjaak

Nouwt (eds.), *Reinventing data protection?* (pp. 207–221). Dordrecht: Springer Netherlands.

Raab, C. D. (2010). Information privacy: Networks of regulation at the subglobal level. *Global Policy*, 1, 291–302. https://doi.org/10.1111/j.1758-5899.2010.00030.x.

Raab, C. D. (2011). Networks for regulation: Privacy commissioners in a changing world. *Journal of Comparative Policy Analysis: Research and Practice*, 13, 195–213. https://doi.org/10.1080/13876988.2011.555999.

Reidenberg, J. R. (2000). Resolving conflicting international data privacy rules in cyberspace. *Stanford Law Review*, 52, 1315–1371. https://doi.org/10.2307/1229516.

Rezende, I. N. (2020). Facial recognition in police hands: Assessing the 'Clearview case' from a European perspective. *New Journal of European Criminal Law*, 11(3), 375–389. https://doi.org/10.1177/2032284420948161.

Righettini, M. S. (2011). Institutionalization, leadership, and regulative policy style: A France/Italy comparison of data protection authorities. *Journal of Comparative Policy Analysis*, 13, 143–164. https://doi.org/10.1080/13876988.2011.555995.

Roussi, A. (2020). Resisting the rise of facial recognition. *Nature*, 587(7834), 350–354. https://doi.org/10.1038/d41586-020-03188-2.

Scassa, T. (2021). Provinces issue orders requiring Clearview AI to comply with data protection laws – But then what?, https://www.teresascassa.ca/index.php?option=com_k2&view=item&id=347:provinces-issue-orders-requiring-clearview-ai-to-comply-with-data-protection-laws-but-then-what?&Itemid=80.

Shackelford, S. J., & Dockery, R. (2019). Governing AI. *Cornell Journal of Law and Public Policy*, 30, 279–333. http://dx.doi.org/10.2139/ssrn.3478244.

Shawoo, Z., & McDermott, C. L. (2020). Justice through polycentricity? A critical examination of climate justice framings in Pakistani climate policymaking. *Climate Policy*, 20(2), 199–216. https://doi.org/10.1080/14693062.2019.1707640.

Spivack, J., & Garvie, C. (2021). A taxonomy of legislative approaches to face recognition in the United States. In A. Kak (ed.), *Regulating biometrics: Global approaches and open questions*, AI Now. https://ainowinstitute.org/publication/regulating-biometrics-global-approaches-and-open-questions.

Stephenson, P. (2013). Twenty years of multi-level governance: 'Where does it come from? What is it? Where is it going?'. *Journal of European Public Policy*, 20(6), 817–837. https://doi.org/10.1080/13501763.2013.781818.

Stevens, Y., & Brandusescu, A. (2021). Weak privacy, weak procurement: The state of facial recognition in Canada. Retrieved from https://static1.squarespace.com/static/5ea874746663b45e14a384a4/t/606c811b9aa6f40dbf84d858/1617723678314/Stevens_Brandusescu_FRT.pdf.

Tarantola, A. (2020). Why Clearview AI is a threat to us all. *Engadet*. Retrieved from https://www.engadget.com/2020-02-12-clearview-ai-police-surveillance-explained.html.

Taylor, Linnet. (2021). Public actors without public values: Legitimacy, domination and the regulation of the technology sector. *Philosophy & Technology*, 34(4), 897–922. https://doi.org/10.1007/s13347-020-00441-4.

Vranaki, A. A. I. (2016). Learning lessons from cloud investigations in Europe: Bargaining enforcement and multiple centres of regulation in data protection. *Journal of Law, Technology and Policy*, 1, 245–275. https://doi.org/10.2139/ssrn.2697171.

8

TRADE AGREEMENTS AND CROSS-BORDER DISINFORMATION

Patchwork or Polycentric?

Susan A. Aaronson

Introduction[1]

Disinformation is not like pornography; most of us do not know it when we see it.[2] While there is some disagreement on an exact definition, disinformation can be defined as information designed to mislead, deceive, or polarize (Nemr and Gangware 2019). Moreover, unlike pornography, disinformation is dangerous to individuals, democracy, and good governance.

We are all complicit without direct intent in the dissemination of disinformation because in almost every country, users, firms, and policy makers perpetuate disinformation. Here's why. Netizens around the world turn to Facebook, Google, WeChat, and other sites, apps, and browsers for news and information.[3] These users provide their personal data to these sites, apps, and browsers provide their services to netizens for free in return for free services. These firms in turn aggregate it and use it to provide users with both tailored advertising and free content (Amnesty International 2019; Zuboff 2021).

But many critics argue that it is not the freemium model that is the problem but firm dependence on ever-growing troves of personal data to utilize and sell to other companies. Critics accuse many of these platforms of feeding their users divisive content to gain their attention and increase their time on the platform, which, in turn, encourages more advertisers (Ghosh et al. 2020). Meanwhile, these ads provide a global revenue stream that both incentivizes and sustains the spread of disinformation within countries and across borders.

Individuals, organizations, and governments have spread propaganda, fake news, and conspiracy theories offline for centuries (Wardle and Derakhshan 2017). However, as life has moved online, so too has disinformation, flowing within and across borders (Vigneault 2021). As a result, the global internet has become both an information platform and a "battlefield" (Weaver 2013).

DOI: 10.4324/9781003388418-10

According to scholar Shoshana Zuboff (2021), advertisers use this data to manipulate us to think, buy, believe, do, or join something that we otherwise would not have done (Angwin 2021).

Disinformation is simultaneously a domestic and an international problem (Ewing 2020). It can be created and disseminated by domestic actors, or it can be created and transferred from individuals in one group or country to another. There are no reliable statistics, but one can see mounting qualitative evidence that disinformation increasingly crosses borders (Nemr and Gangware 2019; Office of the High Commissioner for Human Rights 2021). In fact, disinformation is one of several negative spillovers of a shared internet (a commons) built on cross-border data flows shared by governments, firms, civil society and individuals (Raymond 2012).

Because of its global and continuous nature, disinformation is a "wicked problem" that transcends nations and generations. Wicked problems cannot be "solved," but they can be mitigated (Barclay 2018; Montgomery 2020). According to Brian Pierce (n.d.), former director of the Information Innovation Office at the Defense Advanced Research Projects Agency (DARPA), "wicked problems are typical of open, nonlinear systems that involve people and machines."[4] No one knows how best to counter disinformation at the local, national, or international levels (Tucker et al. 2018).

As Aguerre, Campbell-Verduyn and Scholte note in Chapter 1 of this volume, we can best understand disinformation as a problem of polycentric governance. A polycentric problem in their conception transcends nation states with many different segments of society involved in its governance. Authority is diffused and no one agency, platform, civil society group can effectively govern it. Moreover, there are no shared definitions of the problem of disinformation, nor shared strategies.

Disinformation is built on data which is a resource that requires collective governance to achieve proper functioning. Data has both a commercial/economic and a public good nature. Thus, data governance is not just about policies designed to promote data-based innovation and rules limiting how and when data can be collected, stored, analyzed, and monetized. Data governance is also about strategies to ensure that data serves the common good. So, to govern data in a polycentric manner requires that we treat data as a commons to ensure that the benefits of data are not limited or blocked, but also design and establish institutions that will allow us to better use data to attain societal goals. Therefore, when data is misused, for example, so as to create disinformation, it can affect individuals and communities to whom the data pertains. When data crosses borders, disinformation is best addressed collectively, in a multinational and multi-sectoral manner. Yet in general, governments are not acting collectively, thus revealing limits to polycentric data governance?

Many nations have adopted a wide range of strategies to mitigate disinformation, including platform regulation, data regulation, competition policies, investment rules, technological fixes, and citizen education strategies, among others. With so many different approaches, policy makers are able to achieve a clearer understanding of what works and what does not. However, this polycentric arrangement may not be effective in mitigating cross-border disinformation. Moreover, the lack of coherent approaches could also lead to trade distortions and spillover effects on internet openness and generativity (Organization for Economic Co-operation and Development [OECD] 2016; World Economic Forum 2020). There is growing evidence that the data giants have acted at the national level to weaken and contest domestic regulations aimed at addressing disinformation. These firms may be trying to game the system (Petre et al. 2019).

Given the governance dilemma posed by disinformation, it is incumbent on scholars to suggest not only new ways of thinking about disinformation but also ways the world can collaborate to mitigate it. Herein I argue that trade agreements might help governments deal with cross-border disinformation. When a netizen uses a dating app, searches for information on COVID-19 or watches a movie on Netflix, they are engaging in international trade. To provide the user with this data, firms often use servers located across different countries to improve access speed and reduce network traffic. Moreover, with the adoption of cloud computing, data may be stored and analyzed in many countries simultaneously. In recent years, trade diplomats have included rules to govern these cross-border data flows in a growing number of trade agreements.

Trade agreements are an imperfect and inexact remedy to the challenge of disinformation. First, they can't address domestic disinformation. Secondly, policy makers cannot use trade agreements to directly regulate the business model that underpins the problem of disinformation, although trade agreements could do more to encourage cooperative regulation of the many platforms that fail to sufficiently tackle disinformation. Moreover, I note that trade agreements such as the WTO, are not well-liked or understood. Many people believe that these agreements are negotiated in an opaque process that is indirectly democratic, time consuming, and out of sync with the digital economy (Kilic 2021; Epps 2008).

Despite the limitations of digital trade agreements, many recent digital trade agreements contain language designed to build trust among online market actors. Moreover, trade agreements include useful language on competition policy, as well as provisions designed to ensure that national regulation does not lead to trade distortions. In short, with some refinements, these agreements can help nations coordinate counterweights for cross-border disinformation flows including data protection rules, content moderation and competition policies.

The chapter proceeds as follows: First, I define disinformation and its effects. Then I discuss the role of state actors followed by that of platforms and their business model. The work then discusses several initiatives that have been undertaken by governments to address disinformation. Then I discuss what trade agreements say about data flows, exceptions, competition policy, regulatory coherence, and spam. Finally, I present suggestions for a broader approach to govern cross-border information that nations can use within trade agreements. In doing so, this work traces different levels, institutions, and actors involved to address cross-border disinformation as a polycentric complex of institutions, norms, and national and international policies and practices.

Disinformation and its Global and Social Effects

Researchers traditionally defined disinformation as the purposeful dissemination of information designed to mislead, deceive, harm, and/or polarize people within a country or among countries. It is not the same as misinformation, which is generally understood as the inadvertent sharing of false information that is not intended to cause harm (Derakhshan and Wardle 2018). Governments tend to have similar definitions. For example, the European Union defines disinformation as "false or misleading content that is spread with an intention to deceive or secure economic or political gain and which may cause public harm" (European Commission 2020b). While there may not be a consensus on how to define it, many researchers agree that the data-driven economy and the rise of platforms have facilitated the spread of disinformation. In fact, some scholars call disinformation "computational propaganda" because, increasingly, disinformation is spread by individuals who rely on algorithms, automation, and human curation.[5] As the Technology and Social Change Team (2021) noted,

> opaque algorithms, policies, and enforcement mechanisms determine what information is available to whom ... Social media, especially, brings with it mechanisms and tactics that allow for large-scale coordinated disinformation campaigns that are often hard to recognize and nearly impossible to mitigate once they have reached millions.

The instruments at hand for disinformation are multiple, and diffused across actors, jurisdictions, and technologies.

There is, however, a growing consensus among international human rights bodies and organizations that disinformation is dangerous to both human rights and democracy. If policy makers could develop a coordinated and effective international approach, they could possibly reduce these costs. A recent study found that unilateral data regulations can either raise or reduce global welfare, but a coordinated approach would yield substantial gains (Chen et al. 2020, 4). Policy makers have a long history of trying to develop a coordinated approach to other issues such as environmental protection and labor rights (Aaronson and Zimmerman 2007). Some have also tried to develop a coordinated approach to the governance of cyberspace and cyberthreats (Council on Foreign Relations 2018; Talihärm n.d.).

The Role of State Actors

State actors are both the perpetrators and the victims of disinformation. The Government of Canada's Communications Security Establishment (2019) reported that half of all advanced democracies holding national elections had their democratic process targeted by cyberthreat activity including disinformation, a three-fold increase since 2015. A 2021 study found that foreign actors were most active in disinformation campaigns against the United States, the United Kingdom and Egypt (Goldstein and Grossman 2021).

Researchers cannot easily attribute disinformation directly to a state. A government entity could be the creator and disseminator of disinformation, or it could use bots or trolls or hire a firm to do this dirty work. Government officials may be unable or unwilling to prove attribution because that could require government entities to release information about technical and physical intelligence capabilities and operations. As a result, even when intelligence agencies can attribute disinformation with a high degree of confidence, they face a second attribution problem in the court of public opinion (Newman 2016; Lindsay 2015).

Some governments actively spread disinformation, and firms are organizing to serve their needs. The US Department of Justice found that the Kremlin-backed Internet Research Agency initiated its efforts to interfere in US politics as early as 2014. This privately held Russian company, owned by a friend of President Vladimir Putin, spent US$1.25 million per month on its combined domestic and global operations, which included 76 staffers fluent in English focused on the 2016 US presidential campaign.[6] In 2020, researchers at the Oxford Internet Institute estimated that some 65 firms deployed computational propaganda on behalf of a political actor in 48 countries. These types of activities reveal the failure of the current governance model to develop institutions to protect people from data harm.

The Role of Platforms and Business Model in Fostering Dissemination Across Borders

The purveyors of disinformation—individuals, groups, firms, or governments rely on websites, apps, social networks, and other means to disseminate information. Hence, they are dependent on the large companies that provide the tools for human connection in the internet age – the so-called platforms. Platforms can be defined as digital services that facilitate interactions between two or more distinct but interdependent sets of users (users can be firms, groups, and/or individuals) who interact through the service via the internet (OECD 2019, 11). Platforms present a real challenge to governance of disinformation because they are global and powerful, and they are generally not incentivized to address disinformation.

Although every platform is distinct, and there are several business models used by various platforms, social networking platforms tend to rely on the "freemium" model, where users provide personal data in return for free digital services (Lynskey 2017). But these users are being "used"[7] (United Nations Conference on Trade and Development 2019). After collecting this data, the platforms aggregate users into groups divided by preferences, race, location, income, and other features. Many data firms then make and sell predictions about users' interests, characteristics and, ultimately, behavior to generate advertising revenue (Zuboff 2019; Amnesty International 2019; Snower and Twomey 2020). No one knows if the services that users receive for free are worth the direct and indirect costs of providing such data.

Many researchers have shown that this business model incentivizes platforms to show sensationalistic or otherwise addictive content to keep people using and the ad money flowing. Platforms also gamify usage with like buttons, retweets, and video view counters to keep people hooked. Hence, netizens are also incentivized to share and disseminate disinformation as well as information (Stoller 2021; Donovan 2021; Tworek 2021; Ryan et al. 2020).

Many of the large platforms are under extreme public pressure to moderate content and change their business model, but that is not necessarily what shareholders want. "Social media companies' mission statements focus on sharing, community and empowerment. But their business models are built on ... their ability to grow, as measured in attention and engagement metrics: active users, time spent, content shared" (Etlinger 2019, 24).

Not surprisingly, disinformation seems quite profitable (Ryan et al. 2020). In 2019, the GDI analyzed website traffic and audience information from 20,000 domains it suspected of disinformation and estimated the sites generated at least US$235 million in ad revenue (Price 2019). Harvard University scholar Joan Donavan described disinformation as "a very lucrative business, especially if you're good at it" (Heim 2021).

Platforms have and continue to receive significant revenue from the "freemium" business model, which in turn gives them influence. Some of the biggest platforms have revenues significantly larger than many governments (Babic et al. 2018; Owens 2019). There is growing evidence that firms are using their market power to prevent governments from regulating or to shape such regulations so as not to reduce their dominant positions (Babic et al. 2017). While governments retain significant tools to act against these firms, a coordinated international approach might forestall such bullying of governments by the data giants. But policy makers lack international tools to enable such a coordinated approach.

An Overview of Government Efforts to Tackle Disinformation

Disinformation is a form of speech (self-expression), and nations have evolved different visions of what speech should be regulated online, what should be removed, and who should decide these questions (business, government, civil society). The United States sits on one side of a continuum, where law and culture dictate that there should be relatively few restrictions on speech, and government plays a limited role in regulating social networks. US policies are guided by section 230 of the 1996 Communications Decency Act, which states that "no provider or user of an interactive computer service shall be treated as the publisher or speaker of any information provided by another information content provider." The protected intermediaries include not only regular internet service providers but also a range of "interactive computer service providers," including basically any online service that publishes third-party content from sites such as Amazon, Target, Trip Advisor, and Yelp.[8]

China, Iran, and Vietnam are examples of countries on the other site of the continuum. In these countries, free speech is extremely restricted and government censors decide what is appropriate and inappropriate content (Levush 2019; Morar and Martins dos Santos 2020). Most democracies sit somewhere in between these positions.

But most countries do not have sufficient leverage to influence the practices of the platforms, unless they are large and growing data markets such as India. Moreover, many netizens do not agree with the notion that companies should decide how and when to moderate content online when they profit from monetizing personal data. They want to put forward their own approaches (McCabe and Swanson 2019).

Some countries have advanced domestic strategies to mitigate disinformation, although it is too early to evaluate whether these strategies are effective. For example, Germany created legislation to regulate hate speech, known as the Network Enforcement Act (NetzDG),[9] while the United Kingdom and Australia require firms to remove "online harms" (Hern 2020). Around the world, policy makers[10] (and firms[11] [Chakravorti 2020]) are not only using content moderation regulations to address disinformation but they are also trying to develop technical fixes, regulate political advertising, train citizens to recognize disinformation, fund investigations and enforcement actions, and help other governments address disinformation. Given this patchwork of approaches, policy makers (and executives) recognize the need for collective action. The members of the Group of Seven (G7) who met in Canada in June 2018 agreed to the "Charlevoix commitment on defending democracy from foreign threats." The G7 agreed to "establish a G7 Rapid Response Mechanism to strengthen our coordination to identify and respond to diverse and evolving threats to our democracies, including through sharing information" (Fried 2019). At the initiative of France, some 95 nations have banded together to discuss effective solutions to the problems of disinformation and cyber insecurity (Government of Canada 2021a).

However, these strategies can do little to mitigate cross-border disinformation flows or prod firms to address some of the problems with their current business model. As with labor and the environment, uncoordinated national strategies to address the problem could lead to a race to the bottom among some nations to encourage firms to locate in their countries. Trade agreements, especially at the regional and binational levels, increasingly contain rules that could lead to a more coordinated international approach to directly tackle cross-border disinformation. The next section delineates what trade agreements currently say and how they may provide building blocks for language to govern cross-border disinformation flows.

The State of Digital Trade Agreements and the Governance of Malicious Cross-border Data Flows

This section delineates what trade agreements say about regulating cross-border data flows, competition policies, spam, and the use of trade tools to target entities that disseminate disinformation across borders. The author notes that for the purposes of this writing, they use e-commerce and digital trade agreements simultaneously.

Much of the language in trade agreements is built on and highly influenced by the US approach to governing the internet, the companies that provide its infrastructure and the data that underpins that network of networks. For this reason, the author argues, the free flow of data, with certain exceptions, became the default for almost every trade agreement until recently. The United States was and is home to many of the world's largest digital firms, and it drafted the original principles designed to govern e-commerce and cross-border data flows (Aaronson 2015).

The United States began that effort in 1997 when then president Bill Clinton announced a Framework for Global Electronic Commerce. This framework articulated what the regulatory environment "should" look like if nations wanted to encourage national and global e-commerce. The framework focused on private sector leadership, a limited role for government intervention, and principles to reassure consumers that their data would be protected and secure.[12]

But, to some extent, the effort to build trust in e-commerce by ensuring users that they and their data would be safe took a back seat to the notion of free flow of data across borders. Free flow of data would allow US companies to expand their access to data and grow ever bigger. The Clinton administration made it clear that "the US government supports the broadest possible free flow of information across international borders."[13] This framework very much influenced the OECD Action Plan for Electronic Commerce, which, in turn, influenced the bilateral and regional agreements on e-commerce described below (Aaronson 2015, 2018; Burri 2013).

Unfortunately, almost every trade agreement does not acknowledge the catch-22 underpinning cross-border data flows. Much of the data flowing across borders is aggregated and allegedly anonymized personal data. While users may benefit from services built on data, the people who are the source of that data do not control it. It is their asset, yet they cannot manage, control, exchange, or account for it (World Economic Forum 2011, 11). Individuals' data can essentially be weaponized to create malicious cross-border data flows, whether through disinformation, malware, spam, or other means.

Provisions to Encourage Cross-border Data Flows

In the absence of consensus on how to govern data at the WTO, many countries including Australia, Canada, Chile, EU member states, Japan, Singapore, the United Kingdom, and the United States have placed language governing cross-border data flows in the e-commerce chapters of recent free trade agreements (FTAs). Some 52 percent (182 of 345) of recent (2000–2019) trade agreements have e-commerce or digital trade provisions, and such language is increasingly binding (Burri and Polanco 2020).

Some of these agreements such as the United Kingdom's withdrawal from the European Union (Brexit), the Canada–United States–Mexico Agreement (CUSMA), and the Comprehensive and Progressive Agreement for Trans-Pacific Partnership cover a wide range of sectors. However, some nations including Chile, Japan, New Zealand, Singapore, and the United States have established sector-specific stand-alone digital trade agreements. As noted above, these agreements are built on principles first enunciated by the United States in 1997, in the Framework for Global Electronic Commerce. Trade negotiators focus on rules to govern cross-border data flows and generally rely on nations to enforce their own laws to protect consumers and citizens from harmful or malicious cross-border data flows.

Almost every recent agreement has binding language that makes the free flow of data a default. They contain language such as "Neither Party shall prohibit or restrict the cross-border transfer of information, including personal information, by electronic means, if this activity is for the conduct of the business of a covered person."[14] But policy makers also acknowledge that nations have other important policy objectives such as preserving public order, privacy, consumer welfare, or public morals. Hence, by using the exception as justification, a nation can restrict cross-border data flows.[15]

Nations are supposed to turn to these exceptions only in extraordinary circumstances. However, there are few shared norms and definitions regarding how nations should behave when rules governing data flows conflict with the achievement of other important policy objectives (Aaronson 2018). Consequently, there is a patchwork of strategies to build consumer and user trust at the national level, but less of a focus on shared and/or interoperable strategies.

Moreover, the exceptions were not built for the digital age. Ciuriak (2019) argues that the socially harmful use of data such as "fake news" and disinformation for personally targeted advertising and/or messaging (for example, the exploitation of psychological vulnerabilities for marketing purposes or for political manipulation) should be considered a legitimate exception.

Protecting privacy and personal data is a widely accepted "exception" to the free flow of data. The 2020 Singapore Australia Digital Economy Agreement (SADEA) seems to be the first agreement calling for interoperability of data protection regimes. Interoperability would make data protection more effective, as national approaches would be more coherent.

The exceptions on the free flow of data become sources of authority for digital trade which undermine their authority as other legitimate public policy concerns are brought to the table. This brings another layer of complexity to the arguments and different sets of actors in the national and international environment that are part of a polycentric governing issue in the making.

Intermediary Liability and Content Moderation

As noted above, countries have different ideas on how content should be regulated and what entities – whether business, government, or a combination of the two – should do such regulating. US rules have protected online platforms from lawsuits related to user content and legal challenges stemming from how they moderate content. Not surprisingly, in recent years, the United States tried to include its approach to content moderation in some trade agreements. The United States demanded language on intermediary liability in the US–Japan Digital Trade Agreement and CUSMA.

Provisions to Encourage a Shared Approach to Regulating Platforms (Competition Policies)

The WTO has limited competence on competition/antitrust policies, which could be used by states collectively to tackle the business model. As an example, GATT and GATS contain rules on monopolies and exclusive service suppliers. The principles have been elaborated considerably in the rules and commitments on telecommunications. The agreements on intellectual property and services both recognize governments' rights to act against anti-competitive practices and their rights to work together to limit these practices (Anderson et al. 2018).

Specifically, GATS generally prohibits WTO members from adopting regulations that discriminate among foreign service suppliers ("most favored nation treatment") (GATS article 2.1). GATS, moreover, requires WTO members to regulate reasonably, objectively, and impartially and provide foreign service providers with a possibility to express concerns and have a regulation reviewed (GATS article 6). GATS also requires WTO members to be transparent about regulations that may affect services trade (GATS article 3). These regulations can include labor laws and competition policies (Basedow and Kauffmann 2016).

But policy makers have greater freedom to export their competition policy strategies in their bilateral and regional FTAs. In its FTAs, the European Union requires regional trade agreement parties to prohibit specific anti-competitive practices to the extent that they affect trade; these agreements include obligations to establish or maintain competition laws and to create an institution to enforce them. The United States and Canada require signatories to establish and enforce their own laws (Anderson et al. 2018).[16] The United States and Canada have also added accountability provisions with requirements relating to non-discrimination, transparency, and/or procedural fairness (WTO 2020, 147).

In a 2020 report, the OECD (2020, 3) suggested that "competition authorities seeking to address abuses of dominance in digital markets would benefit from deeper international co-operation, given the international scope of many digital firms." Recent FTAs seem to be moving in that direction with cooperation language.

Taken in sum, given different national objectives and approaches to competition policies, trade agreements have yet to effectively encourage cooperation across borders to tackle the negative spillovers of this new data-driven economy. These approaches could be considered polycentric since they are diffuse, span different levels, and are framed differently but they could also be a sign of patchwork approaches where each center of decision making promotes its own rules and practices.

Provisions to Promote Regulatory Coherence

Policy makers understand that nations have different norms and strategies for regulation, but a patchwork of regulation could cause problems for both producers and consumers of goods and services. In recent years, trade diplomats have drafted provisions in trade agreements to encourage greater coherence.

There are many strategies to achieve coherence, from measures to produce cooperation to mutual recognition and harmonization of regulations. Regulatory coherence includes competition policies, yet these most up-to-date FTAs do not have specific language facilitating such competition cooperation. DEPA, for example, calls for signatories to "pursue the development of mechanisms to promote compatibility and interoperability between their different regimes for protecting personal information. Such strategies can include mutual recognition, regulatory sandboxes (where regulators can experiment) or shared international frameworks."[17] CUSMA, a broader trade agreement, has a regulatory chapter, which states that "each Party should encourage its regulatory authorities to engage in mutually beneficial regulatory cooperation activities with relevant counterparts of one or more of the other Parties in appropriate circumstances to achieve these objectives."[18] EU trade agreements have a section on regulatory cooperation, which notes, "Recognizing the global nature of digital trade, the parties shall cooperate on regulatory issues and best practices through the existing sectoral dialogues."[19] The Brexit agreement simply states, "The Parties shall exchange information on regulatory matters in the context of digital trade."[20]

Taken in sum, these provisions are unlikely to encourage a shared approach to regulation that can serve as a multilateral counterweight to the power of the big firms. Moreover, such strategies cannot prevent a race to the bottom as many countries have no digital regulations or are just learning how to regulate digital firms. For example, developing countries must trade with Europe, which increasingly means they must adopt European standards for data protection. They do not have the time or policy space to develop their own standards (Pisa et al. 2021). Moreover, data governance is expensive and requires good policy governance skills. Data governance will be essential to development, and donor nations have a responsibility to work with developing countries to improve their data governance. Yet trade policy makers have yet to effectively link digital trade governance and data governance capacity building (Aaronson 2019).

This has implications for polycentric governance of digital data, there are some centers of political and economic power that traction more centrality and authority than least developed countries.

Provisions to Reduce Spam

Many, but not all, countries have laws that ban spam.[21] In 2006, members of the OECD issued recommendations on cooperation to address spam. They acknowledged that spam undermined trust and consumer confidence, "which is a prerequisite for the information society and for the success of e-commerce," and that it led to "economic and social costs."[22] They also recognized that "spam poses unique challenges for law enforcement in that senders can easily hide their identity, forge the electronic path of their email messages, and send their messages from anywhere in the world to anyone in the world, thus making spam a uniquely international problem that can only be efficiently addressed through international co-operation."[23] The signatories agreed that they must cooperate to investigate and enforce cross-border spam problems (OECD 2006).

The OECD Recommendations have influenced e-commerce and digital trade language. Almost every trade agreement that covers e-commerce or digital trade includes language to govern spam (Asian Trade Centre 2021). Many FTAs have taken steps to regulate unsolicited commercial electronic communications.

Bans on Certain Practices

Trade agreements create rules to ensure that certain practices do not discriminate between domestic and foreign providers of services or create unfair advantages for domestic companies. Some practices are regulated, and other more egregious practices are banned.

Almost every digital trade agreement or chapter bans two practices: performance requirements and data localization because these practices can discriminate against foreign providers of data services (and in so doing impede market access). The EU–UK Trade and Cooperation Agreement states that cross-border data flows shall not be restricted by data localization strategies and "a Party shall not require the transfer of, or access to, the source code of software owned by a natural or legal person of the other Party."[24]

Trade diplomats have not yet banned other practices. Yet disinformation, such as malware and distributed denial-of-service attacks, can undermine market access and raise costs for firms that must hire researchers to ascertain who is responsible for these attacks while simultaneously correcting disinformation. Moreover, disinformation may have hidden costs, including reducing internet generativity and perceptions that the internet is a safe and stable place to be.

Retaliatory Measures

For example, the United States has used sanctions to deal with "malicious cyber-enabled activities originating from, or directed by persons located, in whole or in substantial part, outside the United States."[25] Since 2016, US law has authorized sanctions related to interfering with or undermining election processes or institutions. In this regard, the United States has sanctioned Russian and Iranian entities. The US process requires an investigation, attribution, and then development of a strategy to target the responsible entities.[26] The United States justifies its actions as legitimate under the national security exceptions.

Conclusion

The World Economic Forum ranks the spread of disinformation and fake news as among the world's top global risks (Edmond 2020). Under current legal frameworks and economic conditions, many of the giant global platforms are unwilling to address the business model that both finances and perpetuates disinformation. These platforms are centers of power and their decisions challenge polycentric arrangements given their gatekeeping positions. In one sense it could be argued that these platforms have more authority than many other actors and instruments. In another, platforms compete for attention and subscribers, none of them control the totality of global data flows but can exercise a great degree of control and authority over their spaces.

At the same time, disinformation is both a global and a national problem that nations must cooperate with each other to mitigate. Rather than constraining governments, international cooperation may help the bulk of nations, many of which lack digital prowess to develop their national policies. Moreover, such language could build trust and, in so doing, expand markets for data, in particular in the developing world.

While trade agreements are not the only answer to the problem of cross-border disinformation, digital trade provisions can provide some tools for mitigating such flows and provide more power to states to address this problem. In addition, while trade agreements cannot address the business model underlying disinformation, they could help policy makers collaborate to challenge platform practices that fuel disinformation. These agreements may also help ensure that policy makers do not avoid regulating for fear of firm bullying. Given the predominant role played by large platforms in disinformation, a more diversified and empowered landscape of actors across the national and international levels with an additional instrument at hand in trade agreements brings more nuance to the polycentric nature of the issue and more choices for global digital cooperation.

Notes

1 This chapter was first published as a paper by the Centre for International Governance Innovation in 2021. The author is grateful for their permission to revise and update the paper as a chapter in this book.

2 In 1964, US Supreme Court Justice Potter Stewart tried to explain "hard-core" pornography by saying, "I shall not today attempt further to define the kinds of material I understand to be embraced ... [b]ut I know it when I see it." See https://corporate. findlaw.com/litigation-disputes/movie-day-at-the-supreme-court-or-i-know-it-when-i-see-it-a.html.

3 As an example, in 2018, some 40 percent of Facebook users got their news from the platform. See www.journalism.org/2018/09/10/news-use-across-social-media-platforms-2018/.

4 Cognitive security is the application of artificial intelligence (AI) technologies patterned on human thought processes to detect threats and protect physical and digital systems.

5 See https://comprop.oii.ox.ac.uk/.

6 *United States of America v. Internet Research Agency LLC*, 18 USC §§ 2, 371, 1349, 1028A.

7 Researchers at the Brown Institute for Media Innovation, a joint initiative between Columbia University and Stanford University, have shown that Amazon, Apple, Facebook, and Google collect more than 450 different pieces of information about their users. See https://brown.columbia.edu/mapping-data-flows/.

8 See https://uscode.house.gov/view.xhtml?req=(title:47%20section:230%20edition:prelim) and www.eff.org/issues/cda230. The Trump administration proposed several reforms; see www.justice.gov/archives/ag/department-justice-s-review-section-230-communications-decency-act-1996.

9 See www.loc.gov/item/global-legal-monitor/2021-07-06/germany-network-enforcement-act-amended-to-better-fight-online-hate-speech/.

10 For a listing of national laws regarding fake news, see www.reuters.com/article/us-singapore-politics-fakenews-factbox/factbox-fake-news-laws-around-the-world-idUSKCN1RE0XN.

11 As an example, Twitter is asking some of its users to point out disinformation (to crowdsource it) (see www.cnn.com/2021/01/25/tech/twitter-birdwatch/index.html); while Facebook is trying to make its campaign advertising business more transparent and making tweaks to its algorithms to support verified news and to curb political advertising during times of political volatility (see www.axios.com/2021/01/27/facebook-to-downplay-politics-on-its-platform).

12 See Framework for Global Electronic Commerce at https://clintonwhitehouse4. archives.gov/WH/New/Commerce/.

13 See Framework for Global Electronic Commerce; see presidential directive at https:// fas.org/irp/offdocs/pdd-nec-ec.htm.

14 See *Agreement between the United States of America and Japan Concerning Digital Trade*, 7 October 2019, art 11 (entered into force 1 January 2020) [*US-Japan Digital Trade Agreement*], online: https://ustr.gov/sites/default/files/files/agreements/japan/Agreement_between_the_United_States_and_Japan_concerning_Digital_Trade.pdf; *DEPA*, 12 June 2020, art 4.2 at 4–1–4–2 (entered into force 7 January 2021), online: www.mfat.govt.nz/assets/Uploads/DEPA-Signing-Text-11-June-2020-GMT.pdf.

15 The exceptions include "measures (a) necessary to protect public morals or to maintain public order; (b) necessary to protect human, animal or plant life or health; (c) necessary to secure compliance with laws or regulations which are not inconsistent with the provisions of this agreement including those relating to: (i) the prevention of deceptive and fraudulent practices or to deal with the effects or a default on services contracts; (ii) the protection of the privacy of individuals in relation to the processing and dissemination of personal data and the protection of confidentiality of individual

records and accounts; [and] (iii) safety." See www.international.gc.ca/trade-comm erce/assets/pdfs/agreements-accords/cusma-aceum/cusma-19.pdf.

16 See e.g., *CUSMA, supra* note 58.

17 Ibid.

18 See *CUSMA, supra* note 58, c 28, art 28.17(1), online: www.international.gc.ca/tra de-commerce/assets/pdfs/agreements-accords/cusma-aceum/cusma-28.pdf.

19 See *Modernization of the Trade part of the EU-Mexico Global Agreement*, not yet signed, art 11(1) [not yet entered into force], online: https://trade.ec.europa.eu/doclib/docs/2018/april/tradoc_156811.pdf.

20 See *Trade and Cooperation Agreement between the European Union and the European Atomic Energy Community, of the one part, and the United Kingdom of Great Britain and Northern Ireland, of the other part*, 30 December 2020, OJ L 149, title III, art 16 (1), (entered into force 1 May 2021) [*EU-UK Trade and Cooperation Agreement*], online: https://assets.publishing.service.gov.uk/government/uploads/system/uploads/atta chment_data/file/948119/EU-UK_Trade_and_Cooperation_Agreement_24.12.2020.pdf.

21 See https://en.wikipedia.org/wiki/Email_spam_legislation_by_country.

22 See https://legalinstruments.oecd.org/en/instruments/OECD-LEGAL-0344.

23 Ibid.

24 See *EU-UK Trade and Cooperation Agreement, supra* note 69, Title III (Digital Trade), art 12(1).

25 See www.whitehouse.gov/briefing-room/presidential-actions/2021/03/29/notice-on-the-continuation-of-the-national-emergency-with-respect-to-significant-malicious-cyber-ena bled-activities/.

26 For more on sanctions against Russian entities, see https://home.treasury.gov/news/p ress-releases/sm1118; on sanctions against Iranian entities, see https://www.state.gov/iran-sanctions/; and on the executive order imposing sanctions against foreign inter-ference in US elections, see https://home.treasury.gov/system/files/126/election_execu tive_order_13848.pdf.

Bibliography

Aaronson, Susan Ariel. 2015. "Why Trade Agreements Are Not Setting Information Free: The Lost History and Reinvigorated Debate over Cross-Border Data Flows, Human Rights and National Security." *World Trade Review* 14 (4): 671–700.

Aaronson, Susan Ariel. 2018. "What Are We Talking about When We Talk about Digital Protectionism?" *World Trade Review* 18 (4): 1–37.

Aaronson, Susan Ariel. 2019. *Data Is a Development Issue.* CIGI Paper No. 223. Waterloo, ON: CIGI. www.cigionline.org/publications/data-development-issue/.

Aaronson, Susan Ariel and Jamie Zimmerman. 2007. *Trade Imbalance: The Struggle to Weigh Human Rights Concerns in Trade Policymaking.* New York: Cambridge University Press.

Aaronson, Susan Ariel and Thomas Struett. 2020. *Data Is Divisive: A History of Public Communications on E-commerce, 1998–2020.* CIGI Paper No. 247. Waterloo, ON: CIGI. www.cigionline.org/publications/data-divisive-history-public-communications-e-commer ce-1998-2020/.

Amnesty International. 2019. *Surveillance Giants: How the Business Model of Google and Facebook Threatens Human Rights.* London, UK: Amnesty International, Ltd. www.amnesty.org/download/Documents/POL3014042019ENGLISH.PDF.

Anderson, Robert D., William E.Kovacic, AnnaCaroline Müller and Nadezhda Spory-sheva. 2018. *Competition Policy, Trade and the Global Economy: Existing WTO Elements, Commitments in Regional Trade Agreements, Current Challenges and*

Issues for Reflection. WTO Staff Working Paper ERSD-2018–12. https://www.wto.org/english/res_e/reser_e/ersd201812_e.pdf.

Angwin, Julia. 2021. "Understanding the Threat of 'Surveillance Capitalism'." *The Markup*, February 13. https://themarkup.org/newsletter/hello-world/understanding-the-threat-of-surveillance-capitalism.

Arbel, Tali and Matt O'Brien. 2021. "Biden Backs Off on Tiktok Ban in Review of Trump China Moves." *PBS News Hour*, February 10. www.pbs.org/newshour/politics/biden-backs-off-on-tiktok-ban-in-review-of-trump-china-moves.

Asian Trade Centre. 2021. "Comparing Digital Rules in Trade Agreements." *Asian Trade Centre*, July 24. http://asiantradecentre.org/talkingtrade/comparing-digital-rules-in-trade-agreements.

Babic, Milan, Jan Fichtner and Eelke M.Heemskerk. 2017. "States Versus Corporations: Rethinking the Power of Business in International Politics." *The International Spectator, Italian Journal of International Affairs* 52 (4): 20–43. doi:10.1080/03932729.2017.1389151.

Babic, Milan, Eelke M.Heemskerk and Jan Fichtner. 2018. "Who Is More Powerful— States or Corporations?" *The Conversation*, July 10. https://theconversation.com/who-is-more-powerful-states-or-corporations-99616.

Banga, Rashmi. 2021. *Joint Statement Initiative on E-Commerce (JSI): Economic and Fiscal Implications for the South.* UNCTAD Research Paper No. 58, UNCTAD/SER.RP/2021/1, February. https://www.researchgate.net/profile/Rashmi-Banga/publication/349313071_F_E_B_R_U_A_R_Y_2_0_2_1_Joint_Statement_Initiative_on_E-Commerce_JSI_Economic_and_Fiscal_Implications_for_the_South/links/602a610892851c4ed57295c3/F-E-B-R-U-A-R-Y-2-0-2-1-Joint-Statement-Initiative-on-E-Commerce-JSI-Economic-and-Fiscal-Implications-for-the-South.pdf?origin=publication_detail.

Barclay, Donald A. 2018. *Confronting the Wicked Problem of Fake News: A Role for Education?* Cicero Foundation Great Debate Paper No. 18/03. www.cicerofoundation.org/wp-content/uploads/Donald_Barclay_Confronting_Fake_News.pdf.

Basedow, Robert and Céline Kauffmann. 2016. *International Trade and Good Regulatory Practices: Assessing the Trade Impacts of Regulation.* OECD Regulatory Policy Working Papers No. 4. doi:10.1787/5jlv59hdgtf5-en. https://www.oecd-ilibrary.org/governance/international-trade-and-good-regulatory-practices_5jlv59hdgtf5-en.

Baye, Michael Roy and Jeffrey Prince. 2020. *The Economics of Digital Platforms: A Guide for Regulators.* The Global Antitrust Institute Report on the Digital Economy 34. doi:10.2139/ssrn.3733754.

BBC News. 2019. "Tackle Tech Giants' 'Bullying Tactics' Review Urges." *BBC News*, March 13. www.bbc.com/news/business-47543107.

Burri, Mira. 2013. *Should There Be New Multilateral Rules for Digital Trade? E15 Expert Group on Trade and Innovation Think Piece.* Geneva, Switzerland: International Centre for Trade and Sustainable Development. https://papers.ssrn.com/sol3/papers.cfm?abstract_id=2344629.

Burri, Mira and Rodrigo Polanco. 2020. "Digital Trade Provisions in Preferential Trade Agreements: Introducing a New Dataset." *Journal of International Economic Law* 23 (1): 187–220. doi:10.1093/jiel/jgz044.

Canadian Security Intelligence Service. 2018. *Who Said What? The Security Challenges of Modern Disinformation.* World Watch: Expert Notes Series Publication No. 2016-2012-05. www.canada.ca/content/dam/csis-scrs/documents/publications/disinformation_post-report_eng.pdf.

Carr, Hope. 2017. "Waging Information Warfare in the 21st Century." *The Three Swords Magazine*, July 17. www.jwc.nato.int/images/stories/_news_items_/2017/InformationWarfare_JWCThreeSwordsJuly17.pdf.

Carvalho, Carlos, Nicholas Klagge and Emanuel Moench. 2011. *The Persistent Effects of a False News Shock*. Federal Reserve Bank of New York Staff Reports No. 374.

Cave, Damien. 2021. "An Australia with No Google? The Bitter Fight Behind a Drastic Threat." *The New York Times*, January 23. www.nytimes.com/2021/01/22/business/australia-google-facebook-news-media.html.

Cedar Partners. 2020. *Platform Accountability: Global Challenges & Opportunities*. https://drive.google.com/file/d/1S4MBS8VmKCiqqBXLdANiF4ijaqfvq-mY/view.

Cellan-Jones, Rory. 2017. "Fake News Worries 'Are Growing' Suggests BBC Poll." *BBC News*, September 22. www.bbc.com/news/technology-41319683.

Chakravorti, Bhaskar. 2020. *Social Media Companies Are Taking Steps to Tamp Down Coronavirus Misinformation—But They Can Do More*. The Conversation, March 30. https://theconversation.com/social-media-companies-are-taking-steps-to-tamp-down-coronavirus-misinformation-but-they-can-do-more-133335.

Chen, Adrian. 2015. "The Agency." *The New York Times Magazine*, June 7. www.nytimes.com/2015/06/07/magazine/the-agency.html.

Chen, Yongmin, Xinyu Hua and Keith E.Maskus. 2020. *International Protection of Consumer Data*. EUI Working Papers RSCAS 2020/42. https://cadmus.eui.eu/bitstream/handle/1814/67583/RSCAS%202020_42.pdf?sequence=1&isAllowed=y.

CIGI. 2019. Models for Platform Governance. Waterloo, ON: CIGI. www.cigionline.org/models-platform-governance/.

Citron, Danielle Keats. 2015. *Hate Crimes in Cyberspace – Introduction*. University of Maryland Legal Studies Research Paper No. 2015–2011. https://ssrn.com/abstract=2616790.

Ciuriak, Dan. 2019. *World Trade Organization 2.0: Reforming Multilateral Trade Rules for the Digital Age*. CIGI Policy Brief No. 152. Waterloo, ON: CIGI. www.cigionline.org/publications/world-trade-organization-20-reforming-multilateral-trade-rules-digital-age/.

Cohen, Noam. 2019. "Will California's New Bot Law Strengthen Democracy?" The New Yorker, July 2. www.newyorker.com/tech/annals-of-technology/will-californias-new-bot-law-strengthen-democracy.

Communications Security Establishment. 2019. *2019 Update: Cyber Threats to Canada's Democratic Processes*. https://www.cyber.gc.ca/sites/default/files/cyber/publications/tdp-2019-report_e.pdf.

Cory, Nigel. 2020. *Censorship as a Non-tariff Barrier to Trade*. Information Technology & Innovation Foundation. www2.itif.org/2020-censorship-non-tariff-barrier-trade.pdf.

Council on Foreign Relations. 2018. *Increasing International Cooperation in Cybersecurity and Adapting Cyber Norms*. www.cfr.org/report/increasing-international-cooperation-cybersecurity-and-adapting-cyber-norms.

Crémer Jacques, Yves-Alexandre de Montjoye and Heike Schweitzer. 2019. "*Competition Policy in the Digital Age*." European Commission. https://ec.europa.eu/competition/publications/reports/kd0419345enn.pdf.

Derakhshan, Hossein and Claire Wardle. 2018. "Information Disorder: Definitions." In *Understanding and Addressing the Disinformation Ecosystem*, pp. 5–12. Philadelphia, PA: Annenberg School for Communication. https://firstdraftnews.org/wp-content/uploads/2018/03/The-Disinformation-Ecosystem-20180207-v4.pdf?x86275.

DiResta, Renée. 2019. "A New Law Makes Bots Identify Themselves—That's the Problem." *Wired*, July 24. www.wired.com/story/law-makes-bots-identify-themselves/.

Donovan, Joan. 2021. "How Social Media's Obsession with Scale Supercharged Disinformation." *Harvard Business Review*, January 13. https://hbr.org/2021/01/how-social-medias-obsession-with-scale-supercharged-disinformation?registration=success.

Durocher, Anthony. 2019. *Competition in the Age of the Digital Giant*. Remarks by Anthony Durocher, Deputy Commissioner, Monopolistic Practices, Competition Bureau, Big Data Toronto 2019, June 13. www.canada.ca/en/competition-bureau/news/2019/06/competition-in-the-age-of-the-digital-giant.html.

Dutch Data Protection Authority. 2013. "Canadian and Dutch Data Privacy Guardians Release Findings from Investigation of Popular Mobile App." News message, January 28. https://www.priv.gc.ca/en/opc-news/news-and-announcements/2013/nr-c_130128/.

Edmond, Charlotte. 2020 "These Are the Top Risks Facing the World in 2020." World Economic Forum, January 15. www.weforum.org/agenda/2020/01/top-global-risks-report-climate-change-cyberattacks-economic-political.

Epps, Tracy. 2008. "Reconciling Public Opinion and WTO rules under the SPS Agreement." *World Trade Review*, 7 (2): 359–392.

Etlinger, S. and Innovation C. for I. G. (2019). "What's So Difficult about Social Media Platform Governance?" In *Models for Platform Governance*, pp. 20–26. Centre for International Governance Innovation. https://www.jstor.org/stable/resrep26127.6.

European Commission. 2020a. *Communication from the Commission to the European Parliament, the Council, the European Economic and Social Committee and the Committee of the Regions: On the European democracy action plan.* COM(2020) 790 final, December 3. https://eur-lex.europa.eu/legal-content/EN/TXT/PDF/?uri=CELEX:52020DC0790&from=EN.

European Commission. 2020b. *The Digital Markets Act*. Retrieved 1 November 2023, from https://digital-markets-act.ec.europa.eu/index_en.

Evans, David S. 2020. "The Economics of Attention Markets." SSRN. doi:10.2139/ssrn.3044858.

Ewing, Philip. 2020. "Report: Russian Election Trolling Becoming Subtler, Tougher to Detect." *NPR*, March 5. www.npr.org/2020/03/05/812497423/report-russian-election-trolling-becoming-subtler-tougher-to-detect.

Freeman, Alan. 2017. "Russia Should Stop Calling my Grandfather a Nazi, says Canada's Foreign Minister." *The Washington Post*, March 9. www.washingtonpost.com/news/worldviews/wp/2017/03/09/canadas-foreign-minister-says-russia-is-spreading-disinformation-about-her-grandfather/.

Fried, Daniel. 2019. *Democratic Defense Against Disinformation 2.0*. Atlantic Council, June 13. https://www.atlanticcouncil.org/wp-content/uploads/2019/06/Democratic_Defense_Against_Disinformation_2.0.pdf.

Ghosh, Dipayan, Lindsay Gorman, BretSchafer and Clara Tsao. 2020. *The Weaponized Web: Tech Policy Through the Lens of National Security*. Alliance for Securing Democracy. https://securingdemocracy.gmfus.org/wp-content/uploads/2020/12/The-Weaponized-Web.pdf.

Goldstein, Josh A. and Grossman, Shelby. 2021. *How disinformation evolved in 2020*. Brookings TechStream, January 4. www.brookings.edu/techstream/how-disinformation-evolved-in-2020/.

Government of Canada. 2021a. "Paris Call for Trust and Security in Cyberspace." www.canada.ca/en/democratic-institutions/services/paris-call-trust-security-cyberspace.html.

Government of Canada. 2021b. "Online disinformation." https://www.canada.ca/en/campaign/online-disinformation.html.

Gu, Lion, Vladimir Kropotov and Fyodor Yarochkin. 2017. "Fake News and Cyber Propaganda: The Use and Abuse of Social Media." *Trend Micro*, June 13. www.

trendmicro.com/vinfo/us/security/news/cybercrime-and-digital-threats/fake-news-cyber-propaganda-the-abuse-of-social-media.

Haggart, Blayne. 2021. "Platform Regulation Is Too Important to Be Left to Americans Alone." [Opinion]. Centre for International Governance Innovation, January 18. www.cigionline.org/articles/platform-regulation-too-important-be-left-americans-alone/.

Heim, Joe. 2021. "'Disinformation Can Be a Very Lucrative Business, Especially If You're Good at It,' Media Scholar Says." *The Washington Post*, January 21. www.washingtonpost.com/lifestyle/magazine/disinformation-can-be-a-very-lucrative-business-especially-if-youre-good-at-it-media-scholar-says/2021/01/19/4c842f06-4a04-11eb-a9d9-1e3ec4a928b9_story.html?mc_cid=b3950438fc&mc_eid=d6ed88c5ef.

Helbing, Dirk, Bruno S. Frey, Gerd Gigerenzer, Ernst Hafen, Michael Hagner, Yvonne Hofstetter, Jeroen van den Hoven, Roberto V. Zicari and Andrej Zwitter. 2017. "Will Democracy Survive Big Data and Artificial Intelligence?" *Scientific American*, February 25. www.scientificamerican.com/article/will-democracy-survive-big-data-and-artificial-intelligence/.

Hern, Alex. 2020. "Online Harms Bill: Firms May Face Multibillion-Pound Fines for Illegal Content." *The Guardian*, December 15. www.theguardian.com/technology/2020/dec/15/online-harms-bill-firms-may-face-multibillion-pound-fines-for-content.

Howard, Philip. 2014. *EAGER: Computational Propaganda and the Production and Detection of Bots*. National Science Foundation Grant Proposal, August 1. https://demtech.oii.ox.ac.uk/wp-content/uploads/sites/12/2015/01/Project-Description.pdf.

Hurst, Daniel. 2020. "Kevin Rudd Says Scott Morrison's 'Public Relations Eggbeater' Is Harming Relationship with Beijing." *The Guardian*, December 4. www.theguardian.com/australia-news/2020/dec/05/kevin-rudd-says-scott-morrisons-public-relations-eggbeater-is-harming-relationship-with-beijing.

Infield, Tom. 2020. "Americans Who Get News Mainly on Social Media Are Less Knowledgeable and Less Engaged." *Pew*, November 16. www.pewtrusts.org/en/trust/archive/fall-2020/americans-who-get-news-mainly-on-social-media-are-less-knowledgeable-and-less-engaged.

Insikt Group. 2019. *The Price of Influence: Disinformation in the Private Sector*. Recorded Future. https://go.recordedfuture.com/hubfs/reports/cta-2019-0930.pdf.

Kilic, Burcu. 2021. *Shaping the Future of Multilateralism - Digital Trade Rules: Big Tech's End Run Around Domestic Regulations*. Heinrich Boell Foundation. https://eu.boell.org/index.php/en/2021/05/19/shaping-future-multilateralism-digital-trade-rules-big-techs-end-run-around-domestic.

Kline, Allison. n.d. "Enhanced Attribution." www.darpa.mil/program/enhanced-attribution.

Knuutila, Aleksi, Lisa-Maria Neudert and Philip N.Howard. 2020. *Global Fears of Disinformation: Perceived Internet and Social Media Harms in 142 Countries*. Computational Propaganda Project Data Memo 2020.8. https://demtech.oii.ox.ac.uk/wp-content/uploads/sites/12/2020/12/Global-Fears-of-Disinformation-v.13.pdf.

Laslo, Matt. 2019. "The Fight Over Section 230—and the Internet as We Know It." *Wired*, August 13. www.wired.com/story/fight-over-section-230-internet-as-we-know-it/.

Lerman, Rachel. 2021. "Social Media Liability Law Is Likely to Be Reviewed under Biden." *The Washington Post*, January 18. www.washingtonpost.com/politics/2021/01/18/biden-section-230/.

Levush, Ruth. 2019. *Government Responses to Disinformation on Social Media Platforms: Comparative Summary*. Congressional Research Service. https://www.loc.gov/item/2019713404/.

Lindsay, Jon R. 2015. "Tipping the Scales: The Attribution Problem and the Feasibility of Deterrence Against Cyberattack." *Journal of Cybersecurity* 1 (1): 53–67.

Lipton, David. 2020. "Cybersecurity Threats Call for a Global Response." *IMF Blog* (blog), January 13. https://blogs.imf.org/2020/01/13/cybersecurity-threats-call-for-a-global-response/.

Lynskey, Orla. 2017. *Regulating 'Platform Power'*. LSE Legal Studies Working Paper No. 1/2017. doi:10.2139/ssrn.2921021.

McCabe, David and Ana Swanson. 2019. "U.S. Using Trade Deals to Shield Tech Giants from Foreign Regulators." *The New York Times*, October 7. www.nytimes.com/2019/10/07/business/tech-shield-trade-deals.html.

Methven O'Brien, Claire, Rikke Frank Jørgensen and Benn Finlay Hogan. 2020. "Tech Giants: Human Rights Risks and Frameworks." SSRN. https://papers.ssrn.com/sol3/papers.cfm?abstract_id=3768813.

Monteiro, José-Antonio and Robert Teh. 2017. *Provisions on Electronic Commerce in Regional Trade Agreements*. ERSD-2017–2011. https://www.wto.org/english/res_e/reser_e/ersd201711_e.htm.

Montgomery, Molly. 2020. *Disinformation as a Wicked Problem: Why We Need Co-Regulatory Frameworks*. Brookings Institution, August. www.brookings.edu/wp-content/uploads/2020/08/Montgomery_Disinformation-Regulation_PDF.pdf.

Morar, David and Bruna Martins dos Santos. 2020. "The Push for Content Moderation Legislation around the World." *Brookings Techtank*, September 21. https://www.brookings.edu/blog/techtank/2020/09/21/the-push-for-content-moderation-legislation-around-the-world/.

Morrison, Sarah, Belinda Barnet and James Martin. 2020. "China's Disinformation Threat Is Real. We Need Better Defences Against State-Based Cyber Campaigns." *The Conversation*, June 23. https://theconversation.com/chinas-disinformation-threat-is-real-we-need-better-defences-against-state-based-cyber-campaigns-141044.

National Endowment for Democracy. 2017. "Issue Brief: Distinguishing Disinformation from Propaganda, Misinformation, and 'Fake News'." *National Endowment for Democracy*, October 17. www.ned.org/issue-brief-distinguishing-disinformation-from-propaganda-misinformation-and-fake-news/.

Needham, Kirsty. 2020. "China Tweet That Enraged Australia Propelled by 'Unusual' Accounts, Say Experts." *Reuters*, December 5. www.reuters.com/article/us-australia-china-tweet/china-tweet-that-enraged-australia-propelled-by-unusual-accounts-say-experts-idUSKBN28E0YI.

Nemr, Christina and William Gangware. 2019. *Weapons of Mass Distraction: Foreign State-Sponsored Disinformation in the Digital Age*. Park Advisors. www.state.gov/wp-content/uploads/2019/05/Weapons-of-Mass-Distraction-Foreign-State-Sponsored-Disinformation-in-the-Digital-Age.pdf.

Newman, Lily Hay. 2016. "Hacker Lexicon: What Is the Attribution Problem?" *Wired*, December 24. www.wired.com/2016/12/hacker-lexicon-attribution-problem/.

Nugent, Clara. 2018. "France Is Voting on a Law Banning Fake News. Here's How it Could Work." *Time*, June 7. https://time.com/5304611/france-fake-news-law-macron/.

Nyst, Carly and Nick Monaco. 2018. *State-Sponsored Trolling: How Governments Are Deploying Disinformation as Part of Broader Digital Harassment Campaigns*. Palo Alto, CA: Institute for the Future. https://legacy.iftf.org/statesponsoredtrolling/.

OECD. 2006. *OECD Recommendation on Cross-Border Co-operation in the Enforcement of Laws against Spam*. 1133rd sess. April 13. www.oecd.org/sti/ieconomy/oecdrecommendationoncross-borderco-operationintheenforcementoflawsagainstspam.htm

OECD. 2016. *Economic and Social Benefits of Internet Openness*. OECD Digital Economy Papers No. 257. Paris, France: OECD Publishing. doi:10.1787/5jlwqf2r97g5-en.

OECD. 2019. *An Introduction to Online Platforms and Their Role in the Digital Transformation*. Paris, France: OECD Publishing. https://www.oecd.org/innovation/an-introduction-to-online-platforms-and-their-role-in-the-digital-transformation-53e5f593-en.htm.

OECD. 2020. *Abuse of Dominance in Digital Markets*. Paris, France: OECD. www.oecd.org/daf/competition/abuse-of-dominance-in-digital-markets-2020.pdf.

Office of the High Commissioner for Human Rights. 2017. *Joint Declaration on Freedom of Expression and 'Fake News,' Disinformation and Propaganda*. www.ohchr.org/Documents/Issues/Expression/JointDeclaration3March2017.doc.

Office of the High Commissioner for Human Rights. 2021. *Disinformation and Freedom of Opinion and Expression: Report of the Special Rapporteur on the Promotion and Protection of the Right to Freedom of Opinion and Expression, Irene Khan*. 47th sess. A/HRC/47/25. https://undocs.org/A/HRC/47/25.

Office of the United States Trade Representative. 2011. *United States Seeks Detailed Information on China's Internet Restrictions*. Press release, October 19. https://ustr.gov/about-us/policy-offices/press-office/press-releases/2011/october/united-states-seeks-detailed-information-china's-i.

Osborne, Charlie. 2019. "Bad Bots Now Make Up 20 Percent of Web Traffic." *ZDNet*, April 17. www.zdnet.com/article/bad-bots-focus-on-financial-targets-make-up-20-percent-of-web-traffic/.

Owens, James. 2019. "The Tech Giants Dominated the Decade. But There's Still Time to Rein Them In." *The Guardian*, December 25. www.theguardian.com/commentisfree/2019/dec/25/2010s-tech-giants-google-amazon-facebook-regulators.

Petre, Caitlyn, Brooke Erin Duffy and Emily Hund. 2019. "'Gaming the System': Platform Paternalism and the Politics of Algorithmic Visibility." *Social Media and Society*, 5 (4). https://journals.sagepub.com/doi/full/10.1177/2056305119879995.

Pierce, Brian. n.d. "A Wicked Problem About Thinking: Cognitive Security." [Media]. Stanford University. https://mediax.stanford.edu/program/thinking-tools-for-wicked-problems/a-wicked-problem-about-thinking-cognitive-security/.

Pinchis-Paulsen, Mona. 2020. "Trade Multilateralism and U.S. National Security: The Making of the GATT Security Exceptions." *Michigan Journal of International Law*, 41 (1): 109–193. https://repository.law.umich.edu/mjil/vol41/iss1/4.

Pisa, Michael, PamDixon and Benno Ndulu. 2021. "Addressing Cross-Border Spillovers in Data Policy: The Need for a Global Approach." February 3. https://www.cgdev.org/blog/addressing-cross-border-spillovers-data-policy-need-global-approach.

Price, Rande. 2019. "Disinformation Is Profitable. That Needs to Change." *Digital Content Next* (blog), August 21. https://digitalcontentnext.org/blog/2019/08/21/disinformation-is-profitable-that-needs-to-change/.

Raymond, Mark. 2012. "The Internet as A Global Commons?" CIGI, October 26. https://www.cigionline.org/publications/internet-global-commons/.

Reuters. 2017. "French Election Contender Macron is Russian 'Fake News' Target: Party Chief." *Reuters*, February 13. www.reuters.com/article/us-france-election-cyber/french-election-contender-macron-is-russian-fake-news-target-party-chief-idUSKBN15S192.

Riley, Michael, Lauren Etter and Pradhan Bibhudatta. 2018. "A Global Guide to State-Sponsored Trolling." *Bloomberg*, July 19. www.bloomberg.com/features/2018-government-sponsored-cyber-militia-cookbook/.

Rossolillo, Nicholas. 2021. "Better Buy: Facebook vs. Google." *The Motley Fool*, January 25. www.fool.com/investing/2021/01/25/better-buy-facebook-vs-google/.

Ryan, Camille D., Andrew J. Schaul, Ryan Butner and John T. Swarthout. 2020. "Monetizing Disinformation in the Attention Economy: The Case of Genetically Modified Organisms (GMOs)." *European Management Journal*, 38 (1): 7–18. doi:10.1016/j.emj.2019.11.002.

Scott, Mark, Thibault Larger and Laura Kayali. 2020. "Europe Rewrites Rulebook for Digital Age. *Politico*, December 15. www.politico.eu/article/europe-digital-markets-act-services-act-tech-competition-rules-margrethe-vestager-thierry-breton/.

Singh, Preeti. 2021. "Inside the Pro-Huawei Influence Campaign." *The New York Times*, January 29. www.nytimes.com/2021/01/29/technology/commercial-disinformation-huawei-belgium.html.

Smeets, Maarten, ed. 2021. *Adapting to the Digital Trade Era: Challenges and Opportunities*. Geneva, Switzerland: WTO Publications. www.wto.org/english/res_e/booksp_e/adtera_e.pdf.

Snower, Dennis and Paul Twomey. 2020. *Humanistic Digital Governance*. CESifo Working Paper No. 8792. https://papers.ssrn.com/sol3/papers.cfm?abstract_id=3754683.

Stoller, Matt. 2021. "Take the Profit Out of Political Violence." *Big*, January 19. https://mattstoller.substack.com/p/take-the-profit-out-of-political.

Talihärm, Anna-Maria. 2013. "Towards Cyberpeace: Managing Cyberwar Through International Cooperation." *UN Chronicle*, August. www.un.org/en/chronicle/article/towards-cyberpeace-managing-cyberwar-through-international-cooperation.

Tech Observer. 2020. "After GDPR, EU Now Goes After Bots and Data Harvesters." *Tech Observer*, January 8. https://techobserver.in/2020/01/08/after-gdpr-eu-now-goes-after-bots-and-data-harvesters/.

Technology and Social Change Team. 2021. "Disinformation at Scale Threatens Freedom of Expression Worldwide." Comment to Irene Khan, Special Rapporteur on the promotion and protection of the right to freedom of expression. https://mediamanipulation.org/sites/default/files/2021-02/Donovan-et-al-TaSC-Comment.pdf.

The Washington Post. 2021. "Opinion: Facebook and Twitter Can Do Something About Deceptive News. So Why Don't They?" *The Washington Post*, February 1. www.washingtonpost.com/opinions/facebook-and-twitter-can-do-something-about-deceptive-news-so-why-dont-they/2021/02/01/da702e0e-626a-11eb-afbe-9a11a127d146_story.html.

Tucker, Joshua A., Andrew Guess, Pablo Barbera, Cristian Vaccari, Alexandra Siegel, Sergey Sanovich, Denis Stukal and Brendan Nyhan. 2018. "Social Media, Political Polarization, and Political Disinformation: A Review of the Scientific Literature." SSRN. https://papers.ssrn.com/sol3/papers.cfm?abstract_id=3144139.

Tworek, Heidi. 2021. "The Dangerous Inconsistencies of Digital Platform Policies." [Opinion]. Centre for International Governance Innovation, January 13. www.cigionline.org/articles/dangerous-inconsistencies-digital-platform-policies.

UK Information Commissioner's Office. 2019. "Adtech Phase 2: Key Findings." https://ico.org.uk/media/about-the-ico/documents/2616754/fff2-info-gathering-201912.pdf.

United Nations Conference on Trade and Development. 2019. "Global efforts needed to spread digital economy benefits, UN report says." UNCTAD, September 4. https://unctad.org/news/global-efforts-needed-spread-digital-economy-benefits-un-report-says.

University of Baltimore and CHEQ. 2019. *The Economic Cost of Bad Actors on the Internet*. https://s3.amazonaws.com/media.mediapost.com/uploads/EconomicCostOfFakeNews.pdf.

US Department of the Treasury. 2017. *Cyber-Related Sanctions Program*. Office of Foreign Assets Control, July 3. https://ofac.treasury.gov/media/8551/download?inline.

Vigneault, David. 2021. "Remarks by Director David Vigneault to the Centre for International Governance Innovation." Canadian Security Intelligence Service speech.,

February 9. www.canada.ca/en/security-intelligence-service/news/2021/02/remarks-by-director-david-vigneault-to-the-centre-for-international-governance-innovation.html.

Wakabayashi, Daisuke, Karen Weise, Jack Nicas and Mike Isaak. 2020. "The Economy Is in Record Decline, But Not for the Tech Giants." *The New York Times*, July 30. www.nytimes.com/2020/07/30/technology/tech-company-earnings-amazon-apple-facebook-google.html.

Wardle, Claire and Hossein Derakhshan. 2017. *Information Disorder: Toward an Interdisciplinary Framework for Research and Policy Making.* Council of Europe Report DGI(2017)09. https://rm.coe.int/information-disorder-toward-an-interdisciplinary-framework-for-researc/168076277c.

Weaver, Nicholas. 2013. "Our Government Has Weaponized the Internet. Here's How They Did It." *Wired*, November 13. www.wired.com/2013/11/this-is-how-the-internet-backbone-has-been-turned-into-a-weapon/.

Wojcik, Stefan, Solomon Messing, Aaron Smith, Lee Rainie and Paul Hitlin. 2018. *Bots in the Twittersphere.* Pew Research Center. www.pewresearch.org/internet/2018/04/09/bots-in-the-twittersphere/.

Woolley, Samuel C. and Philip N.Howard. 2016. "Political Communication, Computational Propaganda, and Autonomous Agents." *International Journal of Communication*, 10: 4882–4890.

World Economic Forum. 2020. *A Roadmap for Cross-Border Data Flows: Future-Proofing Readiness and Cooperation in the New Data Economy.* [White Paper]. Cologne/Geneva, Switzerland: World Economic Forum. www3.weforum.org/docs/WEF_A_Roadmap_for_Cross_Border_Data_Flows_2020.pdf.

World Economic Forum. 2011. *Personal Data: The Emergence of a New Asset Class.* January. http://www3.weforum.org/docs/WEF_ITTC_PersonalDataNewAsset_Report_2011.pdf.

World Economic Forum. 2018. *Report of the Meeting Held on 2 March 2018: Note by the Secretariat.* S/C/M/134. April 5. https://www3.weforum.org/docs/WEF_GRR18_Report.pdf.

World Economic Forum. 2020. *World Trade Report 2020: Government Policies to Promote Innovation in the Digital Age.* Geneva, Switzerland: WTO Publications. www.wto.org/english/res_e/booksp_e/wtr20_e/wtr20_e.pdf.

WTO. 2012. *World Trade Report 2012: Trade and Public Policies: A Closer Look at Non-Tariff Measures in the 21st Century.* Geneva, Switzerland: WTO Publications. www.wto.org/english/res_e/booksp_e/anrep_e/world_trade_report12_e.pdf.

WTO. 2020. *World Trade Report 2020: Government Policies to Promote Innovation in the Digital Age.* https://doi.org/10.30875/60123dd4-en.

Wu, Mark. 2017. *Digital Trade-Related Provisions in Regional Trade Agreements: Existing Models and Lessons for the Multilateral Trade System.* Geneva, Switzerland: International Centre for Trade and Sustainable Development.

Zuboff, Shoshana. 2019. *The Age of Surveillance Capitalism: The Fight for a Human Future at the New Frontier of Power.* New York, NY: Public Affairs.

Zuboff, Shoshana. 2021. "The Coup We Are Not Talking About." *The New York Times*, January 29. www.nytimes.com/2021/01/29/opinion/sunday/facebook-surveillance-society-technology.html.

9

TRACKERS AND CHASERS

Governance Challenges in Disinformation Datafication

Clara Iglesias Keller and Bruna Martins dos Santos

Introduction

This chapter explores the intersection of data governance and digital disinformation also referred to only as "disinformation", to demonstrate how comprehensive approaches to the former allow for insightful regulatory legitimacy assessments of recently proposed regulatory strategies against disinformation. We build our analysis on the polycentric perspective of data governance advanced in this volume, which understands "the roles of digital data as both objects and forms of contemporary governance" (see Chapter 1, this volume). As we will show, this versatility of data is well represented in debates on how to regulate disinformation. First, disinformation itself is a polycentric issue that originates from and is shaped by different centers of information production and decision-making. Furthermore, the polyvalency of data, as prospected in the chapters in this volume, is one of the elements that add yet more layers to the compounded phenomenon that is disinformation. This chapter explores two policy trends that illustrate the versatility of data, particularly in the realm of disinformation regulation. The first one is the regulation of microtargeting, a technique that allows selected distribution of content in accordance with users' pre-expressed preferences – the chasers. The second trend is the institution of traceability obligations, through which digital platforms and other private agents are bound to obligations of data storage and referral to authorities, as a way to allow the identification of disinformation distribution chains – the trackers.

Notwithstanding the blurred lines that distinguish dis- from misinformation and other practices that came to be understood as elements that amount to an "information disorder" (Wardle and Derakhshan, 2017), we refer to disinformation as "false or misleading information that is intentionally spread for

DOI: 10.4324/9781003388418-11

profit, to create harm, or to advance political or ideological goals" (Marwick et al., 2021). As a multidimensional phenomenon, digital disinformation can be better understood through a polycentric perspective. This approach includes comprehending the often-overlapping instances that contribute to its development; this plurality of centers rests at the core of structured disinformation strategies. Disinformation production is often centralized in content clusters (Evangelista and Bruno, 2019), while distribution involves actors of different natures, from marketing agencies to individual users; once distributed, digital disinformation travels through different media and communication channels, which can also shape the way it is presented. This path can also involve different jurisdictions so that coping with disinformation potentially will also involve different centers of state power and policy making.

This polycentric essence is also reflected in the strains of debate that focus on countermeasures towards disinformation. These discussions have already set ground on the premise that disinformation is a phenomenon best captured by polycentric approaches to governance, as it requires different responses from different actors. This implies, for instance, a role for fact-checking and media literacy to be performed by journalistic or civil society organizations, and for digital platforms to implement their own moderation and certification procedures (Iglesias Keller, 2021, p. 488). While principles and structures of data governance hold relevance for several of these fronts, this chapter focuses on how they should inform statutory regulation that targets data.

The importance of exploring such responses to disinformation lies in the relevance of datafication processes for the intentional spread of false content online, as data-based content distribution has been at the centre of disinformation strategies in different national contexts (Cadwalladr, 2017; Evangelista and Bruno, 2019). Together with a number of concerns that accrue from expansive Big Data techniques, disinformation also inspires both general and specifically targeted regulation, urging the need for comprehensive conceptual frameworks on data governance that inform these policy debates with a nuanced perspective and legitimacy standards. For these purposes, we recognize the importance of understanding data governance beyond corporate processes, to include

> the power relations between all the actors affected by, or having an effect on, the way data is accessed, controlled, shared and used, the various sociotechnical arrangements set in place to generate value from data, and how such value is redistributed between actors.
>
> *(Micheli et al., 2020, p. 3)*

Among other implications, this means that data governance for disinformation encompasses different things – including what sort of institutional and technical mechanisms should be in place to safeguard the way private companies handle data; what duties of care these companies should be bound to; what is the role of alternative models of data governance; and the fundamental question that cuts through the biggest dilemmas of our field: what can and what cannot be done with personal data (legitimate uses)? In this chapter, we explore the part of this greater scenario that refers to governments' duties, notably with regard to their role in regulating data in the face of disinformation threats.

Following this Introduction, in Section 1 we bridge data governance and disinformation regulation by exploring the idea of disinformation datafication, as well as the comprehensive and collective approaches to data governance that the phenomenon requires. Section 2 places overarching data protection regulatory frameworks (as a key center of polycentric data governance), within disinformation regulation, to show limitations and contextualize the implementation of the specific policies described in the next sections. In the following sections, we will approach regulatory strategies against disinformation that reflect the polyvalence of data. Section 3 tackles statutory limitation to microtargeting (as the possibility of distribution of content and disinformation tailored to users' preferences) – as well as the relevance of international data protection frameworks in this regard. Section 4 addresses traceability regulations, which entail processes of governance undertaken at various centers. Such strategies were adopted in the realm of disinformation regulation in Brazil and India, but these logics were also considered amidst the debates of the recently approved European Digital Services Act (DSA).

1 Disinformation Datafication and Data Governance

We understand disinformation as an expression of tensions and transformations that, while deeply related to digitalization, result from a broader constellation of technological, social, and political factors. This perspective has challenging implications for disinformation research, a field that aims at understanding practices that originate from various centers while also being inherently mingled with historical circumstances, social practice, and political disputes. This realization sets a departure point for governance debates, whose task is to explore which actors and practices engage (or should engage) in countermeasures against digital disinformation. As a multi-layered and varied phenomenon, containing disinformation requires more than governmental action (in and outside of statutory regulation), encompassing formal and informal responses from different societal actors. Among popular remedies are journalistic and civil society's fact-checking and media literacy initiatives, as well as digital platforms' (sometimes debatable) duties of care in content moderation. Against this wide context, data governance and data regulation are among many mechanisms that operate in the realm of digital communications with the potential to mitigate the implementation and effects of disinformation strategies that rely on the use of personal data, which we refer to as disinformation datafication.

Datafication alone is an overarching concept, broadly used to refer to the ways in which data shapes or reshapes social practices (Steensen, 2019). It can be skeptically approached as the "transformation of information about people into a commodity" (Viljoen, 2021, p. 577), or even associated with "legitimate means to access, understand and monitor people's behavior" (Van Dijck, 2014, p. 198). Beyond its different applications, the relevance of the concept lies in its historical importance as a "new method of quantifying elements of life that until now were not quantified to this extent" (Mejias and Couldry, 2019). Datafication allows us to access knowledge on collective behavior in an unprecedented manner. Even though its essence can be perceived as procedural, the generation of different kinds of value from data (be it financial, participatory, cultural, or epistemological) is an inseparable substantive element of datafication (Mejias and Couldry, 2019).

In the realm of online communications, datafication rests at the core of digital platforms' business models, as it determines information and attention fluxes through access to and processing of user preferences (Jungherr and Schroeder, 2021). The immediate value extracted out of this process is the ability of platforms to monetize their businesses "by using such data to sell products or services to the users, or by selling the data to parties wishing to influence or persuade users towards various goals" (Mejias and Couldry, 2019). In addition, datafication also grants digital platforms with great understanding of users' preferences and their on- and offline behavior, which can be used in a manner beyond microtargeting by advertisements (either for the sake of improving their own services, or to serve other interests). Digital disinformation strategies operate within these very logics. The same techniques that allow for advertising can be used to identify political interests and thus collective and individual tendencies to engage in certain content.

While the empirical evidence on the effects and reach of disinformation datafication are disputed (Barberá, 2020), the misuse of personal data remains a relevant concern for governance, and more specifically, statutory regulation debates. Beyond the fact that said disinformation strategies might operate outside of data protection legal requirements, they also inspire a greater societal conversation about what sort of economic, political, or ideological interests the use of our personal data should support. Depending on how it is shaped, data governance as both a normative framework and institutional arrangement has the potential to mitigate or countermeasure harmful effects of datafication processes that risk individual rights and collective values – especially to the extent to which it can limit the quality of the data being collected and treated in each case (i.e., one's political preferences) or the purpose served by the data usage.

Therefore, exploring the overlap of data and disinformation governance is an exercise that highly benefits from the polycentric approach promoted in this volume, as disinformation countermeasures is also a field where data appears as both an object and a form of governance. Data is an object of governance in this field because disinformation datafication inspires the implementation of structures and norms whose role is to prevent or mitigate the use of data as an instrument of disinformation practice. These measures rest on the key role that personal data plays as fuel to automated systems intended to spread disinformation. In this sense, data governance law (in the form of national frameworks for data regulation) and specific regulations (e.g., the limitation of microtargeting) use data as a target for regulation – i.e., the object to which regulation intends to conform (Iglesias Keller, 2021, p. 501). Other regulatory trends approach data as a form of governance, by implementing obligations of storage or processing of personal data to meet their ends. This is the case of traceability provisions, where data storage is required in order to allow for the production and distribution of disinformation to be traced to its source, and thus sanctioned. Here, data appears as an instrument of disinformation regulation, an element that allows for the implementation of a certain public policy. Under this guise, concerns with misuse of and legitimacy over data are strikingly reshaped in the policy debate (as we will show in our analysis of specific policy initiatives throughout this chapter). Furthermore, data itself, as both object and form of disinformation governance, needs to be considered against its multi-faceted ontological quality (see Chapter 1, this volume). In the realm of disinformation governance, data can be referred to as personal information that allows for identification, or as metadata on information flows. Data can even take non-numerical forms such as images, audio and video, what is currently referred to as 'content' (see Chapter 1, this volume).

Among the varied lenses through which data governance can be understood, we find it particularly important for this analysis to approach data protection as a collective right, besides its enshrined role of assuring individual guarantees. This implies tackling data governance from what Salomé Viljoen calls a "relational" perspective that focuses on how data flows are structured, collected, and produced so as to generate population-level insights on how people relate to one another, thus allowing for inferences on collective behavior (Viljoen, 2021). The author emphasizes the importance of a "horizontal relationship" in datafication, which relates data subjects to each other through "informational infrastructures that make sense of data subjects via group classification and that operationalize classifications to act back on subjects" (Viljoen, 2021, p. 607). On the other hand, the "vertical relationship" is the one between individual data subjects and data collectors, expressed in corporate-centered "hegemonic models" that refer data governance to the forms and mechanisms through which collectors retain control over the data they collect (Carballa Smichowski, 2019, p. 227).

The relationship between corporations and data subjects as key centers of polycentric governance is still relevant to the degree that it reflects the way corporations structure their business models and the type of safeguards over data governance that they put in place in day-to-day activities. But because disinformation datafication is inspired precisely by the intent to identify collective political preferences and influence speech and behavior, governance solutions that focus solely on the rights that individuals exercise over their own data are essentially limited to address the level of social risk entailed in these strategies. This is the core of the problem identified by Viljoen, as "data subjects possess only a fraction of the interests in a certain data flow", while data collectors are motivated to collect as much data as they can, from as many subjects as possible, so they can exploit the insights of horizontal data relations (Viljoen, 2021, p. 613). The main implication of such an approach, for ours and other debates, is that instead of reasserting "individual control over the terms on one's own datafication" data governance debates ought to "develop institutional responses necessary to represent (and adjudicate among) the relevant population-level interests at stake in data production" (Viljoen, 2021, p. 579).

Nevertheless, the regulatory framework developing around data governance and its relation to disinformation is mostly oblivious to this horizontal relationship, as policy solutions continuously replicate individualistic understandings of privacy and mechanisms that either focus on corporate procedures or on controlling and securing individual behavior. In the next section, we provide an overview of this regulatory framework.

2 The Role of Data in Disinformation Regulation

Data is one of the most relevant and promising regulatory targets for statutory regulation that aims to prevent disinformation, both from an efficiency and a legitimacy perspective. The promise of efficiency rests on the idea of disinformation datafication, that is, on the role that the (mis)use of data might play in feeding the dynamics of information distribution in digital platforms. The assumption is that if such processes are embedded with safeguards capable of mitigating social and individuals' risks posed by data usage, so would the initiation and impacts of disinformation strategies. Focusing on regulating data (as opposed to regulating content, for instance) also reaches higher legitimacy standards because it poses lesser threats to a desirably heated digital public sphere.

Governmental action towards digital disinformation mingles with the ever-delicate exercise of regulating freedom of expression – i.e., establishing rules regarding what can and cannot be said, published, and distributed. Even though every right can be subject to restrictions, freedom of expression is an indisputable pillar of modern democracies, and the line that separates these restrictions from state censorship can be thin. This is especially important in the case of legal provisions that assume an element of "truth" to define illegal content, which, together with the elements of harm and intent is usually the case for disinformation. Provisions that establish countermeasures for disinformation based on content essentially rest on an understanding of truth or falsity that can either be pre-established in legislation or left to the discretion of the body responsible for enforcing them. This will ultimately lead to imposing one version of facts – whether it be that from judges, executive authorities, or digital platforms – over others. Strategies based on a concept of disinformation will inevitably steer the dispute over truth and fact away from where it belongs: in society and public debate. For these reasons, it is possible to make a case for prioritizing statutory regulation initiatives that target the use of data and other aspects of platforms' business models, such as transparency standards and due process obligations.

Data regulation that countermeasures disinformation entails a set of mechanisms with different levels of potential to effectively prevent the use of data for the purpose of disinformation distribution. Data governance law refers to legal frameworks that regulate the collection, treatment, and storage of personal data for different purposes. These frameworks approach data protection across sectors to protect rights holders in increasingly digital economies and take shape through the enactment or updating of laws dedicated to data protection, most often based on "the guarantee of a fundamental right and the realization of this right by means of a legal regime of data protection, in the form of a general law on the subject" (Mendes, 2014, p. 47). They pose resistance to disinformation depending on how bound data collectors and processors are to legal requirements. Broad data protection laws can limit collection (e.g., by prohibiting unlawful surveillance or commercialization of voters' personal data), sharing (by prohibiting international data transfer for specific purposes, possibly electoral), and data management, as in cases where there is a deviation from the purposes authorized by the agent. In several countries, these constraints have been carried out by personal data protection rules and by authorities that enforce these rules (Cruz, 2020, p. 377).

Notwithstanding their fundamental role in providing institutional frameworks for the healthy development of digital economies, data protection laws are often built around the "vertical relationship" identified by Viljoen and herein above described. They conceive of data as an individual medium, focusing on legal inquiry and "legal relevance to data's potential to cause personal harm and as therefore appropriately subject to private, individual ordering" (Viljoen, 2021, p. 594). By failing to acknowledge "the role that horizontal data relations play in producing social value and social risk" (Viljoen, 2021, p. 608), general data protection laws are not enough to address social harm caused by disinformation.

Overall, data protection legislation already serves different aspects that regulate the use of data in electoral processes, but the expansion of digital communications that base political communication in and outside of such processes builds up the case for strengthening enforcement of data protection legislation in such contexts (Nenadić, 2019, p. 13). Specific mechanisms may include restrictions on data gathering and accumulation for political microtargeting purposes – like in Japan, where "the capture of personal data on the electorate, and the communication of personalized political messaging" is understood to be "largely prohibited" by the current legislation (Bennett and Oduro-Marfo, 2019, p. 6).

More recently, disinformation datafication has inspired measures particularly directed at the phenomenon, either in or outside of electorals. These initiatives were either inspired by the necessity of, or tailored to, conform or monitor the content distribution dynamics that allow for the spread of disinformation (and possibly other forms of harmful speech that operate within similar logics). It is within these strategies that data presents itself in the most varied roles, as illustrated by the idea of mechanisms for chasers and trackers that we will further approach in the next sections. Beyond exploring the polycentric mechanisms and implications of such strategies, our analysis aims to highlight how, depending on the position occupied by data, different degrees of legitimacy concern are imbued in the debate.

3 The Chasers: Regulation of Microtargeting

Microtargeting is defined as the technique that allows selected distribution of content in accordance with users' pre-expressed preferences. According to the United Kingdom's Information Commissioner's Office, microtargeting is a form of online targeted advertising that analyses personal data to identify the interests of a specific audience or individual to influence their actions. Microtargeting may be used to offer a personalized message to an individual or audience using an online service such as social media.[1]

We refer to microtargeting techniques as chasers because it is a technique that entails the pursuit of granular steps of users' day-to-day lives that will allow for them to be "chased" with content that is likely to be appealing, according to their pre-assessed preferences. This inference of what sort of content is likely to engage a certain user (or, the inference on what user or group of users are likely to engage with certain content) is based on the collection of vast amounts of data regarding users' online experience. When transferred to broader information ecosystems, microtargeting can be a powerful tool to spread disinformation, as the analysis of data such as cookies or social media analytics can help direct disinformation to groups that will potentially be more receptive to the message therein (CITS, 2018).

Every website visit that a user makes is valuable in this scenario, as well as the technologies that allow the collection of data such as cookies, third-party cookies, website navigation, mouse movements, or even keystrokes (Nield, 2017). All of this information is normally connected not just by marketplaces and social media companies, but also by third parties whose business model is based on curating advertisements to users. Such companies are responsible for deploying analytics software that can record an individual's browsing sessions and collect exceptional amounts of user data in ways that are not entirely disclosed to the tracked individual (TIKU, 2017).

As mentioned previously, the same mechanisms that allowed for Internet users' data collection in order to feed targeted ads can be used to attempt to influence electors all over the world. The Cambridge Analytica (CA) case is notorious for shedding light on these practices, as it revealed that a strategic communications company deployed abusive collection and usage of the personal data of electors to, later on, share electoral content through social media platforms (Santos and Varon, 2018). This communication strategy supports the development of "data-driven campaigns" (Rennó, 2018), where data collected through social media platforms and private messaging apps allows companies such as CA to come up with well-defined audiences and prepare political ads according to their references and beliefs (Cadwalladr and Graham-Harrison, 2018). Together with the targeted ads, it was often the case that electors would also be targeted by disinformation (Pallero and Arroyo, 2018). The debate on the role played by the misuse and abuse of personal data in electoral processes, or data-driven elections, was also touched upon by authors such as Colin Bennett and David Lyon when analyzing the CA case. The intersection between the use of data in contemporary campaigns and social media platforms brought a new group of issues regarding process integrity and newer vulnerabilities introduced by the spread of disinformation and "Fake News" (Bennett and Lyon, 2019).

Whereas the CA case was related to political content and attempts to influence elections in countries such as the United States and Brazil, the case also shed light on the relevance of data protection frameworks and dedicated laws to extend some level of protection to users during elections. In this context, the poor level of data protection – or even the absence of user-centric frameworks – is understood to have been one of the factors that facilitated the abuses and malpractices of companies such as CA. In Brazil, the CA case notably contributed to the approval of the current General Data Protection Legislation (LGPD) (Omari, 2020), as it shed light on the need to impose control mechanisms over data processing activities performed in the Country and empower users against the abuses.

Regardless of the content of targeted ads being political or merely commercial (that is, when such a distinction is possible), microtargeting techniques paved the way to forms of political campaigning based on Internet users' constantly monitored behavior. Furthermore, when used for spreading disinformation, microtargeting rests on all sorts of questionable premises, like the idea that disinformation is a legitimate purpose for the use of personal data, or that users' consent to data collection in social media or private messaging platforms would be well informed enough to legitimize this sort of data usage. In light of that, data governance measures can indeed provide interesting arrangements and tools to countermeasure disinformation datafication. General data protection legislation forms relevant frameworks since, by limiting the use of data, they are likely to have (at least some) impact on the reach potential of microtargeting techniques. However, recent policy trends explore other avenues to prevent or mitigate the use of data as an instrument of disinformation practice, notably related to limiting microtargeting. They include acts of legislation that (a) aim to control or ban the use of targeted ads in the electoral context, (b) limit the possibilities of personal data use on microtargeting, and (c) improve platform transparency and accountability with regard to online advertisement and microtargeting.

The recent developments on this topic in the European Union are particularly interesting. In the Digital Services Act (DSA), the European Commission has introduced the discussion of stronger transparency and accountability obligations for platforms, including in the field of targeted advertising (Stolton, 2021). The motivation behind this proposal was to provide Internet users with more information with regard to all ads directed at them, including an explanation on why a certain person was the target of a certain ad. As the DSA discussions moved forward, more provisions introducing the right for an individual to oppose being the subject of profiling activities and a ban on profiling of minors were also introduced to the bill (Lomas, 2022) – following, at least to some extent, the recommendation of the EU data protection supervisor that suggested a European ban on targeted advertising (EDPS, 2021). The final version of the DSA introduced in Article 24 a ban on the presentation of advertisements based on activities such as profiling and the use of certain categories of sensitive data by online platforms that decide to showcase ads to their users (European Parliament, 2022). This measure, according to civil society networks such as the European Digital Rights (EDRi), can represent a turning point for effectively tacking surveillance-based advertisement (EDRi, 2022)

Regulation tailored to contain disinformation distributed specifically through microtargeting could also aim at data collection or at restriction of purpose (i. e., prohibiting microtargeting for political purposes, or during election). In relation to the first aim of microtargeting, data collection often happens broadly, to then be assigned to a certain purpose. So, further restricting data collection thinking about microtargeting, specifically, could have a limited effect. In the second case, depending on how legislation deals with restriction of purpose, limitation or prohibition of the use of data for "political purposes" is likely to lead to another intricate exercise of interpretation regarding what is a political purpose or not. The electoral time frame can provide a more stable criterion – however, in a highly digitalized public sphere, electoral campaigning is submitted to transformations of its own, which means that the relevance of such time frames as the key moment for political communication is diminished. Political content standards based on characteristics of a certain kind of message will probably be fully subjected to the perception of their enforcer, and therefore provide less legal certainty.

Current regulatory approaches on microtargeting also hold some level of convergence to the above-mentioned EDPS opinion as they seem to understand that in order to fight the multitude of risks associated with online targeted advertising, regulatory frameworks need to go beyond rules dedicated exclusively to increasing transparency (EDPS, 2021). On that note, increasing user control and the avoidance of basing recommender systems on individuals' profiling, should and can be two of the possible avenues explored by stakeholders all over the world.

This shows that the regulation of microtargeting is a debate that advances questions of how prepared our data governance, and more specifically, data regulation institutions, are to contain the whole of social risks entailed in disinformation datafication. Beyond that, it inspires a broader, and also very necessary, conversation about what can and cannot be done with our personal data, and what are the mechanisms (currently missing) that can impose de facto barriers to the dissemination of disinformation and other sorts of harmful behavior – as opposed to allowing the practice and application of sanitizing standards, such as transparency. Overall, it mostly flows in the direction of improving individual and collective rights over data. This, however, is not the case with other recent trends for regulating disinformation through data, as we will show in the next section.

4 The Trackers: Traceability Mechanisms

Another set of regulatory obligations that stem from this debate consists of the implementation of obligations that result in the expansion of personal data processing for specific purposes. As referred to in the first section of the present chapter, the deployment of traceability mechanisms on private messaging apps – or the collection of data and/or metadata referring to certain types of content such as the number of shares or the name of the author – is a recurring trend that deserves attention due to the fact that it perceives data as an instrument of disinformation regulation (see Section 1).

Unlike the chasers case, where limiting the data processing and collection activities is key to halting the abuses and misuses, disinformation regulation strategies grounded on traceability mechanisms are responsible for expanding the collection and storage capacities of certain groups of intermediaries, in order to allow authorities to conduct broader law enforcement and investigation activities (Muirhead and Porter, 2019) – we call these mechanisms the trackers. Recent legal provisions referring to traceability mechanisms that have been either proposed or implemented take two forms: (a) traceability of traders (as referred to in the draft EU regulation Digital Services Act) and (b) traceability of disinformation-related content in private messaging apps (as is the case of the Indian legislation and the Brazilian Fake News Bill).

The DSA approaches traceability with regard to the possibility of online platforms allowing the celebration of contracts between traders and consumers in its Article 24c. According to this provision, whenever an online platform allows consumers to conclude contracts with traders, it should ensure that such actors can only offer products within such spaces if they (a) are located within the European Union, (b) provide social media platforms with their details such as name, address, telephone number and electronic address of the trader, (c) a copy of the identification document of the trader or any other electronic identification as defined by Article 3 of Regulation (EU) No 910/2014 of the European Parliament and of the Council (European Commission, 2020, and European Parliament, 2022), (d) the payment account details of the trader and other pre-requisites such as (e) a self-certification by the trader committing to only offer products or services that comply with the applicable rules of Union law. According to policymakers and MEPs who participated at the DSA discussions, whilst the main goal of the above-mentioned provision is to "help combat illegal content online and enhance consumer protection" (Greens-EFA, 2021), it would be important to restrict its application to online marketplaces. A general provision could be problematic considering the "number of potential parties along the supply chain that this term may cover, and that this information would be required at the time of opening an account" (Greens-EFA, 2021). At the same time, stakeholders such as civil society have welcomed the introduction of measures that allow for platforms to verify users who qualify as traders and have the means to conduct checks on these actors' legitimacy and also to further inform customers (BEUC, 2021). Interestingly, the expansion of data collection here refers to personal data that embodies information about users that allows for their identification and localization, like their names and addresses. This is not the case for the other set of traceability policies, whose implementation will require a broader collection of metadata.

By the time this chapter was submitted (mid-2022), two countries have either implemented or at least discussed the concrete options for the application of a traceability-related mechanism in private messaging applications for disinformation regulation purposes: India and Brazil. In India, the "Intermediary Guidelines and Digital Media Ethics Code" started being enforced in 2021, introducing a new set of online intermediary application rules and forcing said applications to track online communications (Ministry of Electronics and Information Technology, 2021). On that note, the Indian legislation demands the following:

> A significant social media intermediary providing services primarily in the nature of messaging shall enable the identification of the first originator of the information on its computer resource as may be required by a judicial order passed by a court of competent jurisdiction or an order passed under section 69 by the Competent Authority as per the Information Technology (Procedure and Safeguards for interception, monitoring and decryption of information) Rules, 2009, which shall be supported with a copy of such information in electronic form.
>
> *(Ministry of Electronics and Information Technology, 2021)*

This provision applies to the majority of private messaging apps that operate in the Country – such as WhatsApp, Facebook Messenger, and others – and, according to civil society organizations, could also be responsible for weakening current end-to-end encryption present in these platforms (Rodriguez, 2021). This provision is also perceived as the construction of a backdoor for current encryption tools (Gopani, 2022) due to the fact that it requires messaging applications to trace users' data in order to facilitate investigations, prosecution, or punishment related to acts practised by them (Katira and Grover,

2022). In May 2021, WhatsApp sued the Indian government over the Intermediary Guidelines and Digital Media Ethics Code claiming that the traceability requirements regarding the origin of the message would "severely undermine the privacy of its users" (Isaac, 2021) and reinforced the claims of civil society organizations about the possibility of the tracing requirement posing a threat to end-to-end encryption (Porter, 2021).

In Brazil, the discussions surrounding Draft Bill n. 2630/2020 in Brazil (a bill intended to regulate social networks and private messengers which is deceivingly referred to as the "Fake News Bill") are currently attempting to introduce traceability of disinformation-related content to the Country's legal scenario. If approved, the draft bill – whose official name is "Brazilian Internet Freedom, Responsibility and Transparency Act" – will introduce a new set of responsibilities for social media platforms, private messaging apps, and search mechanisms operating in the Country (Câmara dos Deputados, 2020), with the general aim of fighting disinformation. So far, this draft bill has seen at least two main versions of the section dedicated to instant/private messaging applications that expanded the obligations for this specific group of actors with regards to transparency and accountability as well as some increased level of users' data collection for the same purposes as the above-mentioned Indian legislation: facilitation of investigations, prosecution activities, or punishment of users.

Initially, the draft bill proposed a traceability mechanism that would require private messaging applications to store, for a period of three months, all metadata related to messages that were sent by "more than five users and reaching out at least 1000 users under the period of 15 days" (Câmara dos Deputados, 2020). The provision required the storage of data such as (a) information on users responsible for broadcasting these messages, (b) time and date stamps, and (c) total number of users who had access to the messages, all in order to canvass and hold liable the group of individuals who would have participated in the dissemination of content deemed illicit (Coalizão Direitos na Rede, 2020). Unsurprisingly, this provision was the object of a lot of discussion between different groups of stakeholders such as Academia and Civil society. On one side, the concerns are concentrated around the possible threat to end-to-end encryption that imposing a requirements of metadata retention could represent (InternetLab, 2020; Rodriguez and Alimonti, 2020), added to that, others also highlight consider the possible "negative impacts on freedom of expression in the Country caused by the constant monitoring of messages" (Coalizão Direitos na Rede, 2021). Despite the critique, some actors also defend the measure as a surgical and relevant approach to halt the dissemination of disinformation and make the case that the metadata collection is not as invasive as some might argue (Hartmann, 2020).

Recently, on the report issued by the congressional working group dedicated to discussing amendments to the proposal at the House of Representatives, this provision was replaced by a new text that states that judicial authorities "may determine instant messaging service providers to preserve and make available records of user interactions determined by a period of up to 15 days, considering the requirements established in the Brazilian law" (Câmara dos Deputados do Brasil, 2021). The new provision also forbids generic requests or ones made outside the scope and technical limits of the services provided by private messaging platforms. Also, to the extent the new wording submits the collection of metadata to a court order based on a specific request, this can be seen as a more limited and less invasive approach to the previously suggested traceability mechanism.

Disinformation datafication has been one of the main inspirations to lawmakers all over the world, resulting in measures and draft provisions directed at halting the spread of disinformation. In cases such as the traceability provisions present in two countries that are important centers of polycentric data governance – Indian and Brazilian – the need to control or monitor the dissemination of viral messages might not be proportional to the level of threats posed to rights such as privacy and freedom of expression for users in both places. Will the ends (or the expansion of prosecution and law enforcement agencies' capacities to conduct investigations online) justify the means (or the possibility of weakened end-to-end encryption and chilling effect on freedom of expression)?

Conclusions

This chapter explored the intersection of data governance and disinformation regulation, in order to address some of the current approaches being deployed at the state level through statutory regulation. Through an analysis of two policy trends surrounding the chasers (microtargeting) and the trackers (traceability) as well as the regulatory efforts dedicated to them, its main finding is that the legitimacy standards currently expected of data as an object are not equally reflected in its implementation as a form of polycentric governance. Data governance measures, particularly in the form of statutory regulation, can ultimately amount to both restrictions and amplification of data collection. While data protection frameworks addressing the abuse and misuse of personal data for microtargeting mostly impose limits on data collection and treatment, traceability obligations expand these activities (that are still to be pursued by private companies) to enable law enforcement, increasing risks for users privacy and data protection rights. It is of utter importance for policymakers to consider how to better coordinate the current strategies and regulatory approaches while upholding rights and avoiding possible threats to speech. A polycentric approach to disinformation, data, and data governance can be particularly helpful in identifying not only the varied dimensions of each of these elements but also the diversity of actors, governance centers, and practices that weigh into the challenge of regulating disinformation.

Note

1 See https://ico.org.uk/for-the-public/be-data-aware/social-media-privacy-settings/microta rgeting/.

References

Barberá, P. (2020) 'Social media, echo chambers, and political polarization', in Persily, N. and Tucker, J.A. (eds) *Social media and democracy: the state of the field, prospects for reform*. Cambridge New York Port Melbourne New Delhi Singapore: Cambridge University Press, pp. 34–55.

Bennett, C.J. and Lyon, D. (2019) Data-driven elections: implications and challenges for democratic societies. *Internet Policy Review*, 8 (4). https://doi.org/10.14763/2019.4.1433.

Bennett, C.J. and Oduro-Marfo, S. (2019) *Privacy, voter surveillance and democratic engagement: challenges for data protection authorities*. UK Office of the Information Commissioner for presentation to the 2019 International Conference of Data Protection and Privacy Commissioners (ICDPPC). University of Victoria. https://privacyconfer ence2019.info/wp-content/uploads/2019/11/Privacy-and-International-Democratic-Engag ement_finalv2.pdf.

BEUC. (2021) *The Digital Services Act proposal: BEUC position paper*. Available at: https:// www.beuc.eu/publications/beuc-x-2021-032_the_digital_services_act_proposal.pdf.

Cadwalladr, C. (2017) The great British Brexit robbery: how our democracy was hijacked. *The Guardian*. Available at: https://www.theguardian.com/technology/2017/may/07/the-great-british-brexit-robbery-hijacked-democracy. Accessed: 10 May 2020.

Cadwalladr, C. and Graham-Harrison, E. (2018) Revealed: 50 million Facebook profiles harvested for Cambridge Analytica in major data breach. *The Guardian*. Available at: https://www.theguardian.com/news/2018/mar/17/cambridge-analytica -facebook-influence-us-election.

Câmara dos Deputados do Brasil. (2020) *PL 2630/2020. Institui a Lei Brasileira de Liberdade, Responsabilidade e Transparência na Internet*. Available at: https://www. camara.leg.br/propostas-legislativas/2256735.

Câmara dos Deputados do Brasil. (2021) *REL 1/2021 do Grupo de Trabalho de Aperfeiçoamento da Legislação Brasileira – Internet (GTNET)*. Available at: https://www. camara.leg.br/propostas-legislativas/2305033.

Carballa Smichowski, B. (2019) Alternative data governance models: moving beyond one-size-fits-all solutions. *Intereconomics*, 54 (4), 222–227. doi:10.1007/s10272-019-0828-x.

CITS. (2018) How is fake news spread? Bots, people like you, trolls, and microtargeting. Citizen's guide to fake news. Center for Information Technology and Society at UC Santa Barbara. https://www.cits.ucsb.edu/fake-news/spread#spread-microtargeting.

Coalizão Direitos na Rede. (2020) *Rastreabilidade*. Available at: https://web.archive.org/ web/20230328124225/http://plfakenews.direitosnarede.org.br/rastreabilidade/.

Coalizão Direitos na Rede. (2021) *Nota sobre o PL 2630/20: Rastreabilidade viola a Constituição ao criar mecanismo de vigilância em massa*. Available at: https://direitosna rede.org.br/2021/10/21/nota-sobre-o-pl-2630-20-rastreabilidade-viola-a-constituicao-ao-criar-mecanismo-de-vigilancia-em-massa/.

Cruz, F.B. (2020) *Novo jogo, velhas regras: democracia e direito na era da nova propaganda política e das fake news*. Belo Horizonte, MG: Grupo Editorial Letramento, Casa do Direito.

EDPS (European Data Protection Supervisor). (2021) *Opinion 1/2021: on the Proposal for a Digital Services Act*. Available at: https://edps.europa.eu/system/files/2021-02/ 21-02-10-opinion_on_digital_services_act_en.pdf.

European Commission. (2020) The Digital Services Act: ensuring a safe and accountable online environment. Available at: https://ec.europa.eu/info/digital-services-act-ensur ing-safe-and-accountable-online-environment_en.

European Digital Rights. (2022) *The DSA should pave the way for systemic change.* Available at: https://edri.org/our-work/the-dsa-should-pave-the-way-to-systemic-change/.

European Parliament. (2022) *Regulation (EU) 2022 of the European Parliament and of the Council of Europe on a single market for digital services (Digital Services Act) and amending Directive 2000/31/EC.* Available at: https://www.europarl.europa.eu/meetdocs/ 2014_2019/plmrep/COMMITTEES/IMCO/DV/2022/06-15/DSA_2020_0361COD_EN.pdf.

Evangelista, Rafael, and Fernanda Bruno. (2019) WhatsApp and political instability in Brazil: targeted messages and political radicalisation. *Internet Policy Review*, 8 (4). https://doi.org/10.14763/2019.4.1434.

Gopani, A. (2022) How India's original traceability requirement acts as a back-door to E2E encryption. *Analytics India Mag (AIM).* Available at: https://analyticsindiamag.com/ how-indias-original-traceability-requirement-acts-as-a-back-door-to-e2e-encryption/.

Greens-EFA. (2021) *Make your voice heard on the Digital Services Act (DSA).* Public Consultation on the Digital Services Act. Available at: https://www.greens-efa.eu/en/ digital-services-act-consultation.

Hartmann, I. (2020) Armazenamento de metadados é medida cirúrgica em projeto contra as fake news. *Jornal Folha de Sao Paulo.* Available at: https://www1.folha.uol.com. br/poder/2020/07/armazenamento-de-metadados-e-medida-cirurgica-em-projeto-contra -as-fake-news.shtml.

Iglesias Keller, C. (2021) Don't shoot the message: regulating disinformation beyond content. *Revista Direito Público*, 18 (99), 486–515.

InternetLab. (2020) *Rastrear o viral? Riscos à privacidade no projeto de lei "de combate às fake news".* São Paulo. Available at: https://www.internetlab.org.br/wp-content/up loads/2020/08/rastrear-o-viral_internetlab.pdf.

Isaac, M. (2021) WhatsApp sues India's government to stop new internet rules. *The New York Times.* Available at: https://www.nytimes.com/2021/05/25/technology/whatsapp -india-lawsuit.html.

Jungherr, A. and Schroeder, R. (2021) Disinformation and the structural transformations of the public arena: addressing the actual challenges to democracy. *Social Media & Society*, 7 (1). doi:10.1077/205630512198892.

Katira, D. and Grover, G. (2022) *How message tracing regulations subvert encryption.* Internet Policy Review. Available at: https://policyreview.info/articles/news/how-m essage-tracing-regulations-subvert-encryption/1642.

Lomas, N. (2022) European parliament backs big limits on tracking ads. *TechCrunch.* Available at: https://techcrunch.com/2022/01/20/meps-vote-to-limit-tracking/.

Marwick, A., Kuo , N., Jones Cameron , S. and Weigel , M. (2021) *Critical Disinformation Studies – a syllabus.* Center for Information, Technology and Public Life – University of North Carolina at Chapel Hill. Available at: https://citap.unc.edu/resea rch/critical-disinfo/ (Accessed: 5 August 2021).

Mejias, U.A. and Couldry, N. (2019) Datafication. *Internet Policy Review*, 8 (4). doi:10.14763/2019.4.1428.

Mendes, L.S. (2014) *Privacidade, proteção de dados e direito do consumidor: linhas gerais de um novo direito fundamental.* São Paulo: Saraiva.

Micheli, M., Ponti, M., Craglia, M. and Berti Suman, A. (2020). Emerging models of data governance in the age of datafication. *Big Data & Society*, 7 (2). doi:10.1177/ 2053951720948087.

Ministry of Electronics and Information Technology. (2021). Information technology (Intermediary Guidelines and Digital Media Ethics Code) rules. *The Gazette of India.* Available at: https://web.archive.org/web/20230502155135/https://egazette.nic.in/Wri teReadData/2021/225464.pdf.

Muirhead, J. and Porter, T.M. (2019). Traceability in global governance. *Global Networks*. doi:10.1111/glob.12237.

Nenadić, I. (2019) Unpacking the "European approach" to tackling challenges of disinformation and political manipulation. *Internet Policy Review*, 8 (4). doi:10.14763/2019.4.1436.

Nield, D. (2017) You probably don't know all the ways Facebook tracks you. *Gizmodo*. Available at: https://gizmodo.com/all-the-ways-facebook-tracks-you-that-you-might-not-kno-1795604150.

Omari, J. (2020,July 19). Undercutting internet governance in Brazil: the "Fake News Bill" and its impact on rights and equality. *VerfassungsBlog*. Available at: https://verfassungs blog.de/undercutting-internet-governance-in-brazil/. doi:10.17176/20200719-235202-0.

Pallero, J. and Arroyo, V. (2018) Your data used against you: reports of manipulation on WhatsApp ahead of Brazil's election. *Access Now*. Available at: https://www.accessnow. org/your-data-used-against-you-reports-of-manipulation-on-whatsapp-ahead-of-brazils-e lection/.

Porter, J. (2021) WhatsApp sues Indian government over new rules it says break encryption. *The Verge*. Available at: https://www.theverge.com/2021/5/26/22454381/ whatsapp-indian-government-traceability-lawsuit-break-encryption-privacy.

Rennó, R. (2018) Brazilian Elections and the public-private data trade. *Tactical Tech*. Available at: https://ourdataourselves.tacticaltech.org/posts/overview-brazil/.

Rodriguez, K. (2021) Why Indian courts should reject traceability obligations. *Electronic Frontier Foundation*. Available at: https://www.eff.org/deeplinks/2021/06/why-india n-courts-should-reject-traceability-obligations.

Rodriguez, K. and Alimonti, V. (2021, February 3) *Despite progress, metadata still under 'second class' protection in Latam legal safeguards*. Electronic Frontier Foundation. https://www.eff.org/deeplinks/2021/02/despite-progress-metadata-still-under-second-class-protection-latam-legal.

Santos, B. and Varon, J. (2018) *Data and politics Brazilian country report: analysis of the playing field for the influence industry in preparation for the Brazilian general elections. Tactical Tech*. Available at: https://cdn.ttc.io/s/ourdataourselves.tacticaltech. org/ttc-data-and-politics-brazil.pdf.

Sombra, T. (2020). The general data protection law in Brazil: what comes next? *Global Privacy Law Review*, 1 (2), 116–119. Available at: https://kluwerlawonline.com/journa larticle/Global+Privacy+Law+Review/1.2/GPLR2020083.

Steensen, S. (2019) Journalism's epistemic crisis and its solution: disinformation, datafication and source criticism. *Journalism*, 20 (1), 185–189. doi:10.1177/1464884918809271.

Stolton, S. (2021) EU executive mulls tougher rules for microtargeting of political ads. *Euractive*. Available at: https://www.euractiv.com/section/digital/news/commission-m ulls-tougher-rules-for-microtargeting-of-political-ads/.

Tiku, N. (2017) The dark side of 'replay sessions' that record your every move online. *Wired*. Available at: https://www.wired.com/story/the-dark-side-of-replay-sessions-tha t-record-your-every-move-online/.

Van Dijck, J. (2014) Datafication, dataism and dataveillance: Big Data between scientific paradigm and ideology. *Surveillance & Society*, 12 (2), 197–208. doi:10.24908/ss.v12i2.4776.

Viljoen, S. (2021) A relational theory of data governance. *The Yale Law Journal*, 131 (2). https://www.yalelawjournal.org/feature/a-relational-theory-of-data-governance.

Wardle, C. and Derakhshan, H. (2017) *Information disorder: toward an interdisciplinary framework for research and policy making*. DGI(2017)09. Council of Europe. https:// edoc.coe.int/en/media/7495-information-disorder-toward-an-interdisciplinary-framework -for-research-and-policy-making.html.

10

PRIVACY GOVERNANCE FROM A POLYCENTRIC PERSPECTIVE

Rotem Medzini and Dmitry Epstein

Introduction

There is growing interest in understanding mechanisms that govern the creation, collection, processing, security, and transmission of identifiable data. A polycentric approach calls for a more institutionally oriented take on privacy governance. Governance, including privacy governance, occurs through multiple types of institutions and involves diverse actors. Most fundamentally, these institutions and actors challenge and transform the central role of the state in governing the internet and information flows. Supranational, intergovernmental, and private institutions attempt to govern and influence data flows through the creation and enforcement of norms, standards, and practices (Raymond and DeNardis 2015; Hofmann 2017). Commercial actors engage in the governance of both internet infrastructure and information flows through their business and operating decisions (Flyverbom et al. 2019). Seemingly technical bodies performing mundane tasks of standardizing and maintaining internet infrastructures are also recognized as spaces where governance occurs, typically outside of the purview of the state (van Eeten and Mueller 2013). Mapping junctions where constitutive decision-making occurs thus becomes an important task in understanding the dynamics of privacy governance.

In this chapter, we focus on regulatory intermediaries as actors with unique capacities and expertise, who are pivotal to the interpretation, monitoring, and implementation of privacy and data policies in organizations (Abbott et al. 2017). We argue that such intermediaries exemplify the polycentric nature of privacy governance. We illustrate that argument with two distinct cases of regulatory intermediation context: institutionalization of the role of data protection officer (DPO) in the EU and technology adoption for remote teaching in the early stages of the COVID-19 pandemic. The two cases are substantially

DOI: 10.4324/9781003388418-12

different. The DPO is a formally structured role that should be applicable across contexts of institutional activity, while educators responsible for technology adoption in the initial chaos of the pandemic often acted as informal, albeit influential, intermediaries. Yet, the cases are also similar in making the polycentric structures of privacy governance explicit, and in demonstrating how privacy governance is shaped through continuous interaction between formal structures and human agency.

We start this chapter by reviewing relevant literature on regulatory governance, information policy, and polycentrism. In doing so, we set the stage to discuss the institutionalization of privacy governance from a polycentric perspective, while accounting for broader structural context. We then proceed to discuss two empirical cases of formal and informal privacy governance arrangements through policy intermediaries. Those cases demonstrate transscalarity and transsectorality, diffusion of knowledge and authority, as well as the dynamic nature and fluidity of privacy governance arrangements. We conclude this chapter with a discussion of potential future research trajectories.

From Regulation to Regulatory Governance

The idea that the ordering of the digital realm spans beyond nation states or a narrow view of regulation is well established, particularly in the context of information policy (Braman 2009; van Eeten and Mueller 2013; Hofmann 2017). While traditionally the concept of regulation has been associated with the state via the premise of command and control regulation, scholarship has moved towards viewing it in terms of regulatory governance. The latter acknowledges plural forms of regulation in which government, industry, civil society, and the public share responsibility for achieving policy goals and promoting social, political, and economic ends (Levi-Faur 2011; Levi-Faur et al. 2021). We position our analysis of polycentric arrangements around digital privacy governance within this conceptual shift.

The political science and legal literature is rich with descriptions and conceptualizations of the shift towards regulatory governance. Some of it focuses on the macro changes in the normative and institutional arrangements describing them as the rise of the regulatory state (Majone 1994), decentring regulation (Black 2001), the post-regulatory state (Scott 2004), and regulatory capitalism (Levi-Faur 2005). Others explore the broadening repertoire of tools of public action (Salamon 2011), the proliferation of instruments for smart regulation (Gunningham et al. 1998), and emerging regulatory mechanisms such as audits (Power 1999) or regulatory intermediation (Abbott et al. 2017). This body of work acknowledges that non-state and transnational actors can have regulatory impact alongside national governments; that such impact can occur not just at the state, but also on supra-national as well as local or regional levels; and that the involved actors and institutions are interconnected, interdependent, and sometimes competing over legitimacy, authority, and power (Levi-Faur 2012; Scholte 2017).

Polycentrism and Regulatory Governance

Within the move towards regulatory governance, polycentrism emerges as a framework that allows for systematic, critical analysis and evaluation of complex, interdependent, and decentralized regulatory systems as transscalar, transsectoral, diffused, and fluid arrangements of actors and institutions with overlapping mandates, ambiguous hierarchies, and lacking a final arbiter (Scholte 2017). Underpinning polycentric regulatory governance arrangements are notions of fragmentation of knowledge and power (Black 2001). First, no single actor has the knowledge necessary to solve what are now complex, dynamic, and sometimes wicked problems. Second, power is also distributed, so that no actor single-handedly controls all critical resources or has a disproportional ability to dictate policy processes, even if it is located in a locus with relatively more power, compared to the rest of the network. The emergent assemblage of interdependencies breaks the dichotomy between the public and private. It acknowledges the interactive nature of relationships among actors and institutions, particularly those between state and non-state actors, and results in shifting normative propositions that recalibrate power structures underpinning governance institutions and processes (Black 2001) as well as mundane practices through which governance is enacted (Epstein et al. 2016).

The notion of actors – both institutional and noninstitutional – is central to a polycentric analysis of governance. We explicitly adopt a broad perspective for the study of polycentric data governance, as we find the institutionalist approach to be overly narrow. While an institutional perspective can depict polycentrism as an immediately perceptible phenomena (Koinova et al. 2021, p. 1991), this tangibility is achieved by focusing on authority relationships between actors as constructed through formal organizations, explicit regulations, and administrative frameworks. A noninstitutional perspective adds intangible practices, by accounting for informal norms, practices, and techniques. Combining the institutionalist and non-institutionalist perspectives allows for examining polycentric governance as a state of ordered chaos – having order without a central authority (Koinova et al. 2021, p. 1992). Untangling the responsibilities, functions, and capacities of actors, while acknowledging that they can perceive and understand regulation differently, is fundamental to mapping polycentric governance.

The classic understanding of regulation focuses on two primary categories of actors – those who make and those who are targeted by rules. The first category consists of actors with the power, resources, and authority to set guidance and structures aimed at modifying the behavior of the latter category of actors, who are the subjects of the regulation (Levi-Faur 2011). This distinction between rule-makers and rule-takers has been used to describe both second-party and first-party regulation. The former refers to an arrangement where rule-makers and rule-takers are socially, politically, economically, and administratively separate from each other. The latter refers to configurations where actors who set the rules and actors who are their subjects are the same actors, as in the case of self-regulation (Black 1996).

Moving towards a regulatory governance perspective calls for expanding the classification matrix of actors involved. Some scholars describe regulatory regimes that explicitly empower rule-beneficiaries – groups of actors whose interests the rules and policies are meant to advance or protect – in their capacity as citizens, consumers, or users. However, rule-beneficiaries may also be actors who stand to benefit indirectly from a particular rule, for example, an interest group that successfully captured a share of the benefits of regulation or even actors affiliated with the rule-makers themselves (Levi-Faur et al. 2021). Polycentrism acknowledges that among the group of citizens, that is, the general public, several sub-groups can capture the benefits of regulation. For example, consumers are a broad group of beneficiaries that profit from food safety regulation, even though they are typically not the direct rule-takers (Havinga and Verbruggen 2017). In some cases, beneficiaries might even be empowered in the regime, as is the case with data subjects invested with information and rights to access, rectify, erase, restrict, and transmit their data. Being empowered, however, does not mean these actors act upon their powers.

Other researchers of regulatory governance focus on third-party regulation – an arrangement where an independent third party acts as a regulatory intermediary between various other actors (Abbott et al. 2017). While intermediaries can be both individuals and organizations acting either formally or informally, they are set apart by unique capacities, resources, expertise, and responsibilities that neither rule-makers nor rule-takers have. Auditors, for example, are viewed as regulatory intermediaries engaged in the evaluation and verification of conformity with a standard. Power (1999, pp. 43–46) notices that many organizations publish reports on their financial performance, yet they require auditors to check the reports to add another level of assurance. A single regulatory regime, however, might simultaneously incorporate different groups of intermediaries with diverse responsibilities and capacities. Focusing on intermediaries in a regime, while controversial and contested, is one way to operationalize polycentrism as a mechanism explaining the dynamics of governance arrangements.

The broad trend of understanding regulation as a multifaceted, iterative process that involves a plurality of actors and evokes a range of sources of power, is arguably more pronounced in the digital realm. As Braman (2009) suggests, in an increasingly digitized society, informational power becomes fundamental in manipulating the informational basis of all other forms of power, such as instrumental, structural, and symbolic power. In relation to privacy, protecting access to and controlling the flow of information about oneself (including derivatives of such information) becomes fundamental for empowering the public and enabling individual autonomy and agency. If governing information and its flows involves "decision-making with constitutive effects" (Braman 2009, p. 3) that occurs across the domain of regulation and technology design in both formal and informal settings, privacy governance is intimately interwoven in the governance of other aspects of the digital domain. Such aspects include governance of the physical and logical resources of the internet, security of and on the network, and platform governance with their diverse institutional arrangements, plurality of actors, and distributed resources. In the following section, we unpack the polycentric dynamics of governing those aspects of the information realm, building towards a conceptualization of polycentric privacy governance.

Polycentrism and Information Policy

In the field of information policy, polycentric tendencies could be found across domains, even when they were not labeled as such. Liberalization and privatization of telecommunication markets in the 1980s both acknowledged that relevant regulatory expertise may lay outside of the purview of nation states (Cowhey 1990) and introduced strong private and transnational actors into formal policy processes (Zacher 2012). With the emergence of the internet, it became increasingly accepted that informal and non-institutionalized forms of regulation, particularly through technology design and maintenance, play important roles in the emerging governance ecosystem (e.g., Braman 2009; Epstein 2013; Epstein et al. 2016; Hofmann et al. 2017; Mueller 2010; van Eeten and Mueller 2013).

When it comes to distributed technology such as the internet, expertise and resources span private and public actors and institutions across local, national, regional, and global levels of operation and analysis. The lack of a single point of control or a dominant rule-making authority over the internet, underpinned the early debates surrounding internet governance (Mueller 2010). The most broadly used (and criticized) formal definition of internet governance, adopted by the UN Working Group on Internet Governance (WGIG 2005), places the plurality of actors and their roles at the core by framing it as "the development and application by *governments, the private sector and civil society, in their respective roles*, of shared principles, norms, rules, decision-making procedures, and programmes that shape the evolution and use of the Internet" (WGIG 2005, p. 4; emphasis added).

Insofar as the internet infrastructure and applications that operate on it underpin data flows (Benkler 2006; Solum and Chung 2004), dynamics of internet governance arrangements are central to understanding privacy governance in the digital realm. One of the most persistent questions in internet governance is who gets to govern. Leveraging the WGIG's definition, scholars engaged in nuanced discussions of multistakeholderism – or the multistakeholder approach – mapping actors, grouping them, and discussing sources of their authority, power, and legitimacy in an attempt to systematically describe and explain the emerging structures ordering the net (DeNardis 2015). Further, they asked questions about where governance happens and through which mechanisms lead to conceptualizations of internet governance in terms of ecosystem (Hofmann 2017), networked governance (Mueller 2010), and co-regulation (Marsden 2011).

Scholte (2017) was one of the first to explicitly apply polycentrism to internet governance, describing it as transpiring through interplays between local, national, and international levels (transscalarity) and involving government, commercial, and civil society actors (transsectorality). Internet governance is also understood as spreading across multiple entities and institutions (diffusion) with unclear chains of command (ambiguous hierarchies) and ever-changing boundaries (fluid; see also Epstein 2013). These latter attributes also result in entities that can simultaneously claim competence over a given regulatory issue (overlapping mandates) with no agreed-upon designated site of ultimate decision-making authority (no final arbiter).

Polycentric tendencies can be observed across internet-related and internet-dependent domains. In cybersecurity literature, for example, scholars have been observing a departure from state-centric views of security towards conceptualizing cybersecurity as "the aggregate of all attempts by organizations and individuals to institutionalize rules, standards and practices that manage and minimize the risks associated with engagement in cyberspace" (Mueller 2017, p. 422). In a rather polycentric fashion, cybersecurity governance involves those stakeholders that are most familiar with both questions of internet governance and questions of security. Devising appropriate rules, and combining relevant policy and technological instruments, require knowledge and appreciation of both domains (Shackelford 2013; Weber and Studer 2016).

Similarly, literature on platform governance argues that traditional and state-centric approaches to the regulation of platforms fall short in addressing concerns about private censorship, abuse of informational power, and human rights harms. Major platform providers (e.g., Facebook, Amazon, Apple, Microsoft, and Google) are global corporations that navigate a plethora of local laws and regulations in order to operate (Gorwa 2019). They also lead standardization efforts for information transmission, storage, and security (Weyrauch and Winzen 2021). They self-regulate by involving a vast range of actors in each economy where they operate (Medzini 2021b). In other words, the understanding of both governance by and governance of the platforms can benefit from a polycentric approach that acknowledges the complexities, interdependencies, and the lack of a single final arbiter. The question comes in two parts: to what extent are polycentric tendencies manifested in digital privacy governance, and what can we learn from identifying them?

Privacy Governance

Literature on privacy governance is vast and diverse. Legal analysis, for instance, focuses on the rights-based premise that individuals are capable of determining for themselves when, how, and to what extent information about them is communicated to others. Informational self-determination is the backbone of European data protection and a vital part of the American information privacy legal framework (Bamberger and Mulligan 2015, p. 21). The regulatory approach, meanwhile, focuses on the role and political power of independent data protection supervisory authorities in Europe, known as DPAs (Newman 2008), which are juxtaposed with inherent limits of private self-regulation (Medzini 2021a), or the relative political power and perceived regulatory strength of US American privacy regulators (e.g., the Federal Trade Commission). An economic perspective zooms in on processes of privacy valuation and calculus involved in resolving the tension between ideal and attainable states of personal information sharing (Acquisti et al. 2016). It is tightly linked to behavioral approaches, which emphasize privacy literacy as a mechanism through which individuals gain agency and autonomy in datafied environments (Masur 2020). While these threads of research do touch on *institutional* aspects of privacy regulation, there is a need for scholarship to map explicitly the loci of control in privacy governance arrangements. This is where a polycentric approach can be particularly insightful.

Institutionally oriented privacy governance research has flagged polycentric tendencies in the past, even if not explicitly labeling them as such. Bennett and Raab (2003), for example, identified four groups of data protection policy instruments: transnational, legal, self-regulatory, and technological. Based on this analysis they explained that privacy governance is exercised through a variety of institutional forms where laws are not the dominant instruments and formal government regulators are not necessarily the most pivotal actors. Thus, when they defined privacy governance as "a complex phenomenon that involves a plurality of actors and a range of methods of operation and coordination" (Bennett and Raab 2003, p. 294), they implicitly acknowledged its polycentricity.

In another example, Mayer-Schonberger (2010) criticized the effectiveness of Western emphasis on empowering individuals to enforce their information rights. He suggested learning from the European experience of relying on privacy professionals for privacy governance arrangements, among other forms of information intermediation. According to Mayer-Schonberger, these information governance intermediaries are pivotal to ensuring information privacy in organizational and societal contexts, thus highlighting their polycentric tendencies.

Yet in another example, Bamberger and Mulligan (2015) used a comparative approach to explore how corporations in five different countries operationalized privacy protections and why. They found that ambiguity in regulatory requirements, activist regulators, and stakeholder scrutiny in the US and Germany resulted in empowering and resourcing privacy professionals. Managers, in turn, relied on privacy professionals' knowledge about risks within the firm and how to manage them (Bamberger and Mulligan, 2015, pp. 222–223). Finally, others have called attention to the practices and, sometimes narrow, perceptions of privacy of technologists and engineers who design information products and factor (or not) privacy into their work products (Waldman 2018; Ribak 2019).

While appealing and versatile, the polycentric approach to privacy governance has been criticized for neglecting the broader structural context within which authority and responsibility are both defined and assigned (Koinova et al. 2021), and, perhaps by extension, inadequately reflecting the empirical reality. Julie Cohen (2012), for example, has found the new privacy governance paradigm that emerged in the U.S. to be ill-equipped to address privacy concerns raised by surveillance capitalism as "it is rooted in a regulatory ideology that systematically downplays the need to hold market actors accountable for harms to the public interest" (Cohen 2012, pp. 1927–1928). According to Cohen, such a paradigm places excessive emphasis on private regulation, notice, and choice, and involves politics that are resistant to critical scrutiny (Cohen, 2012, pp. 1928–1931). Along similar lines, Bennett and Raab (2020) have recently hypothesized that currently, the governance of privacy seems to revert to two-party relationships between regulators and organizations, thus undermining privacy governance as inherently polycentric.

Taken together, we observe polycentric tendencies in privacy governance literature, which acknowledges the plurality of players, distributed power, as well as diverse norms and perceptions of what privacy actually is. At the same time, we also see criticism of the same polycentric tendencies as failing to comprehensively address the concerns of surveillance capitalism and the need to hold market actors – and especially the big tech – to account. To engage with this tension between polycentric tendencies found in privacy governance, and their critique, we paraphrase van Eeten and Mueller (2013) by asking: where is the governance in privacy governance and why does it matter? To answer this question, we analyze two cases – one dealing with formal and another with informal polycentric privacy governance arrangements.

Formal Arrangements – The Case of Data Protection Officers

The case of 'data protection officers,' or the DPOs, is emblematic of the diffusion of regulatory authority in the European data protection regime. Acting as information governance intermediaries in organizations, the DPOs are empowered to interpret laws, manage risks, and strengthen the accountability and responsibilities of rule-takers towards data protection. The path to having such authority delegated from the EU and national rule-makers to an organizational-level role passed through three major milestones: national privacy legislation in Germany in the 1970s, exemptions to the broad registration requirement that empowered national data protection authorities (DPAs) in the 1990s, and the recent adoption of three EU-level data protection reform, including the General Data Protection Regulation (GDPR).

Attempts to institutionalize polycentrism in privacy governance in the EU go back to the German Federal Data Protection Act of 1977 (the Bundesdatenschutzgesetz or BDSG). Responding to the growing use of governmental and corporate databases, BDSG stipulated the mandatory appointment of *independent* compliance officers – the *betriebliche Datenschutzbeauftragten* (a DPO) – in organizations that processed private information and had a certain number of employees. Organizations that failed to appoint a capable officer, ensure their independence, and their ability to fulfill their duties, could face enforcement actions by the data protection supervisory authorities of the German federal states (the Länder). Germany was also the first country to establish an association for DPOs in 1977, followed by Austria in 1983, and then the UK in 1993. At the time, however, the UK and Austria had no requirement for (or even recognition of) the role of DPOs, similar to that of Germany (Medzini 2021a).

DPOs evolved from a national solution to a European policy instrument as part of a political compromise. The broad goal of European rule-makers, and especially national DPAs, was to fight against possible data havens. The compromise at the time, however, limited the ability to effectively delegate authority to DPOs. On one side of this political struggle was a French-led coalition that sought to concentrate power with national DPAs. Members of this coalition had already empowered their national DPAs by establishing an extensive notification scheme for most, if not all, automatic processing operations in organizations. On the other side was the German delegation that favored a more diffused regulatory approach. They suggested a notification exemption either by permitting organizations to appoint their own supervisory authority or by enabling national supervisory authorities to delegate responsibilities to DPOs (Medzini 2021a, p. 372). The Council Presidency reached a compromise between the two approaches by promoting *an exemption* where, instead of registering their databases, organizations appoint and register a data protection *official* with the DPA. As such, this compromise reflected an attempt to formalize transscalar and transsectoral diffusion of authority.

At the national level, however, rule-makers and regulators refrained from both delegating responsibilities to DPOs and providing them with formal authority. First, European policymakers limited the scope of responsibilities of the DPOs to the national level. They bound DPOs to the application of only *national* data protection legislation, and tasked them to maintain publicly accessible registries of processing operations as well as notify national DPAs in cases when individuals' freedoms or rights were being jeopardized. Second, the Directive gave member states extensive discretion in adopting the DPOs' exemption into their national legislation. National politics and regulatory culture governed these arrangements (Bignami 2011). For instance, in Belgium and in the UK, the parliaments adopted a DPO provision into national legislation, but the governments did not issue the implementing decree or ordinance. Finally, when member states and national DPAs adopted provisions regarding DPOs, most of them continued with a centralized approach – they considered the DPOs as the DPAs' eyes and ears within the organization or as a tool for sanctioning problematic organizations by excluding their officers from national registries. Such sanctioned organizations had no choice but to re-register their processing operations with the DPAs. The limited scope of the DPOs' responsibilities and the broad discretion assigned to member states had been the bane of the polycentric recognition of the DPOs as a mechanism of regulatory intermediation until the adoption of three European data protection regulations and directives.

The adoption of three European regulations and directives, including the GDPR, altered the role of DPOs in governing privacy. This step was possible due to the adoption of the Lisbon Treaty, which allowed European policymakers to address the regulatory shortcomings harming the free movement of personal data in the EU. The most significant decision the European Commission made at that time was to reform the data protection framework around a directly applicable regulation (Medzini 2021a). While the Commission considered a regulation that comes into force and is legally binding without any need for national implementation legislation as the best policy alternative to achieve a high degree of harmonization, it also created a disruption in how member states rely on DPOs. Among the many provisions in the proposed regulation, the European Commission, with the later support of the European Parliament, offered to mandate the appointment of DPOs. This suggestion was part of a more significant proposition to simplify the notification system, increase managerial responsibilities, and implement additional self-regulatory mechanisms. The European Commission relied on its suggestion about the practices and experiences concerning DPOs already established by the member states, especially Germany, and by the European data protection supervisor, the DPA for European institutions.

The proposal to appoint DPOs, however, met intra-European politics. The European Council offered the most vigorous opposition. Delegates of the member states at the Working Party on Information Exchange and Data Protection (DAPIX) debated whether DPOs should become a mandatory requirement or whether to take a granular approach that considers the characteristics of relevant organizations and sectors. The delegates further negotiated which entitlements the officers should receive. Most importantly, the delegates strongly disagreed with the Commission's proposal to legislate a directly applicable regulation and to include in it about fifty provisions that empower the Commission to adopt either delegated or implementing acts, including in regard to DPOs. The deciding factor between the Commission and the Council was the European Parliament. While it sided with the Commission on the functionality of DPOs and the need to incorporate them into the regime, it sided with the Council against empowering the Commission with the competence to issue delegated and implementing acts, including regarding DPOs. The three institutions reached a compromise in December 2015, but the legislation was delayed until April 2016.

The adoption of the new legislation advanced polycentric tendencies of the European data protection regime. The new legislation limited the discretion of the member states by requiring a range of institutions, public authorities, and private organizations to designate a DPO or contract one externally as a service. European and national policymakers can decide what additional categories of organizations must assign DPOs, but they cannot withdraw from the predefined cases set by European policymakers. European policymakers also entrusted the DPOs with monitoring compliance, guiding managers and employees on how to process private information, and indicating to managers when and which appropriate organizational and technical measures they need to implement. Organizations are permitted to assign additional tasks to the officers, as long as these tasks do not conflict with their primary role/core activities/core tasks.

European policymakers also require that organizations appoint proficient and knowledgeable DPOs and protect them from being dismissed or penalized for performing their tasks. Nevertheless, DPOs are not formally required to hold any one type of academic degree or receive formal certification. Whereas national DPAs, like the French CNIL, develop schemes to accredit providers of professional training courses and recognizable certifications to prove the officers' skills and knowledge, these national authorities cannot require certification as a prerequisite for practice. In conclusion, while the European data protection regime is still organized around roles and responsibilities held by supranational and national rule-makers and regulators, their decision to delegate authority to DPOs created a diffused and polycentric regime. As such, in contrast to an ideal model of polycentric governance (Scholte 2017), the current arrangement maintains a degree of hierarchy as DPAs act as arbiters for DPOs' decisions on data protection in non-standard cases, with the court system acting as a final arbiter on both in times of crises. In this regime, DPOs interpret rules and manage risks as a mundane practice; in doing so, they rely on actors who are neither rule-makers nor regulators to share knowledge, gain credibility and proficiency, and in some cases, promote professional interests.

Informal Arrangements – The Case of Remote Learning Technology Adoption During COVID-19

In the spring of 2020, over 1.2 billion pupils and over 200 million college and university students worldwide found their institutions abruptly seizing in-person classes due to the COVID-19 pandemic (Li and Lalani 2020; Salmi 2020). In the more resourceful places, the solution was moving to distance learning, joining a broader shift towards remote, computer-mediated social, cultural, political, and economic activities (Vargo et al. 2021). Such a move required the rapid adoption of information technologies, which inevitably involved digital privacy considerations, thus exposing the underlying informal governance arrangements.

Since the beginning of the pandemic, scholars have paid substantive attention to the pedagogical aspect of this rapid move to distance learning (e.g., Babbar and Gupta 2021; Khanal et al. 2021). Less attention has been paid to privacy implications or to privacy considerations given to decisions about the adoption and implementation of technological solutions for remote learning (e.g., Komljenovic 2021; Macgilchrist et al. 2021). Only a handful of projects tackled those questions explicitly (e.g., Bergdahl and Nouri 2021; Chang 2021; Cohney et al. 2021; Epstein et al. 2021; John et al. 2022). Yet, moments of crisis like this expose the implicit governance structures insofar as they refer to decision-making with constitutive effect (Braman 2009, p. 3; see Fortun et al. 2017 for a discussion of studying moments of crisis). The emerging picture is that of a mostly informal polycentric arrangement, where knowledge, expertise, agency, resources, and authority are distributed across and within institutions.

While empirical evidence is still emergent and focused mostly on Western, educated, industrialized, rich, and democratic (WEIRD) countries, a number of case studies have documented how schools, universities, and educators renegotiated privacy boundaries when quickly adopting digital tools for remote learning. Institutional privacy concerns associated with this rapid shift primarily involved the loss of control over student data when adopting commercial platforms, which leverage personal information for profit. Those concerns highlighted the shift of power within privacy governance arrangements away from the state towards commercial platform providers (Cohney et al. 2021; Komljenovic 2021). Social and pedagogical concerns centered on privacy boundary turbulence caused by the collapse of professional and personal settings when learning and teaching from home. Those concerns foregrounded the role of street-level bureaucratic practices and epistemic communities in shaping privacy governance arrangements on the ground (Cohney et al. 2021).

The initial wave of lockdowns in the spring of 2020 created a sense of chaos for educators in both schools and higher education (Macgilchrist et al. 2021; John et al. 2022). On the one hand, it pushed the actors to fall back on existing, default structures that were often reflective of privacy cultures dominant in their states and institutions. Here, one could observe the path dependency set by hierarchical decision-making about which technologies to adopt and how to use them in educational settings (Cohney et al. 2021; Komljenovic 2021). In Israel, for example, teachers and pupils (and their parents) in schools had been extensively using WhatsApp for day-to-day communication prior to the pandemic, paying little attention to privacy, but making it readily available as a major communication channel in the early stages of the pandemic (John et al. 2022). In Germany, on the other hand, while the overall sensitivity to privacy was higher, educators had no readily available means to reach pupils, and sometimes even no contact details other than a postal address. Adopting WhatsApp, even under the circumstances, was perceived as an act of rebellion, thus exposing privacy confounds of considerations about that confounded technology adoption (John et al. 2022).

Similarly, when institutions made decisions about the adoption of remote learning platforms, those decisions reflected both the top-down prescriptive nature of national privacy culture and the institutional autonomy to consider or disregard vertical privacy concerns. For example, while some relied on centralized, closed, commercial products such as Blackboard, Canvas (Cohney et al. 2021) or Google Classroom (Bergdahl and Nouri 2021; John et al. 2022), either ignoring or accepting potential privacy risks (Rubel and Jones 2016), others opted out for more localized, self-hosted, and open-source solutions such as Moodle (Epstein et al. 2021; John et al. 2022). As the pandemic progressed, centrally supplied solutions, such as institutionally funded Zoom, Webex or Teams accounts, or BigBlueButton servers, further demarcated the realm of solutions available by default to teachers and lecturers. At the same time, at least in the US, data protection principles have often been regulated through institutional level Data Protection Addenda in lieu of central regulation (Cohney et al. 2021). Contrary to the case of the DPO regime described above, which was developed to govern the mundane, here, privacy governance structures emerged from a crisis and under the dual pressures of time and span.

The same initial sense of chaos also created room for exercising both organizational and individual agency, as it interacted with broader, structural arrangements. When it comes to the development of norms and practices around technology adoption and privacy management, the exercise of individual agency, as the basis of developing said norms and practices, highlighted the role of professional networks and epistemic communities, as well as that of educators as policy entrepreneurs and street-level bureaucrats (Taylor 2007). First, in relation to knowledge and expertise, educators reported learning about new tools and the ways to adopt them through their personal and professional networks, often at the expense of information coming from formal sources (Epstein et al. 2021; John et al. 2022). Particularly interesting in this regard is the emergence of hyperlocal, authentic expertise, such as colleagues teaching their peers about using technology for remote learning, with each such decision evoking (or not) privacy concerns (Bergdahl and Nouri 2021; John et al. 2022).

Second, there is a sense of enhanced agency among educators when it comes to privacy practice within their classrooms. On the one hand, teachers and lecturers require their students to use additional digital tools for pedagogical reasons, but in ways that may expose them to data collection by third parties (Bergdahl and Nouri 2021; Cohney et al. 2021; Epstein et al. 2021). On the other hand, they may either enforce or circumvent established centralized policy. This was evident, for example, in the case of camera usage in Israeli schools, where teachers were both confused about formal policy for the use of a camera during classes and established policy based on their interpretation of their class's needs (John et al. 2022). Another example is the eventual dominance of Zoom as the primary video-conferencing tool for remote learning in places like Estonia, where the point of departure was more towards GDPR-friendly solutions such as BigBlueButton (Bergdahl and Nouri 2021; Epstein et al. 2021).

Taken together, this emerging body of evidence draws a picture of distributed knowledge, expertise, agency, resources, and authority, as well as a multiplicity of interrelated public and private actors involved in renegotiating privacy boundaries during the COVID-19 crisis. While institutional decisions both reflect and reify broader structures of legitimation and power with regards to privacy, the individual agency of educators and hyperlocal expertise result in decisions with constitutive effects on remote learning environments. Especially in times of turbulence, such decisions establish path dependency for future decision-making concerning ed-tech adoption and privacy. As such, the polycentric view of privacy governance, in this case, allows unpacking informal institutionalization processes expressed through interaction between individual agency, social structures, and socio-technical systems within which street-level bureaucrats operate.

Conclusions and Future Research

In this chapter we asked to identify polycentric tendencies in digital privacy governance. Such tendencies have been observed in other areas of policymaking, as the research of governance has progressively moved from a top-down, state-centric view of regulation, towards a broader view of governance as an ensemble of decentralized, distributed, and dynamic systems. Particularly, in internet governance, as Aguerre, Campbell-Verduyn, and Scholte suggest in Chapter 1 of this volume, the polycentric perspective has been found useful for systematic analysis of constitutive structures lacking a single point of control or a dominant rule-making authority, including in areas such as cybersecurity and platform governance. It is important that privacy researchers, also, pay greater attention to the question of locating governance in privacy governance.

The two cases presented above – institutionalization of the formal role of the DPOs in the EU and the emergence of informal rules and practices around the adoption of technologies for remote learning in the early stages of COVID-19 – were selected as distinct examples of polycentric tendencies in privacy governance. Both cases involve actors that are pivotal to the regulatory process without being rule-makers or rule-takers in the classic, state-centric sense. What makes those cases intriguing is that despite their apparent topical differences, both exhibit similar elements identified by Scholte (2017) as markers of polycentrism.

First, the two cases demonstrate the transscalarity and transsectorality of privacy governance arrangements. Both DPOs and educators exercise a degree of agency when making decisions about the flow of personal information. Yet they make these decisions while acting outside of the formal institutions of government but within the shadow of hierarchical decisions by state regulators or technology designers. The DPOs have a formally delegated authority to interpret the law and establish organization-level practices. Educators, who have a limited ability to make choices between commercial shelf products, erect informal governance structures through norms-in-practice when it comes to surveilling and datafying their students' experience or regulating the use of video in remote teaching. In both cases, decisions made at the organizational level require interpretive flexibility that may exploit gaps or challenge existing rules, thus creating tensions between organizational-level practice and a top-down order. While our analysis focuses just on two main groups of actors, a broader look at the privacy complex would include additional players, particularly engineers designing privacy into their products (Waldman 2018; Ribak 2019) or certification and monitoring bodies as another source of constitutive decision-making (Medzini 2021c). Further research can help identify how, and possibly also why, additional actors expand the transscalarity and transsectorality of privacy governance.

Second, the two cases illustrate the diffusion of knowledge and authority within emerging privacy governance arrangements. The DPOs and educators in our examples, rely on epistemic communities and professional networks for expertise and for the legitimacy of their actions. DPOs heavily rely on their professional networking as they must demonstrate that they were designated based on professional qualities and knowledge. Professional associations, for-profit and nonprofit organizations, and even academic institutions that provide certifications offer a space for professional networking and enable knowledge exchange. Some professional associations even act as interest groups that defend and promote favorable policies on the national and European levels. Educators, meanwhile, rely on peers in lieu of formal, top-down advice about technology adoption, or respond to pressure from other stakeholders, such as parents, when making decisions about adopting technology at the expense of, or in the name of, privacy protection. This dynamic was further pronounced in the adoption of practices of technology use, such as requirements about the (non)use of webcams. One way to think about this observation is a new type of network effect: one that leverages the epistemic networks to augment literacy deficits, information overload, and lack of clearer authority or arbiter. Future research should study the isomorphic tendencies of the epistemic communities and professional networks, as well as how and to what effect they become political actors and interest groups.

Finally, the two cases emphasize the dynamic nature and the fluidity of privacy governance arrangements. The evolution of formalization of the role of the DPOs in the EU, is in itself an example of a dynamic process. The legislation adopted at the state or the union level at different points in time reflected bottom-up technological developments and how the emergent practices utilized them. The case of education technology adoption during the pandemic condensed similar dynamics in a much shorter period of time. One of the more vivid examples of the change introduced through this shock is the acceptance in Israeli higher education institutions of recording lectures, a practice that departed from previously established norms of respecting the privacy of the classroom, thus establishing a new norm and an expectation of having recordings available also after the emergency has passed. This observation emphasizes the need for more longitudinal research, as well as the utility of studying crises, and disasters where privacy governance structures get revealed more vividly.

The analysis presented in this chapter is the proverbial 'tip of the iceberg' of polycentric privacy governance arrangements. The two cases we used to demonstrate polycentric tendencies are a proof of concept, which can and should be leveraged in future work. The dynamic nature of the phenomenon, and repeated exogenous shocks, such as major data breaches or a pandemic, continue to alter the structures of legitimation and domination in privacy governance. Moreover, regulatory thought itself continues to evolve, responding to both technological and economic changes in increasingly datafied societies. For instance, there is a growing interest in the role of algorithms in communication, including algorithmic regulation, and governance of and by algorithms (Latzer and Just 2020).

Further, the growing importance of (often informal) networks and the aforementioned dynamic nature of the field calls for expanding the methodological repertoires of privacy policy researchers beyond the emerging and existing methods of studying internet governance (DeNardis et al., 2020). In addition to tracing regulatory processes and analyzing policy outcomes, understanding the polycentrism in privacy governance requires mapping the dynamic networks that produce the norms, language, and practice which affect digital privacy. Finally, as we can see, even based on analysis of just two cases, comparative analysis holds the potential of revealing meta structures that underpin decision-making processes with constitutive effects for privacy. Future research should engage in a more systematic comparative analysis of polycentrism across cultural, social, political, economic, and technological structures.

References

Abbott, K.W., Levi-Faur, D. and Snidal, D. (2017) 'Theorizing regulatory intermediaries: The RIT model', *The ANNALS of the American Academy of Political and Social Science*, 670 (1), pp. 14–35.

Acquisti, A., Taylor, C. and Wagman, L. (2016) 'The economics of privacy', *Journal of Economic Literature*, 54 (2), pp. 442–492.

Babbar, M. and Gupta, T. (2021) 'Response of educational institutions to COVID-19 pandemic: An inter-country comparison', *Policy Futures in Education*, pp. 1–23.

Bamberger, K.A. and Mulligan, D.K. (2015) *Privacy on the ground: Driving corporate behavior in the United States and Europe.* Cambridge, MA: The MIT Press.

Benkler, Y. (2006) *The wealth of networks: How social production transforms markets and freedom.* Yale University Press.

Bennett, C.J. and Raab, C.D. (2003) *Governance of privacy: Policy instruments in global perspective.* Routledge.

Bennett, C.J. and Raab, C.D. (2020) 'Revisiting the governance of privacy: Contemporary policy instruments in global perspective', *Regulation & Governance*, 14 (3), pp. 447–464.

Bergdahl, N. and Nouri, J. (2021) 'Covid-19 and crisis-prompted distance education in Sweden', *Technology, Knowledge and Learning*, 26 (3), pp. 443–459.

Bignami, F. (2011) 'Cooperative legalism and the non-Americanization of European regulatory styles: The case of data privacy', *The American Journal of Comparative Law*, 59 (2), pp. 411–461.

Black, J. (1996) 'Constitutionalising self-regulation', *The Modern Law Review*, 59 (1), pp. 24–55.

Black, J. (2001) 'Decentring regulation: Understanding the role of regulation and self-regulation in a "post-regulatory" world', *Current Legal Problems*, 54 (1), pp. 103–146.

Braman, S. (2009) *Change of state: Information, policy, and power*. Cambridge, MA: MIT Press.

Chang, B. (2021) 'Student privacy issues in online learning environments', *Distance Education*, 42 (1), pp. 55–69.

Cohen, J. E. (2012). What privacy is for. *Harv. L. Rev.*, 126, 1904–1933.

Cohney, S., Teixeira, R., Kohlbrenner, A., Narayanan, A., Kshirsagar, M., Shvartzshnaider, Y. and Sanfilippo, M. (2021) 'Virtual classrooms and real harms: Remote learning at {U.S}. universities', in *Seventeenth Symposium on Usable Privacy and Security (SOUPS 2021)*, pp. 653–674. https://www.usenix.org/conference/soups2021/presentation/cohney.

Cowhey, P.F. (1990) 'The international telecommunications regime: The political roots of regimes for high technology', *International Organization*, 44 (2), pp. 169–199.

DeNardis, L., Cogburn, D., Levinson, N. S. and Musiani, F. (eds.). (2020). *Researching internet governance: Methods, frameworks, futures*. The MIT Press.

van Eeten, M.J. and Mueller, M. (2013) 'Where is the governance in Internet governance?', *New Media & Society*, 15 (5), pp. 720–736.

Epstein, D. (2013) 'The making of institutions of information governance: The case of the Internet Governance Forum', *Journal of Information Technology*, 28 (2), pp. 137–149.

Epstein, D., John, N., Wilhelm, C., Barats, C. and Silbak, A. (2021) '*Privacy, COVID-19 and online teaching: A comparative study in Estonia, France and Israel*', Association of Internet Researchers (AoIR) 22nd Annual Conference, remote.

Epstein, D., Katzenbach, C. and Musiani, F. (2016) 'Doing internet governance: How science and technology studies inform the study of internet governance', *Internet Policy Review*, 5 (3).

Flyverbom, M., Deibert, R. and Matten, D. (2019) 'The governance of digital technology, big data, and the internet: New roles and responsibilities for business', *Business & Society*, 58 (1), pp. 3–19.

Fortun, K., Choi, V.Y. and Jobin, P. (2017) 'Researching disaster from an STS perspective', in Felt, U., Fouché, R., Miller, C.A. and Smith-Doerr, L. (eds.) *The Handbook of Science and Technology Studies*. 4th edn. Cambridge, MA: MIT Press, pp. 1003–1028.

Gorwa, R. (2019) 'What is platform governance?', *Information, Communication & Society*, 22 (6), pp. 854–871.

Gunningham, N., Grabosky, P.N. and Sinclair, D. (1998) *Smart regulation: Designing environmental policy*. Oxford: Oxford University Press.

Havinga, T. and Verbruggen, P. (2017) 'Understanding complex governance relationships in food safety regulation: The RIT Model as a theoretical lens', *The ANNALS of the American Academy of Political and Social Science*, 670 (1), pp. 58–77.

Hofmann, J. (2017) 'Constellations of trust and distrust in internet governance', in European Commission and Directorate-General for Research and Innovation (eds.) *Trust at risk: Implications for EU policies and institutions*. Luxembourg: European Commission, Directorate-General for Research and Innovation (Research policy and organisation), pp. 85–98.

Hofmann, J., Katzenbach, C. and Gollatz, K. (2017) 'Between coordination and regulation: Finding the governance in Internet governance', *New Media & Society*, 19 (9), pp. 1406–1423.

John, N., Joeckel, S., Epstein, D. and Dogruel, L. (2022) Privacy and distance learning in turbulent times: A comparison of German and Israeli schools during the beginning of the COVID-19 pandemic. *Learning, Media and Technology*, 48(3), pp. 514–527. https://doi.org/10.1080/17439884.2022.2089682.

Khanal, P., Bento, F. and Tagliabue, M. (2021) 'A scoping review of organizational responses to the COVID-19 pandemic in schools: A complex systems perspective', *Education Sciences*, 11 (3), Article# 115.

Koinova, M., Deloffre, M.Z., Gadinger, F., Mencutek, Z.S., Scholte, J.A. and Steffek, J. (2021) 'It's ordered chaos: What really makes polycentrism work', *International Studies Review*, 23 (4), pp. 1988–2018.

Komljenovic, J. (2021) 'The rise of education rentiers: Digital platforms, digital data and rents', *Learning, Media and Technology*, 46 (3), pp. 320–332.

Latzer, M. and Just, N. (2020) 'Governance by and of algorithms on the Internet: Impact and consequences', in Nussbaum, J.F. (ed.) *Oxford Research Encyclopedia of Communication*. Oxford, UK: Oxford University Press.

Levi-Faur, D. (2005) 'The global diffusion of regulatory capitalism', *The ANNALS of the American Academy of Political and Social Science*, 598 (1), pp. 12–32.

Levi-Faur, D. (2011) 'Regulation and Regulatory Governance', in Levi-Faur, D. (ed.) *Handbook on the Politics of Regulation*. Northampton, MA: Edward Elgar Publishing, pp. 3–21.

Levi-Faur, D. (2012) 'From "Big Government" to "Big Governance"?', in Levi-Faur, D. (ed.) *The Oxford Handbook of Governance*. Oxford University Press, pp. 3–18.

Levi-Faur, D., Kariv-Teitelbaum, Y. and Medzini, R. (2021) 'Regulatory governance: History, theories, strategies, and challenges', in *Oxford Research Encyclopedia of Politics*. New York: Oxford University Press.

Li, C. and Lalani, F. (2020) 'The COVID-19 pandemic has changed education forever: This is how', *World Economic Forum*, 29 April. https://www.weforum.org/agenda/2020/04/coronavirus-education-global-covid19-online-digital-learning/.

Macgilchrist, F., Potter, J. and Williamson, B. (2021) 'Shifting scales of research on learning, media and technology', *Learning, Media and Technology*, 46 (4), pp. 369–376.

Majone, G. (1994) 'The rise of the regulatory state in Europe', *West European Politics*, 17 (3), pp. 77–101.

Marsden, C.T. (2011) *Internet co-regulation: European law, regulatory governance and legitimacy in cyberspace*. Cambridge: Cambridge University Press.

Masur, P.K. (2020) 'How online privacy literacy supports self-data protection and self-determination in the age of information', *Media and Communication*, 8 (2), pp. 258–269.

Mayer-Schonberger, V. (2010). Beyond privacy, beyond rights - Toward a systems theory of information governance. *California Law Review*, 98 (6), pp. 1853–1886.

Medzini, R. (2021a) 'Credibility in enhanced self-regulation: The case of the European data protection regime', *Policy & Internet*, 13 (3), pp. 366–384.

Medzini, R. (2021b) 'Enhanced self-regulation: The case of Facebook's content governance', *New Media & Society*, 24 (10), pp. 2227–2251.

Medzini, R. (2021c) 'Governing the shadow of hierarchy: Enhanced self-regulation in European data protection codes and certifications', *Internet Policy Review*, 10 (3). https://doi.org/10.14763/2021.3.1577.

Mueller, M.L. (2010) *Networks and states: The global politics of Internet governance*. Cambridge, MA: MIT Press.

Mueller, M.L. (2017) 'Is cybersecurity eating internet governance? Causes and consequences of alternative framings', *Digital Policy, Regulation and Governance*, 19 (6), pp. 415–428.

Newman, A.L. (2008) 'Building transnational civil liberties: Transgovernmental entrepreneurs and the European Data Privacy Directive', *International Organization*, 62 (1), pp. 103–130.

Power, M. (1999) *The audit society*. Oxford University Press.

Raymond, M. and DeNardis, L. (2015) 'Multistakeholderism: Anatomy of an inchoate global institution', *International Theory*, 7 (3), pp. 572–616.

Ribak, R. (2019) 'Translating privacy: Developer cultures in the global world of practice', *Information, Communication & Society*, 22 (6), pp. 838–853.

Rubel, A. and Jones, K.M.L. (2016) 'Student privacy in learning analytics: An information ethics perspective', *The Information Society*, 32 (2), pp. 143–159.

Salamon, L.M. (2011) 'The new governance and the tools of public action: An introduction', *Fordham Urban Law Journal*, 28 (5), pp. 1611–1674.

Salmi, J. (2020) *COVID's lessons for global higher education*. Indianapolis, IN: Lumina Foundation.

Scholte, J.A. (2017) 'Polycentrism and democracy in internet governance', in Kohl, U. (ed.) *The net and the nation state: Multidisciplinary perspectives on internet governance*. Cambridge: Cambridge University Press, pp. 165–184.

Scott, C. (2004) 'Regulation in the age of governance: The rise of the post regulatory state', in Jordana, J. and Levi-Faur, D. (eds.) *The politics of regulation: Institutions and regulatory reforms for the Age of Governance*. Edward Elgar Publishing, pp. 145–174.

Shackelford, S.J. (2013) 'Toward cyberpeace: Managing cyberattacks through polycentric governance', *American University Law Review*, 62 (5), pp. 1273–1364.

Solum, L. B. and Chung, M. (2004) The Layers Principle: Internet architecture and the law. *Notre Dame Law Review*, 79 (3), pp. 815–948. https://doi.org/10.2139/ssrn.416263.

Taylor, I. (2007) 'Discretion and control in education: The teacher as street-level bureaucrat', *Educational Management Administration & Leadership*, 35 (4), pp. 555–572.

Vargo, D., Zhu, L., Benwell, B. and Yan, Z. (2021) 'Digital technology use during COVID-19 pandemic: A rapid review', *Human Behavior and Emerging Technologies*, 3 (1), pp. 13–24.

Waldman, A.E. (2018) 'Designing Without Privacy', *Houston Law Review*, 55 (3), pp. 659–727.

Weber, R.H. and Studer, E. (2016) 'Cybersecurity in the Internet of Things: Legal aspects', *Computer Law & Security Review*, 32 (5), pp. 715–728.

Weyrauch, D. and Winzen, T. (2021) 'Internet fragmentation, political structuring, and organizational concentration in transnational engineering networks', *Global Policy*, 12 (1), pp. 51–65.

WGIG (2005) *Report of The Working Group on Internet Governance*. Chateau de Bossey: United Nations.

Zacher, M.W. (2012) 'Capitalism, technology, and liberalization: The international telecommunications regime, 1865–1998', in Rosenau, J.N. and Singh, J.P. (eds.) *Information technologies and global politics: The changing scope of power and governance*. Albany, NY: SUNY Press, pp. 189–210.

PART III

Technologies

11

GLOBAL DATA GOVERNANCE BY INTERNET INTERCONNECTION

Nathalia Sautchuk Patrício

Introduction

Global data governance needs Internet interconnection. Internet interconnection policies, as well as technical protocols and standards, are an integral but still poorly understood part of data governance debates. These matters are central to interoperability, as Chapter 3 by Aguerre in this volume has illustrated. The present chapter contributes to what Sacks and Sherman characterize as a need for "deeper study and mapping of the standards landscape across categories such as internet architecture, company activities, people, and governments ... as a basis for any international framework for data governance" (Sacks and Sherman 2019). I argue that polycentric lenses offer a way to foreground the typically obscure "Internet interconnection layer" and its data governance tensions. Emphasizing interconnection to deal with the mechanisms that allow the transmission of data between different networks on the Internet is a recognition of polycentric arrangements governing data globally. Ultimately, the data used by platforms from their users rely on the Internet for both data production and circulation.

Digital data travel through multiple protocols and pass through different networks (also referred to as Autonomous Systems, or ASes) as well as various physical media such as fiber optic cable and satellite radio spectrum. The definition of what is allowed (or not) to be sent is based on interconnection policies set and maintained among networks that shape the possibilities of using and retaining data across platforms. In addition, data specifically related to sender and receiver communication can be retained and updated at the interconnection level. This means that, when content is sent on the Internet, it is "inserted" in a standardized data packet, containing data related to sender and receiver. These data are read during routing processes and updated by the routers from the

DOI: 10.4324/9781003388418-14

interconnection points. Global data governance is thus polycentric: through interconnections between seemingly autonomous but highly interconnected systems that enable data to 'travel'. The interconnection of these networks on the Internet represents an important but understudied form of global polycentric data governance.

The chapter proceeds in three sections. The first section unpacks data governance by Internet interconnection. The second section then elaborates on how polycentric governance helps to understand "global data governance by Internet interconnection". Specifically, it traces the role (and interconnections) between routing policies, Internet Exchange Points (IXPs), and Content Delivery Networks (CDNs). Finally, the third section presents some considerations on challenges and future research regarding global polycentric data governance.

Data governance by internet interconnection

What are data in the digital age? This definitional question remains at the heart of existing global digital data governance debates. The term data governance first focused on the corporate environment making use of data. One structured literature review synthesized a definition of data governance as follows:

> Data governance specifies a cross-functional framework for managing data as a strategic enterprise asset. In doing so, data governance specifies decision rights and accountabilities for an organization's decision-making about its data. Furthermore, data governance formalizes data policies, standards, and procedures and monitors compliance.
>
> *(Abraham, vom Brocke and Schneider 2019)*

More recently, however, data governance debates are identifying the role of different actors and the broader social implications about data. Particularly the role of governments has contributed to *international* dimensions of data governance, including the issue of data flow between different jurisdictions (see Chapter 3, Aguerre in this volume). Government involvement is also important to Internet interconnectivity. Sacks and Sherman (2019) recognize this point in conceiving data governance as rules for how governments interact among themselves as well as with the private sector in order to manage data, understand the access and use patterns, and what should be included in the design and enforcement of standards, policies, and laws.

Others, however, insist that the Internet's network architecture is data governance. A change in the design of the networks, encompassing Internet-based services, as well as the global Internet itself, exemplifies how the politics of the Internet are affected, such as "the balance of rights between users and providers, the capacity of online communities to engage in open and direct interaction, the fair competition between actors of the Internet market" (Musiani 2013). As Musiani (2013) goes on to suggest, technical architecture appears as one of the strongest, if not the strongest structuring element of internet governance: what is shaped into architecture and infrastructure can seldom be undone by institutional negotiation and dialogue alone, and institutions find it increasingly complicated to keep up with "creative" governance by architecture and by infrastructure.

Musiani and collaborators (DeNardis and Musiani 2016) point to an aspect of Internet governance that is more broadly relevant to global digital data governance: the ways in which the interconnection of the network of networks operate, both through specific policies and technical implementation. The formulation and implementation of such policies *is* the key way of doing Internet governance, and not just an indirect influence. Internet governance is not just influenced by aspects of the network architecture, the very design of this architecture is a form of Internet governance. Arguably, it *is* Internet governance, something that is also central to data governance.

Building on these insights points to how the Internet layer becomes a crucial 'site' for data governance and polycentricity allows us to see and connect these sites of power. Data governance is not only influenced by aspects of Internet architecture, such as network interconnections, but also fundamentally involves the design of this architecture and implementation of network interconnection policies. Hence a key under-recognized aspect of digital data is governance *by* Internet interconnection. The likes of the 70,000 ASes that constitute the Internet today thus form an important basis not only for the understanding of the interconnections of the network of networks, but also data governance more generally.

The technical architecture of the Internet thereby forms a central structuring element of data governance. Moreover, the Internet's polycentric interconnection architecture both affects and is affected by data production and flows. What is implemented in the architectural layers of the Internet often ends up going unnoticed, as key interconnection agreements are mostly informal and even handshake agreements (Van Eeten and Mueller 2013). This informality contributes to obscurity that in turn renders change by formal institutional and governmental·negotiations less, but not entirely, infrequent.

There are two main types of network interconnection at stake in data governance: peering and transit. A peering arrangement involves two Internet providers that exchange their own traffic data with each other. That is, peering involves the exchange of traffic between two or more networks. Generally, a network has some peering policies with conditions that other networks have to meet in order to be considered as 'peers', and to exchange traffic without payment between the parties. One of the factors to be considered when establishing a peering agreement is that both networks send each other approximately the same volume of data traffic. Those policies can be open, when a network is interested in peering with any other network; or restrictive, when a network is generally not interested in new peering; or selective, when the network chooses its peering partners on a case-by-case basis (Meier-Hahn 2016; Kende et al. 2021). In a peering arrangement, a network does not allow a practice known as 'transit', which means that the peer cannot use the network as a "bridge" to achieve content in a third network. To obtain access to the entire Internet, a network needs to have many peering agreements with various networks. An alternative for many peering agreements is to make a transit arrangement. This is normally a business relationship between networks, where a fee is provided. In general, a smaller network buys traffic from a larger one, which delivers this traffic to and from its peers and any other transit arrangement it may have (Kende et al. 2021). Figures 11.1, 11.2, and 11.3 show three scenarios of network interconnection: pointing, peering, and transit agreements among networks.

Analyzing Network A, we see that it has access to data from Network B directly via peering agreement and can reach data from Network D through Network C via transit agreement. When looking at Network E, we see that it has access to networks B and D, via a peering agreement. However, Network E cannot access data from Network C and A, since it has no transit agreement that allows this interconnection.

FIGURE 11.1 Peering agreement between Network A and B. Network A can reach data from Network B directly, and vice versa.

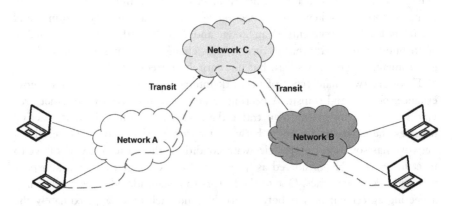

FIGURE 11.2 One transit agreement between Network A and C, and another between B and C. Network A can reach data from Network B through Network C, and vice versa.

FIGURE 11.3 Example of network interconnection with peering and transit agreements. Analyzing Network A, it is possible to see that it has access to data from Network B directly via peering agreement and can reach data from Network D through Network C via transit agreement. When looking at Network E, we see that it has access to networks B and D, via a peering agreement. However, Network E cannot access data from Network C and A, since it has no transit agreement that allows this interconnection.

Although the price of transit has dropped in recent years, it is still more financially and strategically advantageous to connect via peering. Internet Exchange Points (IXPs) were created to facilitate traffic exchange between multiple networks, rather than on a bilateral basis, as well as to make the exchange more efficient. IXPs have been growing in many regions of the world and have become one of the centres of power at the interconnection level that can be clearly identified with a polycentric lens. According to the Internet Exchange Federation (IX-F), an IXP is a network facility that enables the interconnection of more than two independent Autonomous Systems, primarily for the purpose of facilitating the exchange of Internet traffic. At this point, it is important to make a distinction between Internet Exchanges (also known as peering) from bilateral network interconnection, in which one network connects directly to another. In an IXP there are numerous participants interconnected (at least three) and the data traffic passing between any pair of participating Autonomous Systems is not required to pass through any third Autonomous System, nor does the IXP alter or otherwise interfere with such traffic (Internet Exchange Federation n.d.). Figure 11.4 displays an example of network interconnection through an IXP. According to Figure 11.4, networks A, B, C, and D can access data from each other directly via IXP. However, only Network B can access data from Network E, since E is not connected to the IXP and only has a peering agreement with Network B.

Another key aspect of interconnection has to do with sharing routing tables. Interconnection means not only having physical infrastructures connected through cables or other physical media, but "logical connection" between networks. This means that network actors need to be aware of the routes that can be used to reach other networks. It is in this context that the Border Gateway Protocol (BGP) has an important role. In the RFC 1771, Rekhter and Li (1995) say that the primary function of the BGP is the exchange of network reachability information with other BGP systems. The shared information contains the list of ASes (the numbers for the networks) that reachability information traverses. Basically, it could be seen as a map of the connections among ASes, since each AS is not connected to all others and depends on the collaboration of other ASes to send and receive information to those that do not have a direct connection. It means that a connection exists between two ASes when there is a physical connection and/or a BGP connection among them (Rekhter and Gross 1995).

Having laid out the basics of interconnectivity it is now essential to note the paradigm shift in Internet interconnection. The open and public Internet as an open platform in which resources are publicly shared and permissionless innovation is fostered has gradually been supplanted by proprietary (or closed) and private networks dominated by large private cloud ecosystems, operated by a few big tech companies and an array of providers offering non-public connectivity services (Stocker et al. 2021). There remains a more public Internet, which uses interconnection mechanisms such as peering and transit, also relying on the use of IXPs, and is connected to the more private Internet, in which the

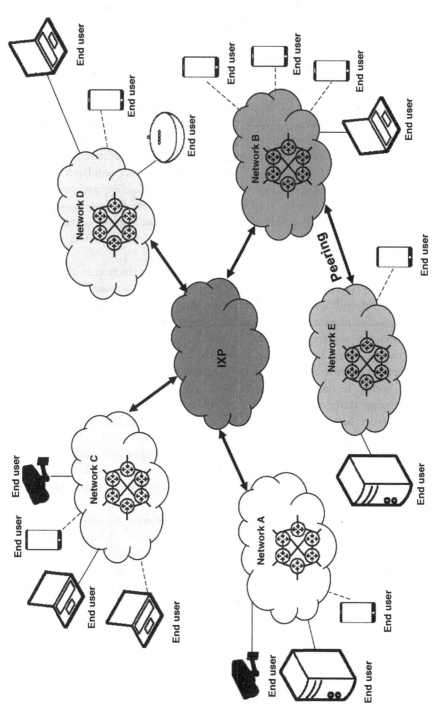

FIGURE 11.4 Network interconnection through IXP.

data distribution occurs within closed or internal networks with the massive use of Content Delivery Networks (CDNs). This paradigm shift is of vital importance for polycentric approaches in data governance as it entails a growing concentration of power centres.

CDNs have emerged to deploy and distribute data once static content is developed, such as videos (Kende et al. 2021). Cloudflare, one of the better-known companies to offer CDN, provides a service defined as "a geographically distributed group of servers which work together to provide fast delivery of Internet content" all allowing for a quick transfer of assets needed for loading Internet content including pages, images, and videos (Cloudflare n.d.). CDNs are used as a means to improve website load times, reduce bandwidth costs to content and application providers, increase content availability and redundancy, as well as to improve website security. Commonly, there are two main types of CDN: they can be independent players who distribute content (data) of other companies, and the largest content providers who develop CDNs to deliver their own content (Kende et al. 2021).

With content being closer to end users, there is a reduction in the distance data needs to travel physically between endpoints, which is manifested in fewer network borders (hops) that need to be crossed on the public Internet. There is also a growing phenomenon that are zero-hop and one-hop networks. In zero-hop scenarios, servers are deployed within networks where they terminate traffic to end users. For example, the CDN servers in this scenario are on the Internet Service Providers' own networks, allowing users to have direct access to the content. In one-hop scenarios, two networks are directly interconnected and exchange traffic. In this scenario, CDN companies are located close to the main Internet Service Providers (ISPs) and have direct interconnection with them, either through peering agreements or by being connected to IXPs (Stocker et al. 2021). Figure 11.5 illustrates the use of CDN in network interconnection. As we can see in Figure 11.5, Network A is a zero-hop network, having a CDN inside its own network, while Networks B, C, and D are one-hop networks.

Analyzing the aspects of Internet interconnection, through peering, transit, IXPs, and CDNs, it becomes possible to identify the ways that data governance takes place through the coordination of different centres of power that affect interconnection arrangements. Three cases where data governance is exercised by Internet interconnection will be explored in depth below.

The first case is of the initial IXP in Mexico. This illustrates the various challenges to the operation and the motivation for large ISPs around the world to connect to an IXP (Rosa 2021). Large ISPs generally sell data transit to smaller providers and, for them, participation in an IXP is meaningless, as they will lose an income stream by peering for free to these same networks. To force the connection of large ISPs to the IXP, Mexico enacted legislation. As a result, Mexico's largest ISP, Telmex, physically connected to the IXP in 2019. Yet, until now, Telmex has not activated the logical part of the connection, the BGP session for exchanging information about routes. The company justifies this

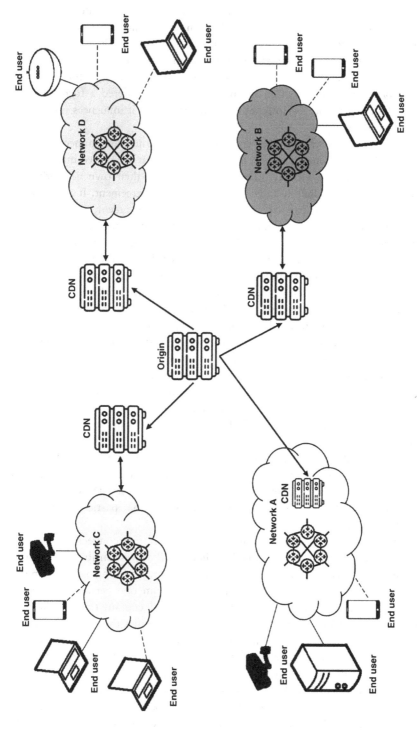

FIGURE 11.5 Network with CDN infrastructure.

lack of information exchange at the IXP for not having the route tables, since formally it is another company from the same economic group that has these tables, but does not have a license to operate in the telecommunications market. The logic is that IXP affects the population in that area, and the fewer the operators in the exchange, the smaller the network effects that this exchange can enable. Thus, participation in an IXP can be considered a form of polycentric data governance by Internet interconnection, as it influences the flow of data in the network.

A second case illustrating data governance by Internet interconnection is the use of CDNs. As discussed earlier, there are CDNs that are placed internally on the ISPs' networks as well as other CDNs that have their own networks and connect to the larger ISPs usually through a peering agreement. It remains difficult for small ISPs to participate in this type of arrangement, as large CDNs are not interested in hosting their servers on these networks or in making a peering agreement with them. Another difficulty for ISPs operating in regions where CDNs have no commercial interest in establishing their servers is that small providers end up depending on transit offered commercially by large ISPs to access the CDNs' content that is hosted on their networks or with which they have peering. In some cases, CDNs are able to connect to the largest IXPs in the country or region in which the most important ISPs may be connected. This tends to increase the operational cost of these small operators in addition to the tendency to increase the number of hops needed to reach the content, which increases the load time of content and becomes a competitive disadvantage. One solution to this scenario is shown by the NIC.br OpenCDN initiative. Through this project, CDNs have incentives to make their content available in different IXPs in Brazil. The initiative offers space in a data centre for hosting their servers, Internet traffic, and connection to the biggest Brazilian IXP in São Paulo to feed the caches, as well as connection to the IXP from several locations so that they can distribute their content locally. Local ISPs are offered the possibility to obtain the content of the largest CDNs on the local IXPs, through the provision of connectivity to the participating CDNs (OpenCDN.br n.d.).

A third example of data governance by Internet interconnection is linked with routing security. As explained earlier, BGP is responsible for sharing information related to routes, a mechanism known as 'routing announcement'. Routing announcements are statements passed from one network operator's routers to other operators' routers using BGP and contain the Autonomous System Number (ASN), a number that uniquely identifies the network, and the IP addresses associated with that network. BGP is susceptible to errors and security attacks because these announcements are highly distributed and decentralized. These problems can be caused by the intentional publication of false information about origin IP addresses or by configuration errors in routers. They happen partly because the BGP protocol does not intrinsically validate route information. With this, over time, different solutions were thought of to mitigate these problems, but without losing the flexibility and autonomy of a distributed data governance model. One of the oldest and most widely used solutions is Internet Routing Registries (IRRs), a set of databases in which network operators voluntarily share their routing policy information – including operator contact, ASN, and route – in a semi-standardized format based on the Routing Policy Specification Language (RPSL). The information published in IRRs can be used by operators to validate some route announcements and to discard others that are invalid. But there are several problems with IRRs (Kuerbis and Mueller 2017), such as the issue of encouraging the maintenance of updated information, the difficulty of verifying the authenticity and accuracy of the routing data, and the possibility of a unilateral change in the data by an operator may have undesirable and unexpected operational consequences for other networks. Kuerbis and Mueller also compare IRRs to other methods of governing routing data in a way that enhances Internet security, such as BGPSEC, the Resource Public Key Infrastructure (RPKI), and the Mutually Agreed Norms for Routing Security (MANRS). In general, the way networks engage in sharing and updating route information in IRRs or even using these other current methods is a form of data governance by interconnection.

As these three cases highlight, data governance by Internet interconnection takes place in polycentric ways. From the choice to connect and how this interconnection takes place (peering, transit, IXP), through to the use of CDNs and arriving at issues such as the quality and reliability of the information shared by the networks in this interconnection, there are multiple actors and centres of decision-making. The next section will elaborate on the polycentric modes of governance by interconnection. Table 11.1 gives a summary of data governance strategies and practices.

Polycentric Data Governance by Internet Interconnection

Polycentricity is useful for explaining and understanding data governance by Internet interconnection. As detailed in Chapter 3 of this volume, global polycentric governance is not tied up with any one geographical area but occurs in interactions of agencies at regional, national, and local levels defined as trans-scalarity. There are combinations of governmental, commercial, and civil society actors, sometimes acting together in a 'multi-stakeholder' institution, which is especially true in the case of Internet governance where the feature of

TABLE 11.1 Summary of data governance strategies and practices

Strategies to Interconnect	Interconnection Practices
Peering	
Transit	BGP/BGPSEC,
IXP	IRR, RPKI,
	MANRS
CDN	

trans-sectorality is present. Data governance by interconnection is highly changeable over time with "continual arrivals of new regulatory bodies, as well as frequent adjustments to the structures and mandates of existing institutions" (Scholte 2017). Polycentric governance involves multiple agencies claiming competence over a given regulatory situation, which illustrates the overlapping mandates and jurisdictions. The precedence among regulatory bodies is also often not very clear, leading to contestable lines of command between those institutions and ad hoc arrangements to reconcile ambiguous hierarchies. Not only that: polycentric governance lacks an ultimate decision point, which further illustrates data governance by interconnection as Table 11.2 summarizes.

Despite the apparent disorder in polycentricity, Koinova et al. (2021) argue that norms, micro-patterns of practice, and macro-frameworks of social structure generate governance effects which make polycentricity work. Scholte (2021) reflects that polycentric governance contains three different layers of structure to ordering dynamics in this context: norms, practices, and underlying orders. Each layer of structure will now be explored in turn.

Polycentric Data Norms

Koinova et al. (2021) argue that "norms are general articulated principles that inform the process of governing". Some examples of norms are democracy, economic growth, gender equality, human rights, peace, rule of law, sovereignty, sustainable development, transparency, and accountability (Koinova et al. 2021).

TABLE 11.2 Polycentric attributes and Internet interconnection

General Attributes of Polycentric Governance	Specific Attributes in Data governance by Internet Interconnection
Trans-scalarity	Not confined to any one geographical area; interactions of agencies at global, regional, country, and local levels.
Trans-sectorality	Different stakeholders across spheres of activity, such as companies (ISPs, telecommunication companies, CDNs), government, technical community, and civil society.
Diffusion	No central decision-making point in a diffusion in different bodies for sharing and maintaining route information in IRRs as well as in the peering and transit policies among networks.
Fluidity	International, regional, and national bodies that have been stable for several years without major adjustments or the creation of new bodies.
Overlapping mandates	Numerous private entities, such as IXPs and CDNs, and others are not formally constituted, having only a community character.
Ambiguous hierarchies	No clear precedence among the various actors.
Absence of a final arbiter	While in some countries there is regulation that ends up imposing a national final arbitrator, such as the Mexican case mentioned above, this is largely not the case around the world.

A key norm guiding polycentric data governance by interconnection is economic growth. One of the commonly agreed goals is to encourage market competition even if, in the case of Internet interconnection, not everything can be based on competition. When looking specifically at IXPs, routing policies, and CDNs, the norm of growth is disputed. On the one hand, there is a need for the growth of non-market collaboration between networks, even among those that compete for the same market. This means both sharing data of the most up-to-date routes possible between networks, as well as having routing policies that favor peering relationships, usually with no cost, especially between market-dominant and small networks. On the other hand, there is little incentive for the biggest companies to be collaborative, such as peering with smaller networks or participating in IXPs, since they prefer to keep a paid transit relationship instead of free peering.

A related norm usually overlooked when talking about Internet interconnection is the rule of law. While there is a common conception that there are only formal laws and regulations in countries considered authoritarian and/or with a non-free economy, there are several countries considered democratic and free market that do have some regulation to encourage the interconnection of networks, with the goal of maintaining competition in this market. Meier-Hahn (2016) surveyed internet interconnection professionals and found that nine out of ten existing regulations have been encountered by more than half of these actors (see also Rosa 2021).

Polycentric Data Practices

The second type of structure in a polycentric mode of governance concerns practices. Practices are what people do either tacitly or unconsciously. Koinova et al. (2021) classify practices in four dimensions. The first, comprising routines, words, phrases, and narratives, takes on discursive dimensions. The second is referred to as behavioral dimensions and is related to routine forms of bodily interaction. Third, material dimensions have objects as common reference points for a polycentric governing complex. The last one is generally referred to as institutional dimensions of practice and covers the ways in which organizations build and execute their policy processes.

The first discursive dimension of practices refers to the same elements present in Internet governance in general, such as the use of acronyms, the issue of bottom-up multistakeholder participation, and shared insider jokes, among others. Thinking about governance arenas at an international level more related to interconnection, there are several informal groups known as NOGs (Internet Operators Groups), which bring a sense of community to professionals working in the area (Meier-Hahn 2017). In this context, there is a discourse linked to this idea of community, for example, the sharing of good practices associated with routing, as is the case with MANRS. Other ideas that appear commonly in the discourse have to do with the fact that the more interconnections a network has, the better it is for the Internet as a whole, just as the more networks connected in an IXP, the more robust and sustainable is that IXP. Related to the IXPs there is also a discourse that they are neutral points for traffic exchange, and that they do not interfere with traffic.

The behavioral dimension of practices presents a certain ambiguity in bodies involved with data governance by Internet interconnection. Several spaces have the same dress code (more casual) and forms of deliberation that are predominantly observed in the Internet governance field in general. The NOGs have mailing lists for exchanging experiences, organize technical events with related topics, and have working groups that produce and share reports of best practices on routing and interconnection. These groups do not have the power to decide which protocols will be used in the interconnections or which policies will be adopted by individual networks, but they serve as a forum that brings together people from different networks in various regions, especially those responsible for the technical implementation of policies. There are also nodes of this network of governance bodies in which different behaviors are presented, especially when analyzing Internet interconnection in its regulatory approach. In these spaces, there is a much greater formalism, which is exemplified both in the dress code and in the forms of deliberation themselves (such as proposals and votes on laws by legislators).

There is further ambiguity in the third material dimension of governance by Internet interconnection. These arenas lack materials that are commonly distributed in other Internet governance bodies as well as in NOG meetings, such as t-shirts, tote bags, stickers, pins, and other freebies. This contrast may be explained by the fact that the Internet interconnection field rarely brings in new players, so there is less need to integrate newcomers into the community. There is still a large adherence to the use of open source or free tools. For example, for communication between the participants of a NOG, the use of mailing lists is very common. Even for the implementation of network management, several open tools are widely used. Regulatory bodies prefer to use their own solutions or those in which they may have greater control or sovereignty in relation to data. For example, some countries develop specific or customized platforms for their purpose. These practices tend to be in line with other Internet governance spaces, such as ICANN and the IGF.

The fourth institutional dimension of practices is strongly influenced by the multistakeholder discussion and presents further ambiguity in data governance by interconnection. As in other Internet governance bodies, those in which Internet interconnection debates take place end up presenting similar bureaucratic layouts, with executive boards, secretariats, and working groups. Normally, participation in these instances takes place as voluntary work on behalf of the community. Even in this context, there is no central coordination or "control" body that aggregates all the existing routes on the Internet. As discussed earlier, there are several IRRs operated by different institutions (such as private organizations, including those that offer Internet connection services, in addition to the Regional Internet Registries) as a voluntary mechanism that can be more or less reliable in the recorded data (Kuerbis and Mueller 2017). On the other hand, when analyzing the regulatory bodies around the world, they generally do not have the same structures as the other bodies of Internet governance. Nevertheless, in some countries, there is an attempt by the regulatory bodies to emulate multistakeholderism through the creation of working groups and committees with external experts serving a multistakeholder distribution, similar to those observed in other bodies.

Polycentric Data Underlying Orders

The third layer of structure in polycentric governance, underlying orders, is systemic, permeating all locations and connections in a polycentric regime. Scholte (2021) notes key aspects such as the hegemonic leadership of the leading government, capitalism, and techno-rationalism as underlying orders that permeate Internet governance.

There is an embedded view that Internet governance should be something done by private entities, with the least possible interference from national states, as it could lead to a scenario of "less efficiency", understood in this case as a network with fewer interconnections (ten Oever 2021). This reasoning can also be extended to data governance by interconnection. In relation to capitalism, it has also shaped much of what data governance is today. In addition to the points cited by Scholte in relation to commodification and surplus accumulation, there is also the private ownership of the means of production and the need for competitive markets. These characteristics are related to Internet interconnection since the vast majority of the networks are private entities and, since they have the prerogative to implement their interconnection and routing policies as they wish, one of the biggest concerns in this area is the guarantee of competition, through the interconnection access for small networks. Reflecting on the issue of techno-rationalism in the Internet interconnection debate, there is an ambiguity. On the one hand, this issue is manifested in the discourse on the existence of fundamental properties of the Internet, which comes from this vision of problem-solving through technology. However, Internet interconnection ends up taking a regulatory approach in many countries, in a way, from an assumption that technology alone is not addressing existing problems. This foregrounds that there are many centres of power addressing interconnection issues, some of them closer between them and with other Internet governance processes, others more detached and external to other Internet governance issues but that emerge as traditional centres of authority and power.

Conclusion

Internet interconnection is not an indirect influence on, but rather central to Internet governance and data governance more generally. Polycentric theorizing brings in a more nuanced lens to the different actors and mechanisms involved in the deployment of this interconnection. It helps point to and make sense of complex, varied, and fluid arrangements involving not only different actors but also technological practices. Whether networks connect through peering or transit, whether the largest ISPs participate in local IXPs, whether or not networks update routing information in IRRs or whether or not they have agreements with CDNs are some examples of how global data governance by Internet interconnection is done. As pointed out by Musiani (2013) in relation to Internet governance, data governance by interconnection is more difficult to unravel through institutional and governmental negotiation.

Future research on global data governance must consider the continually changing nature of Internet interconnection. In particular, studies must trace how the Internet has increasingly become a closed network dominated by a few companies operating large private cloud ecosystems, with particular emphasis on the growing role of CDNs in this scenario. In the same direction, the usual mechanisms of peering and transit, as well as the IXPs, have been confronted with the reality of zero-hop and one-hop networks, which end up diminishing the importance of these mechanisms and of the public Internet itself. The increasingly less distributed, decentralized, and collaborative data governance by Internet interconnection needs to be studied and linked with needs for collaboration between multiple networks and a potential shift in forms of doing data governance.

This chapter has highlighted the analytical usefulness of exploring data governance by Internet interconnection through the characteristics of the polycentric governance, such as trans-scalarity, trans-sectorality, diffusion, overlapping mandates, and ambiguous hierarchies. While polycentric governance is important to highlight underlooked aspects of data governance at the interconnection level, it may not sufficiently explain the whole phenomenon. As such further studies are needed to build on polycentricity with other concepts and theoretical approaches in order to better understand the global data governance by Internet interconnection. How can polycentric data governance thrive at the interconnection level of the Internet is still not only a theoretical but a policy issue to be pursued.

Acknowledgements

I gratefully acknowledge the support of the Alexander von Humboldt Foundation that, through the German Chancellor Fellowship program, made the present study possible. Also, I acknowledge the Centre for Global Cooperation Research at the University of Duisburg-Essen for hosting me during my fellowship time, as well as the volume editors for their feedback on earlier versions of this chapter. A special acknowledgment goes to Carolina Aguerre and Malcolm Campbell-Verduyn for their very kind contributions and insights.

References

Abraham, R., vom Brocke, J. and Schneider, J. (2019). Data Governance: A Conceptual Framework, Structured Review, and Research Agenda, *International Journal of Information Management (IJIM)*, 49, 424–438 (ABDC: A; ABS: 2; VHB: C; ISI: 4.713).

Cloudflare (n.d.). *What is a CDN? How do CDNs work?*, (https://www.cloudflare.com/learning/cdn/what-is-a-cdn/), accessed 11 Feb. 2022.

Couldry, N. and Mejias, U. A. (2019). Data Colonialism: Rethinking Big Data's Relation to the Contemporary Subject, *Television & New Media*, 20 (4), 336–349. doi:10.1177/1527476418796632.

DeNardis, L. and Musiani F. (2016). 'Governance by Infrastructure'. In *The Turn to Infrastructure in Internet Governance*, edited by D. L. Musiana, D. L. Cogburn, & N. S. Levinson, 3–21. Palgrave Macmillan.

Internet Exchange Federation (n.d.). *Definition of an Internet Exchange Point*, (http://www.ix-f.net/ixp-definition.html), accessed 11 Feb. 2022.

Kende, M., Kvalbein, A., Allford J. and Abecassis D. (2021). *Study on the Internet's Technical Success Factors*, Report for APNIC and LACNIC, Analysis Mason (https://report.analysysmason.com/internet_success_factors/#internet-study), accessed 11 Feb. 2022.

Koinova, M., Deloffre, M. Z., Gadinger, F., Mencutek, Z. S., Scholte, J. A., Steffek, J. (2021). It's Ordered Chaos: What Really Makes Polycentrism Work, *International Studies Review*, 23 (4), 1988–2018.

Kuerbis, B. and Mueller, M. (2017). Internet Routing Registries, Data Governance, and Security, *Journal of Cyber Policy*, 2 (1), 64–81. doi:10.1080/23738871.2017.1295092.

Meier-Hahn, U. (2016). *Exploring the Regulatory Conditions of Internet Interconnection – A Survey Among Internet Interconnection Professionals*. HIIG Discussion Paper Series No. 2016–03. http://dx.doi.org/10.2139/ssrn.2740312.

Meier-Hahn, U. (2017). When Internet Interconnection Trouble Occurs, Immediate Coordination Kicks In, *Internet Policy Review* (https://policyreview.info/articles/news/when-internet-interconnection-trouble-occurs-immediate-coordination-kicks/713), accessed 11 Feb. 2022.

Musiani, F. (2013). Network Architecture as Internet Governance, *Internet Policy Review*, 2 (4). https://doi.org/10.14763/2013.4.208.

OpenCDN.br (n.d.). *About OpenCDN* (https://opencdn.nic.br/en/about/.), accessed 11 Feb. 2022.

Rekhter, Y. and Gross, P. (1995). *Application of the Border Gateway Protocol in the Internet*, Request for Comments – RFC 1772, Internet Engineering Task Force (https://tools.ietf.org/html/rfc1772), accessed 11 Feb. 2022.

Rekhter, Y. and Li, T. (1995). *A Border Gateway Protocol 4 (BGP-4)*, Request for Comments – RFC 1771, Internet Engineering Task Force (https://tools.ietf.org/html/rfc1771), accessed 11 Feb. 2022.

Rosa, F. R. (2021). Internet Interconnection Infrastructure: Lessons from the Global South, *Internet Policy Review*, 10 (4). https://doi.org/10.14763/2021.4.1583.

Sacks, S., and Sherman, J. (2019). *Global Data Governance. Concepts, Obstacles, and Prospects*. New America Foundation.

Scholte, Jan Aart. (2017). 'Polycentrism and Democracy in Internet Governance'. In *The Net and the Nation State: Multidisciplinary Perspectives on Internet Governance*, edited by Uta Kohl, 165–184. Cambridge: Cambridge University Press.

Stocker, V., Knieps, G. and Dietzel, C. (2021). The Rise and Evolution of Clouds and Private Networks – Internet Interconnection, Ecosystem Fragmentation. TPRC49: The

49th Research Conference on Communication, Information and Internet Policy. http://dx.doi.org/10.2139/ssrn.3910108.

ten Oever, N. (2021). 'The Metagovernance of Internet Governance'. In *Power and Authority in Internet Governance*, edited by B. Haggart, N. Tusikov, & J. A. Scholte, 56–75. London: Routledge.

van Eeten, M. and Mueller, M. (2013). Where Is the Governance in Internet Governance?, *New Media & Society*, 15 (5), 720–736.

12

THE DISTRIBUTIONS OF DISTRIBUTED GOVERNANCE

Power, Instability and Complexity in Polycentric Data Ordering

Malcolm Campbell-Verduyn

Introduction

Periodic bursts of techno-euphoria have surrounded experiments with a set of supposedly 'new' forms of 'distributed' digital data governance over the past decade. The establishment of the 'cryptocurrency' Bitcoin in 2009 prompted ever-widening attempts after about 2013 to 'distribute' the ability to undertake, verify and publish digital transactions. In this rush of experimentation with Bitcoin's underlying technology, blockchain, a specific version of what is more generally labelled 'distributed ledger technologies' sparked trials with distributed forms of data governance in what had become highly centralized areas of activity. Distributed databases were proposed and piloted the verification and publication of digital transactions of everything from art and intellectual property to more concrete materials such as land, minerals and agricultural commodities. With great fanfare and support from start-ups, non-governmental, international and governmental organizations from around the world, competition and collaboration across a host of experiments with distributed data governance spawned sectors and levels of activity.

Common to this techno-experimentation with distribution governance is a shared desire to escape the pathologies of data centralization. The most well publicized and longstanding problems with data produced and held in more centralized data repositories is the nearly continual threat of breaches, hacks and leaks. Afflicting organizations of all types, breaches at leading multinational firms like the American credit scoring firm Experian attracted worldwide attention.[1] As debates over data centralization persisted in app-based responses to the COVID-19 pandemic (Porter and Rani 2023), a search for distributed alternatives turn to experimentation with blockchains for contact tracing, supply chain management and a host of other governance functions (Bernards et al. 2022; Campbell-Verduyn 2021).

DOI: 10.4324/9781003388418-15

Distributed data governance, generally, and blockchain technologies, specifically, have been positioned by their promoters as providing 'new' and more 'effective' forms of governance. Distribution aims to enact order through the more or less equal dispersion of power amongst the plurality of 'nodes' making up digital networks. These claims are emphasized in continual references to novel forms of democratic 'user empowerment' (Magnuson 2020; Weber 2018) and its purported ability to serve as data "antigravity" spurring tendencies towards centralization across existing data governance forms (Vergne 2020). In short, distributed data governance is said to *disperse* decision-making power, as well as *reduce* the instabilities and uncertainties associated with leaks, hacks and breaches of centralized data governance.

These claims warrant far more interrogation than has been forthcoming in studies of blockchain technology where proclamations of the benefits of 'distribution' are often uncritically taken at face value. Granted, scholarship has struggled to keep up with the continually widening efforts to 'scale-up' blockchain-based forms of distributed data governance into increasingly intricate – and sensitive – applications ranging from 'self-sovereign identities' for refugees to digital coins and 'non-fungible tokens' (NFTs) of athletes and artists (Cheesman 2022). As a result, larger questions of power have often been overlooked.

In repoliticizing this 'space' of activity, this chapter asks: how can we understand and assess claims to the novelty and efficacy of distributed data governance? This question is of some urgency to investigate in lieu of the considerable human and non-human resources being put into 'distributing' ever more activities whose governance has remained more centralized historically. These experiments in distributed data governance are attracting limited attention of not only 'geeks in basements' but that of policy-makers, public administrators, media organizations and financiers worldwide as the hype around a blockchain-based Web3 grows (Campbell-Verduyn and Huetten 2022). Moving past plentiful scandals and frauds that are often dismissed by developers as mere 'costs of doing business' when experimenting with novel technology, this chapter assesses patterns of continuity and change regarding two inter-related structural issues in blockchain-based 'distributed data governance': power concentration and instability.

The main argument advanced in this chapter is that distributed data governance is neither new nor devoid of the pathologies of more centralized digital data governance. Far from a panacea to existing problems, blockchain-based distributed data governance extends instabilities and power concentration, continuities that are often rendered unclear due to the considerable complexities surrounding these activities.

This contention is grounded in polycentric theorizing. Polycentricity embraces the complexity of "ordered chaos" in recognizing the fluidity and dispersion of decision-making power across scales and sectors of activity (Koinova et al. 2021). In turn, three structures of polycentric data ordering – norms, practices and "underlying orders" (Scholte 2021) – are drawn upon in this chapter to, first, map the less-than-original underpinnings of distributed data governance and, second, illustrate how distributed data governance extends both instabilities and concentrations of power.

Polycentric Distributed Data Ordering

Polycentrism serves as a useful heuristic for understanding contemporary data governance in dispersed geographical locations and across scales of activity. It stresses the dynamic and relational processes wherein linkages between in and across sites of activity are continually made and remade. Scholte (2021) produced such apparent "ordered chaos" from three central structures:

> *Norms*, the overarching "aspirational visions" guiding "the shared expectations for actor behavior" (Deloffre 2021).

> *Practices*, the everyday "activities, material objects and governing tools" as well as other "mundane matters" (Gadinger 2021: 1999) that Scholte (2021) divides into discursive, material, institutional and behavioural forms.

> *Underlying orders*, the "deeper structures" identified by Scholte (2021) in the relevant example of Internet governance as consisted by capitalism, techno-rationalism and embedded hierarchies of "age, ethnicity/race, gender, North-South geopolitics, and English language".

Examining each of these three structures, the following subsections illustrate how 'ordered chaos' is being produced in blockchain-based distributed data governance. In doing so, each subsection stresses the far longer lineages of such data ordering that contrast starkly with claims of novelty.

Distributed Data Norms

> [D]istributed modes of organisation [...] can be understood either as an engineering *principle*, a design *aim*, or an aspirational *claim*.
>
> *(Bodó et al. 2020)*

The formation of an overarching "aspirational vision" (Deloffre 2021) for distributed data governance did not emerge with the creation of Bitcoin in 2009. Rather, the initial cryptocurrency and subsequent competitors are best understood as the latest effort to "return to the origins" of the early Internet while maintaining standards of informational security that have developed since (Musiani and Méadel 2016). As the Internet evolved and became more centralized towards the turn of the millennium, in part to address informational security problems, discussions of 'distributed networked architectures' periodically re-surfaced. Like Bitcoin, experiments in 'distribution' sparked various scandals and controversies. In the 1990s controversy surrounded the music sharing service Napster. In the 2000s video and other file sharing services like BitTorrent courted controversy. These and other attempts to 'distribute' data inspired, and were inspired by, continual efforts at re-distributing power in wider data governance.[2] The following elements of blockchain and post-2008 distributed governance experimentation's 'origin story' form continuities with earlier attempts to 'distribute' data:

a   the initial attempt proposed by the author(s) of the Bitcoin white paper's proposal for producing, verifying and publishing digital coins with "no central authority" (Nakamoto 2008: 4);
b   subsequent discussions on the cryptography mailing list that the white paper was originally circulated in;[3] and
c   Internet forum discussions that led to the production of the first cryptocurrency in 2009.

The 'crypto' in cryptocurrency is illustrative here. Emphasizing cryptography rather than the novelty of a 'digital currency' points to the aspirational vision guiding Bitcoin's proposal and subsequent development. It situates Bitcoin as one experiment in a lineage of attempts to counter an important pathology of the increasingly centralized Internet: the growing ability of governments and large corporations to surveil online activities – what Roger Clarke (1988) identified as 'dataveillance'. Active in the 1990s and into the early new millennium so-called cypherpunks experimented with ways to counter such dataveillance. These included 'cryptocredits' and other forms of cryptographically "untraceable digital currency" (Jeong 2013). Nakamoto's aspirations for Bitcoin are thereby better understood as "a throwback" to these and other evolving efforts to counter the affordances of the 'network of networks' (Jeong 2013).

Metagovernance norms are those understood by Deloffre (2021: 1997) as emerging "through reflexive and iterative processes during which actors discuss, formulate and implement the values and principles of governance". Such discussions occurred in the mailing lists and chatrooms where Bitcoin was initially proposed. Over the course of 2008–9 (Champagne 2014), these discussions reiterated the "aspirational vision" of attaining distributed governance through "shared expectations for actor behavior" and notions of "what activities should be governed, by whom, and how" (Deloffre 2021: 1996). Implementations of these norms then occurred through the development of Bitcoin in 2009. Such metagovernance further materialized in subsequent extensions of Bitcoin's underlying blockchain technology in distributed data practices traced in the next subsections.

Distributed Data Practices

Distributed data governance is often reduced to "pirate practices" (Musiani and Méadel 2016). Specific discursive and material practices are identifiable in various versions of "pirate culture" (Lindgren and Lundström 2011). These cultures include 'cypherpunk' that centrally inspired the development of Bitcoin.[4]

Blockchain-based distributed data governance involves core *discursive* practices. These emphasize the possibilities of 'informational security' beyond centralization (Brekke 2020). Just as with the wider libertarian emphasis on achieving "structural decentralization" of the Internet (Schneider 2019), a shared discursive stress in distributed governance projects is found in the flurry of white papers published in the aftermath of Bitcoin's 2008 white paper.[5] Common to most, if not all, of these documents is a view that "the key problem of our era is the role of 'intermediaries' in all areas of society" (Swartz 2017: 90). A discursive stress on security through transparency – all transactions are legible on a shared digital ledger – spans blockchain projects at all scales, from local efforts to distribute monetary governance to planetary ambitions of climate finance (Campbell-Verduyn 2021).

However, discursive emphasis on (re-)distributed solutions to the 'middlemen problem' is far from new. Chinese cryptographer Wei Dai already in 1998 envisioned what Plassaras (2013) summarizes as a "system of untraceable medium of exchange that avoided the need for intermediaries in electronic transactions, and one in which government involvement was permanently forbidden and unnecessary". A decade prior, American cypherpunk David Chaum (1985) had proposed an electronic cash transaction system that would provide information "security without identification". Bitcoin white paper author Satoshi Nakamoto and blockchain-based projects since have followed in an established discursive tradition foregrounding distributed solutions "with the explicitly stated goal of making each and every institution obsolete" (Musiani and Méadel 2016).

Taken to the extreme, this discursive tradition has culminated in distributed data governance projects whose white papers conjure the likes of Borderless Voluntary Nations, as Bitnation (2017) calls for in constructing "the first ever digitally-constituted nation that represents both a reputation system which is managed by an algorithm named Lucy, and a monetary system which rewards participants according to their virtuous behaviour" (Faustino et al. 2021: 7). The centrality of sets of instructions that are algorithms provide information security points to the *entanglements* in distributed data governance between discursive and material practices to which the analysis now turns.

Material practices of blockchain-based informational security are just as central to distributed data governance as their discursive counterparts. The profound entanglements of the two are exemplified in Bitcoin. In the first 'cryptocurrency', for instance, algorithms materialize discursive emphasis on distribution by enabling the following:

a   the scrambling into cryptographic 'hash' codes of the identities of users and objects that are transacted directly in 'peer-to-peer' fashion;[6]

b   the verification that digital transactions have occurred in a 'distributed consensus' that relies on algorithms to resolve increasingly complex mathematical equations;

c   the publication of 'blocks' of verified digital transactions in sequential order on a 'distributed ledger'.

None of these algorithmically assisted material practices are new. As Narayanan and Clark (2017) argue in *Bitcoin's Academic Pedigree: The concept of cryptocurrencies is built from forgotten ideas in research literature*, "nearly all of the technical components of bitcoin originated in the academic literature of the 1980s and '90s". Existing material applications of knowledge were bundled together to form "[n]ew blockchain databases" that are "laid on top of diverse knowledge and material networks, involving newer and older record-keeping devices and stakeholders from formal and informal sectors" (Rodima-Taylor 2021: 149). The material practices involved in this constant negotiation between new and existing material applications of knowledge are likened by even leading blockchain developers to "a methodology for building systems that try to guarantee certain kinds of information security properties" (Vitalik Buterin cited in Brekke 2020).

In other words, blockchain-based data governance is underpinned by longstanding discursive and material practices that have attempted to enable the secure undertaking, verifying and publishing of digital transactions with varying levels of anonymity. This modality of distributed data governance is also far from novel. Rather, it extends several orders underlying what Scholte (2021) identifies as profit-oriented techno-solutions for largely young, male, Global North actors in Internet governance more generally. Drawing on Bitcoin and other post-2009 experiments with blockchain technology the next subsection further illustrates how the most recent iterations of distributed data governance extend much longer standing capitalist, gendered and colonial relations.

Distributed Underlying Orders

Hold onto your hats, boys and girls! It's a new world – a financial system without intermediaries, that anyone can access 24 hours a day with only a mobile phone and a wallet!

Dr. Jane Thomason (2021), Blockchain 'thought leader'

The original Bitcoin 'genesis' block contained the historical note: UK 'chancellor on brink of second bailout for banks'. Satoshi Nakamoto and later Bitcoin developers positioned the original cryptocurrency against the unprecedentedly large forms of state support provided to financial intermediaries in the 2007–8 global financial crisis, both through unprecedented monetary policies, such as quantitative easing programmes, and fiscal policies undertaken in rescuing insolvent firms. What economist Saifedan Ammous (2018) calls the "Bitcoin standard" is intended to provide "the decentralized alternative to central banking". Providing some support for more communal, social and post-capitalist activities,[7] such as 'solidarity finance' (Scott 2016), Bitcoin and related distributed data projects in practice mainly advance attempts at developing 'freer' versions of capitalism. In a passage from *Blockchain and the distributed reproduction of capitalist class power*, which is worth citing at length, legal scholar Robert Herian (2018) elaborates how

> [u]nder the duel banners of 'innovation' and 'progress' blockchain has become the means *du jour* for the reproduction of capitalist class power through 'world changing' technology in the so-called fourth-industrial age in which advanced Western capitalist societies now imagine themselves [... The] blockchain horizon is one in which more capitalism and with it the further and deeper entrenchment of capitalist class power are likely outcomes based on the present course of blockchain research, development and implementations. This is perhaps unsurprising however as blockchain is self-evidently a capitalist organizational form, or more specifically, to refer to capital's contemporary 'mutant form', a neoliberal one.
>
> *(Herian 2018)*

Blockchain-based distributed data projects, such as the aforementioned Bitnation, provide clear examples of how this vision of 'unfettered capitalism' materializes in projects that generally propose a "global free market for governance services" (Tempelhof 2017: 4 cited in Faustino et al. 2021). Supposedly 'novel', these twenty-first century projects extend the project of 'neoliberal' capitalist order of the late twentieth century.

The novelty of blockchain-based distributed data governance is equally challenged by continuities with longstanding gendered and colonial relations underpinning global capitalism and recently (identified) versions of 'computational capitalism' (Beller 2017) and 'data colonialism' (Couldry and Mejias 2020). Start-ups and large multinational firms, NGOs, governments as well as a flurry of individual entrepreneurs from the Global North undertake increasingly wide ranges of blockchain-based experimentation in and across the Global South (Kshetri 2017; Campbell-Verduyn and Giumelli 2022). These have ranged from trials in aid provision (Reinsberg 2021) and land reform (Rodima-Taylor 2021) to refugee identification (Cheesman 2022) and 'sustainable' supply chain management (Bernards et al. 2020). Attracting charges of what Herzfeld (2002), in an earlier pre-blockchain age, referred to as "crypto-colonialism", libertarian utopia projects like Sol in Puerto Rico took advantage of inequalities heightened by the 2018 hurricane that devastated this US territory (Yarovaya and Lucey 2018). Early speculation about possibilities for blockchain technologies to contribute to decolonial struggles, for instance with 'indigenous cryptocurrencies' experimented with by the First Nations in Canada (Alcantara and Dick 2017; Tekobbe and McKnight 2016), gave way to a growing stress on how experiments with this technology extend neo-colonial patterns of extraction and dependence as well as perpetuate wider North-South inequities (Calvão and Archer 2021; Crandall 2019; Howson 2020; Jutel 2021; Scott 2016). Blockchain, in short, is marked by "uneven geographies" (Zook and McCanless 2021).

Similarly, supposedly 'novel' post-2009 experiments in distributed data governance have extended existing 'digital gaps' such as in age and gender. Early national-level studies indicated that in countries like Canada cryptocurrency ownership and usage have largely remained the domain of young men (Huynh et al. 2020; Zhao 2017). These findings prompted continual industry attempts to improve age, and especially gender, gaps not only in the usage of blockchain applications but in participation in distributed data governance (Adams et al. 2020; Wolfson 2021). Some blockchain applications have purposely been geared towards women[8] while training programmes have been set up by the likes of the CryptoChicks Academy.[9] These efforts, however, largely advance an 'add-and-stir' approach to bringing women into male-dominated, blockchain and Internet governance more widely (Youngs 2007). They also typically fail to materialize any intersectional linkages between gender and the aforementioned colonial and "computational capitalist" underlying orders.[10]

In sum, the blockchain-based version of distributed data governance emerging since 2008 is not divorced from the underlying orders structuring poly-centric governance of the Internet more generally. While not *exclusively* doing so, Bitcoin and other experiments with blockchain technologies extend the capitalist, gendered and unequal underlying orders Scholte (2021) identified in Internet governance more widely. The libertarian discourses and practices dominating 'the space', as the industry is typically referred to, are firmly part of an underlying order that attempts to mask power relations, including through technical complexities that the next section turns to discuss.

The Complexities, Inequalities and Instabilities of Distributed Data Governance

This section argues that rather than reducing key pathologies of centralized data governance, distributed data ordering *extends* instabilities and power concentrations. Concentration-decision-making and instability are enhanced as these pathologies are largely masked by the complexities of polycentricism's 'ordered chaos'.

Despite endeavouring to distribute power, blockchain-based data governance in practice concentrates various forms of power. Since the advent of Bitcoin in 2009 tensions have continually risen between distributed data governance norms, as well as discursive and material practices, on the one hand, and both institutional and behaviour practices, on the other. Initially framed in technical jargon, these strains became more prominently political as tensions surfaced between discursive stress of Bitcoin as an "alternative to the oligopolistic market structure of third-party intermediaries in established payment systems"

(Weber 2016) and its re-production of centralized intermediaries. The production, or 'mining', of new Bitcoin wherein new tokens are accrued by the fastest node to accurately verify that transactions in the network have indeed occurred, rapidly became dominated by large mining pools. As new 'big crypto' intermediaries accumulated tokens they gained decision-making power.[11] Fears grew that their majority control could enable a '51% attack', the majority consensus required for the supposedly permanent ledger of transactions to be altered. Such fears were repeated in Ethereum, the leading rival blockchain developed "to take the internet to its logical conclusion: total decentralization" (Stephen Tual cited in Swartz 2017). In practice, however, over half of the Ethereum blockchain became hosted on corporate servers, including those of American tech behemoth Amazon Web Services (Beaumier and Kalomeni 2022). While this concentration of power in Ethereum has not attracted wider attention, the 'civil war' that occurred within 'distributed' communities surrounding the original cryptocurrency exemplified the extension of this pathology of centralized data governance.

The 2017 Bitcoin civil war revolved around the growing size of the permanent ledger. Increasing usage of the first cryptocurrency was being held back by the slowing down of transaction processing and verification times. One group, made up of pools of producers ('miners') and other larger companies, sought to develop an offshoot or 'fork' of Bitcoin to encourage even wider usage. Over 50 companies signed the so-called New York Bitcoin Scaling Agreement in May 2017.[12] This agreement, however, attracted the ire of individual users keen on maintaining the (libertarian) 'spirit of Satoshi'. Tampering with the original protocol underlying Bitcoin was regarded as sacrilege. However, this latter group of 'protocol purists' lost out to the former group of cryptocurrency 'expansionists'. The original Bitcoin was split into two, with a new token called Bitcoin Cash emerging from Bitcoin Core with an enhanced transaction processing speed.

The bitterly fought Bitcoin Civil War illustrated both the agenda-setting and decision-making power of a concentrated group of industry insiders that have come to more widely represent the key bureaucrats of blockchains, or "blockocrats" (Kavanagh and Ennis 2021). In chatrooms and industry events as well as in the comments on news sites, an issue initially regarded as 'off limits' – tampering with the protocol – was put forward and eventually acted upon by a small group, the 0.01% of 'community' members said to control more than a quarter of the cryptocurrency (Makarov and Schoar 2021). The split was a decision at odds with the distributed decision-making ethos stressed in both discursive practices and norms of distributed data governance (Campbell-Verduyn and Goguen 2019). It was a decision that revealed tensions in the core goals and objectives that have not been resolved as cryptocurrencies, including Bitcoin Cash, further split to enhance their broader 'usability'.

The extension of power concentration in distributed data governance is further illustrated in the other manner through which cryptocurrencies are procured: via formal exchanges. Since their origins, the practices of crypto-currency exchanges have stood in stark contrast with the wider norms, as well as discursive and material practices of distributed data governance. This is because these organizations do not distribute but rather concentrate data on servers. They provide bank-like custodial services for their clients. Like banks, they have also suffered hacks and other attacks on what are centralized 'honeypots' of customer data (Ogundeij 2016).[13] Unlike individual bank hacks, however, attacks of crypto-exchanges have sparked turmoil across the 'distributed' space. These instabilities emerged most spectacularly when leading crypto-exchange Mt. Gox announced in 2014 that it had lost nearly $500 million worth of Bitcoin over a period of three years. The Tokyo-based exchange suspended trading and filed for bankruptcy, leaving clients in a protracted battle to recover part of their funds. Despite efforts at improving cyber security, leading exchanges have continued to follow a centralized data storage model in providing custodial services to clients. As the size of these and other exchanges has grown, along with their increasing interconnectedness with the existing system the likes of NASDAQ-listed Coinbase have been identified by global financial regulators as conduits to wider global financial instability (Bank for International Settlements 2015; Chimienti et al. 2019; Financial Stability Board 2022). Although instability remained largely confined to cryptocurrency markets when the world's second largest exchange, FTX, declared bankruptcy in late 2022 and was hacked the day after, these events and earlier comparable events were likened to the fall of Lehman Brothers in 2008 and highlighted inequalities in various ways the inside investors were able to recoup funds (Rogers 2022; Young 2022).

The twin pathologies of concentrated power and instabilities are not *automatically* extended into blockchain-based attempts at distributed data governance. Continual efforts have been made to re-enforce distributed data governance practices. This is most clearly revealed in so-called 'Decentralized Finance' (DeFi), the so-called 'wild west' of finance (Kruppa and Murphy 2019). Here Decentralized Exchanges (DEXs) provide forums where the exchange of cryptocurrencies occurs in peer-to-peer manners with little to no data retained, thereby better reflecting the original ethos of distributed data governance. Nevertheless, as they have grown in size[14] (with the largest DEX Uniswap facilitating nearly half the volume as Coinbase, the largest 'centralized exchange' [CEX]), DEXs have become subjected to more concentrated forms of decision-making. DEXs have come under the remit of AML/CFT standards promulgated by the Financial Action Task Force (FATF), an intergovernmental organization based in Paris, France. While its deliberations are for the most part open – FATF draft guidance is typically published for public comment – FATF decisions are ultimately undertaken by a concentrated group of member state representatives. Other global financial regulators, such as the Bank for International Settlements have referenced the 'decentralisation illusion' of DeFi pointing to widespread reproduction of centralized intermediaries in and across 'the space' (Aramonte et al. 2021) that has replicated the kinds of 're-intermediation' seen in 'financial technology' (fintech) more generally (Langley and Leyshon 2021).

Thus, despite these and further attempts at ensuring distribution in the 'space',[15] blockchain-based distributed data governance has remained replete with tensions between centralized institutional and behavioural practices, on the one hand, and the norms as well as discursive and material practices of distributed data governance on the other. Industry organizations have emerged as centralized focal points for ordering 'distributed activities'. The Bitcoin Foundation was an early attempt by leading industry figures to form a concentrated governing council. The Ethereum Foundation has similarly concentrated decision-making within a small group of 'core' developers and coders. Meanwhile, industry bodies spanning blockchains have emerged to develop 'solutions' for complying with the likes of anti-money laundering and counter the finance of terrorism (AML/CFT) standards promulgated by the FATF. These bodies have closely resembled the very centralized activities that distributed data governance originally arose to bypass and counter (Campbell-Verduyn and Huetten 2021). Finally growing attention to the environmental impacts of Bitcoin production led to the formation of a Bitcoin Mining Council. Led by two CEOs of American multinationals, Tesla's Elon Musk and Micro-Strategy's Michael Saylor, this council sought to establish standards between large mining pools for energy reporting in line with a wider stress on Environmental, Social, Governance (ESG). This proposal in May 2021 was compared to a 'cartel' like the Organization of Petroleum Exporting Countries (OPEC), as well as to the centralized decision-making that led to the aforementioned 2017 New York Bitcoin Scaling Agreement (Hochstein and Harkin 2021).

These further examples are indicative of how blockchain-based distributed data governance has extended since 2009 the very pathologies of centralized data governance that blockchain-based governance has been discursively positioned as overcoming. Pathologies of instability and concentration of power overlap, with the former feeding into the latter and vice versa. For example, the hack of what in 2016 was $120 million worth of crowdfunded-raised tokens through the original Decentralized Autonomous Organization, The DAO, was resolved after calls for Vitalik Buterin, the 24-year-old founder of the Ethereum blockchain, and a 'core' group of developers to formally adopt a previously informal set of rules[16] that standardized interactions between the disparate applications on this blockchain (Buntix 2017). While much attention fixated on the instability of this and other hacks in blockchain-based 'distributed' data projects, far less attention has been granted to the potential for wider instability and growing concentration of power this episode illustrated. This inattention is in part due to the growing complexity of 'ordered chaos'. As layer upon layer of governance practices have been added within and between blockchain projects, concentrations of power have become increasingly difficult for users, developers and regulators alike to pinpoint. A growing 'patchwork' (Kiviat 2015: 575) of standards have long been

TABLE 12.1 Polycentricity in blockchain-based global digital data governance

Actor Type	Examples
Industry Associations	Digital Chamber of Commerce, Ethereum Enterprise Alliance, Global Blockchain Business Council, Hyperledger, International Association of Trusted Blockchain Applications, Financial Blockchain Shenzhen Consortium
Internet Governance Organizations	International Telecommunication Union, Internet Corporation for Assigned Names and Numbers (ICANN), World Wide Web Consortium (W3C)
Multinational Technology Firms	Amazon Web Services, Microsoft, IBM, Tencent
International Organizations	Bank for International Settlements, International Monetary Fund, Financial Stability Board, Organization for Economic Cooperation and Development

identified in the private industry associations, public and quasi-public international organizations whose activities were described above. Added to this have been the (re-)entry of longstanding Internet governance organizations into blockchain activities that, as previously noted, built on previous experiments in Internet governance (see overview in Table 12.1). In this growing market for ordering, with a growing number of centers of decision-making, locating concentrations of power and the kinds of 'fault lines' emerging across what are increasingly complex 'informational infrastructures' has become increasingly difficult (Campbell-Verduyn et al. 2019).

Far from the panacea to multifold problems involved with centralized data governance, therefore, the distribution of distributed data governance exemplified by Bitcoin and blockchains since 2009 has remained concentrated and unstable. Growing complexity in both governance practices and behaviours such as the on-going 'blockchainization' of everything from abstract art to greenhouse gases renders the very recognition of such pathologies increasingly difficult. This is a problem as contrary to claims of individual empowerment, users subjected to rampant hacks and scams in 'the space' are left with little clear recourse once transactions have been rendered permanent on distributed ledgers. Claims of enhanced stability and power distribution all too often taken at face value fall well short of when a polycentric lens is employed to scrutinize efforts to distribute data governance.

Conclusion

Overlooked in the techno-hype surrounding 'novelty', blockchain-based experiments in distributed data governance have since 2009 extended and enhanced the pathologies of centralized data governance. This chapter first outlined continuities between the pre- and post-2009 norms, practices and underlying orders informing blockchain experiments. In a second instance the polycentric approach illustrated continuities and complexities in the pathologies afflicting data governance, both in its more centralized and 'distributed' forms.

A host of questions to be explored in future research arise from this chapter's identification of overlaps between (de)centralized and distributed forms of data governance: can the pathologies of power concentration and instability genuinely be overcome? Or are these pathologies unchangeable structural features of digital data governance in an age of centralized platforms? Can we expect chronic instabilities and concentration in power to ever be overcome in further data governance experiments? Does their digital nature preclude remedies? Is socio-technical experimentation in data governance inevitably unstable and a conduit to concentrations of power?

In investigating these questions, further research will benefit from a stress on norms, practices and underlying orders that a polycentric lens on governing draws attention to. Polycentricism usefully alerts us to how the distribution of 'distributed data governance' is continually shaped by underlying structures, as well as by norms and practices whose inner workings and interrelations are becoming increasingly complex and difficult for even the most socio-technically attuned research to navigate. Polycentric frameworks, generally, can help to pierce through the widespread hype surrounding techno-experimentation in a hyper-capitalist age. On-going research will do well to draw on insights from polycentricism in heeding Herian's (2018) call to consider experimentation against the "backdrop of continuing struggles to achieve meaningful and stable regulation and governance over commercial platforms, within networks, and in consideration of interoperability and the broader architecture of the Internet".

Notes

1 Experian's 2017 server breach exposed personal and transactional data on almost half of the US population over a period of three months.
2 Most famously Barlow (1996) but also for instance https://dci.mit.edu/decentralizedweb.
3 For instance, Nakamoto's response that the underlying Bitcoin "proof-of-work chain is how all the synchronisation, distributed database and global view problems you've asked about are solved" (cited in Champagne 2014: 69).
4 A more elaborate history of these "pirate cultures" can be found in Brunton (2019).
5 White papers are promotional documents largely intended for marketing to investors but that also wax lyrically about their philosophical grounding.
6 See Monsees (2019: 62) for a detailed description of public key cryptography.
7 These alternatives have struggled to scale and overcome tensions with capitalist counterparts (Dallyn and Frenzel 2021).
8 www.womenscoin.com.
9 https://cryptochicksacademy.com see also https://blockchainbywomen.com and https://globalwomeninblockchain.org.
10 For an intersectional analysis of cryptocurrency see Henshaw (2022).
11 A marine animal theme is typically used to categorise large holders of BTC. Those possessing around 1000 BTC are known as sharks, those with around 5000 BTC as whales, and those with more than 5000 BTC as humpbacks. A January 2021

estimate found these three categories to add up to more than a third of the Bitcoin network, at 13.3%, 18.4% and 6.6%, respectively (Schultze-Kraft 2021).

12 https://dcgco.medium.com/bitcoin-scaling-agreement-at-consensus-2017-133521fe9a77.

13 For a list up see https://bravenewcoin.com/insights/36-bitcoin-exchanges-that-a re-no-longer-with-us.

14 For an overview see www.theblockcrypto.com/data/decentralized-finance/dex-non-custodial.

15 Including with 'cross-chain interoperability' projects proposing bridges between increasingly concentrated blockchains and non-blockchain activities. Yet even here projects such as Polychain have been hacked, losing some $12 million in 2021.

16 The "Ethereum Request for Comment" number 22.

Acknowledgements

Feedback from Angie Raymond, Carolina Aguerre, Daniel McCarthy and Tony Porter helped to substantially improve this chapter and is gratefully acknowledged.

References

Adams, P.R., Frizzo-Barker, J., Ackah, B.B. and Chow-White, P.A. (2019) Meetups: Making space for women on the blockchain. In *Blockchain and Web 3.0.*, Ragnedda, M., and G. Destefanis, eds. New York: Routledge, pp. 48–61.

Alcantara, C. and Dick, C. (2017) Decolonization in a digital age: cryptocurrencies and indigenous self-determination in Canada. *Canadian Journal of Law & Society*, 32 (1): 19–35.

Ammous, S. (2018) *The bitcoin standard: the decentralized alternative to central banking*. John Wiley & Sons.

Aramonte, S., Huang, W. and Schrimpf, A. (2021) DeFi risks and the decentralisation illusion. *Bank for International Settlements Quarterly Review*, 6 December. Available at: https://www.bis.org/publ/qtrpdf/r_qt2112b.htm.

Bank for International Settlements (2015) *Digital currencies*. Available at: https://www.bis.org/cpmi/publ/d137.pdf.

Barlow, J.P. (1996) A declaration of the independence of cyberspace. Available at: http s://www.eff.org/cyberspace-independence.

Beaumier, G. and Kalomeni, K. (2022) Ruling through technology: politicizing blockchain services. *Review of International Political Economy*, 29(6): 2135–2158.

Bernards, N., Campbell-Verduyn, M., Rodima-Taylor, D., Duberry, J., DuPont, Q., Dimmelmeier, A., Huetten, M., Mahrenbach, L.C., Porter, T. and Reinsberg, B. (2020) Interrogating technology-led experiments in sustainability governance. *Global Policy*, 11(4): 523–531.

Bernards, N., Campbell-Verduyn, M. and Rodima-Taylor, D. (2022) The veil of transparency: blockchain and sustainability governance in global supply chains. *Environment and Planning C: Politics and Space*, earlyView. https://doi.org/10.1177/23996544221142763.

Beller, J. (2017) *The message is murder: Substrates of computational capital*. Pluto Press.

Bodó, B., Brekke, J.K. and Hoepman, J.H. (2021) Decentralisation in the blockchain space. *Internet Policy Review*, 10(2). https://doi.org/10.14763/2021.2.1560.

Brekke, J.K. (2020) Hacker-engineers and their Economies: The political economy of decentralised networks and 'cryptoeconomics'. *New Political Economy*. Epub ahead of print 12 August 2020. doi:10.1080/13563467.2020.1806223.

Brunton, Finn (2019) *Digital cash: The unknown history of the anarchists, utopians, and technologists who created cryptocurrency.* Princeton University Press.

Buntix, J. P. (2017) ERC20 token standard officially formalized by Ethereum developers. Available at: https://themerkle.com/erc20-token-standard-has-now-been-officially-formalized-by-the-ethereum-developers/ [Accessed 6 November 2020].

Calvão, F. and Archer, M. (2021) Digital extraction: Blockchain traceability in mineral supply chains. *Political Geography*, 87(May): 1–12.

Campbell-Verduyn, M. (2021) The pandemic techno-solutionist dilemma. *Global Perspectives*, 2(1): 1–5.

Campbell-Verduyn, M. (2023) Conjuring a cooler world? Imaginaries of improvement in blockchain climate finance experiments. *Environment and Planning C: Politics and Space*. OnlineFirst. Available at: https://doi.org/10.1177/23996544231162858.

Campbell-Verduyn, M. and Goguen, M. (2019) Blockchains, trust and action nets: Extending the pathologies of financial globalization. *Global Networks*, 19(3): 308–328.

Campbell-Verduyn, M., Goguen, M. and Porter, T. (2019) Finding fault lines in long chains of financial information. *Review of International Political Economy*, 26(5): 911–937.

Campbell-Verduyn, M. and Huetten, M. (2021) The formal, financial and fraught route to global digital identity governance. *Frontiers in Blockchain*, 4: 1–12.

Campbell-Verduyn, Malcolm, and Francesco Giumelli (2022) Enrolling into exclusion: African blockchain and decolonial ambitions in an evolving finance/security infrastructure. *Journal of Cultural Economy*, 15(4): 524–543.

Campbell-Verduyn, M. and Huetten, M. (2022) From peer-regulated divisions to unity in Web3: Implications of blockchain's evolution for internet governance. *Global Cooperation Research Quarterly*, 2–3. Available at: https://www.gcr21.org/publications/gcr/gcr-quarterly-magazine/global-cooperation-research-2-3-/-2022.

Champagne, P. (2014) *The book of Satoshi.* Lexington, KY: e53 Publishing.

Chaum, D. (1985) Security without identification: Transaction systems to make big brother obsolete. *Communications of the ACM*, 28(10): 1030–1044.

Cheesman, M. (2022) Self-sovereignty for refugees? The contested horizons of digital identity. *Geopolitics*, 27(1): 134–159.

Chimienti, M.T., Kochanska, U. and Pinna, A. (2019) Understanding the crypto-asset phenomenon, its risks and measurement issues. *European Central Bank Economic Bulletin*. Available at: https://www.ecb.europa.eu/pub/economic-bulletin/articles/2019/html/ecb.ebart201905_03~c83aeaa44c.en.html.

Clarke, R. (1988) Information technology and dataveillance. *Communications of the ACM*, 31(5): 498–512.

Couldry, N. and Mejias, U.A. (2020) *The costs of connection: How data are colonizing human life and appropriating it for capitalism.* Stanford University Press.

Cowen, N. (2020) Markets for rules: The promise and peril of blockchain distributed governance. *Journal of Entrepreneurship and Public Policy*, 9(2): 213–226.

Crandall, J. (2019) Blockchains and the "Chains of Empire": Contextualizing blockchain, cryptocurrency, and neoliberalism in Puerto Rico. *Design and Culture*, 11(3): 279–300.

Dallyn, S. and Frenzel, F. (2021) The Challenge of Building a Scalable Postcapitalist Commons: The Limits of FairCoin as a Commons-Based Cryptocurrency. *Antipode*, 53(3): 859–883.

De Filippi, Primavera and Aaron Wright (2018) *Blockchain and the law: The rule of code.* Harvard University Press.

Deloffre, Maryam (2021) Metagovernance norms and polycentricity in global humanitarian governance. *International Studies Review*, 23(4): 1996–1999.

DuPont, Quinn (2019) *Cryptocurrencies and blockchains.* Polity

Faustino, Sandra, Inês Faria and Rafael Marques (2021) The myths and legends of King Satoshi and Knights of Blockchain. *Journal of Cultural Economy*, 5(1): 67–80.

Financial Stability Board (2022) *Assessment of risks to financial stability from crypto-assets.* Available at: https://www.fsb.org/wp-content/uploads/P160222.pdf.

Gadinger, Frank (2021) Polycentric governance through the lens of practice. *International Studies Review*, 23(4): 1999–2002.

Golumbia, David (2016) *The politics of Bitcoin: Software as right-wing extremism.* Forerunners – Ideas First: University of Minnesota Press.

Henshaw, A. (2023) "Women, consider crypto": Gender in the virtual economy of decentralized finance. *Politics & Gender*, 19(2): 560–584.

Herian, Robert (2018) Blockchain and the distributed reproduction of capitalist class power. In *MoneyLab Reader 2: Overcoming the hype*, Gloerich, Inte, Geert Lovink, and Patrick de Vries, eds. Amsterdam: Institute of Network Cultures, pp. 43–51.

Herian, Robert (2019) *Regulating blockchain.* London: Routledge.

Herzfeld, M. (2002) The absent presence: Discourses of crypto-colonialism. *South Atlantic Quarterly*, 101: 899–926.

Hochstein, M. and Harkin, C. (2021) 'This isn't the start of OPEC': New Bitcoin Mining Council just wants to promote greener practices, member says. *Coindesk*, 25 May. Available at: https://www.coindesk.com/business/2021/05/25/this-isnt-the-start-of-opec-new-bitcoin-mining-council-just-wants-to-promote-greener-practices-member-says/.

Howson, P. (2020) Climate crises and crypto-colonialism: Conjuring value on the blockchain frontiers of the Global South. *Frontiers in Blockchain*, 3. Available at: https://www.frontiersin.org/articles/10.3389/fbloc.2020.00022/full.

Huynh, K., Henry, C., Nicholls, G. and Nicholson, M. (2020) Benchmarking bitcoin adoption in Canada: Awareness, ownership and usage in 2018. *Ledger*, 5: 74–88.

Jeong, S. (2013) The Bitcoin protocol as law, and the politics of a stateless currency. Available at SSRN: https://papers.ssrn.com/sol3/papers.cfm?abstract_id=2294124.

Jutel, O. (2021) Blockchain imperialism in the Pacific. *Big Data & Society*, 8(1): 1–14.

Kavanagh, D. and Ennis, P.J. (2020) Cryptocurrencies and the emergence of blockocracy. *The Information Society*, 36(5): 290–300.

Kiviat, T.I. (2015) Beyond bitcoin: Issues in regulating blockchain transactions. *Duke Law Journal*, 65: 569–608.

Koinova, Maria, Maryam Z. Deloffre, Frank Gadinger, Zeynep S. Mencutek, Jan Aart Scholte, and Jens Steffek (2021) It's ordered chaos: What really makes polycentrism work. *International Studies Review*, 23(4): 1988–2018.

Kruppa, M. and Murphy, H. (2019) 'DeFi' movement promises high interest but high risk. *Financial Times*, 30 December.

Kshetri, N. (2017) Will blockchain emerge as a tool to break the poverty chain in the Global South? *Third World Quarterly*, 38(8): 1710–1732.

Langley, P. and Leyshon, A. (2021) The platform political economy of fintech: Reinter-mediation, consolidation and capitalisation. *New Political Economy*, 26(3): 376–388.

Lindgren, S. and Lundström, R. (2011) Pirate culture and hacktivist mobilization: The cultural and social protocols of #WikiLeaks on Twitter. *New Media & Society*, 13(6): 999–1018.

Magnuson, W. (2020) *Blockchain democracy: Technology, law and the rule of the crowd.* Cambridge University Press.

Makarov, I. and Schoar, A. (2021) Blockchain analysis of the Bitcoin market. *National Bureau of Economic Research.* doi:10.3386/w29396.

Monsees, L. (2019) *Crypto-politics: Encryption and democratic practices in the digital era*. New York: Routledge.

Musiani, F. and Méadel, C. (2016) "Reclaiming the Internet" with distributed architectures: An introduction. *First Monday*, 21 (12). https://doi.org/10.5210/fm.v21i12.7101.

Nakamoto, S. (2008) Bitcoin: A peer-to-peer electronic cash system. Bitcoin.org [Online]. Available at: https://bitcoin.org/bitcoin.pdf.

Narayanan, A. and Clark, J. (2017) Bitcoin's academic pedigree: The concept of crypto-currencies is built from forgotten ideas in research literature. *Queue*, 15(4): 20–49.

Ogundeij, O. (2016) Centralized exchanges are "honeypots for thieves", says expert. *Cointelegraph*, 9 August. Available at: https://cointelegraph.com/news/centralize d-exchanges-are-honeypots-for-thieves-says-expert.

Plassaras, N.A. (2013) Regulating digital currencies: Bringing Bitcoin within the reach of IMF. *Chicago Journal of International Law*, 14(1): 377–407.

Porter, T. and Rani (2023). Legitimacy and space in the use of technologies for environmental and social governance: The cases of human trafficking and COVID-19 contact tracing. *Environment and Planning C: Politics and Space*. OnlineFirst. https://doi.org/10.1177/23996544231184053.

Reinsberg, B. (2019) Blockchain technology and the governance of foreign aid. *Journal of Institutional Economics*, 15(3): 413–429.

Rodima-Taylor, D. (2021) Digitalizing land administration: The geographies and temporalities of infrastructural promise. *Geoforum*, 122(June): 140–151.

Rogers, T. (2022) Crypto collapse reverberates widely among black American investors. *Financial Times*, 5 July.

Schneider, N. (2019) Decentralization: An incomplete ambition. *Journal of Cultural Economy*, 12(4): 265–285.

Scholte, J. A. (2021) Structuring polycentrism: Norms, practices and underlying orders in internet governance. *International Studies Review*, 23(4): 1999–2018.

Schultze-Kraft, R. (2021) No, bitcoin ownership is not highly concentrated – but whales are accumulating. *Glassnode Insights*, 2 February. https://insights.glassnode.com/bit coin-supply-distribution/.

Scott, B. (2016) How can cryptocurrency and blockchain technology play a role in building social and solidarity finance? (No. 2016–1). United Nations Research Institute for Social Development Working Paper. Available at: https://www.econstor.eu/handle/10419/148750.

Swartz, L. (2017) Blockchain dreams: Imagining techno-economic alternatives after Bitcoin. In *Another economy is possible: Culture and economy in a time of crisis*, Castells, M. ed. Cambridge: Polity.

Tekobbe, C. and McKnight, J.C. (2016) Indigenous cryptocurrency: Affective capitalism and rhetorics of sovereignty. *First Monday*. https://doi.org/10.5210/fm.v21i10.6955.

Thomason, J. (2021) DeFi: Who, what and how to regulate in a borderless, code-governed world? *Cointelegraph*, 25 September. https://cointelegraph.com/news/defi-who-what-and-how-to-regulate-in-a-borderless-code-governed-world.

Vergne, J.P. (2020) Decentralized vs. distributed organization: Blockchain, machine learning and the future of the digital platform. *Organization Theory*, 1(4): 1–26.

Weber, Beat (2016) Bitcoin and the legitimacy crisis of money. *Cambridge Journal of Economics*, 40(1): 17–41.

Weber, Beat (2018) *Democratizing money? Debating legitimacy in monetary reform proposals*. Cambridge University Press.

Westermeier, C. (2020) Money is data–the platformization of financial transactions. *Information, Communication & Society*, 23(14): 2047–2063.

Wolfson, R. (2021) WEF report suggests women underrepresented in blockchain, points to solutions. *Cointelegraph*, 4 April. Available at: https://cointelegraph.com/news/wef-report-suggests-women-underrepresented-in-blockchain-points-to-solutions.

Yarovaya, L. and Lucey, B. (2018) Bitcoin rich kids in Puerto Rico: Crypto utopia or crypto-colonialism. *The Conversation*, 14 February. Available at: https://theconversation.com/bitcoin-rich-kids-in-puerto-rico-crypto-utopia-or-crypto-colonialism-91527.

Young, M. (2022) FTX hacker is now the 35th largest holder of ETH. *Cointelegraph*, 16 November. Available at: https://cointelegraph.com/news/ftx-hacker-is-now-the-35th-largest-holder-of-eth.

Youngs, G. (2007) *Global political economy in the information age: Power and inequality.* Routledge.

Zhao, T. (2017) Blockchain for babyboomers: What stops older generation from using Bitcoin? *Cointelegraph*, 16 July. Available at: https://cointelegraph.com/news/blockchain-for-babyboomers-what-stops-older-generation-from-using-bitcoin.

Zook, M. and McCanless, M. (2021) Mapping the uneven geographies of digital phenomena: The case of blockchain. *Canadian Geographer*, 66(1), 23–36.

13

POLYCENTRIC THEORY DIFFUSION AND AI GOVERNANCE

Janet Hui Xue

Introduction

Discussion of the development and evolution of artificial intelligence (AI) technologies tends to focus on big tech companies and the confrontational positioning of the so-called powerhouses of AI technologies: the USA and China. However, their focus on either big tech or big countries risks oversimplifying the complexity of AI governance. Polycentricity's focus on multiple centres of power and authority, this chapter argues, provides theoretical lenses through which to explain new features associated with using AI applications, such as distributed data networks across jurisdictions. The lens of polycentric governance adds much-needed nuance concerning the use of digital data within human–machine co-existence. Stress on multiple centres of so-called AI hubs brings into focus a growing area of debate on how to redefine the roles of human beings in a digital world. In other words, polycentric governance may widen the debate over AI to the roles humans play in data-informed automated decision-making, human-robot in production lines, and algorithmic decision-making based on chatbots.

This chapter makes two contributions. First, it explains the attributes of polycentricity shaping the global implementation of AI technology. It highlights two levels of complexity – namely computing complexity and social complexity – caused by the features of multiple centres of power implementing AI technologies, as well as the tension between individual human beings' interventions (e.g., the human in the loop) and automated decision-making. Second, the chapter argues that norms, code, laws, and markets in the development of an AI commons will aim to guide the development of technologies that maximise their social benefits to society at large instead of favouring a few corporations' or governments' interests. Polycentricity helps guide the empowerment of individuals to participate

DOI: 10.4324/9781003388418-16

cooperatively with the aim of reducing the risk of the concentration of power in a world in which the roles of humans are being redefined.

1 Polycentric AI Governance

The Bloomington School explains how polycentricity has three features: (1) multiple centres of semiautonomous decision-making; (2) the existence of a single system of rules (be they institutionally or culturally enforced); and (3) the existence of a spontaneous social order as the outcome of evolutionary competition between different ideas, methods, and ways of life (Aligica and Tarko 2011; Carlisle and Gruby 2017). In polycentric governance, there is no single decision centre with ultimate authority (Stephan et al. 2019), but instead multiple decision-making centres. The attributes of polycentric AI emerge as two key aspects: diverse definitions of AI and multiple centres of policy discourse.

The attributes of polycentricity are first shown in definitions for AI emerging across communities. The dispersion of the technical definition-making process also reflects an attempt to order this technology, which builds a foundation for its formal governance. The term "artificial intelligence" is often used to describe many different things – from big data to data analytics to deep learning. Various definitions of AI are used by several different communities, such as scientific communities, regulatory communities, and corporate communities. AI was originally quite broadly defined. John McCarthy (2007) described AI as "the science and engineering of making intelligent machines, especially intelligent computer programs." However, discipline-based definitions limit the complexity of social realities. According to the High-Level Expert Group on AI of the European Commission:

> AI systems are software (and possibly also hardware) systems designed by humans that, given a complex goal, act in the physical or digital dimension by perceiving their environment through data acquisition, interpreting the collected structured or unstructured data, reasoning on the knowledge, or processing the information, derived from this data and deciding the best action(s) to take to achieve the given goal.
>
> *(European Commission 2021, ft. 1)*

AI systems may consist of networks, data, computing power, and applications with features of "learning, reasoning, or modelling implemented with the techniques and approaches" (Council of the European Union 2021). Examples here are automated recommendation systems of communication, or remote biometrics access for identification management. The common attributes to certain AI systems, such as systems that include unsupervised machine learning (ML), reflect on what Polanyi called "self-coordination" (1951, p. 176) in the dynamic of a constantly evolving, "self-learning" system. A known problem for most

ML and AI technologies is their "black-box" nature, which means it is not possible generally to explain the characteristics of a model or its biases by inspecting the trained model or the algorithms used. One distinction is between systems that enforce rules as opposed to those making recommendations; another is between systems that search for a match to input information as opposed to systems that classify information (Gorwa et al. 2020). ML can also be differentiated into systems that automate routine operations and systems that improve decision-making (Veale and Brass 2019). The different approaches of the algorithmic design and platform logic that embeds most of these ML models underscore the diverse rules, semi-autonomous decision-making centres, and to some extent some spontaneity in the organisation of these systems which account for the polycentric characteristics of the Bloomington School developed earlier.

A second aspect of polycentricity in the emergence of AI are the multiple centres of policy discourse and of authority. Big companies have acted rapidly and have taken the lead in the conversation on ethical AI and responsible AI. For example, Microsoft's Responsible AI Standard is a guide for building AI systems (Microsoft 2022). Even traditionally non-digital companies like IKEA are also taking a leap into digital transformation, which not only participates in developing ethical principles of developing AI but also dedicates efforts to operationalise the AI blueprint to its business model (Stackpole 2021). International governmental organisations have begun to promote their policy frameworks. Standardisation bodies such as the International Organization for Standardization (ISO)/International Electrotechnical Commission (IEC), the Institute of Electrical and Electronics Engineers (IEEE), and the National Institute of Standards and Technology (NIST) have introduced industrial development benchmarks for AI. In addition, numerous self-regulatory initiatives, such as the Global Partnership for AI, have also called for a more inclusive policy framework. Other international AI policy frameworks are prominent, including the AI principles agreed upon by the Organisation for Economic Co-operation and Development (OECD) members and subsequently adopted by the G20. Yet, the 142 United Nations (UN) Member States are not represented in many of these initiatives (Cihon et al. 2020). These countries often lack sufficient technical capacity such as sophisticated digital infrastructure to support large-scale computing power, and they are also unable to leverage sufficient power to render their national interests visible within global policy schemes.

UNESCO's Recommendation on the Ethics of Artificial Intelligence, approved by 193 Member States in November 2021, is a landmark that has to a certain extent centralised some of the discursive dispersion and repetition of previous policy discussions. It aims to become an "ethical compass" as well as a "normative bedrock" for what is yet envisioned in an increasingly watchful environment on the advances of AI, for which from a polycentric perspective more visible and authoritative institutional actors are needed at a global and national level.

Furthermore, currently available policies mostly centre on consumer-based applications, but guidelines are still not available concerning the industrial use of these technologies, where human employees are also involved. In response to national AI strategies and international technical standards, organisations are still left on their own to attend to the implementation of these systems and they are centres of decision-making as such, configuring a diverse landscape of actors. While some leading corporations have made more explicit their rules and procedures about AI, and are advocating for self-regulation, smaller organisations and individuals affected by AI technologies are excluded from central debates.

2 Attributes of the Polycentricity of "Personal Data" in AI Applications

Developing AI demands constant data acquisition. This practice is not always aligned with and is even often in opposition to some basic principles of data governance worldwide, such as data minimisation, standardisation of the quality of data, and transparency of data use. Personal data are valuable for developing AI as a general-purpose technology for personalised services, such as the conversational AI, because personal data are used to identify, profile, and predict users' online or offline behaviours, facial expressions, and emotions. Users' behavioural data are collected and distributed by multiple data centres.

However, not all data related to a person are treated as personal data subject to data protection laws. From a legal regulation perspective, identifiability is the critical feature for determining whether personal data are treated and protected under data protection laws, such as the General Data Protection Regulation (EU) 2016/679 (GDPR). According to Article 4(1) of GDPR, "personal data" refers to any information relating to an identified or identifiable natural person ("data subject") – a person who can be identified, directly or indirectly, by reference to an identifier such as a name, an identification number, location data, an online identifier, or one or more factors specific to the physical, physiological, genetic, mental, economic, cultural, or social identity of that person. The legal definition also serves as a starting point to guide app developers in their application of privacy-preserving technology to minimise data collection and in the anonymisation of data to make such data subjects less identifiable. However, some circumstances may incentivise personal data to be collected and used for the public interest, such as during a public health crisis like a pandemic. In a pandemic, users' travel histories could be used to monitor whether they have come into contact with carriers of the disease or virus, perhaps in the form of heat maps tracking community mobility. Similarly, such applications can also be used to track energy consumption and medical facility supplies (e.g., vaccination distribution at the local level). AI also challenges traditional regulatory approaches based on distinguishing between "general personal data" (e.g., email addresses) and "sensitive personal data" (e.g., biometric data such as facial data).

TABLE 13.1 Key attributes of the polycentricity of "personal data" in AI applications

Complexity of reality	Classifying data	Processing data	Sense-making	Intelligence
Computing complexity	Structured data Unstructured data	Cleaning data Converting data to the right format Clearing and tokenising data Labelling data Modelling data	Big data analytics Machine learning Deep learning	Digital identity Digital profiles Semi-autonomous/fully autonomous conversation/work–life management Augmented digital life
Social complexity	Structured social realities Unstructured social realities	Quantified Measured Predictable Racial hatred Augmented disinformation Ideological division Social transformation	Cultural tribes Political opinion Community formulation	Code Laws Markets Norms

Traditional approaches to governing data use tend to focus on compliance within their jurisdictions. However, jurisdiction-focused compliance is not compatible with the features of data stored and processed across national borders for AI applications. Analysing nuanced interpretations of laws in an applicable context becomes increasingly challenging in terms of reaching a mutual understanding between legislators and legal practitioners, engineers, and citizens. These difficulties lie in the complexity of computing on top of the complexity of social reality because the data used in AI applications are now distributed to more diverse digital agents than ever before.

The polycentric nature of data use in AI applications massively varies among dataset formats, and their existence in distributed data centres across jurisdictions introduces more problems in terms of governing AI applications. While scrutinising the details of polycentric diffusion that are featured in data use within AI applications, this section highlights complexities at two levels: computing complexity and social complexity. These are summarised in Table 13.1.

2.1 Computing Complexity

Computing complexity refers to situations dealing with vast datasets and diverse approaches to analysing enormous volumes of digital data. The complexity normally occurs in four processes: classifying data, processing data, sense-making, and intelligence. Regarding classifying data, categorising data in different forms – text, image, video, and voice –can be automatically generated into or from expressions of emotion by using sentiment analysis or by understanding online behaviour. Future AI applications could use new types of computing data to offer users immersive, composite experiences through emerging technologies such as virtual reality, augmented reality, and mixed reality (Reiners et al. 2021). Very broadly, such data exist in two forms: structured and unstructured. While structured data are highly organised and are easily decipherable by ML algorithms, it is not easy to apply ML to unstructured data such as the text generated via chatbots.

Furthermore, processing of data, including clearing, labelling, and tokenising data, occurs before data are ready to meet the specific requirements of ML goals. This preparation is critical for the next stage of making sense of data. ML processes could lead to innovative ideas or intelligent solutions based on systematic evaluations and predictions rather than using discrete, observed inputs. Compared to widely distributed digital sensors that collect and transmit data at low cost, the real challenge of computing complexity is sensitively adapting such data to local norms and to local social and cultural traditions. An example is the predication of the possibility of a patient having skin cancer based on ML comparing the patient's medical imaging with a database of skin cancer images.

The four processes of complexity described above mean that AI applications constantly challenge the legal meaning of the "identification of an individual" through their definition of personal data within data protection laws, and they may even breach users' rights. Both industry and governments are still in the process of operationalising non-identifiable data use in practice. The simple reason for this is that AI applications introduce challenges to common principles of data governance such as data minimisation, informed consent, and transparency of data use. Attempts by regulators to increase user protection based on these principles have often proved ineffective. Companies are driven to use automatic means to maximise data collection and to capitalise on data, and this process is exacerbated in business models built on monetising data (Xue 2022).

By contrast, technology companies are fighting to harvest more data across more sectoral fields, even though these data may not yet be used in their current products and services. Although some AI applications aim to recognise patterns instead of re-identifying individuals, they can still reinforce algorithmic vulnerability in certain social groups that are proportionally unrepresented in a predesigned database or predesigned algorithm (Pasquale 2015).

One typical governance problem which arises from the existence of multiple centres of power is that a single mistake made during development may be repeated millions of times due to automation, while no good way to trace the error data points. The compromised data sources as such can cause long-term algorithmic vulnerability in groups of individuals who are at risk of group profiling and thus unfair treatment (Xue 2021). Such algorithms can be designed and used to target individuals for commercial purposes. AI technology can scale up personalisation at even lower costs and at rapid speed based on "individual profiling" or "group profiling" (Wachter 2020). Furthermore, even when the design of an ML algorithm aims to recognise patterns instead of re-identifying individuals, the capability of such an algorithm to predict the behaviours of groups of individuals and make automatic decisions without their consent (e.g., bank loans or health insurance) can cause harm to groups of individuals at scale. Obtaining such consent is impossible in most cases when data are collected from a public space.

2.2 Social Complexity

Despite the growth of advanced technologies to preserve and analyse massive amounts of data, AI technologies may introduce a more chaotic order, reshaping the existing power dynamic currently concentrated in a few hands. They also reveal new solutions that allow more actors to participate in governing processes and to benefit from their social value. Effective governing of digital data often depends on the consequences of the interplay between many social complexity factors. "Social complexity" refers to the fact that individuals frequently interact in many different contexts (cultural environment, political opinion, see Table 13.1) with many diverse individuals, and often they repeatedly have exchanges with many of the same individuals over time (Freeberg et al. 2012). For analytical convenience, this can be understood in both a structured and an unstructured way (Ostrom 2010) – social complexity arises because of organisational culture, market dynamics, and operational processes, increasing the challenges faced when processing these data. The reality is that while prevailing AI applications bring people together to communicate with each other, they also divide people along lines of language and cultural values, beliefs, and interests (Scholte 2021b).

I used the structured complexity for analytical consistency in comparison with structured complexity of data as mentioned in Section 2.1. In my work "structured complexity" means that organisations function in a mixed structure when allocating resources, coordinating nodes, and implementing operations. In this chapter, this term refers to the social structural change associated with growing human–machine co-existence, not only in the workforce, but also as life mates. For example, the European Union (EU) is preparing to adapt its technical infrastructure and coordinating mechanisms across organisations to ensure that digital services are ready to enable EU residents to access digital healthcare services with equal convenience across the EU. The traditional organisational structure that consists of hospitals, general practitioner networks, and pharmacies may be greatly changed in their staffing and work types, evolving towards a new system of human–robotic collaboration, consisting of telehealth, social robot care, and AI-aided self-care management. The COVID-19 pandemic has accelerated such demands, requiring that this transformation rapidly takes place. An example from this pandemic was Our World in Data, developed by the Oxford School of Government, which provided online tracking and analytics of the timely reporting of cases of COVID-19. This helped policymakers to develop vaccination strategies (Oxford University n.d.). Processing such data may revitalise traditional institutions, such as the World Bank, and different national statistical offices and think tanks which aim to use and reuse data to understand the global population, manage local traffic, better utilise water resources, and improve "smart" neighbourhoods, to mention but a few examples.

By contrast, unstructured complexity may be embedded in policy diffusion (Koinova et al. 2021). Governing the use of personal data by AI is more than a technical or economic question; it also involves ideological competition and the negotiation of cultural interests. The fragmentation (Biermann et al. 2009) of several ideologies, such as technocracy and central planning-based forms of socialism, may reinforce the existing digital divide between and within the Global North and Global South. Research shows that algorithmic fairness as understood within Western norms is not easily translated to, for example, the cultural values of people from India (Sambasivan et al. 2021). Furthermore, when we accept common ethical principles such as transparency and fairness, the gap between perceptions and enforceability may increase due to the process of implementing these policies in local contexts. For instance, collecting personal data for the purposes of overcoming public crises should be proportionate and always involve thinking ahead about exit plans to end such use when these crises end. However, preventing the repurposing of massive, valuable datasets is not an easy task.

Being aware of social complexity does not guarantee a fairer representation of ML network design, nor a lower risk of social exclusion. Nevertheless, it is helpful to have such an awareness during development and before the designing of a technical system. An algorithmic impact assessment follows this approach to help companies consider their social impacts during the early stages of development and to help them incorporate greater social consideration into their business structures. Such assessments help companies consider where best to position humans in the loop to make the most sense of data, thereby enabling human self-realisation and not devaluing human abilities (Floridi et al. 2018).

For instance, a company such as Mercedes uses human–machine teams – so-called cobots – to customise their production of cars to cater to each customer's personal preferences. In the plant, working with human beings, the cobots can be reprogrammed easily using a tablet, allowing them to handle different tasks depending on changes in the workflow through the digitising of vehicle production in response to the real-time data records of dealerships and changes of components. Similar situations to this raise questions as to whether we should use algorithms to determine the "employability" of humans based on pseudoscientific analyses of human work records. As non-governmental organisations, governments, and activity groups must rely on the data or even the data analytics provided by big corporations, at least for the foreseeable future, an approach must be found to mitigate the biases generated from datasets, ML algorithms, and data analytics for public purposes such as upskilling and preparing the future workforce.

Such a situation is even more striking when we think that many Global South countries are absent from the current global AI policy map (Cihon et al. 2020). While many Global South countries have actively embraced AI applications, and many have even adopted data privacy laws, this does not mean that these populations and the diverse social values and subcultures they represent are included in databases. When companies from the Global North or even those from the Global South deploy AI technologies, insufficient resources are available to protect marginalised people. The COVID-19 pandemic brings in additional examples when several countries used AI-empowered applications to read X-ray images, such as the AI Based Intelligent COVID-19 detector Technology for Medical Assistance (ATMAN) in India (Ministry of Defence, Government of India 2020).

3 Revisiting the Debate on "Code, Laws, Norms, and Markets" From a Polycentric Perspective

Scholte (2021b) substantiated the "ordered chaos" of the current tech scene to norms, practices, and underlying orders as the three "systemic ordering forces." This section discusses how "code" and "laws" can be implemented when dealing with human–machine collaborative governance against the division between Global North and Global South. Such a combination in regulation creates underlying demands to implement existing technical standards, interrelating the meaning of existing laws and demonstrating the counter-power of previously either human-dominant or machine-dominant discursive practices across different societies. These complexities, as explained in the previous sections, may force self-coordination in the self-learning of future AI systems.

Each regulatory approach identified in the seminal work of Lawrence Lessig (1999) – laws, code, markets, and norms – has its strengths and limitations regarding the initiation, accumulation, and implementation of symbolic power resources. Each of these four regulatory approaches represents different norms, actors, and sometimes overlapping centres of authority, following polycentric 2.0 perspectives outlined in the introduction to this volume. Law, codes, markets, and norms may also be considered as systemic ordering forces, each with their own distinct, but also coinciding normative background, repertoire of practices, and underlying orders as developed by Scholte (2021b) and discussed in other chapters in this volume (see Chapter 12 and Chapter 11, this volume). What Lessig's conceptualisation allows for is an imbrication of polycentricity 2.0 and 3.0, which will be discussed in the next paragraphs of this last section in the case of AI governance and data.

Generally speaking, law faces enormous difficulties in AI regulation due to the high cost of implementation and the uncertainty regarding the interpretation of the conditions to apply for each legal term. National laws have certain advantages in this regard. A unified framework may offer a solution by pooling sovereignty to create standards that support effective code and protect users' rights. National laws acknowledge a legal foundation that empowers individuals to control data about themselves, to access information, or to express their opinions freely, such as by promoting privacy-enhancing technologies nationwide. However, when old rules are applied in new scenarios, such as automated decision-making in judiciary systems, judges need to understand these applications of AI and make sense of such automated processes. Reidenberg's research has focused on the constitutionalisation of neutral technology, implying that regulating this digital architecture requires compatible law (Reidenberg 1997). Although many regulatory technologies are available for determining the outcomes of cases automatically, a judiciary is still required to interpret the law in such a way that preserves meaning by mapping the law from one technology to another.

Another common view involves questioning whether territory-based national laws can be well implemented in non-territorial cyberspace, where data flow across borders every second. While legal institutions are made to last, economic institutions are designed for rapid adaptation to changing economic and technological realities. Uncertainties occur at three levels in the translation and interpretation of symbolic exchanges. The highest level of uncertainty resides in what Lasswell (1948) called "symbolic exchange," which eventually adds up to social complexity. Symbolic exchanges at the highest level of abstraction in a system of laws and policies are: (1) some standard, goal, or set of values against which perceptions of what is happening within the environment to be controlled are compared through (2) some mechanism of monitoring or feedback, which in turn triggers (3) some form of action that attempts to align the controlled variables as they are perceived by monitoring the implementation component along with the goal component.

Regulation by code increasingly prevails not only in the private sector but also in the public sector. Governments use code-based rules and algorithmic ML to determine national tax declarations in tax offices, to process Medicare, and to predict jail sentences or crime rates. The term "code" here refers to software code (i.e., code developed through computer programming). National laws can also take power away from particular groups of people, such as by making certain privacy-related transactions illegal. Laws can send signals emphasising the importance of the traceability, accessibility, and accuracy of stored data. New principles that lay out the rules regarding liability, accountability, transparency, and explicability, for example, may be translated into future laws that are more compatible with AI technologies. Consequently, engineers can translate these legal requirements into code that is used to define the technical systems, software, or architecture of AI applications. Code can be used to program the setting of an AI application in order to improve the capacities of individuals to control certain types of their data.

Lessig (1999) saw two regulatory regimes – code and law – that compete with each other. Some scholars view code differently from the law; they see code as having originated in market behaviour and reflecting the spirit of liberty (Cohen 2012). By contrast, other scholars see code as metaphorically equal to law; they believe that code lays the foundations of the digital architecture of control as an extra-legal regime. However, these two views might not solve the problems relating to the competing interests of different actors. As Lessig asserted, "cyberspace is regulated by its code." However, the internal forces exerted by code might not be independent of external forces, such as laws. The possibilities and constraints that cyberspace affords users are rooted in particular values. The code embedded in the programs, protocols, and platforms that make up online social life is subject to the regulation of site builders and owners. Evidence shows that it is not easy either to translate code into law to address new social justice issues or to execute law in code to improve regulatory efficiency. Smart contracts, on the one hand, can scale up processes of online dispute resolution; on the other hand, such processes carry risks of perpetuating mistakes, such as unfair treatment and incorrect reasoning, which require the intervention of a human arbitrator (Xue and Holz 2019). In this respect, using code-driven automatic regulatory approaches to execute current laws does not necessarily guarantee efficiency. Often, automated decision-making increases complexity at all levels. Once the decision is triggered and proceeds, it is not easy to reverse it.

Often, humans face a challenging situation of there being no flaws in the technical design of code which nonetheless has profound, large-scale social implications. Scandals lead us to question whether we should include sensitive data such as nationality in all databases and to consider how best to design an algorithm to process data related to nationality in order to assess an individual's tax declaration. In December 2021, the Dutch Data Protection Authority (Autoriteit Persoonsgegevens) announced a fine of €2.75 million against the Tax and Customs Administration because it unnecessarily processed the nationality of applicants using an ML algorithm to combat fraud. The Tax and Customs Administration used the nationality of applicants as an indicator in a system that automatically designated specific applications as "high risk." The Tax and Customs Administration focused their attention on people with "a non-Western appearance," and those of Turkish or Moroccan nationality in particular. Using such an algorithm automatically singled out people with these parameters and labelled them as having a higher risk score in the childcare benefits system, preventing them from claiming the childcare benefits they deserved.

Such risks can cross national boundaries due to global market forces. Commercial innovation, combined with the global promotion of technical standards facilitated by code, constantly challenges the constraints put in place by domestic laws through the goal of relaxing regulation. The commercial forces underlined by code mediate and formalise user behaviours. Facebook (now rebranded as Meta) shows how code can change social norms by mediating daily online social behaviours. Online exchanges influence people's perceptions of what behaviours are expected as norms amongst their "imagined audiences" (Marwick and Boyd 2011), including their views on data subject rights, digital identity, information sharing, and approaches to dealing with machine agents.

Final Words

This chapter brought together different strands of polycentric governance literature to understand a rapidly shifting landscape of AI governance. Many problems surrounding the governance of AI emerge due to issues with data: its origins, the types of actors and their decisions, as well as the effects of this data for algorithmic governance, among other issues. Yet, against the backdrop of these tensions and omissions, polycentric theories and the socio-legal cyberspace regulatory approaches of Lessig can bring some greater coherence to a rapidly moving thematic, technological, and institutional environment surrounding AI. The analysis of Lessig's four regulatory modalities, traditional to cyberspace governance debates with the main categorisations of the Bloomington School of polycentric governance and the more fluid and global perspectives of polycentric theorising (Koinova et al. 2021), all suggest that there are many ways in which regulatory approaches can help understand AI tensions by stressing the sources of power that shape these debates.

References

Aligica, P.D. and Tarko, V., 2012. Polycentricity: from Polanyi to Ostrom, and beyond. *Governance*, 25 (2), pp.237–262.

Amjad, M., Sidorov, G. and Zhila, A., 2020. Data augmentation using machine translation for fake news detection in the Urdu language. In: *Proceedings of the 12th Language Resources and Evaluation Conference*. Marseille, France: European Language Resources Association, pp.2537–2542.

Ansell, C. and Gash, A., 2008. Collaborative governance in theory and practice. *Journal of Public Administration Research and Theory*, 18 (4), pp.543–571.

Autoriteit Persoonsgegevens, 2020. *Methods used by Dutch tax administration unlawful and discriminatory*. [online] Available at https://web.archive.org/web/20230326191954/https://autoriteitpersoonsgegevens.nl/en/news/methods-used-dutch-tax-administration-unlawful-and-discriminatory.

Autoriteit Persoonsgegevens, 2021. *Tax Administration fined for discriminatory and unlawful data processing*. [online] Available at https://gdprhub.eu/AP_(The_Netherlands)_-_Tax_Administration_fined_for_discriminatory_and_unlawful_data_processing?mtc=hubasmtw.

Benkler, Y., 2006. *The wealth of networks: how social production transforms markets and freedom*. New Haven, CT: Yale University Press.

Biermann, F., Pattberg, P., van Asselt, H. and Zelli, F., 2009. The fragmentation of global governance architectures: a framework for analysis. *Global Environmental Politics*, 9 (4), pp.14–40.

Carlisle, K. and Gruby, R.L., 2019. Polycentric systems of governance: a theoretical model for the commons. *Policy Studies Journal*, 47 (4), pp.927–952.

Cihon, P., Maas, M.M. and Kemp, L., 2020. Fragmentation and the future: investigating architectures for international AI governance. *Global Policy*, 11 (5), pp.545–556.

Cohen, J.E., 2012. *Configuring the networked self*. New Haven, CT: Yale University Press.

Council of the European Union, 2021. *Proposal for a Regulation of the European Parliament and of the Council laying down harmonised rules on artificial intelligence (Artificial Intelligence Act) and amending certain Union legislative acts – Presidency compromise text*. [online] Available at https://data.consilium.europa.eu/doc/document/ST-14278-2021-INIT/en/pdf.

Curran, J., 2002. *Media and power*. Abingdon-on-Thames: Taylor & Francis.

Durkheim, E., Brookfield, C. and Turner, B.S., 1991. *Professional ethics and civic morals*; Translated by C. Brookfield; with a New Preface by B.S. Turner. New ed. Routledge Sociology Classics. New York: Routledge.

European Commission, 2021. *AI Watch: AI standardisation landscape state of play and link to the EC proposal for an AI regulatory framework*. [online] Available at https://op.europa.eu/en/publication-detail/-/publication/36c46b8e-e518-11eb-a1a5-01aa75ed71a1/language-en.

Floridi, L., Cowls, J., Beltrametti, M., Chatila, R., Chazerand, P., Dignum, V., Luetge, C., Madelin, R., Pagallo, U., Rossi, F. and Schafer, B., 2018. AI4People – an ethical framework for a good AI society: opportunities, risks, principles, and recommendations. *Minds and Machines*, 28 (4), pp.689–707.

Forlano, L., 2021. *A New AI Lexicon: Human Exploring the Boundaries of Humans and Machines*. [online] Available at https://ainowinstitute.org/publication/a-new-ai-lexicon-human.

Freeberg, T.M., Dunbar, R.I. and Ord, T.J., 2012. Social complexity as a proximate and ultimate factor in communicative complexity. *Philosophical Transactions of the Royal Society B: Biological Sciences*, 367(1597), pp.1785–1801.

Global Partnership on Artificial Intelligence (GPAI), 2020. *Joint Statement from Founding Members of the Global Partnership on Artificial Intelligence*. [online] Available at https://www.diplomatie.gouv.fr/en/french-foreign-policy/digital-diplomacy/news/article/launch-of-the-global-partnership-on-artificial-intelligence-by-15-founding.

Gorwa, R., Binns, R. and Katzenbach, C., 2020. Algorithmic content moderation: technical and political challenges in the automation of platform governance. *Big Data & Society*, 7 (1), doi:205395171989794.

Hood, C., Rothstein, H. and Baldwin, R., 2001. *The government of risk: understanding risk regulation regimes*. New York: Oxford University Press, pp.23–27.

Jones, J. and Trice, M. eds., 2020. *Platforms, protests, and the challenge of networked democracy*. London: Palgrave Macmillan.

Kim, R.E., 2020. Is global governance fragmented, polycentric, or complex? The state of the art of the network approach. *International Studies Review*, 22 (4), pp.903–931.

Koinova, M., Deloffre, M.Z., Gadinger, F., Mencutek, Z.S., Scholte, J.A. and Steffek, J., 2021. It's ordered chaos: what really makes polycentrism work. *International Studies Review*, 23 (4), pp.1988–2018.

Lasswell, H.D., 1948. The structure and function of communication in society. *The Communication of Ideas*, 37 (1), pp.136–139.

Lessig, L., 1999. *Code and other laws of cyberspace*. New York: Basic Books.

Marwick, A.E. and Boyd, D., 2011. I tweet honestly, I tweet passionately: Twitter users, context collapse, and the imagined audience. *New Media & Society*, 13 (1), pp.114–133.

McCarthy, J., 2007. What is Artificial Intelligence? [online] Available at http://www-formal.stanford.edu/jmc/whatisai.pdf.

Microsoft, 2022. Microsoft's framework for building AI systems responsibly. [online] Available at https://blogs.microsoft.com/on-the-issues/2022/06/21/microsofts-framework-for-building-ai-systems-responsibly/.

Ministry of Defence, Government of India, 2020. AI Based Intelligent COVID-19 detector Technology for Medical Assistance (ATMAN). [online] Available at https://www.drdo.gov.in/ai-based-intelligent-covid-19-detector-technology-medical-assistance-atman.

Noble, S.U., 2018. *Algorithms of oppression*. New York: NYU Press.

Ostrom, E., 2010. Beyond markets and states: polycentric governance of complex economic systems. *American Economic Review*, 100 (3), pp.641–672.

Oxford University, n.d. Coronavirus (COVID-19) Vaccinations. [online] Available at https://ourworldindata.org/covid-vaccinations.

Parsons, T., 1996. The theory of human behavior in its individual and social aspects. *The American Sociologist*, 27 (4), pp.13–23.

Pasquale, F., 2015. *The black box society*. Cambridge, MA: Harvard University Press.

Polanyi, M., 1951. *The logic of liberty*. Chicago, IL: University of Chicago Press.

Reidenberg, J.R., 1997. Lex informatica: the formulation of information policy rules through technology. *Texas Law Review*, 76, (553–593). https://ir.lawnet.fordham.edu/faculty_scholarship/42.

Reiners, D., Davahli, M.R., Karwowski, W. and Cruz-Neira, C., 2021. The combination of artificial intelligence and extended reality: a systematic review. *Frontiers in Virtual Reality*, 2. https://www.frontiersin.org/articles/10.3389/frvir.2021.721933/full.

Sambasivan, N., Arnesen, E., Hutchinson, B., Doshi, T. and Prabhakaran, V., 2021. Re-imagining algorithmic fairness in India and beyond. In: *Proceedings of the 2021 ACM Conference on Fairness, Accountability, and Transparency*, pp.315–328. https://doi.org/10.48550/arXiv.2101.09995.

Sava, D., 2020. Google Cloud AI and Harvard Global Health Institute Collaborate on new COVID-19 forecasting model. [online] Available at https://cloud.google.com/blog/products/ai-machine-learning/google-cloud-is-releasing-the-covid-19-public-forecasts.

Scholte, J.A., 2021a. Beyond institutionalism: towards a transformed global governance theory. *International Theory*, 13 (1), pp.179–191.

Scholte, J.A., 2021b. Structuring polycentrism: norms, practices and underlying orders in internet governance. In: It's ordered chaos: what really makes polycentrism work. *International Studies Review*, 23 (4), pp.1988–2018.

Smith, C., 2022. 'No-code' brings the power of A.I. to the masses, *New York Times*. [online] Available at https://www.nytimes.com/2022/03/15/technology/ai-no-code.html.

Stackpole, T., 2021. Inside IKEA's Digital Transformation. [online] Available at https://hbr.org/2021/06/inside-ikeas-digital-transformation.

Stephan, M., Marshall, G. and McGinnis, M., 2019. An introduction to polycentricity and governance. In: *Governing Complexity: Analyzing and Applying Polycentricity*, pp.21–44. Cambridge: Cambridge University Press.

UNESCO, 2021. *Recommendation on the Ethics of Artificial Intelligence—UNESCO Digital Library*. UNESCO. Available at https://unesdoc.unesco.org/ark:/48223/pf0000380455.

Veale, M. and Brass, I., 2019. Administration by algorithm? Public management meets public sector machine learning. In: *Algorithmic regulation*, Karen Yeung and Martin Lodge, eds, pp.121–149. Oxford: Oxford University Press. https://papers.ssrn.com/sol3/papers.cfm?abstract_id=3375391.

Wachter, S., 2020. Affinity profiling and discrimination by association in online behavioural advertising. *Berkeley Technology Law Journal*, 35 (2). [online] Available at https://doi.org/10.2139/ssrn.3388639.

Webb, A., 2019. *The big nine: how the tech titans and their thinking machines could warp humanity*. London: Hachette UK.

Xue, J.H., 2021. Algorithmic vulnerability in deploying vaccination certificates in the European Union and China. *European Journal of Risk Regulation*, 12 (2), pp.332–342.

Xue, J.H., 2022. Delegitimising data subjects' economic interests during automatic propertisation of their data: a comparative study of data protection on social media platforms in the UK and China. *Journal of Global Media and China*. [online] Available at https://doi.org/10.1177/20594364211060874.

Xue, J.H. and Holz, R., 2019. Applying smart contracts in online dispute resolutions on a large scale and its regulatory implications. In: *Blockchain and Web 3.0: social, economic, and technological challenges*. London: Routledge, pp.177–191.

14

CONCLUSION

The End of a Beginning

Carolina Aguerre, Malcolm Campbell-Verduyn and Jan Aart Scholte

Introduction

This concluding chapter summarizes how polycentric perspectives offer a rich interdisciplinary understanding of governing digital data. We consolidate the main insights and contributions gained across the book's studies of diverse sectors of activity and diverse jurisdictions worldwide. We finish with suggestions for further research both on digital data governance and on polycentric approaches to global cooperation more generally. Overall, we see that polycentric perspectives are not a singular theory to steer analysis of, and prescriptions for, digital data governance. Rather, polycentric approaches allow us to compare and bring into conversation diverse perspectives, thereby offering potentials for a deeper synthetic knowledge.

Through a unifying focus on polycentricity, the book has brought together academic fields that understand data and their governance quite differently. Singly and in combination, this set of perspectives clarifies a growing variety of actors, structures, and processes at subnational, national, regional, and global levels that crucially shape digital data governance. Polycentricism generally provides nuanced ways to understand this complexity (Gadinger and Scholte, 2023; Scholte, 2017). It provides a set of perspectives to navigate the many debates around digital data governance, helping to establish what digital data governance currently involves, as well as what it could be and should become in the future.

Key Contributions of this Volume

Turning to more specific contributions, the following section highlights three main innovations that this book brings to knowledge (and by extension policy) concerning digital data governance. The first overarching contribution, already

DOI: 10.4324/9781003388418-17

broached above, has been bringing polycentric perspectives to bear on a more encompassing understanding of digital data governance. The second major contribution has been to underline power hierarchies coexisting with, and shaping, the diffusion and fluidity in polycentric governing of digital data. The third central contribution of this volume has been to promote policy diversity in the practice of digital data governance.

Promoting Synthetic Knowledge

This book has built on the notion of polycentrism to draw together highly varying understandings of digital data governance. As we saw in the introductory chapter, the concept of polycentrism has evolved over time, starting with the generic insight of Michael Polanyi, moving on to the political economy conceptions of the Bloomington School, and recently developing the theme of 'ordered chaos', where deeper structures bring considerable regularity to institutional messiness. Yet all variants of the concept have, in their different ways, emphasized that governance is diffuse and complex across multiple sites and layers.

Given that the concept has this openness and malleability, a focus on polycentrism has allowed this volume to bring together highly diverse perspectives on digital data governance. In its general formulation, the idea of polycentrism highlights certain broad attributes (transscalarity, transsectorality, diffusion, fluidity, overlapping mandates, ambiguous lines of command, no final arbiter) that a wide range of approaches perceive in contemporary governance. These arguments may diverge in their more detailed analyses – indeed, sometimes quite considerably – but these broad defining features of polycentrism offer a common starting point for comparisons, conversations, and potentially, also, combinations of approaches.

Such potentials for fruitful exchange and synthesis are illustrated within and between a number of the book's chapters. For example, Raymond and Shackelford (Chapter 2) in elaborating a Bloomington School perspective on polycentric governing of digital data do not pursue an inward-looking conversation that is limited to the School itself, but rather develop an outward-looking engagement with other perspectives on complex governance. Li and Yang (Chapter 7) take a more generic institutionalist approach to polycentrism in their examination of data protection regimes. Meanwhile, Iglesias Keller and Martins dos Santos (Chapter 9) with their exploration of the regulation of disinformation adopt a more 'ordered chaos' perspective on polycentrism, in the process combining insights from legal knowledge, political analysis, and science and technology studies. Even when eschewing the term 'polycentrism', Aaronson (Chapter 8) develops ideas of 'patchwork' that readily speak to other analyses in the volume. In all of these cases and more, the concept of polycentrism invites larger conversations and more encompassing understandings.

Spotlighting Power

A second main innovation of this book has been to reveal that governance of digital data is not so horizontal and flat as some interpretations of polycentrism might suggest. The fact that polycentric governing is diffuse (scattered) and fluid (unsettled) does not mean that it lacks power hierarchies. On the contrary, the various studies in this volume have repeatedly indicated that the absence of unified and centralized regulatory arrangements for digital data does not remove relations of dominance and subordination. Specific actors, norms, practices, and underlying orders have more power than others in digital data governance – with important and potentially negative consequences for cooperation, democracy, effectiveness, and fairness.

Several chapters in this volume – including those by Medzini and Epstein, Li and Yang, and Iglesias Keller and Martins dos Santos – have emphasized efforts by state authorities to assert more regulatory power in the digital data domain. Rodima-Taylor (Chapter 5) shows how platformization and datafication involve both corporate and state power, increase subordination of the Global South, and prompt grassroots resistance around data rights. Campbell-Verduyn (Chapter 12) traces how forms of distributed data governance in ongoing experiments with blockchain technologies have (inadvertently) reproduced and extended the very concentrations of power they arose to counter. Xue (Chapter 13) further highlights hierarchies in both state and corporate power across the polycentric governance of artificial intelligence. This volume has repeatedly shone a spotlight on the ubiquity of power hierarchies through polycentric perspectives on the governance of digital data.

Embracing Policy Diversity

The third main contribution of this book has been to welcome a variety of policy approaches to digital data governance. Prevailing tendencies in global governance research and practice seek to achieve uniformity in regulatory arrangements across the world. In contrast, this volume has eschewed a single normative framework, rejecting one-size-fits-all understandings and instead embracing a multiplicity of possible governance arrangements for digital data.

Illustrating this point, Verhulst (Chapter 6) urges that digital data governance should develop from questions rather than assertions, thereby inviting multiple rather than singular answers to regulatory challenges. Medzini and Epstein (Chapter 10) highlight how broadly shared norms for digital data governance can be developed on different lines in different national contexts. Rocha da Siqueira and Ramalho (Chapter 4) critique the predominantly extractive character of existing digital data governance, even when it is motivated by well-intended objectives such as the Sustainable Development Goals of the 2030 Agenda. They urge a fundamental rethinking of policies so as to empower marginalized communities and achieve more systemic justice.

In sum, the three main innovations of this book have all foregrounded poly-centric perspectives not as a singular analytical and normative approach to steer digital data across varying spaces and scales of governance. Rather, polycentric perspectives allow us to develop conversations among a variety of explanatory frameworks as well as different normative prescriptions suited for democratic concerns.

Research Paths Ahead

This book has provided in-depth analyses of a broad spectrum of specific pro-blems in digital data governance, making the trio of general contributions ela-borated above. Still, no volume can on its own fully cover all the issues at stake. More remains to be explored in further research. The following final paragraphs identify four avenues for future work, related respectively to multi-stakeholderism, sociological theory, temporality, and normative concerns.

Regarding multistakeholderism, future research can fruitfully further probe the relationship between polycentrism and multistakeholder initiatives. Whereas polycentrism concerns a multiplicity of sites within a regulatory complex, mul-tistakeholderism involves a multiplicity of constituencies within a single reg-ulatory institution. To that extent, polycentrism and multistakeholderism are respectively macro and micro versions of governance arrangements marked by transscalarity, transsectorality, diffusion, fluidity, overlapping mandates, ambiguous hierarchies, and the absence of a final arbiter. Indeed, many indivi-dual sites within today's polycentric complexes of digital data governance have a multistakeholder character. Examples include standard-setting mechanisms, infrastructure projects for blockchain data in Latin America (LACNet), cloud services in Europe (GAIA-X), and data platforms (such as AgriData in Senegal and Citizens' Biometric Councils in the UK). An important path for future research is to explore such macro-micro relationships to better understand, for example, how polycentrism and growing multistakeholderism might be mutually reinforcing trends.

Regarding sociological theory, future research on digital data governance could also benefit from drawing on practice theories and global political sociology theories. While contributions to this volume have underlined how polycentric governance occurs through social structures as well as through actors (inter alia in Chapters 3, 9, and 12), much more can be gained from tracing how everyday practices (as micro structures) and larger systemic pat-terns (as macro structures) interact in ordering digital data in contemporary society. Practice theories can further elucidate informal features within poly-centric governing: for instance, around behavioural routines (such as crowd-sourcing initiatives) and discourses (such as talk about 'digital sovereignty'). Global political sociology can help to show how the micro connects and works through larger social forces in digital data governance, such as capitalism, core-periphery relations, a hegemonic state, and patriarchy.

Regarding temporality, further research on polycentrism in digital data governance can bolster this volume's attention to scales, local to global, by further exploring questions of time. A stress on temporality involves both future-oriented and historically sensitive analysis, placing present trends in medium- and longer-term perspectives. Even though digital data technologies emerged relatively recently, many of the organizations, norms, practices, and macro structures that govern them have deeper historical roots. Temporality also figures around digital data in terms of the sheer speed of their processing and circulation, where control of that speed constitutes a major source of power (Virilio 1996). Timewise, too, policy struggles to keep up with the high speed at which digital data technologies develop. Could demands for fast policy action also risk to compromise time-consuming democratic deliberation?

Two explicitly normative questions can also guide further research on polycentric digital data governance. One relates to the implications of polycentrism for democracy in the governance of digital data. From Michael Polanyi onwards – and in many of this volume's chapters – a presumption has held that the decentralized character of polycentrism enhances democracy. Yet today's polycentric governing of digital data includes many authoritarian players. Meanwhile, liberal regimes also often curtail or bypass democratic processes in making rules for digital activities. Democratic access, transparency, and accountability are all themes that need to figure more centrally in the analysis of purportedly 'bottom-up' multistakeholder processes, as well as larger polycentric networks.

A second normative concern that deserves greater attention going forward relates to knowledge power and risks of epistemicide (i.e., the death of certain kinds of understanding) through digital data governance. Online spaces are often celebrated as being open to all perspectives. Yet digital data governance may – whether by design or, more usually, through subtle workings of structural power – favour dominant ways of knowing (such as Western rationalism) and marginalize and silence others (such as indigenous life-worlds). Additionally, the notion of data justice (Taylor, 2017) foregrounds the need to address more squarely structural inequalities in the production and use of knowledge in digital data.

In ending this beginning of what we hope will be growing interdisciplinary research on digital data governance, we have outlined four issues for future work. Additional questions undoubtedly exist. Our hope is that this volume's bringing together of polycentric perspectives to study digital data governance is a start and not the end of a fruitful endeavour.

References

Gadinger, F. and Scholte, J.A. (eds) (2023). *Polycentrism: How Governing Works Today.* Oxford: Oxford University Press.

Scholte, Jan Aart. (2017). Polycentrism and Democracy in Internet Governance. In *The Net and the Nation State: Multidisciplinary Perspectives on Internet Governance*, edited by Uta Kohl, 165–184. Cambridge: Cambridge University Press.

Taylor, L. (2017). What Is Data Justice? The Case for Connecting Digital Rights and Freedoms Globally. *Big Data & Society*, 4(2), doi:2053951717736335. https://doi.org/10.1177/2053951717736335.

Virilio, P. (1996). *Speed and Politics*. Cambridge, MA: MIT Press.

INDEX

Locators in *italics* refer to figures and those in **bold** to tables.

the 100 questions initiative 92–94

2030 Agenda *see* UN 2030 Agenda

Aaronson, Susan 30

accountability, data responsibility 96–97, 98

action research 92

activism *see* grassroots data activism

Ada Lovelace Foundation 28–29

advertising: and disinformation 125; microtargeting 155–158

Africa: balancing data privacy and open data 76–79, 82; grassroots data activism 74–78

agency: data responsibility 97, 98; grassroots data activism 70, 71–72, 81–83; privacy governance 168, 171, 177–178

algorithmic coloniality 69

algorithmic transparency 80–81, 82

algorithms for personal data 227–231

antitrust policies 134

Appadurai, A. 51–52, 54–55

application programming interfaces (API) 79

artificial intelligence (AI) 13; definition 224–225; development and evolution 223; personal data 226–231; polycentric AI governance 223–231

authority, diffusion of 39–40

Autonomous System Number (ASN) 196–197

Berkes, Fikret 23

big data: availability of 54, 59–60; grassroots data activism 71–72, 81–82; power in the datascape 53–55; role in regulating disinformation 149, 153–155; role of citizen-generated data 55–58; statistics about 4

bilinguals (domain experts and data science experts) 92–93

Bitcoin 207–214

blockchain 12, 209–210, 212–213, 215–216, 241

Bloomington School 6–7, 224, 239

Border Gateway Protocol (BGP) 192, 196–197

Brazil, law on trackers 160–161

Brazilian Institute of Geography and Statistics (IBGE) 60

Bundesdatenschutzgesetz (BDSG) 172–173

Cambridge Analytica (CA) case 155–156

Centre for Global Cooperation Research (CGCR) 10

chasers (microtargeting) 155–158

Christchurch Call 38, 40, 45

Cinnamon, Jonathan 61–62, 74

citizen-generated data (CGD): challenges of alternative data sources 58–62; the datascape 51–52, 55–65; and disinformation 125; polycentricism and non-extractivist methodologies 62–63

Clearview AI 113–115, **116–117, 118**
Clinton, Bill 132
Cloudflare 194
Cohen, Julie 172
collective action: algorithmic transparency
  80–81; common pool resources 22–23,
  68–69; disinformation policies 131;
  grassroots data activism 71, 73–74,
  80–81
common pool resources: and cyber
  infrastructure 24–25; digital commons
  26–28; global data as a resource 28–30;
  Governing the Commons (Ostrom)
  22–23, 28; polycentrism 68–69, 82;
  tragedy of the commons 22–23
competition policies 134
computational propaganda 128
computing complexity, personal data **227**,
  227–229, 229–231
Content Delivery Networks (CDNs)
  194–196, *195*
content moderation 134 *see also*
  disinformation
Court of Justice, European Union 41,
  109, 119
COVID-19 pandemic: acceleration of
  technology use in the Global South 75;
  AI technology 229–230, 231; remote
  learning 175–178; Sustainable
  Development Goals (SDGs) 52
credit data 78
cross-border data flows 41; bans on certain
  practices 136; digital trade agreements
  132–134; promoting regulatory
  coherence 135–136; provisions to reduce
  spam 136; retaliatory measures 137; a
  shared approach to regulating platforms
  134–135
crowdsourcing: alternative finance 73–75;
  data responsibility 90, 91–92
cryptocurrencies 12, 207–214
CUSMA (Canada-United States-Mexico
  Agreement) 133, 135
Cyber Peace Accord 25
cyber sovereignty 11
cybersecurity: digital infrastructure 24–25;
  overlapping mandates 41; state-centric
  vs. polycentric 170

data activism *see* grassroots data activism
Data Economy Lab 28
data minimization 94–95, 98
data privacy *see also* data responsibility:
  AI governance 226–231; balancing with
  open data 76–81, 82; by design 89;

future research 178–180; governance
  approaches 170–178; polycentric
  perspective 165–169; from regulation to
  regulatory governance 166–170; trackers
  158–161
data protection authorities (DPAs)
  105–107; AI governance 233;
  cross-border enforcement 108–113,
  119–121; cross-border enforcement –
  case studies 113–119; European Data
  Protection Board (EDPB) 12, 106–107,
  109–113, **111–112**, 118–120; polycentric
  data governance 107; privacy
  governance 172–175
data protection legislation 108–113,
  154–157
data protection officers (DPOs) 165–166,
  172–173, 174–175, 178–179
data responsibility 88–90; the 100
  questions initiative 92–94;
  accountability 96–97, 98; data
  minimization and proportionality
  94–95, 98; participation
  (democratization) 95–96, 98; problem
  definition and formulating questions
  90–91; questions, crowdsourcing, and
  polycentricism 91–92; toward a new
  movement and science of questions
  98–99
data retention policies 95
datafication of contemporary society 1;
  from datafication to data activism
  71–72; disinformation datafication and
  data governance 150–153; meaning of
  150–151; role of data in regulating
  disinformation 153–155
data_labe 59–61
the datascape: challenges of alternative
  data sources 58–62; and citizen-
  generated data 51–52, 55–65;
  polycentricism and non-extractivist
  methodologies 62–63; power in 53–55;
  UN 2030 Agenda as 51, 52–53, 57,
  62–65
"datasphere" 1, 4
de Sousa Santos, B. 51, 63
Decentralized Exchanges (DEXs) 214–215
Decentralized Finance (DeFi) 214–215
decolonial knowledge-making 70
Defense Advanced Research Projects
  Agency (DARPA) 126
democracy, and disinformation 130–131
democratization of data governance 95–96,
  98, 242
diffusion of authority 39–40

digital data, in contemporary society 1–3
digital disinformation see disinformation
Digital Economy Report 42
digital governance model 28–29
Digital Services Act (DSA) 157, 158–159
digital trade agreements 127, 131–134, 136
Digital Trade and Data Governance
    Hub 30
digitization see also datafication of
    contemporary society: as global
    transformation 1; Internet Governance
    Forum (IGF) 5; statistics about 4; as
    very recent trend 4
discursive practices (distributed data
    governance) 209
disinformation 12, 125–128; bans on
    certain practices 136; definition 128;
    digital trade agreements 127, 131–134;
    disinformation datafication and data
    governance 150–153; global and social
    effects 128; governance challenges
    148–150; government efforts to tackle
    130–131; microtargeting 155–158;
    promoting regulatory coherence
    135–136; provisions to reduce spam 136;
    retaliatory measures 137; role of data in
    regulating 153–155; role of platforms
    and business model 129–130; role of
    state actors 128–129; a shared approach
    to regulating platforms 134–135;
    traceability mechanisms 158–161
dispersed governance 6–7
distributed governance 205–207;
    complexities, inequalities and
    instabilities 212–216; data norms
    207–208; data practices 208–210;
    polycentric distributed data ordering
    207, 216; underlying orders 210–212
distributed technology 169–170
distribution of digital data 5
diversity 91

e-commerce agreements 132–133
encryption 159–160
enforcement of data protection 105–107;
    cross-border enforcement 108–113,
    119–121; cross-border enforcement –
    case studies 113–119; polycentric data
    governance 107
Environmental, Social, Governance
    (ESG) 215
equity 91
Ethereum Foundation 215
European Data Protection Board (EDPB)
    12, 106–107, 109–113, 111–112, 118–120

European Union see also General Data
    Protection Regulation (GDPR): Court
    of Justice 41, 109, 119; cross-border
    data flows 134, 135; cross-border
    enforcement 108–113, 119–121;
    cross-border enforcement – case studies
    113–119; data protection authorities
    (DPAs) 105–107, 119–120; digital
    healthcare services 229–230; Digital
    Services Act (DSA) 157, 158–159

Facebook: content moderation 35; data
    held by 5; encryption 74–75, 159–160; in
    the Global South 74–75, 76; potential
    for disinformation 125; social norms
    233–234
Fair Information Practice Principles
    (FIPPs) 94 see also data responsibility
fake news 125, 133, 137 see also
    disinformation
finance platforms, grassroots data activism
    69, 74–75, 78–81
Financial Action Task Force (FATF)
    214–215
FinTech platforms 69, 76–80, 215
fluidity of data governance 40, 92, 198
fractioned global system 51–52
free trade agreements (FTAs) 133, 135
freedom of speech, and disinformation
    130–131 see also grassroots data
    activism
freemium content 125, 129, 130

General Agreement on Tariffs and Trade
    (GATT) 134
General Agreement on Trade in Services
    (GATS) 134
General Data Protection Regulation
    (GDPR) 12; "adequacy agreement" 41;
    balancing data privacy and open data
    76–81; data minimization and
    proportionality 94; and EDPB 110–113;
    legal predecessors 108–110; local
    enforcement 105; polycentric AI
    governance 226; privacy governance
    172–173
Global South: balancing data privacy and
    open data 76–81, 82; grassroots data
    activism 72–76, 81–82; technology
    platforms and alternative finance 69,
    74–75, 78
globalization, the "datasphere" as part of 1
Google: market share 5; online learning
    177; potential for disinformation 125;
    QUIC protocol 38–39, 40

governance of digital data 2, 3–6 *see also* disinformation; challenges and responsibility 88–89; common pool resources and cyber infrastructure 24–25; controversies in 12; data privacy 170–178; digital commons 26–28; dispersed governance 6–7; global data as a resource 28–30; history of the Internet 34; Internet Governance Forum (IGF) 5; Internet interconnection policies 188–197, **198**, 199–201; misuse of data 126; polycentric AI governance 223–231; polycentric attributes 37–43; polycentric perspective 238–239

Governing the Commons (Ostrom) 22–23, 28

grassroots data activism 68; from datafication to data activism 71–72; in the Global South 72–76; pluriversal perspective 81–83; polycentric data governance 70–71; precarious balance of data privacy and open data 76–81, 82

Group of Seven (G7) 131

Group of Twenty (G20) 7–8

hate speech 131

Hathaway, Oona 25

healthcare, digital healthcare services 229–230

Hess, Charlotte 21, 26–27, 69

IETF (Internet Engineering Task Force) 40

India, Intermediary Guidelines and Digital Media Ethics Code 159–160

indigenous knowledges 62–63

industry associations **216**

information governance 26–28 *see also* disinformation; governance of digital data

information policy 169–170

informational power 168–169

infrastructure, digital: architectural principles of the Internet 35–43, 46–47; cybersecurity 24–25; data protection 152; the datascape 64; grassroots data activism 71, 73–74; privacy governance 165, 169, 189; as a public good 26, 29; self-regulatory initiatives 225; UN 2030 Agenda 53, 58

institutional privacy 176–178

interdisciplinarity 9–10, 13, 242

intermediary liability 134

International Governmental Organizations (IGOs) 41

the Internet: architectural principles and data policies 35–36; blackout/

shutdowns 39, 40, 44; cryptocurrencies 207–214; and data governance 34–35; global model of interconnectivity 45–46; as an information commons 25–26, 45–46; interoperability 34–35, 36, 44; polycentric attributes of digital data governance 37–43; systemic ordering forces 43–46

Internet Corporation for Assigned Names and Numbers (ICANN) 7–8

Internet Exchange Points (IXPs) 192–196, *193*, 199, 200

Internet Governance Forum (IGF) 5

Internet interconnection policies 187–188; data governance 188–197; peering and transit agreements 189–194, *190*, *191*; polycentric data governance 197–198; polycentric data norms 198–199; polycentric data practices 199–201; polycentric data underlying orders 201

Internet Protocol (TCP/IP) 35, 45

Internet Routing Registries (IRRs) 197

Internet Service Providers (ISPs) 39–40, 76, 131, 194, 196

Internet Society (ISOC) 46

interoperability: cross-border data flows 133; data flows across the Internet 11, 34–35, 36, 44; the datascape 55; Internet interconnection policies 187

Ireland, Data Protection Commission (DPC) 118–119

"knowledge commons" 29–30

lead supervisory authority (LEAs) 108–109, 112, 118–119

legal context: AI governance 231–234; data privacy 166–170; data protection 108–113, 154–157; policy diversity 240–241

Lessig, Lawrence 231, 233

M-Pesa 78

machine learning 80–81, 224–225, 230–231 *see also* artificial intelligence (AI)

marble-cake federalism 22

Mayer-Schonberger, V. 171

McGinnis, Michael 22

Meta 115–119

metagovernance norms 208

microtargeting 155–158

misleading information *see* disinformation

misuse of data 126 *see also* disinformation

Montreal Protocol 25

multi-centrism *see* polycentricity

multinational technology firms **216**
multistakeholderism 241
Musiani, F. 188–189, 202
Mutually Agreed Norms for Routing
Security (MANRS) 197, 199

National Household Sample Survey
(PNAD) 60
National Statistical Offices (NSOs) 64
network interconnection *see* Internet
interconnection policies
NOGs (Internet Operators Groups)
199, 200
non-extractive methodologies 51, 62–64
non-fungible tokens (NFTs) 4, 206
normative concerns 243

one-stop-shop mechanism (OSS) 106,
108–110
online learning 175–178
Onuoha, Mimi 59
open data, balancing with data privacy
76–81, 82
Organization for Economic Co-operation
and Development (OECD): AI
governance 225; cross-border data flows
127, 132, 134, 136; provisions to reduce
spam 136
Ostrom, Elinor 6–7, 21–28, 30–31, 57,
68–69
Ostrom, Vincent 6–7, 21, 22–25, 30–31
overlapping mandates
ownership of digital data: in contemporary
society 4; intellectual land grabs 69

Paris Call for Trust and Security in
Cyberspace 25
participation in data governance 95–96, 98
pirate practices (distributed data
governance) 208–209
pluralism 91
pluriversal perspective 81–83
Polanyi, Michael 6, 22, 224–225, 242
policy diversity 240–241
polycentric attributes of digital data
governance 37–43; ambiguous
hierarchies 42, **198**; diffusion of
authority 39–40, **198**; fluidity 40, **198**;
no final arbiter 42–43, **198**; overlapping
mandates 41–42, **198**; transscalar 37–38,
198; transsectoral 38–39, **198**
polycentric data governance: challenges of
alternative data sources 58–62; common
pool resources 68–69; cross-border
enforcement 108–113, 119–121;

cross-border enforcement – case studies
113–119; data norms 198–199; data
privacy 165–169; distributed governance
207, **216**; grassroots data activism
70–71; Internet interconnection policies
197–198; a primer 107
polycentricity 2–3, 6; artificial intelligence
(AI) governance 223–231; citizen-
generated data 62–63; code, laws, norms,
and markets 231–234; data protection
enforcement 105–107; data responsibility
91–92; as dispersed governance 6–7;
importance of concept 8–10, 238–242;
information policy 169–170; institutional
dynamics 12, 165–167, 171; as "ordered
chaos" 7–8, 11, 13, 207, 231
power: the datascape 53–55; distribution
of decision-making power 107, 113,
119–120; informational 168–169;
profitable digital platforms 130;
spotlighting 240
prisoner's dilemma 22–23
privacy *see* data privacy
private messaging apps 159–160
proportionality in data 94–95

question science 89; the 100 questions
initiative 92–94; problem definition and
formulating questions 90–91; questions
as tools for data responsibility 94–97;
questions, crowdsourcing, and
polycentricism 91–92; toward a new
movement 98–99
QUIC protocol 38–39, 40

regulation *see* legal context
relationality 52
remote learning 175–178
Resource Public Key Infrastructure
(RPKI) 197
responsible data *see* data responsibility
Routing Policy Specification Language
(RPSL) 197

Scholte, Jan Aart 170, 201, 207, 212, 231
search engines 5
self-expression, and disinformation 130–131
Siddarth, Divya 27
Singapore Australia Digital Economy
Agreement (SADEA) 133
social complexity, personal data **227**
social justice: citizen-generated data 59, 62;
and data governance 4, 51, 57, 59;
grassroots data activism 72; in a legal
context 233

social media: datafication of contemporary
society 1; grassroots data activism 68,
72–76, 81–82; microtargeting 155–156;
mission statements 130; potential for
disinformation 125, 128, 130, 160;
terrorist content 38, 45; traceability
mechanisms 158–159, 161
sociological theory 241
spam, provisions to reduce 136 *see also*
disinformation
stakeholders, multistakeholderism 241
state actors 128–129
structural inequalities 11
Sustainable Development Goals (SDGs):
challenges of alternative data sources
58–62; the datascape 51, 52–53, 57,
62–65; power in the datascape
53–55
synthetic knowledge 239–240

targeted advertising 155–158
temporality 242
terrorist content, on social media 38, 45
traceability mechanisms 158–161
trackers 158–161
trade agreements, digital 127, 131–134
tragedy of the commons 22–23
transscalarity 37–38, **198**
transsectoral data 38–39, **198**

UN 2030 Agenda: challenges of alternative
data sources 58–62; the datascape 51,
52–53, 57, 62–65; power in the
datascape 53–55
UNESCO's Recommendation on the
Ethics of Artificial Intelligence 225
United States: Clearview AI 114, 115;
competition policies 134; content
moderation 134; CUSMA 133, 135;
grassroots data activism 70, 73; privacy
protection 41; sanctions against
international entities 137; tackling
disinformation 130–131, 132; trade
agreements 133–135; US-Japan Digital
Trade Agreement 134
Ushahidi 73–74

Vienna Declaration 110
Viljoen, Salomé 152–153
violent datafication 61–62

Western, educated, industrialized,
rich, and democratic (WEIRD)
countries 176
Weyl, E. Glen 27
WhatsApp: encryption 159–160; in the
Global South 74, 75–76
wicked problems 126, 167
Working Group on Internet Governance
(WGIG) 169–170
World Economic Forum 137
World Trade Organization (WTO):
cross-border data flows 41, 42,
132–133, 134

Printed in the United States
by Baker & Taylor Publisher Services